Cengage

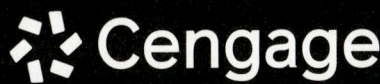

QuickBooks® Online for Accounting 6E

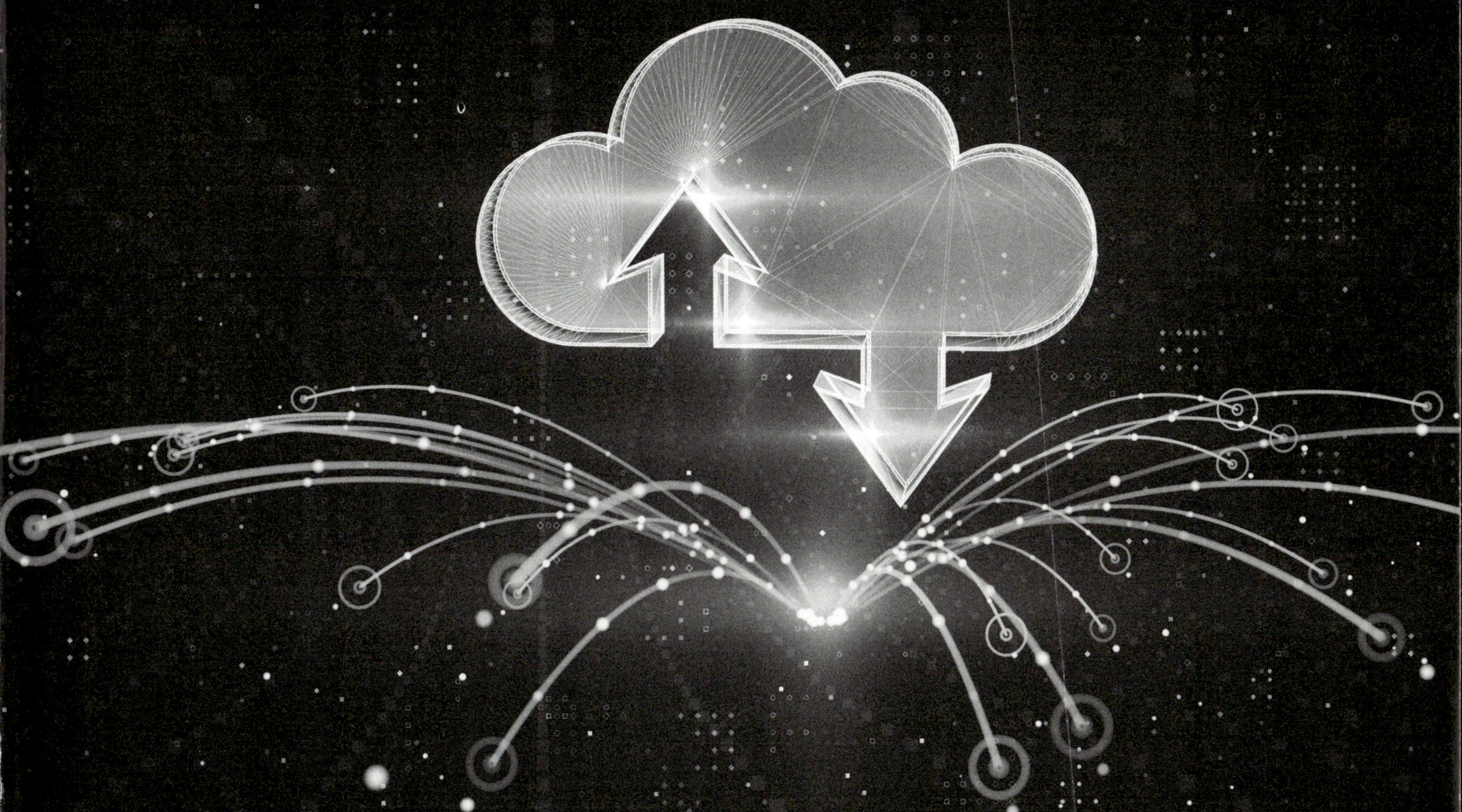

Glenn Owen

Australia • Brazil • Canada • Mexico • Singapore • United Kingdom • United States

QuickBooks® Online For Accounting, Sixth Edition

Glenn Owen

Senior Vice President, Higher Education & Skills Product: Erin Joyner

Product Director: Joe Sabatino

Product Manager: Jonathan Gross

Vendor Content Manager: Valarmathy Munuswamy, Lumina Datamatics, Inc.

Product Assistant: Flannery Cowan

Marketing Manager: Colin Kramer

Intellectual Property Analyst: Ashley Maynard

Intellectual Property Project Manager: Anjali Kambli, Lumina Datamatics, Inc.

Production Service: Lumina Datamatics, Inc.

Art Director and Cover Designer: Christopher Doughman

Cover Image: Zfl/Moment/Getty Images

© 2023, 2022, 2021 Cengage Learning®

No part of this work covered by the copyright herein may be reproduced or distributed in any form or by any means, except as permitted by U.S. copyright law, without the prior written permission of the copyright owner.

For product information and technology assistance, contact us at
Cengage Customer & Sales Support, 1-800-354-9706 or
support.cengage.com.

For permission to use material from this text or product, submit all requests online at **www.cengage.com/permissions**.

Intuit and QuickBooks are trademarks and service marks of Intuit Inc., registered in the United States and other countries.

Library of Congress Control Number: 2022901604

ISBN: 978-0-357-72221-3

Cengage
200 Pier 4 Boulevard
Boston, MA 02210
USA

Cengage is a leading provider of customized learning solutions with employees residing in nearly 40 different countries and sales in more than 125 countries around the world. Find your local representative at: **www.cengage.com**.

To learn more about Cengage platforms and services, register or access your online learning solution, or purchase materials for your course, visit **www.cengage.com**.

Printed in the United States of America
Print Number: 01   Print Year: 2022

Brief Contents

Chapter 1 An Introduction to QuickBooks Online Using the Sample Company 1

Chapter 2 An Overview of QuickBooks Online 22

Chapter 3 Setting Up a New Company: Establishing a Chart of Accounts, Beginning Balances, Customers, Vendors, and Products/Services 41

Chapter 4 Recording Operating Activities: Sales and Cash Receipts 76

Chapter 5 Recording Operating Activities: Purchases and Cash Payments 104

Chapter 6 Recording Investing and Financing Activities 134

Chapter 7 Recording Payroll 155

Chapter 8 Establishing Budgets and Preparing Bank Reconciliations 182

Chapter 9 Analysis and Recording of Adjusting Entries 206

Chapter 10 Preparing Financial Statements and Reports 223

Appendix 1 Sales Tax 246

Appendix 2 Comprehensive Case Problems 249

Appendix 3 Overview—Do I Need to Become QuickBooks Online Certified? 269

Index 271

Contents

Preface		vii
About the Author & Dedication		xx

Chapter 1 An Introduction to QuickBooks Online Using the Sample Company — 1

Overview	1
Begin Your Sample Company Walkthrough	1
Customers, Vendors, and Employees	3
Banking Transactions	7
Sales and Expense Transactions	9
Settings	11
Chart of Accounts	13
Lists	14
Reports	16
Company Settings	18
End Note	20
Chapter 1 Practice	21
Chapter 1 Questions	21
Chapter 1 Matching	21

Chapter 2 An Overview of QuickBooks Online — 22

Overview	22
What Is QBO?	22
How Is QBO Similar to/Different than the Desktop Version of QuickBooks Accountant?	23
How to Open the QBO Company You Created in the Preface	24
Navigating QBO	31
Assigning an Instructor as the Company's "Accountant"	36
Video Tutorials for QuickBooks Online (Developed and Maintained by Intuit)	37
End Note	39
Chapter 2 Practice	40
Chapter 2 Questions	40
Chapter 2 Matching	40

Chapter 3 Setting Up a New Company: Establishing a Chart of Accounts, Beginning Balances, Customers, Vendors, and Products/Services — 41

Overview	41
Company Settings	42
Modify the Chart of Accounts and Establish Beginning Balances	43
Close Opening Balance Equity and Create a Balance Sheet	51
Create, Print, and Export a Transaction Detail by Account	53
End Note	54
Chapter 3 Practice	55
Chapter 3 Questions	55
Chapter 3 Matching	55
Chapter 3 Cases	55
Case 1	56
Case 2	59
Case 3	61
Case 4	64
Case 5	68
Case 6	72

Chapter 4 Recording Operating Activities: Sales and Cash Receipts — 76

Overview	76
Services, Products, and Customers	76
Sales Receipts and Invoices	80
Cash Receipts	83
Transaction Detail by Account	86
End Note	87
Chapter 4 Practice	88
Chapter 4 Questions	88
Chapter 4 Matching	88
Chapter 4 Cases	88
Case 1	89
Case 2	91

Case 3	93
Case 4	95
Case 5	98
Case 6	101

Chapter 5 Recording Operating Activities: Purchases and Cash Payments — 104

Overview	104
Vendors	104
Purchase Orders	105
Bills	108
Payment of Bills, Use of a Credit Card, Payments for Items Other Than Bills	112
Trial Balance	115
End Note	118
Chapter 5 Practice	119
Chapter 5 Questions	119
Chapter 5 Matching	119
Chapter 5 Cases	119
Case 1	120
Case 2	122
Case 3	124
Case 4	127
Case 5	129
Case 6	131

Chapter 6 Recording Investing and Financing Activities — 134

Overview	134
Fixed Assets	134
Long-Term Investments	136
Equity Transactions (Common Stock, Dividends, Owner Investments, and Owner Withdrawals)	138
Long-Term Debt	140
Acquisition of a Fixed Asset in Exchange for Long-Term Debt	141
End Note	142
Chapter 6 Practice	143
Chapter 6 Questions	143
Chapter 6 Matching	143
Chapter 6 Cases	143
Case 1	144
Case 2	145
Case 3	147
Case 4	149
Case 5	151
Case 6	153

Chapter 7 Recording Payroll — 155

Overview	155
Employees	155
Payroll Accounts	157
Pay Employees	158
End Note	164
Chapter 7 Practice	165
Chapter 7 Questions	165
Chapter 7 Matching	165
Chapter 7 Cases	165
Case 1	166
Case 2	168
Case 3	171
Case 4	174
Case 5	177
Case 6	179

Chapter 8 Establishing Budgets and Preparing Bank Reconciliations — 182

Overview	182
Budget Creation	182
Budget Reports	185
Bank Reconciliation	189
End Note	192
Chapter 8 Practice	193
Chapter 8 Questions	193
Chapter 8 Matching	193
Chapter 8 Cases	193
Case 1	194
Case 2	196
Case 3	198
Case 4	200
Case 5	201
Case 6	204

Chapter 9 Analysis and Recording of Adjusting Entries — 206

Overview	206
Trial Balance	207
Adjusting Journal Entries: Prepaid Expenses	208
Adjusting Journal Entries: Accrued Expenses	211
Adjusting Journal Entries: Unearned Revenue	212
Adjusting Journal Entries: Accruing Revenue	213
Adjusting Journal Entries: Depreciation	214
End Note	216
Chapter 9 Practice	217
Chapter 9 Questions	217
Chapter 9 Matching	217

Chapter 9 Cases 217
Case 1 218
Case 2 218
Case 3 219
Case 4 220
Case 5 221
Case 6 222

Chapter 10 Preparing Financial Statements and Reports 223

Overview 223
Income Statement 224
Balance Sheet 226
Statement of Cash Flows 229
Accounts Receivable Aging Summary 231
Accounts Payable Aging Summary 233
Inventory Valuation Summary 235
Customizing and Saving Reports 237
End Note 239

Chapter 10 Practice 240
Chapter 10 Questions 240
Chapter 10 Matching 240
Chapter 10 Cases 240
Case 1 241
Case 2 242
Case 3 242
Case 4 243
Case 5 244
Case 6 245

Appendix 1 Sales Tax 246

Appendix 2 Comprehensive Case Problems 249

Appendix 3 Overview—Do I Need to Become QuickBooks Online Certified? 269

Index 271

Preface

Overview

Accounting has arrived in the Cloud and its time has come. *Cloud computing* is a general term for anything that involves delivering hosted services over the Internet. According to a recent study by KPMG (a global network of professional firms), businesses—large, medium, and small—are using the Cloud to drive cost efficiencies, better enable a mobile workforce, and improve alignment with their customers and vendors.

Imagine being able to update your business's accounting information system from anywhere on any device using any operating system. That is where the global economy is going. Are you on the path?

Is This Text for You?

This text is for you if you are an instructor who desires a self-paced, self-directed environment for your students to learn the essentials of QuickBooks Online (QBO) and to review their understanding of financial accounting and reporting.

This text is for you if you are a business owner looking for a self-paced, self-directed environment for yourself to learn the essentials of QBO as well as a means to refresh your understanding of financial accounting and reporting.

This book focuses on QBO. It is not designed for users of QuickBooks Pro, Accountant, or any other desktop version of QuickBooks. In that case, Glenn Owen's QuickBooks Accountant books are a better fit. The desktop version and online versions are different, and though you can import files created in the desktop version into the online version, significant differences exist as discussed in Chapter 1.

Multiple Companies

Intuit has finally seen the light and has agreed to give students and instructors the ability to create more than one company. They have also developed a more streamlined means to access QBO.

See overview at: https://www.intuit.com/partners/education-program/products/quickbooks/

Instructors

To give your students access to creating multiple companies:

1 First step, register yourself as a QBO Educator: Access the Educator Portal by navigating your web browser to https://www.intuit.com/partners/education-program/products/quickbooks/educator-qbo-signup/

2 Intuit will then attempt to validate you as an instructor at your educational institution.

3 After validation, navigate your web browser to https://accounts.intuit.com/index.html?redirect_url=https%3A%2F%2Feducation-portal.app.intuit.com%2Fapp%2Fdashboard&appfabric=true

Figure Preface 1

Sign in to the Education Portal

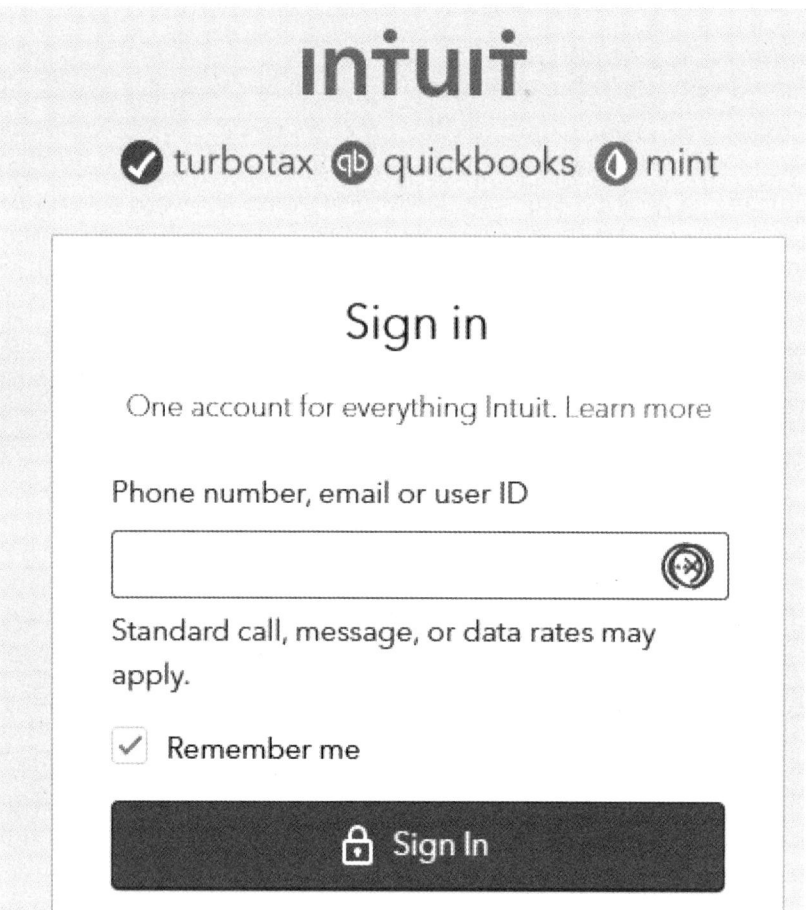

4 Provide your email in the space shown in Figure Preface 1 above and then click **Sign In**.

5 Provide your password in the window presented next and then click **Continue**. A Welcome to the Intuit Educator Portal window should appear as shown in Figure Preface 2.

6 Click the video box titled **How the Educator Portal Works** to see an overview of the Educator Portal.

7 To access the Sample Company this text uses to demonstrate QBO features, you will click **QuickBooks Online test drive**. Don't do this now.

8 To access QBO tutorials, you will click **Tutorials**. Don't do this now, instead proceed to the next step below.

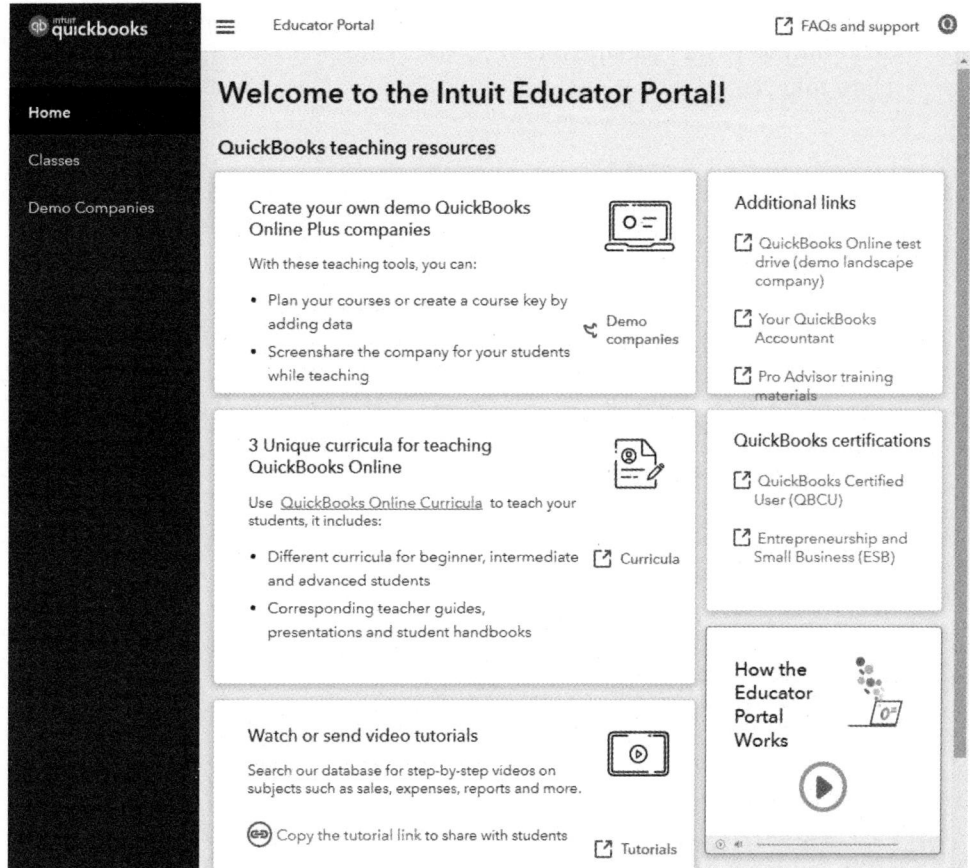

Figure Preface 2

Welcome to the Intuit Educator Portal

9 Click **Classes** from the navigation bar on the left to view the screen shown in Figure Preface 3. Ignore the reference to an existing Account 100 class. Your screen will not show the Accounting 100 class.

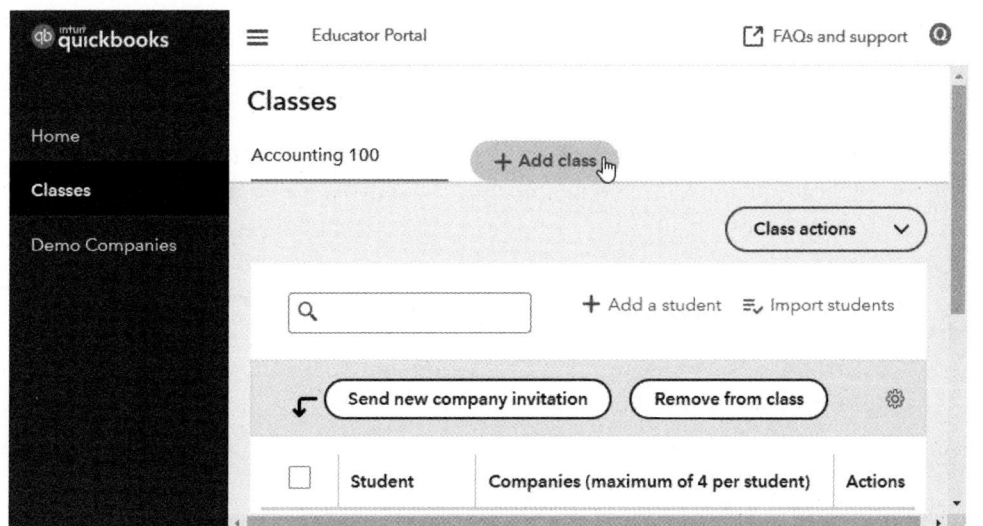

Figure Preface 3

Classes

10 Click **+ Add class** to create a class as shown in Figure Preface 3.

11 Type a name for your class. For example, Figure Preface 4 shows Accounting 101 as the class name. Once you've entered a class name click **Add class**.

Figure Preface 4

Add class

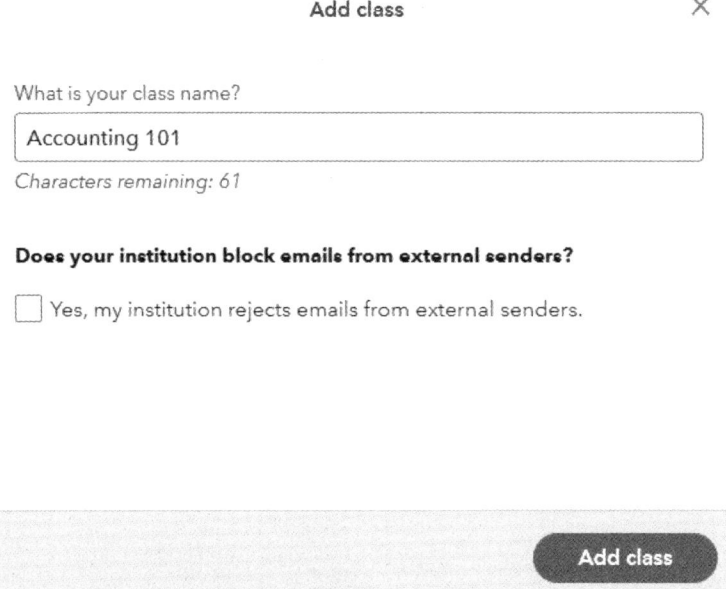

12 Click **Add class**. Your window should look like Figure Preface 5. Add your students to a class either by uploading a roster or clicking Add students manually.

Figure Preface 5

Add students

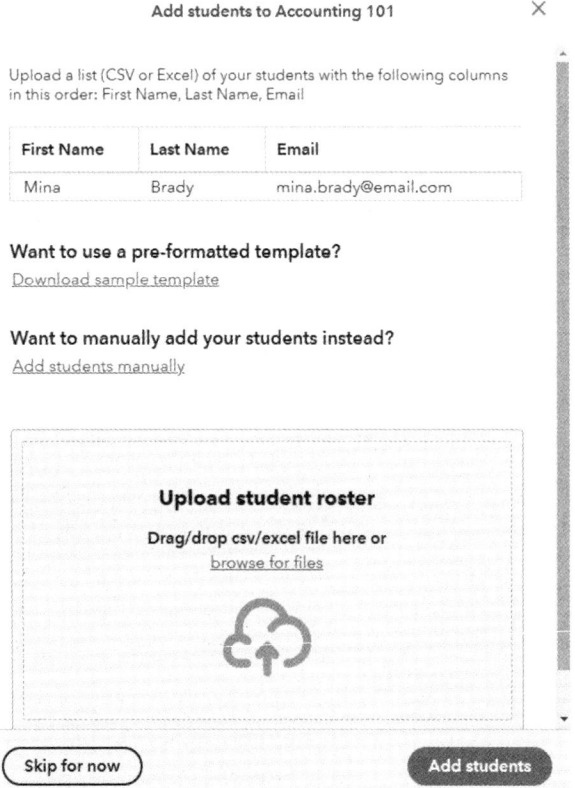

13 In this example click **Add students manually** to view Figure Preface 6. The student information will be empty until you perform step 14.

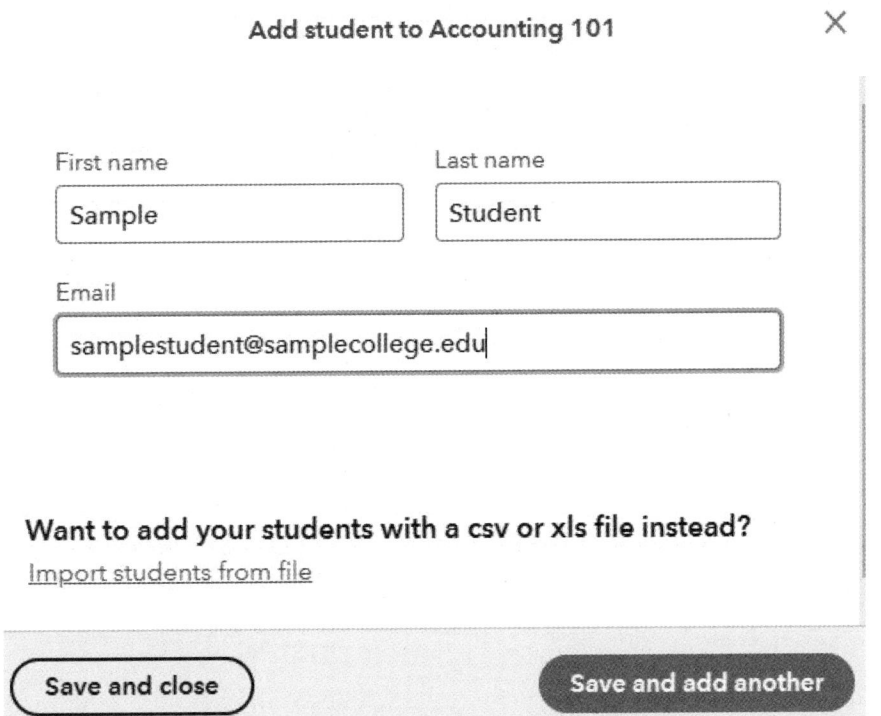

Figure Preface 6

Adding students manually

14 Type your student's first name, last name, and email address, then click **Save and close**. A sample student was added in this example.

15 To assign a company to a student, place a **check** next to a student's name and then click **Send new company invitation** as shown in Figure Preface 7.

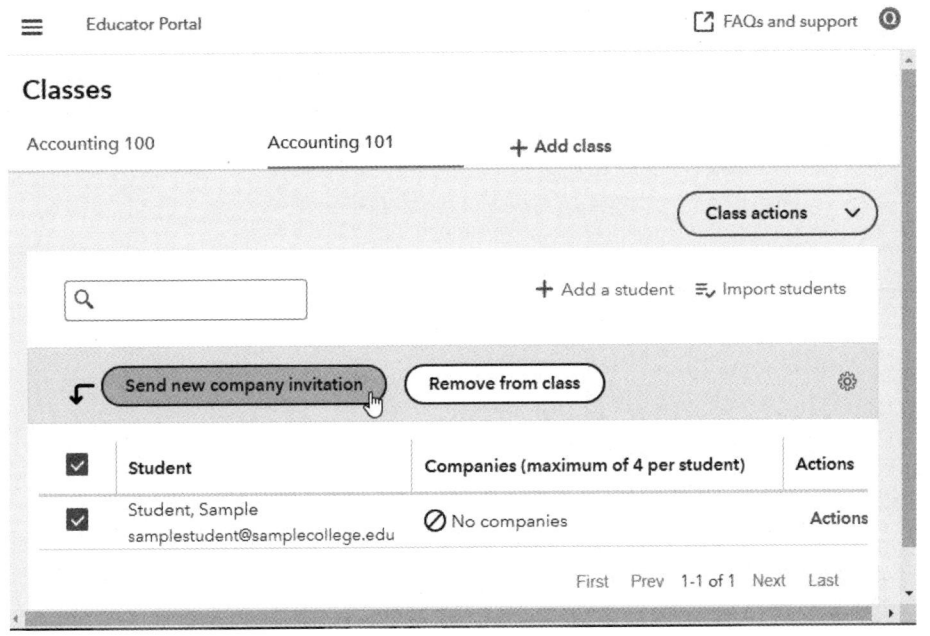

Figure Preface 7

Sending an invitation to a student to complete a case

16 Type **Case 1** in the Choose a name text box as shown in Figure Preface 8. As an instructor you get to choose the name, however, it is recommended that you match the name with the case you've chosen to assign from the text (either Case 1, 2, 3, 4, 5, or 6).

Figure Preface 8

Entering a name for the company you're assigning to a student

17 Click **Next: Preview invitation** to view Figure Preface 9.

Figure Preface 9

Partial view of invitation preview

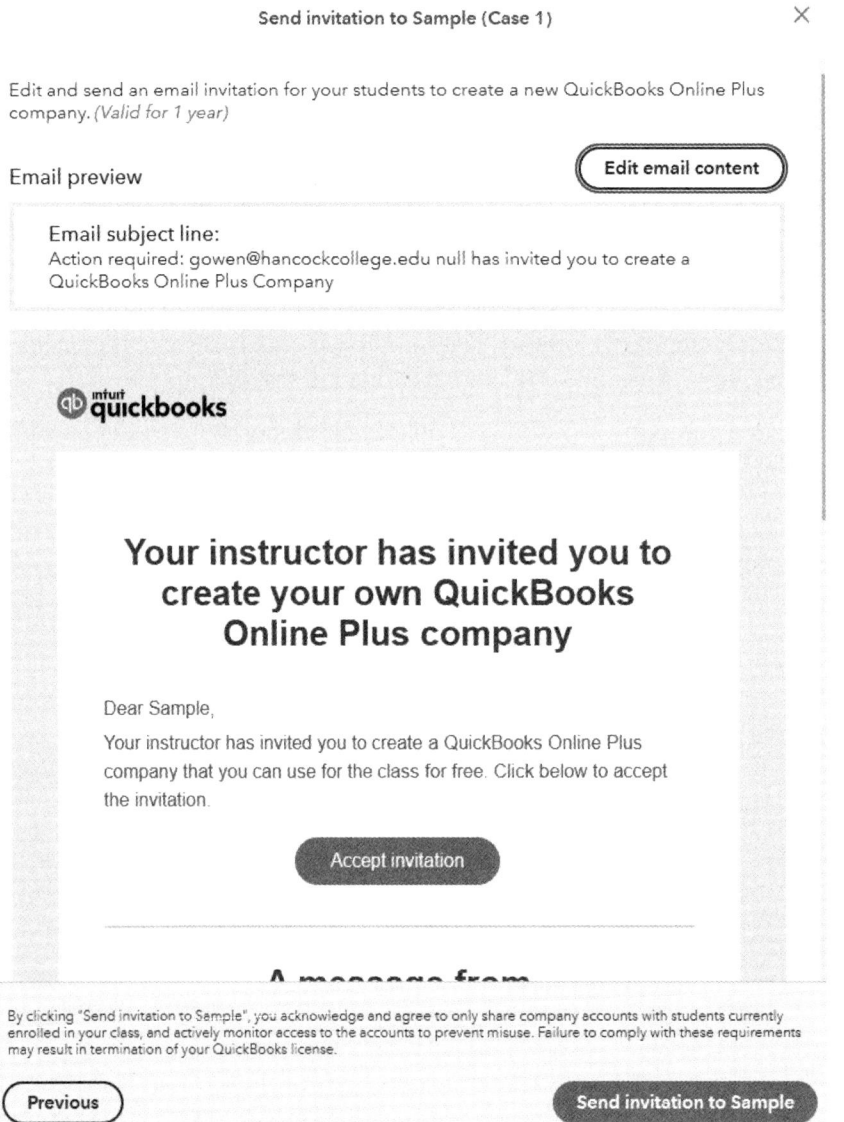

18 Click **Send invitation to Sample** (replacing your student's first name in place of Sample).

19 You should receive confirmation that your invitation was sent. Your student listing should then be updated to indicate an invitation was sent and give you the opportunity to resend the invitation if necessary. This update should look like Figure Preface 10.

Figure Preface 10

Updated student information

	Student	Companies (maximum of 4 per student)
☐	Student, Sample samplestudent@samplecollege.edu	✓ Case 1: Invitation sent Resend invitation

20 Click your account information icon located in the upper right-hand corner of the QBO window, then click **Sign out**.

Keep in mind that you, as an instructor, may assign your class up to 4 companies. There are 6 cases found at the end of each chapter of this text, but you can only assign 4 to a class. However, if you have a second class, you may assign those students only 4 companies as well, but they can be different than those assigned in a different class.

Students

If you have not received an invitation from your instructor read the following to get access to QBO to create one or more companies. Students at accredited academic institutions are eligible for a one-year student registration.

1 First step, register yourself as a student: Access the Educator Portal by navigating your web browser to https://www.intuit.com/partners/education-program/products/quickbooks/student-qbo-signup/

2 Intuit will then attempt to validate you as a student at your educational institution.

3 After validation, navigate your web browser to https://quickbooks.intuit.com/sign-in-offer/

4 Provide your username and password to login.

If you have received an invitation from your instructor, read the following to get access to QBO. Students at accredited academic institutions are eligible for a one-year student registration.

1 Click **Accept Invitation** in the email you received from your instructor as shown in Figure Preface 11.

Figure Preface 11

Accepting an instructor's invitation to create a QBO company

Your instructor has invited you to create your own QuickBooks company

Dear Sam,

Your instructor has invited you to create a QuickBooks Online Plus company that you can use for the class for free. Click below to accept the invitation.

Accept invitation

2 If you have already registered and been validated (see above), click **Sign In** and provide Intuit with your username and password as shown in Figure Preface 12. If you have not registered, provide your information as shown below and click **Create Account**.

Figure Preface 12

Creating a QBO account

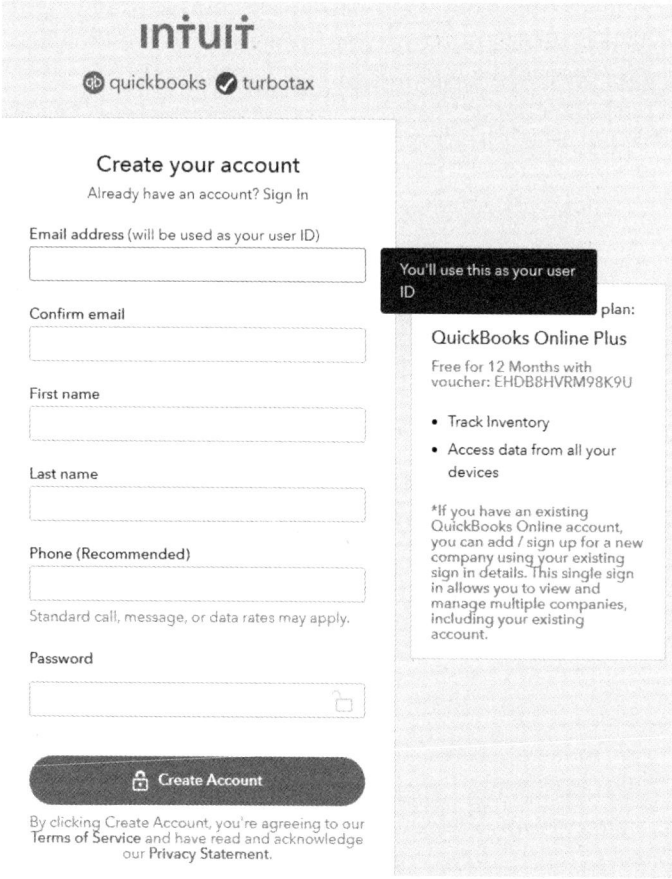

3 Type your **email address** twice, **first name**, **last name**, **phone** (if you wish), a **password** twice, and then click **Create Account**. You should now see a QBO window like Figure Preface 13.

Figure Preface 13

QBO Welcome

4 For now, do not click Next, instead just close the browser window. You will return to your company in Chapter 2.

Payroll

The text and related data files created for this book were constructed using QBO. In this version of QuickBooks, Intuit continues its use of a basic payroll service but has made it more accessible by having it live on its Cloud-based system. QBO initially comes with the current tax tables; however, these tables soon become outdated, and the payroll feature is disabled unless the user subscribes to the payroll service.

The author decided to use the manual payroll tax feature, which requires that students manually enter the tax deductions. This alleviates the discrepancies between the solutions manual and the students' data entry and removes the burden of having to purchase the tax table service for each copy of QBO used. Instructions on how to set up payroll for manual calculation of payroll taxes are provided in the text. For more information, see your QBO documentation.

All reports have a default feature that identifies the basis in which the report was created (e.g., accrual or cash) and the date and time the report was printed. The date and time shown on your report will, of course, be different from that shown in this text.

Instructional Design

Each chapter of this text begins with a listing of expected student learning outcomes followed by a step-by-step explanation of how to obtain those outcomes. In most chapters, the explanations utilize a Sample Company created by Intuit in which the author demonstrates how various operating, investing, and financing activities of a business are captured and then reported in QBO.

End-of-chapter questions, matching, and student cases follow these explanations. The questions help you to review the text-explained concepts and processes, whereas the matching section helps with terms and definitions. The student cases provide the information necessary to add data to the student's company file. Each chapter requires the student to add information to the previous chapter's rendition. Thus, for success in learning, each student must complete the previous chapter's student case before attempting the next chapter's student case.

Solutions to each chapter's student cases are provided in the instructor manual. The following is a matrix of all end-of-chapter cases that identifies key differences between cases key processes assessed. For example, Cases 1, 2, 4, and 6 are corporations, whereas Cases 3 and 5 are sole proprietors. Cases 1 and 2 do not require sales tax collections, whereas Cases 3, 4, and 5 do. All cases involve business entities that sell products, provide services, and have checking accounts, customers, vendors, employees, and so on.

	Case 1	Case 2	Case 3	Case 4	Case 5	Case 6
Company Setup:						
Date company started using QBO	1/1/24	1/1/25	1/1/26	1/1/21	1/1/22	1/1/23
Location	La Jolla, CA	La Jolla, CA	La Jolla, CA	Hollywood, CA	Huntsville, AL	Sumner, WA
Company organization	Corporation	Corporation	Sole Proprietor	Corporation	Sole Proprietor	Corporation
Business	Distributor	Distributor	Retail	Sports Gym	Engineering	Automotive Dealer
Inventory products sold	Surf boards	Toys	Cell Phones	T-Shirts	Computers	Recreational Vehicle
Services provided	Consulting	Repairs	Repairs	Monthly Fees	Program Support	Repairs
Track expenses	Yes	Yes	Yes	Yes	Yes	Yes
Bill payment terms (default)	Net 30	Net 30	Net 30	Net 30	Net 30	Net 30
Hourly employees	Yes	Yes	Yes	Yes	Yes	Yes
Salary employees	Yes	Yes	Yes	Yes	Yes	Yes
Sales tax applicable	No	No	Yes	Yes	Yes	Yes
Add customers	Yes	Yes	Yes	Yes	Yes	Yes
Add employees	Yes	Yes	Yes	Yes	Yes	Yes
Add inventory items	Yes	Yes	Yes	Yes	Yes	Yes
Add service items	Yes	Yes	Yes	Yes	Yes	Yes
Add vendors	Yes	Yes	Yes	Yes	Yes	Yes
Add/delete accounts	Yes	Yes	Yes	Yes	Yes	Yes
Enter beginning balances	Yes	Yes	Yes	Yes	Yes	Yes
Accounts Used:						
Checking account	Yes	Yes	Yes	Yes	Yes	Yes
Accounts receivable	Yes	Yes	Yes	Yes	Yes	Yes
Prepaid expenses/supplies	Yes	Yes	Yes	Yes	Yes	Yes
Investments	Yes	Yes	Yes	Yes	Yes	Yes
Fixed assets	Yes	Yes	Yes	Yes	Yes	Yes
Accounts payable	Yes	Yes	Yes	Yes	Yes	Yes
Notes payable	Yes	Yes	Yes	Yes	Yes	Yes
Common stock	Yes	Yes	No	Yes	No	Yes
Owner's equity	No	No	Yes	No	Yes	No
Business Transactions:						
Record additional investment by owners	No	No	Yes	No	Yes	No
Record adjusting (accrual) entries	Yes	Yes	Yes	Yes	Yes	Yes

Record bills	Yes	Yes	Yes	Yes	Yes	Yes
Record bills received with purchase orders	Yes	Yes	Yes	Yes	Yes	Yes
Record bills received without purchase orders	Yes	Yes	Yes	Yes	Yes	Yes
Record checks	Yes	Yes	Yes	Yes	Yes	Yes
Record journal entries	Yes	Yes	Yes	Yes	Yes	Yes
Record payments made on account	Yes	Yes	Yes	Yes	Yes	Yes
Record payments received on accounts	Yes	Yes	Yes	Yes	Yes	Yes
Record payroll	Yes	Yes	Yes	Yes	Yes	Yes
Record purchase orders	Yes	Yes	Yes	Yes	Yes	Yes
Record sales invoices	Yes	Yes	Yes	Yes	Yes	Yes
Record sales receipts	Yes	Yes	Yes	Yes	Yes	Yes
Record the sale of common stock	Yes	Yes	No	Yes	No	Yes
Reports Created:						
Reports—A/P Aging Summary	Yes	Yes	Yes	Yes	Yes	Yes
Reports—A/R Aging Summary	Yes	Yes	Yes	Yes	Yes	Yes
Reports—Balance Sheet	Yes	Yes	Yes	Yes	Yes	Yes
Reports—Export Reports to Excel	Yes	Yes	Yes	No	No	Yes
Reports—Income Statement	Yes	Yes	Yes	Yes	Yes	Yes
Reports—Inventory Valuation Summary	Yes	Yes	Yes	Yes	Yes	Yes
Reports—Statement of Cash Flows	Yes	Yes	Yes	Yes	Yes	Yes
Reports—Transaction Detail by Account	Yes	Yes	Yes	Yes	Yes	Yes
Reports—Trial Balance	Yes	Yes	Yes	Yes	Yes	Yes

Comprehensive Problems

Additional transactions for Cases 1, 2, 3, 4, and 6 can be found in Appendix 2. Students who have successfully completed a case in the text through Chapter 10 can be assigned these comprehensive problems. Each pick up in the month following the chapter work. For example in Case 1, chapter work occurred in January 2024, thus the comprehensive problem will describe transactions occurring in February 2024. The transactions included in February are similar in nature to those described in Chapters 3 to 10. Students assigned Case 1 would be able to complete comprehensive Case 1. Those assigned Case 2 would only be able to complete comprehensive Case 2 and the like.

Textbook Goals

This textbook takes a user and a preparer perspective by illustrating how accounting information is created and then used for making decisions. QBO is user-friendly and provides point-and-click simplicity and sophisticated accounting reporting and analysis tools. The textbook uses proven and successful instructional design (described earlier) to demonstrate the application's features and elicit student interaction.

The first and foremost goal of this text is to help students review fundamental accounting concepts and principles through the use of the QBO application and the analysis of business events. The content of this text complements the first course in accounting principles or financial accounting. Thus, this text should either be used concurrently with an accounting principles or financial accounting course or be used subsequent to completion of such a course.

A second goal of this text is to teach students how to set up QBO for a business, use it to record business events, and use it to generate financial statements and reports. Acquiring these skills will help students improve their job prospects whether the company they work for uses QuickBooks or not.

A third goal of this text is to teach students the value of a computerized accounting information system and how it can be used to communicate important information to business owners, investors, and creditors.

Date Warning

The Sample Company (created and maintained by Intuit) is used to demonstrate many aspects of QBO in this text. The author has no control over the dates used by Intuit and those dates may change depending on when you are accessing the file online. The dates that appear in the figures supplied by the author in this text may not be the dates that appear on your screen. Instructions to generate reports in this text often suggest the user set the report period to the month before or in the month of the current system date. If you are entering data at the beginning of the month (your system date is between the 1st and the 15th of a month), you should set your report period to the month prior to your current system date. If you are entering data at the end of the month (your system date is between the 15th and the 31st of a month), you should set your report period to the current month of your current system date. For example, if you are entering data on 10/09/2022, use 09/01/2022 to 09/30/2022 as your reporting period. For example, if you are entering data on 10/21/2023, use 10/01/2023 to 10/31/2023 as your reporting period.

The student cases (Cases 1–6) are set in 2024, 2025, 2026, 2021, 2022, and 2023, respectively. If transactions are entered into the student case in other than the proper period, answers will be wrong. Be careful about entering dates into QBO when you are working on this case. The default date when entering new transactions into QBO is the computer's system date that may or may not be in those years.

Update Warning

QBO is frequently upgraded by Intuit to provide new features, correct errors, or improve functionality. This book was written in late 2021 and early 2022, and all figures are based on how QBO looked at that time. If you are using this text in 2022 or later, Intuit may have made modifications in how QBO looks and feels or functions. Differences will occur, which are out of the author's control.

Keep in mind that sales tax rates change year to year, state to state. The solutions provided by the author for each case were based on tax rates in effect for that particular year. If a rate changes your answers for sales tax payable and related accounts may be different.

Instructor as Your Accountant

Your instructor may choose to have you assign them as your accountant so that they can see your work and progress at their convenience without having you to "send" the file. In fact, you cannot "send" your file, since all the files are on the Cloud. Instructions on how to set your instructor as your accountant are provided in Chapter 2.

Alternative means by which instructors can view your work.

Video Tutorials Developed by Intuit

Intuit, developer of QBO, and others have made video tutorials to help you get started with QBO. These tutorials can be viewed and/or sent to students from the Welcome to the Intuit Educator Portal described earlier in this text.

Instructors

To access these tutorials:

1 Login to the Educator Portal as shown in Figure Preface 8.

2 Click **Tutorials** shown at the bottom of the window to view Figure Preface 9.

3 View as many tutorials as you like and send them to students if you desire.

Students

To access these tutorials:

1 Navigate your browser to https://quickbooks.intuit.com/learn-support/en-us/tutorials?product=&tutorial=

2 Type a topic for a video into the text box labeled **Search for anything**.

3 View the video.

About the Author

Glenn Owen is a retired member of Allan Hancock College's Accounting and Business faculty, where he lectured on accounting and information systems from 1995 to 2016. In addition, he is a retired lecturer at the University of California at Santa Barbara, where he taught accounting and information systems courses from 1980 to 2011. His professional experience includes five years at Deloitte & Touche as well as vice president of finance positions at Westpac Resources, Inc., and ExperTelligence, Inc. Mr. Owen completed his fourth edition of Using Microsoft Excel and Access in Accounting text in 2016, which gives accounting students specific, self-paced instruction on the use of spreadsheets (Excel 2016) and database applications (Access 2016) in accounting. He has also written the 15th edition of his *Using QuickBooks Accountant for Accounting 2018* text, which is also a self-paced, case-based instruction on the use of a commercial accounting application (QuickBooks 2018). His innovative teaching style emphasizes the decision maker's perspective and encourages students to think creatively. His graduate studies in educational psychology and 41 years of business experience yield a balanced blend of theory and practice. Mr. Owen was presented the Lifetime Achievement Award in August 2016 by the Two-Year Section of the American Accounting Association.

Dedication

I would like to thank my wife Kelly for her support and assistance during the creation of this and previous editions of this text. Though our boys are out of the house and pursuing their own interests, she continues to listen to my often crazy ideas for new cases and experiences with college students, providing an excellent sounding board and reality check. You, the boys, their wives, and our grandchildren continue to define what life is all about.

An Introduction to QuickBooks Online Using the Sample Company

chapter 1

Student Learning Outcomes

Upon completion of this chapter, the student will be able to do the following:

- Open the Sample Company provided by Intuit to explore QBO
- Access customer, vendor, and employee information
- Explore banking transactions
- Explore sales and expense transactions
- Explore the chart of accounts
- Explore lists
- Access reports
- Use the Gear icon to view company settings

Overview

Intuit has provided a Sample Company online to provide new users a test-drive of its QBO product. You will open this Sample Company and explore various features of QBO. In this chapter, you will be viewing the Sample Company looking at customer, vendor, and employee information. You will also be viewing banking, sales, and expense transactions and will be looking at the chart of accounts, lists, reports, and company settings. You will not be making any changes, such as adding a customer, invoice, check, and so on. That will occur in the next chapter.

The author has no control over the dates used by Intuit, and those dates may change, depending on when you are accessing the file online. The dates in the figures supplied by the author in this text may not be the dates on your screen.

Begin Your Sample Company Walkthrough

You can use this Sample Company to explore QBO as often as you like. No matter what you do to modify this Sample Company, you will be unable to save it. When you leave and later return, it will look the same as it did initially. Each time you open this Sample Company, it will retrieve your current system date (the actual date you are working on your computer) and place that date under the company name on the home page.

2 Chapter 1 *An Introduction to QuickBooks Online Using the Sample Company*

To open the Sample Company, do the following:

1. Open your Internet browser.

2. Type **https://qbo.intuit.com/redir/testdrive** into your browser's address text box, press **[Enter]** to view the Sample Company Dashboard shown in Figure 1.1. Transaction dates may differ on your screen from the figures shown throughout this text.

Figure 1.1

Sample Company Dashboard

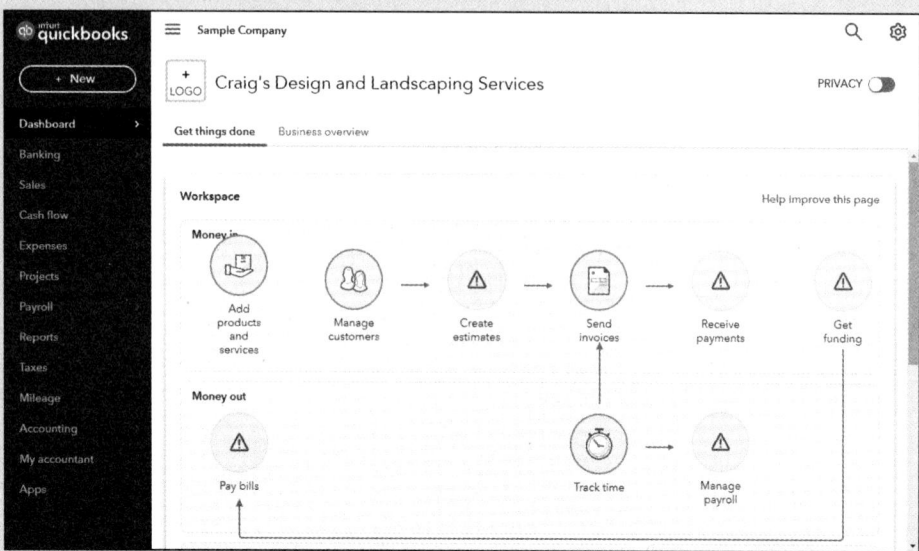

3. Click the [+ New] icon to view the Create menu shown in Figure 1.2.

Figure 1.2

Create menu

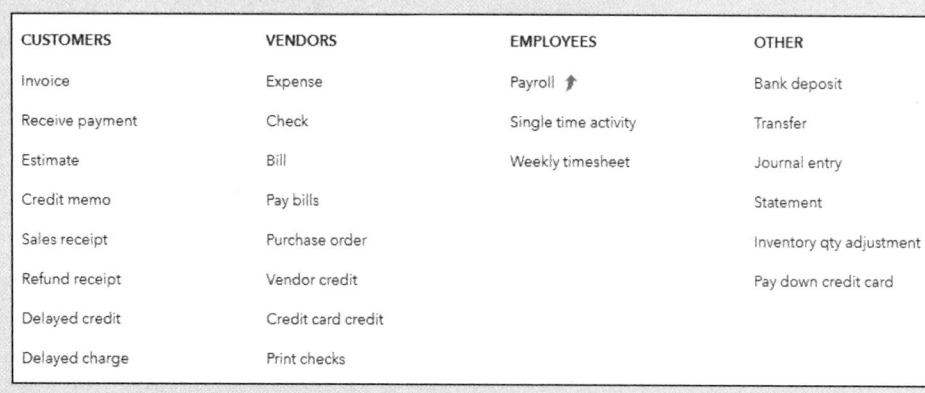

An Introduction to QuickBooks Online Using the Sample Company Chapter 1   3

Customers, Vendors, and Employees

QBO provides easy access to customer information using the navigation bar. In this section, you will open the Customers section in a new tab and drill down to a specific customer and specific transactions related to that customer.

To access customer information, do the following:

1 Click **Sales** and then click **Customers** as shown in Figure 1.3.

Trouble? If the navigation menu does not appear, click the **Show Navigation** icon located next to the words Sample Company. Clicking this icon should reveal and hide the navigation menu each time it's clicked.

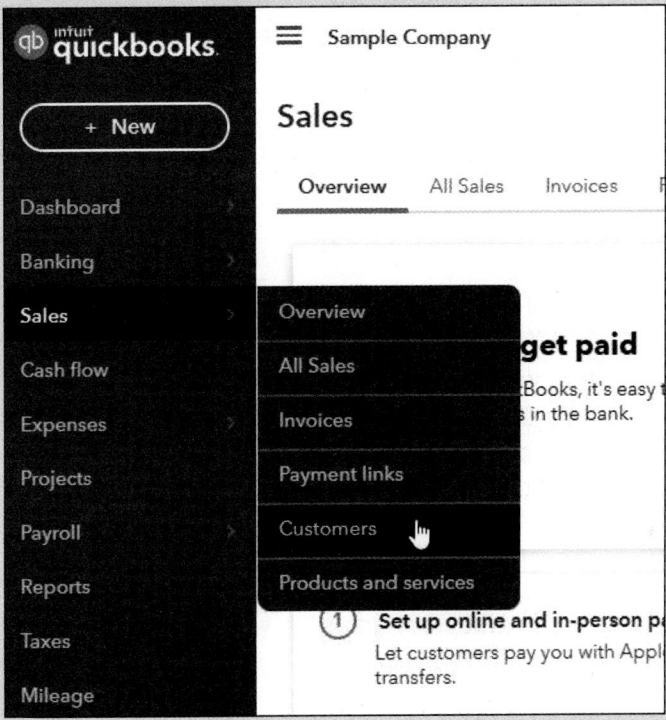

Figure 1.3

Accessing the Customers window

2 The resulting Customers window is then revealed as shown in Figure 1.4.

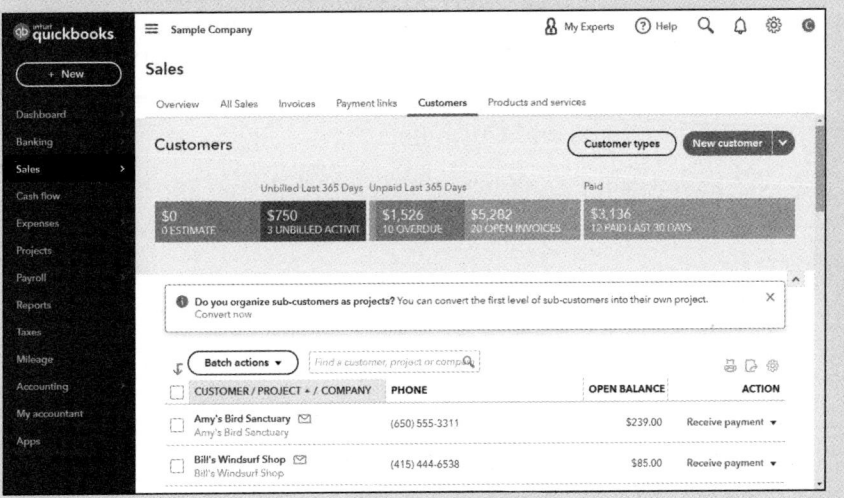

Figure 1.4

Customers window

3   Click on the **Amy's Bird Sanctuary** text to view detailed transactions related to that particular customer shown in Figure 1.5.

Figure 1.5

Amy's Bird Sanctuary

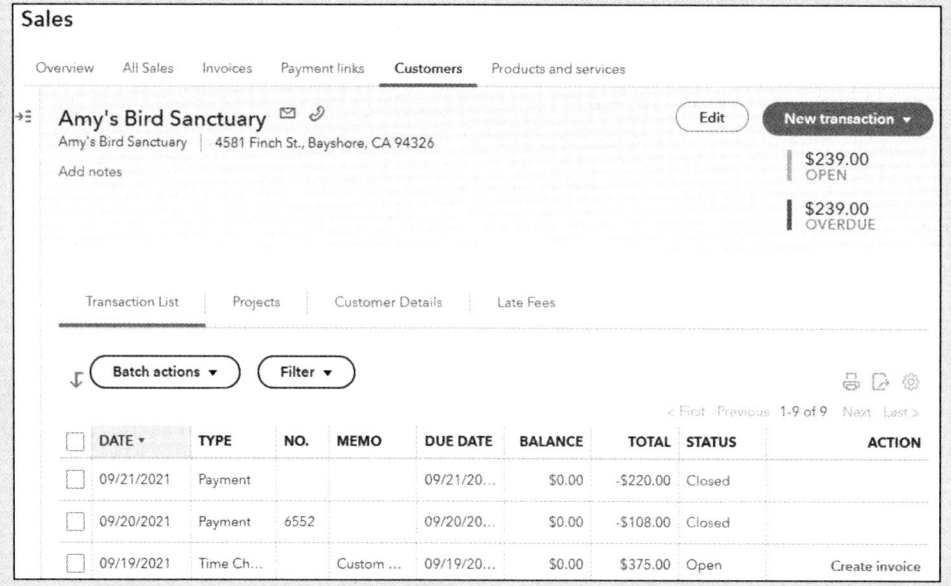

The $239.00 overdue balance noted at the top of the window correlates to invoice 1021 shown near the bottom of the list. To view it, scroll down the transactions list for Amy's Bird Sanctuary. (The author has no control over the dates used by Intuit, and those dates may change depending on when you are accessing the file online. The dates, which appear in the figures supplied by the author in this text, may not match the dates that appear on your screen.)

QBO provides easy access to vendor information using the navigation bar. In this section, you will open the Vendors section in a new tab and drill down to a specific vendor and specific transactions related to that vendor.

To access vendor information, do the following:

1   Click **Expenses** and then click **Vendors** (in a manner similar to what you just did for Sales and Customers previously).

2   A vendor listing as shown in Figure 1.6 should appear.

An Introduction to QuickBooks Online Using the Sample Company   **Chapter 1**   5

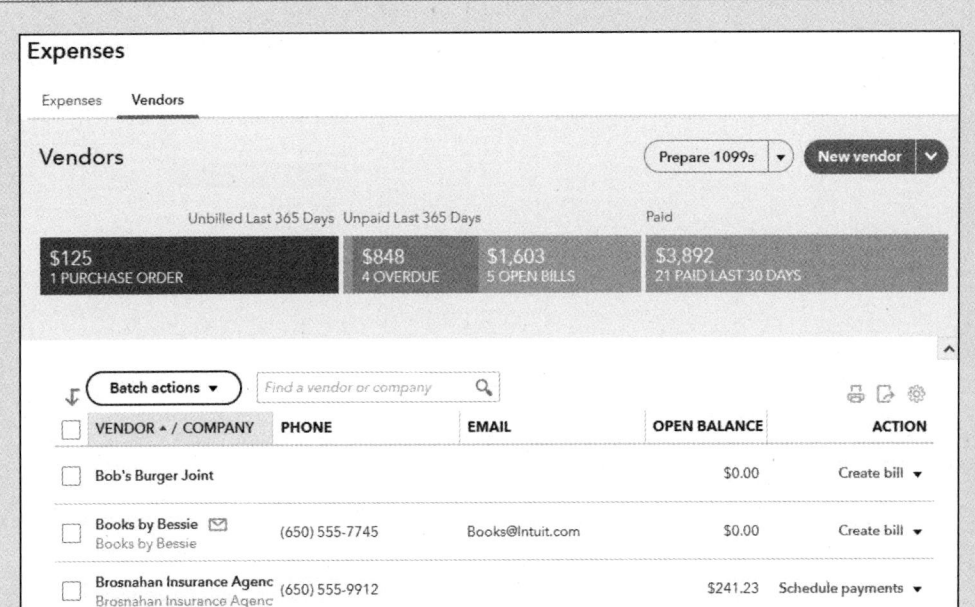

Figure 1.6

Vendors information

3 Click on the **Brosnahan Insurance Agency** text to view detailed transactions related to that particular vendor shown in Figure 1.7.

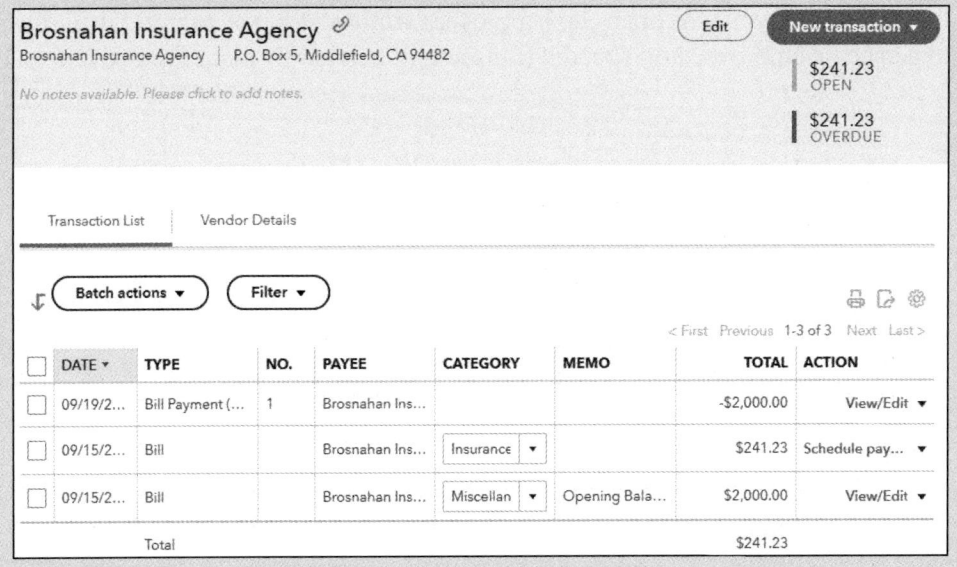

Figure 1.7

Brosnahan Insurance Agency

4 Click on the **$241.23** balance to view the bill received as shown in Figure 1.8.

Figure 1.8

Bill from Brosnahan Insurance Agency

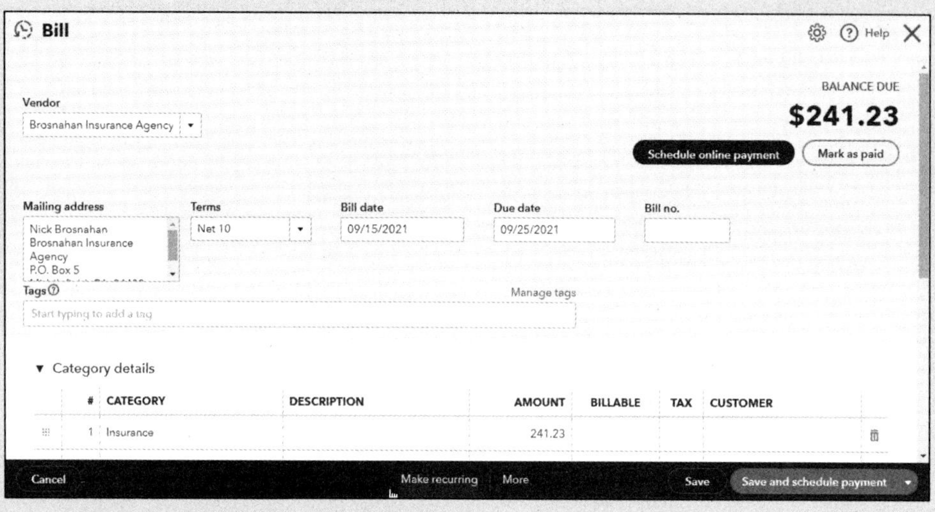

The $241.23 overdue balance noted at the top of the window correlates to a bill received from an earlier month.

QBO provides easy access to employee information using the navigation bar. In this section, you will open the Employees section in a new tab and drill down to a specific employee and specific transactions related to that employee.

To access employee information, do the following:

1. Click the **X** in the upper-right corner of the Bill to close it.
2. Click **Payroll** and then select **Employees** to reveal an employee listing as shown in Figure 1.9.

Figure 1.9

Employees information

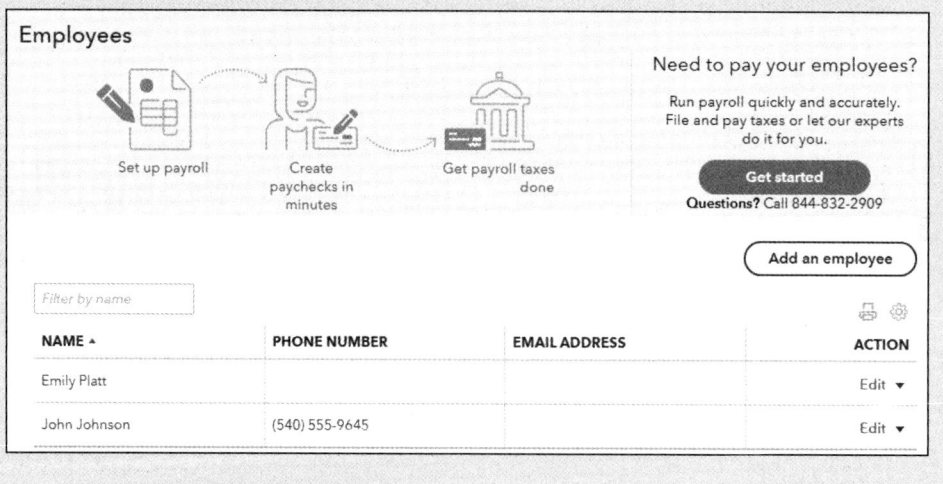

3 Click **Edit** for John Johnson to view employee information for John Johnson as shown in Figure 1.10.

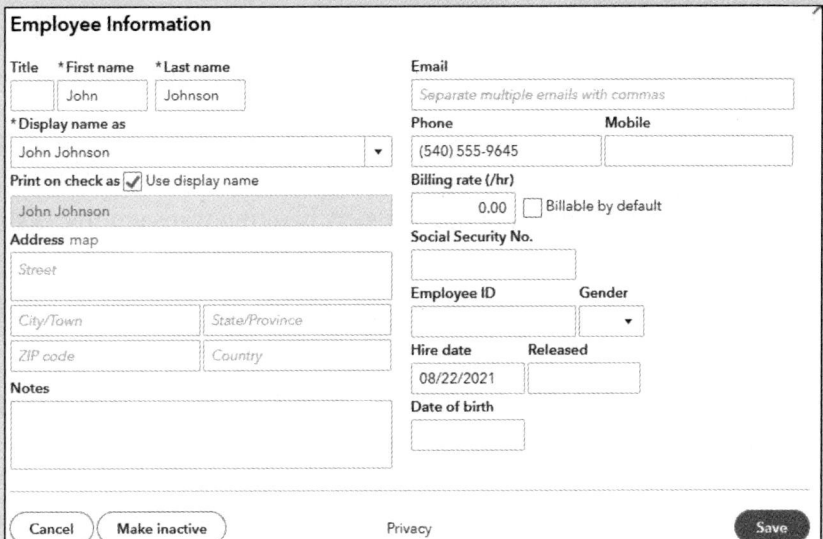

Figure 1.10

Employee Information for John Johnson

4 Click **Cancel** to close this window.

5 Click the **C** icon located in the upper right-hand corner of your window, and then click **Sign out** to close the Sample Company.

Banking Transactions

QBO has an online banking feature that lets you automatically connect to your bank and download banking-related transactions. The application automatically matches the banking transaction with a previously recorded QBO transaction. QBO calls this "Recognizing." This feature is briefly reviewed as this text is academically based and no "real" bank account is linked to this sample, and no "real" bank account will be linked to your student company.

To view banking transactions, do the following:

1 Open your Internet browser.

2 Type **https://qbo.intuit.com/redir/testdrive** into your browser's address text box and then press **[Enter]** to view the Sample Company home page shown in Figure 1.1. You may be asked to provide security information before proceeding. Click **Continue**.

3 Click **Banking** from the navigation bar and then click the **X** in the Your bank connection is all set window to view the Checking page as shown in Figure 1.11.

2 Double-click on Invoice No. **1036** to reveal the invoice shown in Figure 1.15.

Figure 1.15

Invoice #1036

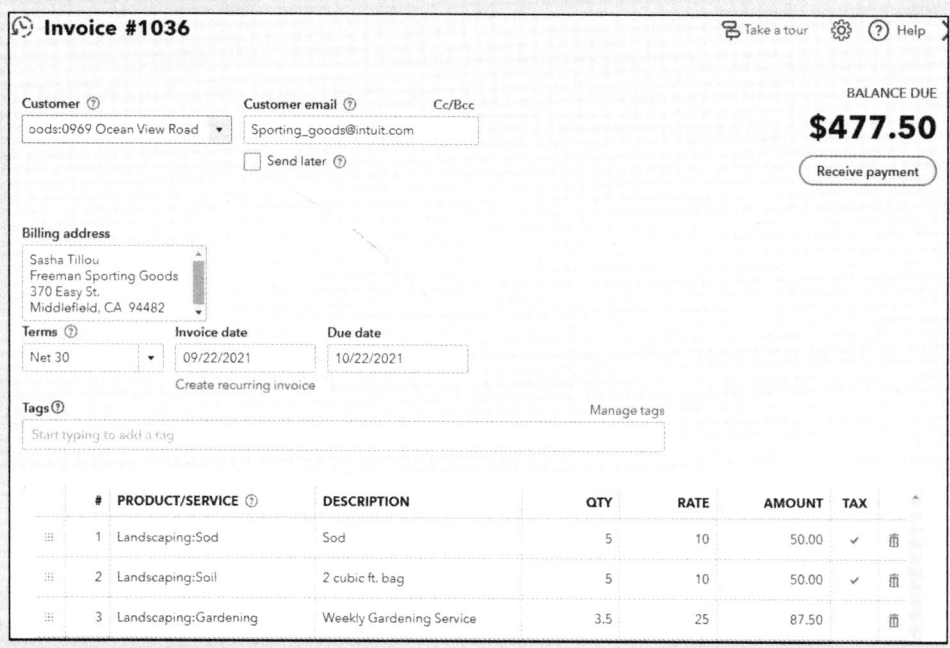

3 Click **Cancel** to close Invoice No. 1036.

The Expense Transactions section will provide a listing of recent credit card charges, bills, expenses, purchase orders, checks, bill payments, and cash payments. You can decide to drill down to view a particular credit card transaction.

4 Click **Expenses** and then click **Expenses** again from the navigation bar to view the Expense Transactions section shown in Figure 1.16.

Figure 1.16

Expense Transactions (partial view)

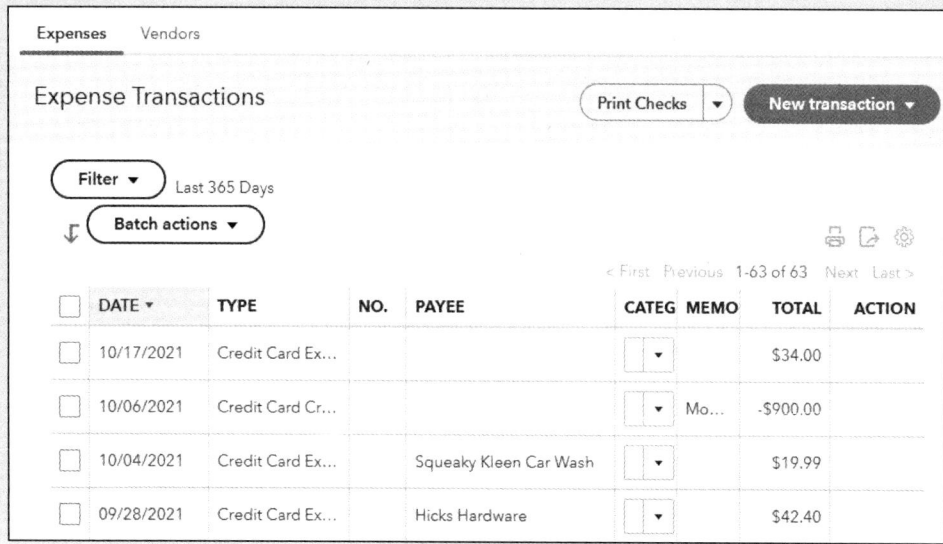

An Introduction to QuickBooks Online Using the Sample Company Chapter 1

5   Click **Squeaky Kleen Car Wash** to reveal the charge as shown in Figure 1.17.

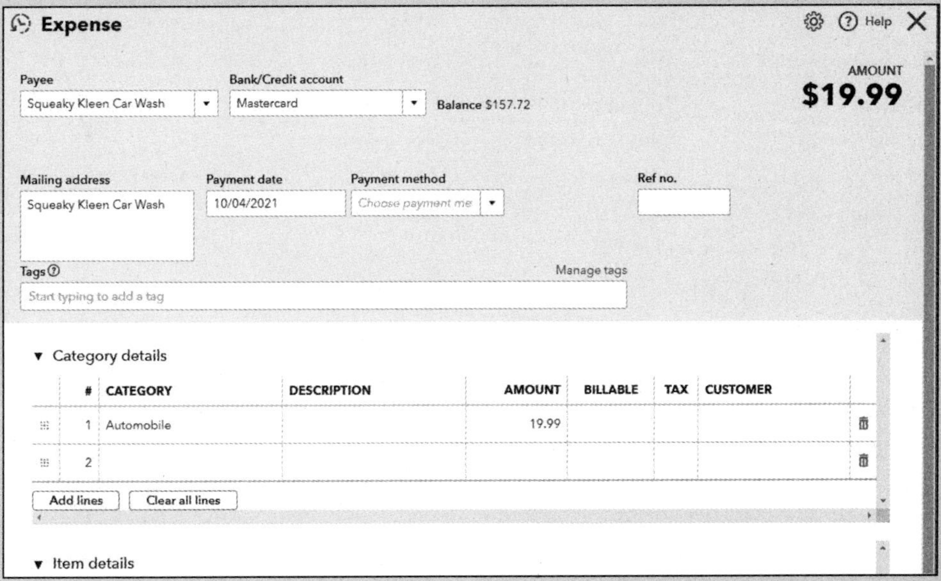

Figure 1.17

Expense window (credit card charge for $19.99)

6   Click **Cancel** to close the credit card charge window.

Settings

The Settings window (also known as the Gear window) is accessed by clicking the Gear icon located in the upper-right portion of the QBO window. Here you can modify your company settings, products and services, and budgets as well as reconcile bank accounts.

To view the Settings window and examine the Sample Company's settings:

1   Click the **Gear** icon as shown in Figure 1.18.

Figure 1.18

Company Settings window

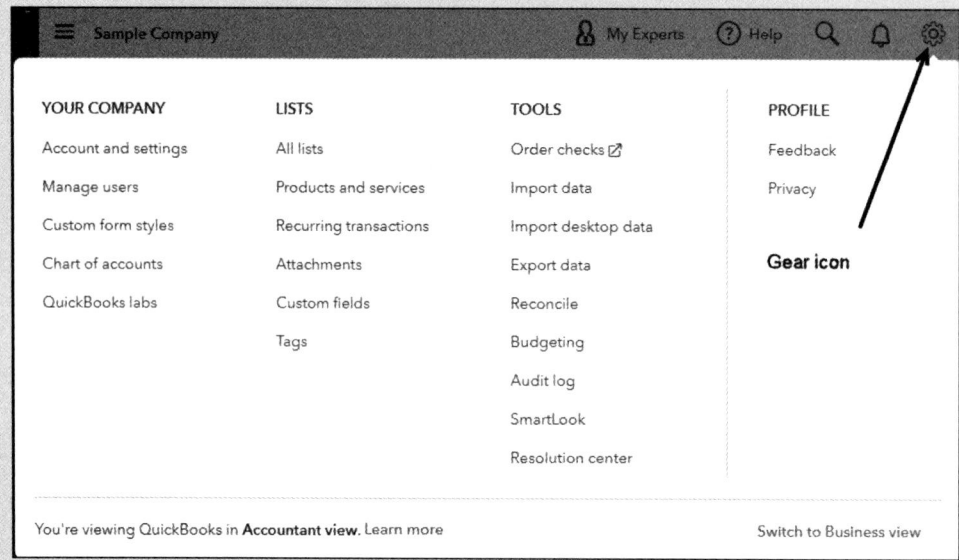

2. Click **Account and settings** to view company name, type, address etc. as shown in Figure 1.19.

Figure 1.19

Account and Settings window

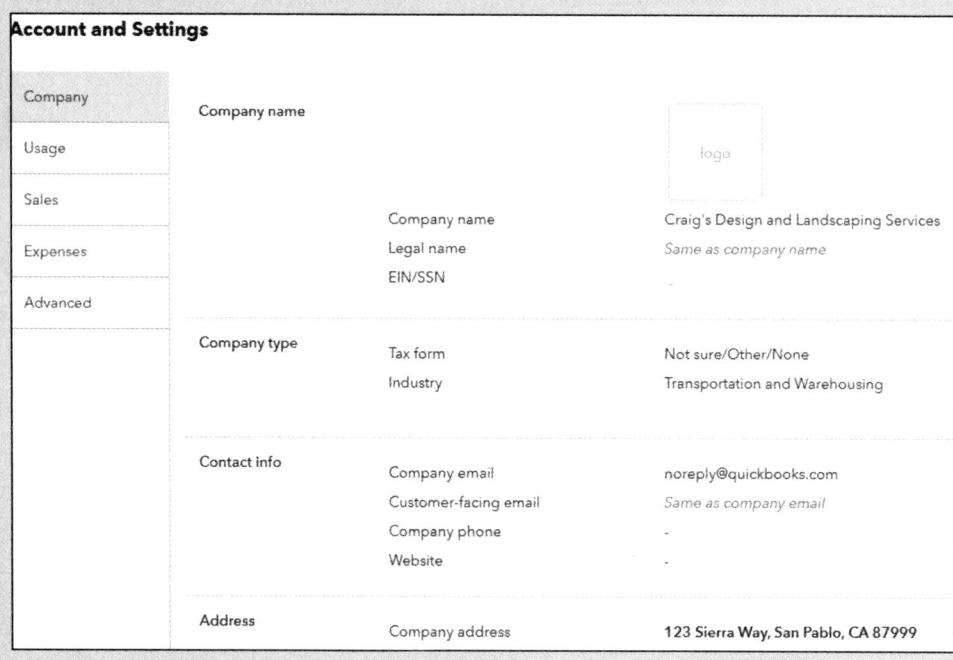

3. Click **X** to close the Account and Settings window.

Chart of Accounts

A chart of accounts is a listing of all accounts available. Each account is assigned a type and a detailed type. The Sample Company's chart of accounts has been modified from the default chart of accounts and tailored to this company's needs. Not all companies need these particular accounts, and some will need additional accounts.

To view the Sample Company's chart of accounts, do the following:

1. Click the **Gear** icon and then click **Chart of Accounts** to view the Chart of Accounts section. Then click **See your Chart of Accounts** to view the Sample Company's chart of accounts as shown in Figure 1.20.

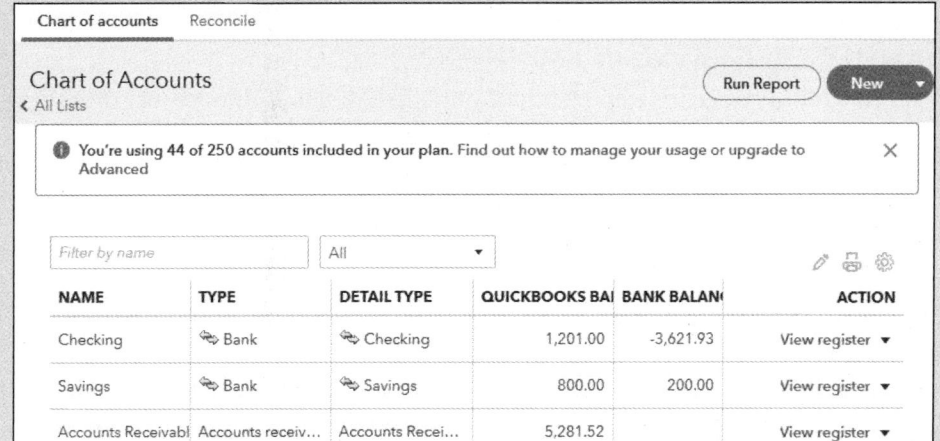

Figure 1.20

Chart of Accounts (partial view)

2. Scroll down the chart of accounts. Each asset, liability, and equity account has a View register action item listed.

3. As you scroll down, you will see that the balance in the chart of accounts for accounts payable (A/P) is $1,602.67.

4. Click **View register** on the Accounts Payable line of the chart of accounts to view the register for accounts payable shown in Figure 1.21. The ending balance in the A/P Register matches the $1,602.67 balance specified in the chart of accounts listing. (Remember to ignore dates in this Sample Company problem.)

Figure 1.21

A/P Register

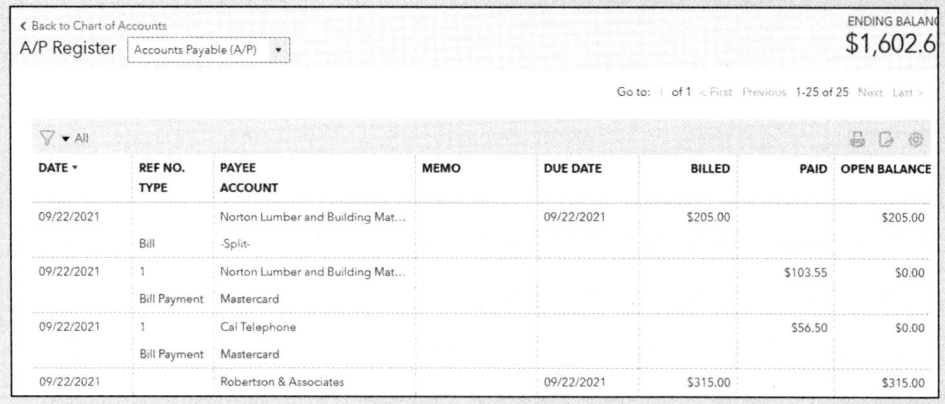

5. Click **Back to Chart of Accounts** located at the top of the A/P Register.

6. Scroll down the chart of accounts to see that each revenue and expense account has a Run Report action item listed. Click **Run Report** on the Landscaping Services account line to view an Account QuickReport for this account.

7. Scroll to the top of this Account QuickReport report. Select **This Year-to-date** from Report period drop-down list, and then click **Run report** to view the report shown in Figure 1.22.

Figure 1.22

Account QuickReport

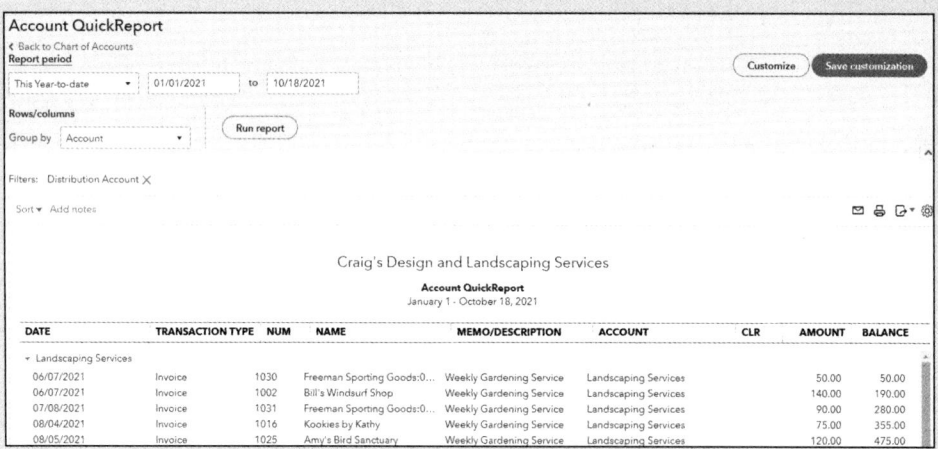

Lists

Lists in QBO provide you with an easy and quick way to view a collection of common items. Some of the more common lists include the chart of accounts, products and services, and terms. You can decide to view a summary of all the lists available in QBO and explore the list of terms.

An Introduction to QuickBooks Online Using the Sample Company   **Chapter 1**   15

To view a list of lists and the list of terms, do the following:

1. Click the **Gear** icon and then click **All Lists** to view a list of lists shown in Figure 1.23.

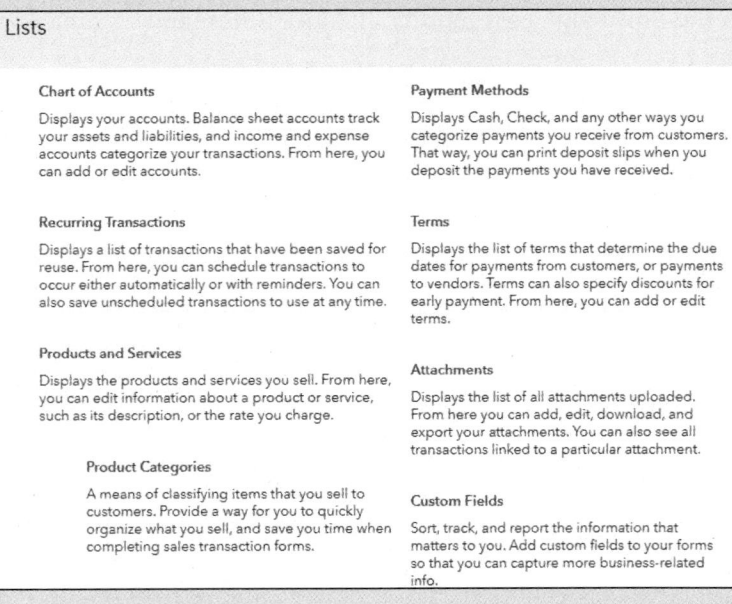

Figure 1.23

Lists

2. Click **Terms** to view the list shown in Figure 1.24.

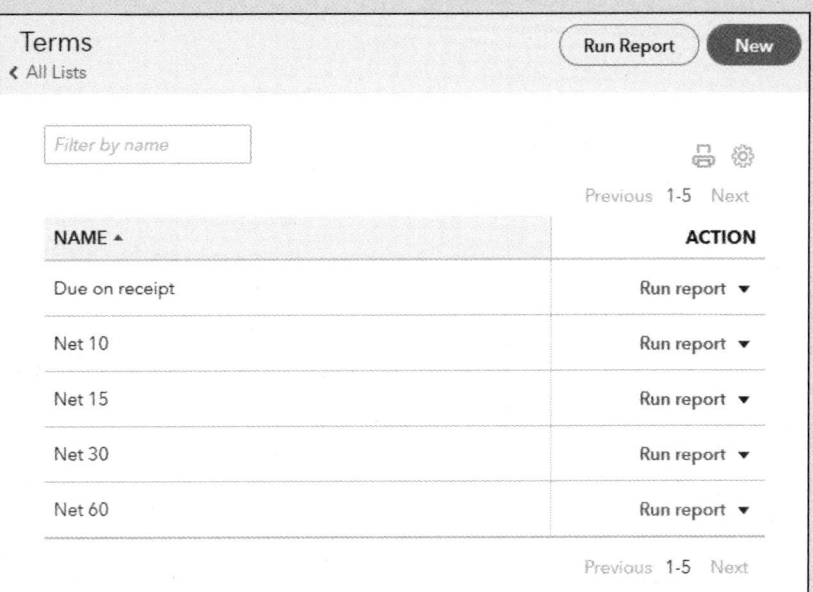

Figure 1.24

Terms

Reports

QBO comes with many predesigned reports for use in business, all of which you can customize for your particular needs. For instance, you can decide to focus on the common financial statement reports: the Income Statement (known in QBO as the Profit and Loss report), Balance Sheet, and Statement of Cash Flows.

1 Click **Reports** from the navigation bar.
2 Click **Standard** and then click **Favorites** to hide any reports QBO had tagged as a favorite.
3 Scroll down the page to see Business overview report options shown in Figure 1.25.

Figure 1.25

Business overview reports

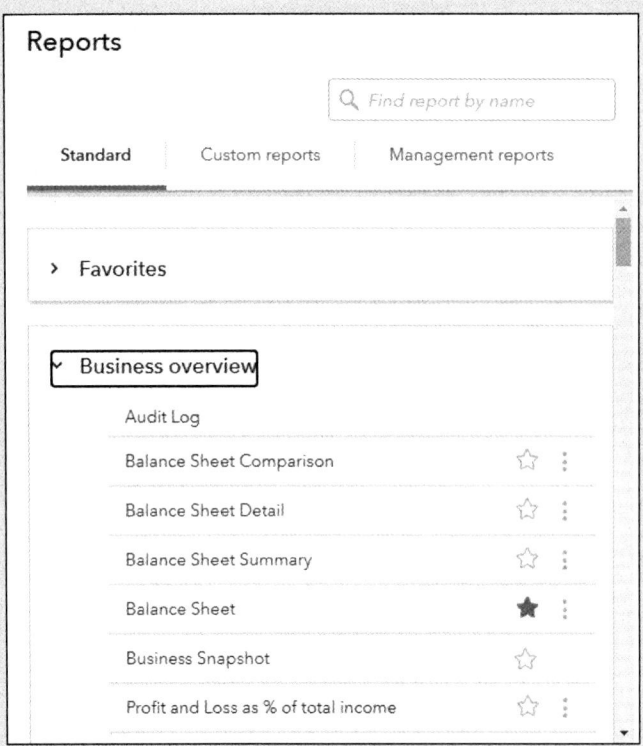

4 Scroll down the page and then click **Profit and Loss**. Click **Collapse** and then scroll to the top of the report to view the top part of the Profit and Loss Report shown in Figure 1.26. (If you view the entire report, you would note that clicking the **Collapse** text summarizes details under a heading. For example, Landscaping Services is shown as one number when Collapse is selected. Clicking **Expand** would show more detail. You will learn more about customizing and creating other reports in Chapter 10. Remember, the dates on your screen may differ from those shown in the figure.)

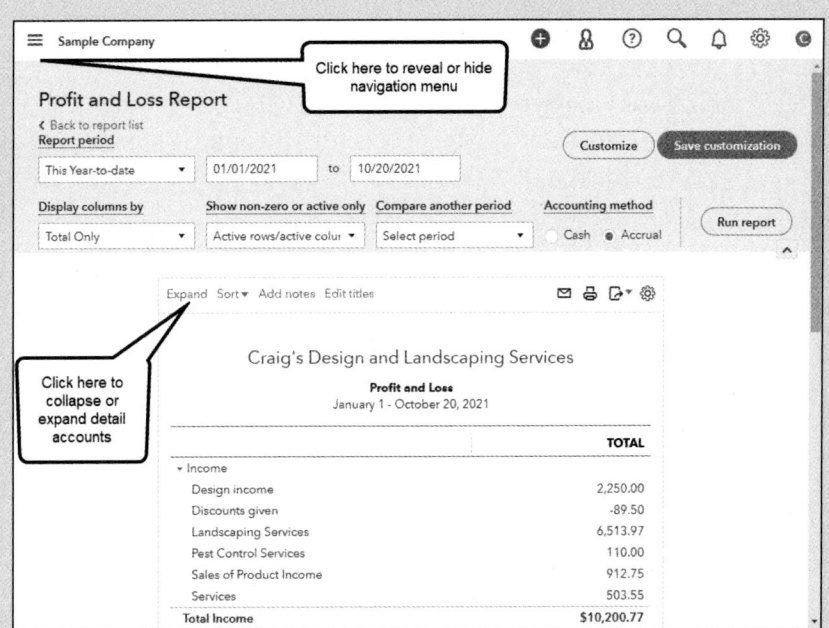

Figure 1.26

Profit and Loss Report (partial view)

5   Click **Reports**, then scroll to find and click **Balance Sheet**, and then scroll to the top of the report to view the top part of the Balance Sheet Report shown in Figure 1.27.

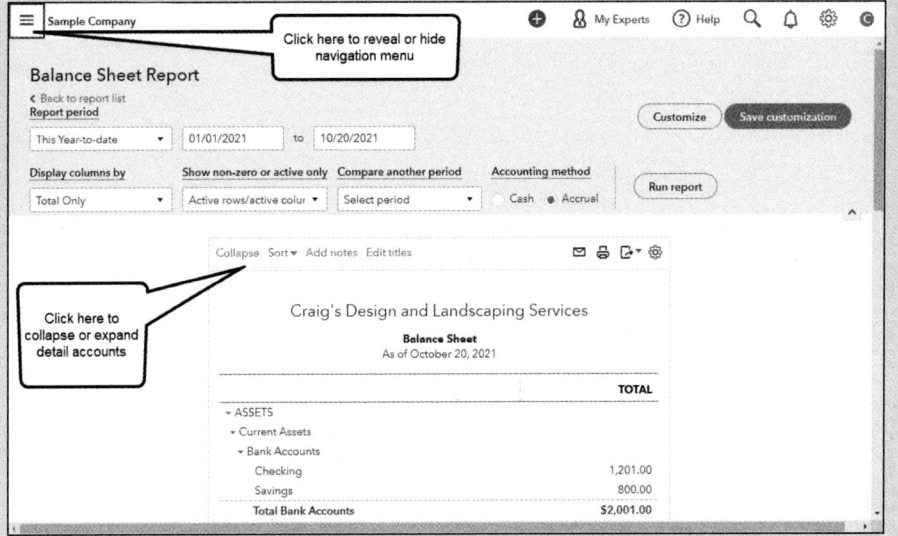

Figure 1.27

Balance Sheet Report (partial view)

6   Click **Reports**, then scroll to find and click **Statement of Cash Flows**, and then scroll to the top of the report to view the top part of the Statement of Cash Flows Report shown in Figure 1.28.

Figure 1.28

Statement of Cash Flows Report

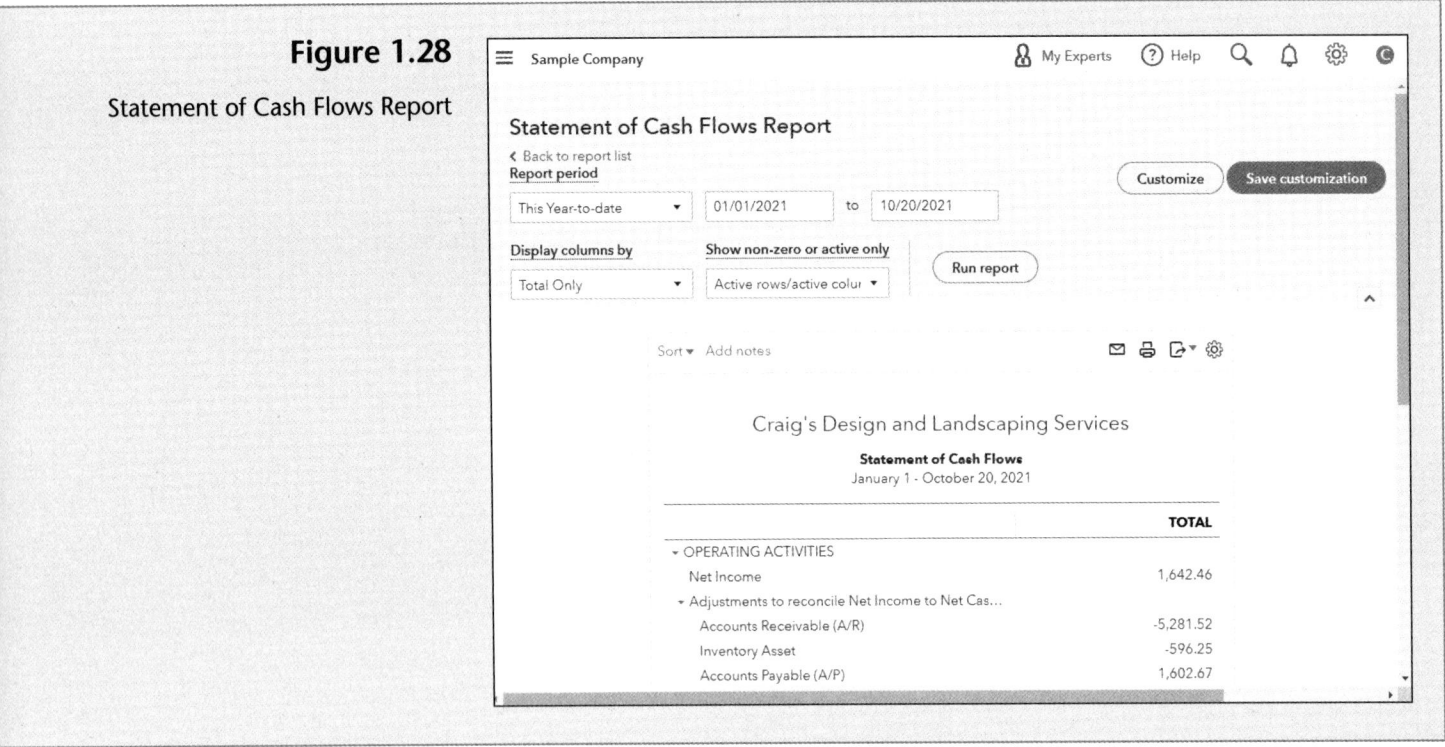

Alternatively, you can easily find a report if you know its name or part of its name. For example, if you wanted to access a report dealing with accounts receivable (A/R), you would type Accounts receivable into the report search box located in the Reports section.

To find a report related to accounts receivable, do the following:

1 Click **Reports** and type **Accounts receivable** in the Find report by name search box. Note the two reports that match your search as shown in Figure 1.29.

Figure 1.29

Reports

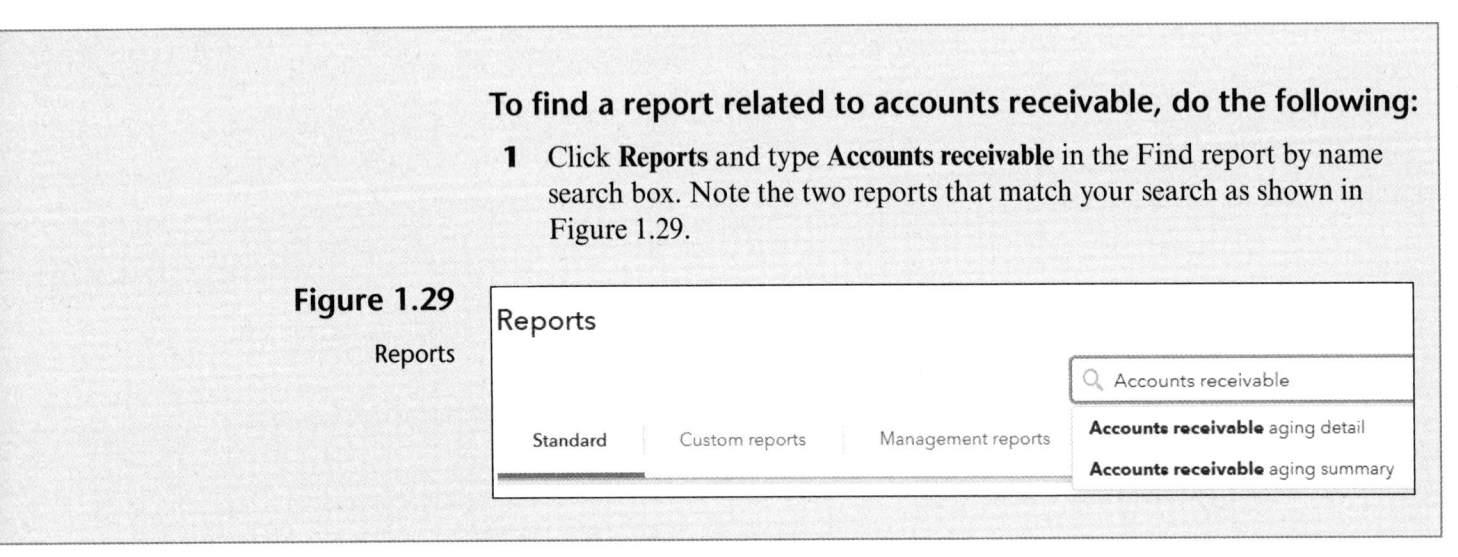

Company Settings

Five tabs are in the Settings section of QBO: Company, Usage, Sales, Expenses, and Advanced. You can edit these by clicking on the Pencil icon to the right of each section. The settings for the Sample Company have been modified from the default settings provided when QBO first creates a company. These options in the Settings section change the way QBO appears to the user. For example, in the Advanced section, if time tracking is turned off, no time tracking features will be available in QBO. Also, if purchase orders are turned off in the Expenses section, no purchase orders will be available in QBO. You can decide to view each of these sections to learn more about what options you are given in QBO.

1. Click the **Gear** icon and then click **Account and settings**, and click the **Company** tab to view the Company Settings section shown in Figure 1.30.

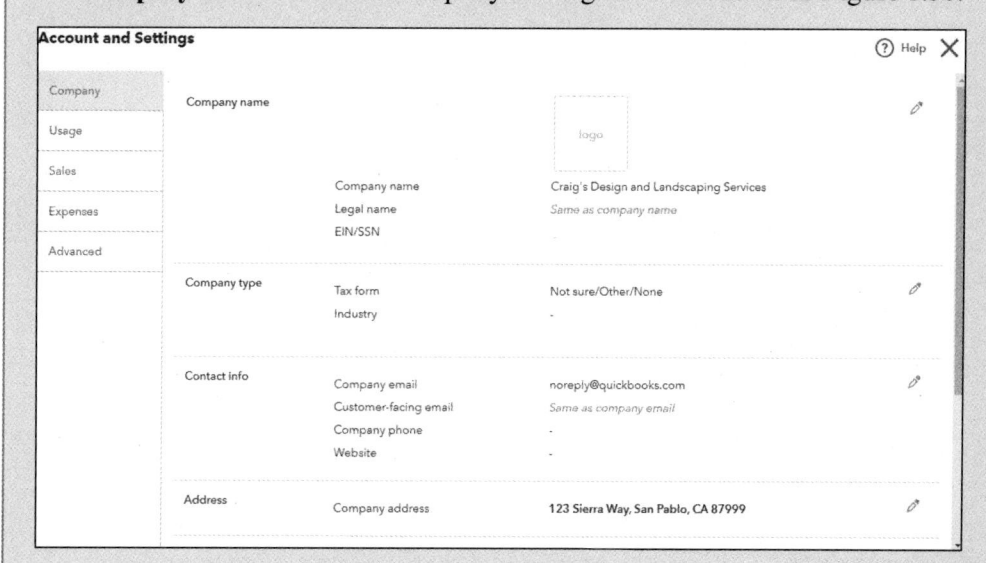

Figure 1.30

Company settings

2. Click the **Sales** tab in the Account and Settings window to view options provided as shown in Figure 1.31.

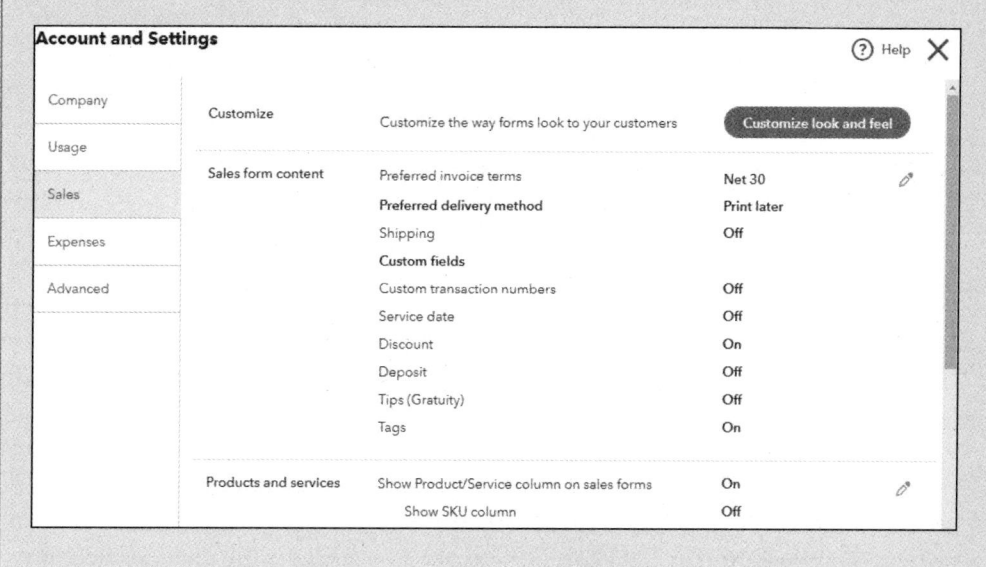

Figure 1.31

Sales settings

3   Click the **Expenses** tab in the Account and Settings window to view options provided as shown in Figure 1.32. Note that this is where you can turn purchase orders on or off.

Figure 1.32

Expenses settings

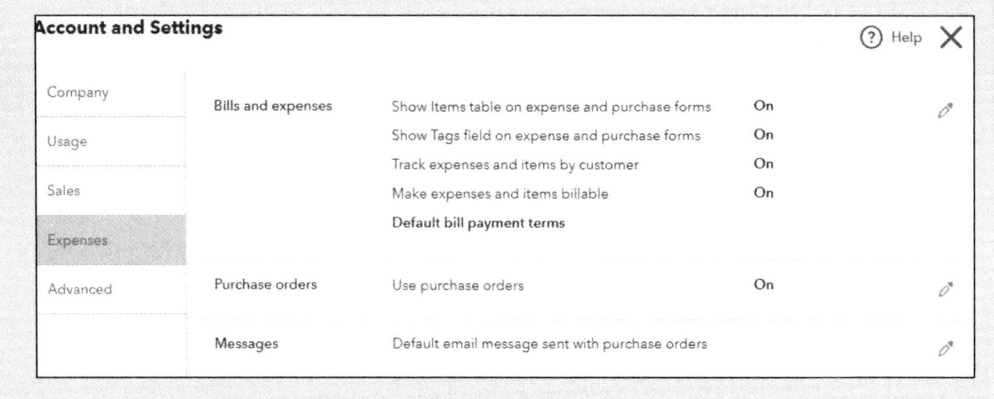

Account and Settings				
Company	Bills and expenses	Show Items table on expense and purchase forms	On	
Usage		Show Tags field on expense and purchase forms	On	
		Track expenses and items by customer	On	
Sales		Make expenses and items billable	On	
Expenses		Default bill payment terms		
Advanced	Purchase orders	Use purchase orders	On	
	Messages	Default email message sent with purchase orders		

4   Click the **Advanced** tab in the Account and Settings window to view options provided as shown in Figure 1.33. Note that this is where you change your company type to corporation, sole proprietor, etc.

Figure 1.33

Advanced settings

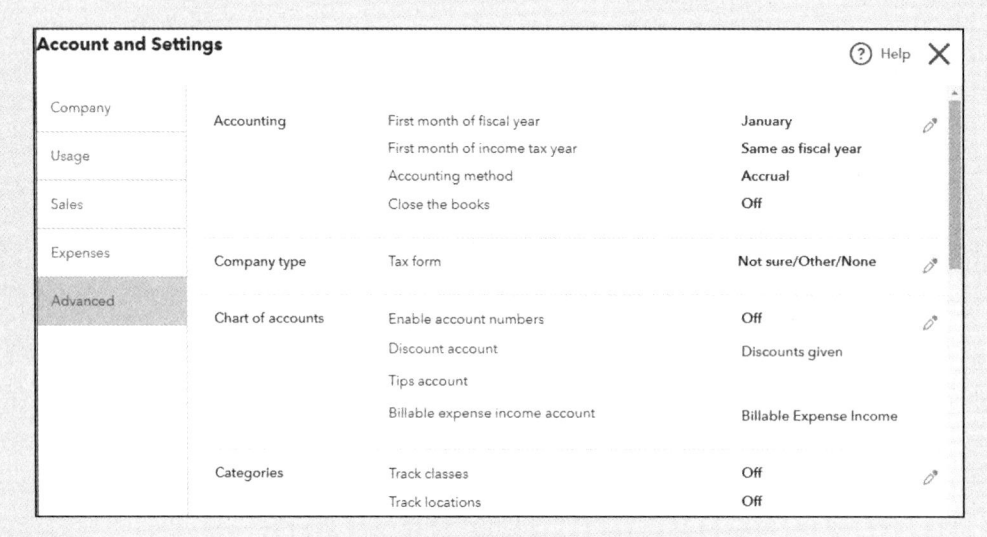

Account and Settings				
Company	Accounting	First month of fiscal year	January	
Usage		First month of income tax year	Same as fiscal year	
		Accounting method	Accrual	
Sales		Close the books	Off	
Expenses	Company type	Tax form	Not sure/Other/None	
Advanced	Chart of accounts	Enable account numbers	Off	
		Discount account	Discounts given	
		Tips account		
		Billable expense income account	Billable Expense Income	
	Categories	Track classes	Off	
		Track locations	Off	

5   Click **Done** to close the Settings window.

End Note

In this chapter, you have used Intuit's Sample Company to practice navigating QBO. You have accessed customer, vendor, and employee information; viewed various transactions; and viewed the chart of accounts, lists, reports, and company settings. In Chapter 2, you will either register as a new student or accept an invitation to work a case your instructor assigns you. In Chapter 3, you will use the Sample Company to learn how to modify settings, the chart of accounts, beginning balances, and products and services. In Chapters 4 through 10, you will use the same Sample Company to learn how to add operating, investing, and financing activities; reconcile a bank account; create a budget; add adjusting entries; and prepare financial statements and reports.

Chapter 1 Questions

1. What steps do you take to view customer information?
2. What steps do you take to view detail transactions related to a particular customer?
3. What steps do you take to view a specific bill from a specific vendor?
4. What steps do you take to view a specific employee's information?
5. How are bank deposits, which have not been recorded in QBO, classified?
6. How are bank charges, which have not been recorded in QBO, classified?
7. Opening the Sales Transaction section of QBO will provide a listing of _____.
8. Opening the Expense Transaction section of QBO will provide a listing of _____.
9. What lists are available in QBO?
10. What steps do you take to view all reports related to accounts payable (A/P)?

Chapter 1 Matching

a. Navigation bar
b. Amy's Bird Sanctuary
c. Brosnahan Insurance Agency
d. Recognizing
e. Uncategorized Income
f. Uncategorized Expense
g. Registers
h. John Johnson
i. Terms
j. Chart of accounts

_____ An employee in the Sample Company
_____ Bank deposits not yet recognized
_____ Exist for all asset, liability, and equity accounts
_____ Specify due dates for payment to/from vendors/customers
_____ Used to access a list of sales and expense transactions
_____ A vendor in the Sample Company
_____ A listing of all accounts available
_____ Bank charges not yet recognized
_____ A customer in the Sample Company
_____ Matching a banking transaction with a QBO transaction

chapter 2
An Overview of QuickBooks Online

Student Learning Outcomes

Upon completion of this chapter, the student will be able to do the following:

- Identify the basic features of QuickBooks Online (QBO)
- Explain how QBO is similar to and differs from the desktop version of QuickBooks
- Open the QBO company you created in the Preface to this text
- Provide information to QBO about your company
- Successfully navigate the QBO Dashboard
- Assign their instructor as their "Accountant"
- Use QBO's help feature

Overview

The focus of this chapter is to introduce you to QuickBooks Online (QBO) and get your account and company established. A description of QBO will be provided along with a brief comparison of how QBO differs from its desktop version. This text includes instructions provided by Intuit to create your own personal account with Intuit and create one and only one company. You will assign your company a name that includes your name for identification purposes. Welcome to the journey.

What Is QBO?

VIDEO LINK
Navigate your browser to the Video Tutorials provided by Intuit (see website address specified in the Preface to this text) and then search on how to get started in QuickBooks Online.

QBO is an online version of the popular QuickBooks accounting software developed by Intuit. The software is designed to capture common business events like purchases from and payments to vendors; sales to and collections from customers; payments and receipts to/from other operating, investing, and financing activities; period end accrual adjustments; and reports. Reports include the standard financial statements, including the income statement, statement of stockholders' equity, balance sheet, statement of cash flows, and other useful reports like accounts receivable aging. All interaction with QBO is done via an Internet connection. In other words, if you have not connected to the Internet, you will have no QBO. In other words, QBO cannot work offline.

All interaction with QBO is done online; there are no files to maintain on a computer, and everything is saved online. Thus, there is no need for backup files. The monthly fee for using QBO covers one and only one company. This text includes access codes for the user to create one company online for a limited amount of time.

How Is QBO Similar to/Different than the Desktop Version of QuickBooks Accountant?

Even though these two products share the name "QuickBooks," they are unrelated. QBO isn't a copy of QuickBooks that has been web enabled. They are different products with different database structures and approaches to solving problems even though both were developed in-house by Intuit to capture and report on accounting events.

Not all features available in QBO are available in the Windows desktop version of QuickBooks Accountant (QBDT). Likewise, not all features of QBDT are available in QBO. QBO requires an Internet connection. QBDT requires installation of software on to a computer. QBO requires a monthly fee. QBDT requires a one-time purchase and no monthly fees.

A key difference is that because QBO is online, it works on multiple operating systems (Windows, Apple, etc.) and multiple devices (desktops, laptops, smart phones, or tablets). The same cannot be said for QBDT. Intuit requires different software for QBDT to run on a Windows-based or an Apple-based computer. In this text, QBDT will always mean the Windows version of QuickBooks Accountant.

Some additional notable differences are the following:

- QBDT can be used for an unlimited number of companies; QBO limits you to four companies as assigned by your instructor. Need to manage more than four company outside of your class using QBO? Each will cost you another monthly fee.
- QBO can automatically download bank transactions for no additional cost.
- QBDT can track inventory purchases and sales based on an average cost assumption or a first-in-first-out assumption.
- QBO can track inventory purchases and sales based only on a first-in-first-out assumption.
- QBDT can account for the receipt of inventory items (receive items function) based on a purchase order; QBO cannot and calls inventory products and services.
- QBO can automatically schedule and send invoices, whereas QBDT cannot.
- QBDT can perform manual payroll without paying Intuit a monthly payroll processing fee. QBO encourages you to sign up for its payroll service and makes manually processing payroll difficult.
- QBO can be accessed from anywhere in the world where you have access to the Internet. QBDT requires a computer with the QuickBooks application and data files installed.
- QBDT provides for profit and loss as well as balance sheet budgeting. QBO only provides for profit and loss budgeting.
- QBO operates irrespective of platform (desktop, laptop, mobile device, or tablet) or operating system (Microsoft Windows or Apple iOS). QBDT does have a version of QuickBooks for both of those operating systems, but they are different and require two separate application purchases.

- QBDT includes a fixed asset management system, which will calculate depreciation and maintain detailed fixed asset records by individual asset, whereas QBO does not calculate depreciation and does not maintain detailed records of fixed assets.
- QBO provides automatic upgrades; this is a good and a bad feature. With QBO, you are almost always running the most current version (whether you want to or not).

How to Open the QBO Company You Created in the Preface

Instructions for both instructors and students are found in the Preface to this text. You must complete this registration process before you can proceed in this chapter.

Once you completed your QBO registration, you were presented with a QBO company shell (meaning a QBO company without any details). You were then instructed to sign out of QBO. In this section of the text, you are to return to that QBO company and add some additional information. When you return to that company you will be presented a series of questions to set up your company in QBO. Since you exited QBO before answering questions in the Preface, QBO automatically returns you to the setup questions. Once you have completed this setup process, QBO will open your company dashboard.

To login to the company you created in the Preface to this text:

1. Type **https://qbo.intuit.com/** into your web browser.
2. Enter your User ID and password and then click **Sign In**.
3. Click **Skip for now** when asked to verify your number. Your company welcome window should now appear and look like Figure 2.1.

Figure 2.1
Welcome window

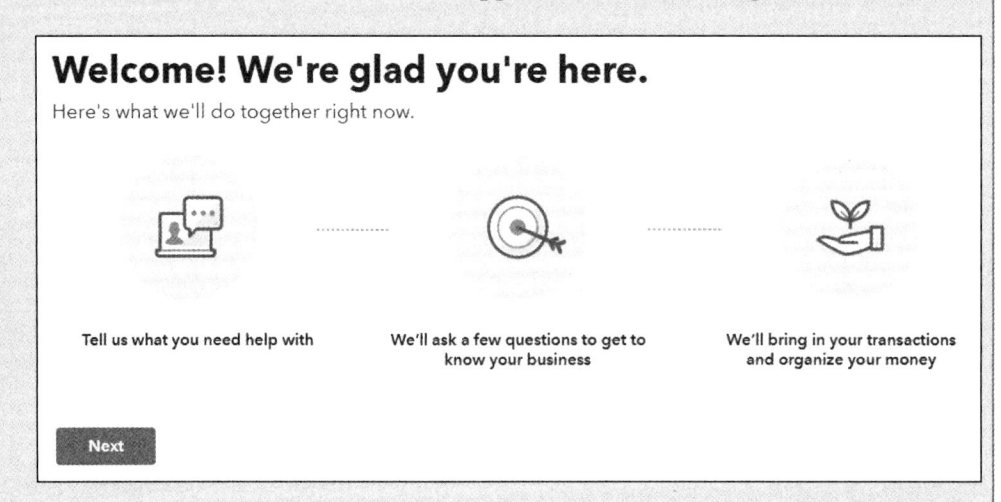

4. Click **Next** to answer the business name question. Type **Case 01 - Student Name (ID Number)** or whatever name your instructor specifies as shown in Figure 2.2.

An Overview of QuickBooks Online **Chapter 2** 25

Figure 2.2

Business name

What's your business name?

We'll use this to get you started in QuickBooks.

Legal business name

Case 01 - Student Name (ID Number)

☐ I'm moving from QuickBooks Desktop™ and want to bring in my data.

Back   Next

5 Click **Next** to answer the industry question. Click **Skip for now**.

6 Click **C Corp** to answer the type of business question as shown in Figure 2.3.

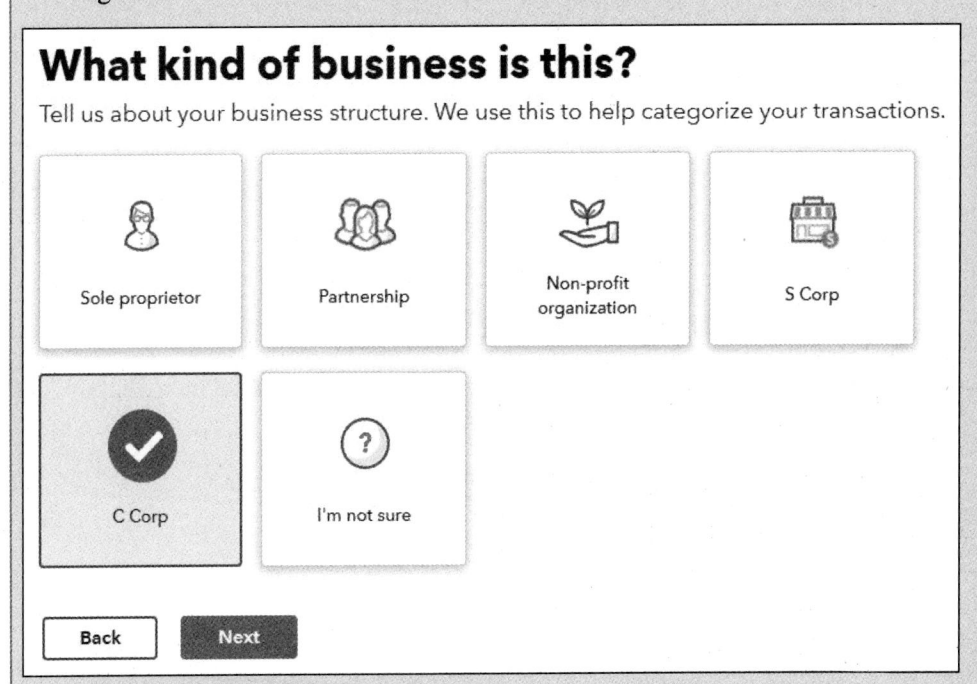

Figure 2.3

Type of business

What kind of business is this?

Tell us about your business structure. We use this to help categorize your transactions.

Sole proprietor   Partnership   Non-profit organization   S Corp

C Corp   I'm not sure

Back   Next

7 Click **Next** to answer the question about how your business makes money. Click **Provides services** and **Sells products** as shown in Figure 2.4.

Figure 2.4

How your business makes money

How does your business make money?

We tailor your accounting categories based on your answer. Select all that apply.

- Provides services
- Sells products
- Something else

Back Next

8 Click **Next** to answer the question about your main role. Click **Bookkeeper or Accountant** as shown in Figure 2.5.

Figure 2.5

Your main role

What's your main role at Case 01 - Student Name (ID Number)?

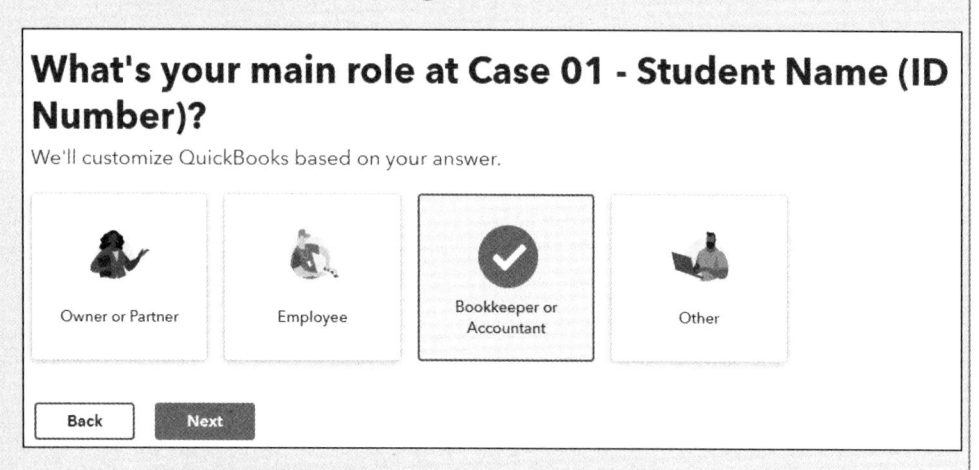

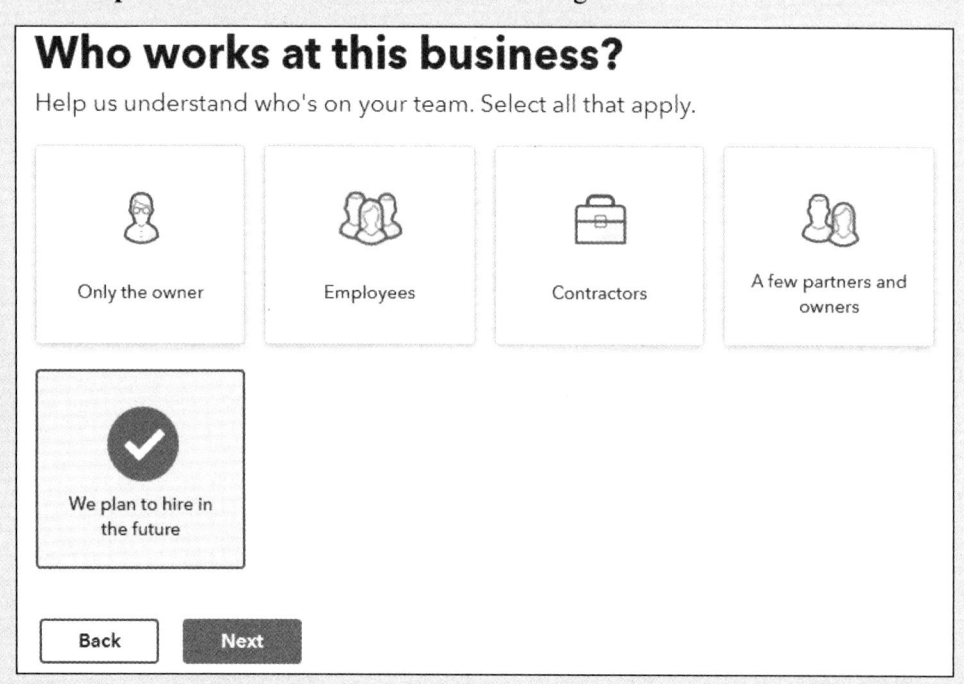

We'll customize QuickBooks based on your answer.

- Owner or Partner
- Employee
- Bookkeeper or Accountant
- Other

Back Next

9 Click **Next** to answer the question about who works at this business. Click **We plan to hire in the future** as shown in Figure 2.6.

Figure 2.6

Who works at this business

Who works at this business?

Help us understand who's on your team. Select all that apply.

- Only the owner
- Employees
- Contractors
- A few partners and owners
- We plan to hire in the future

Back Next

10 Click **Next** to answer the question about what apps you use. Click **Skip for now**.

11 Click **Skip for now** in the Link your accounts window.

12 Click the choices specified in Figure 2.7. Click **Next** to move to the next window.

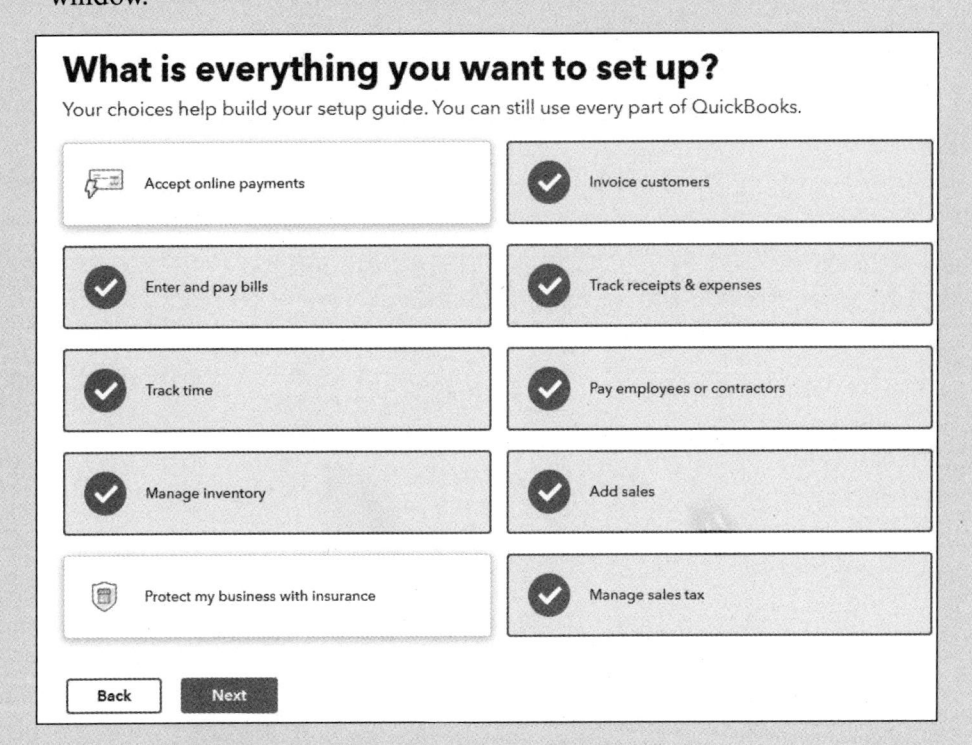

Figure 2.7

Choices to build your setup guide

13 Click **No, I don't want a free trial** when asked if you are ready for a free trial of QuickBooks Payroll, then click **Next**.

14 Click **Let's go** to complete the setup process. At this point, click **Take a quick tour** or close the Welcome to QuickBooks window to view your company dashboard as shown in Figure 2.8.

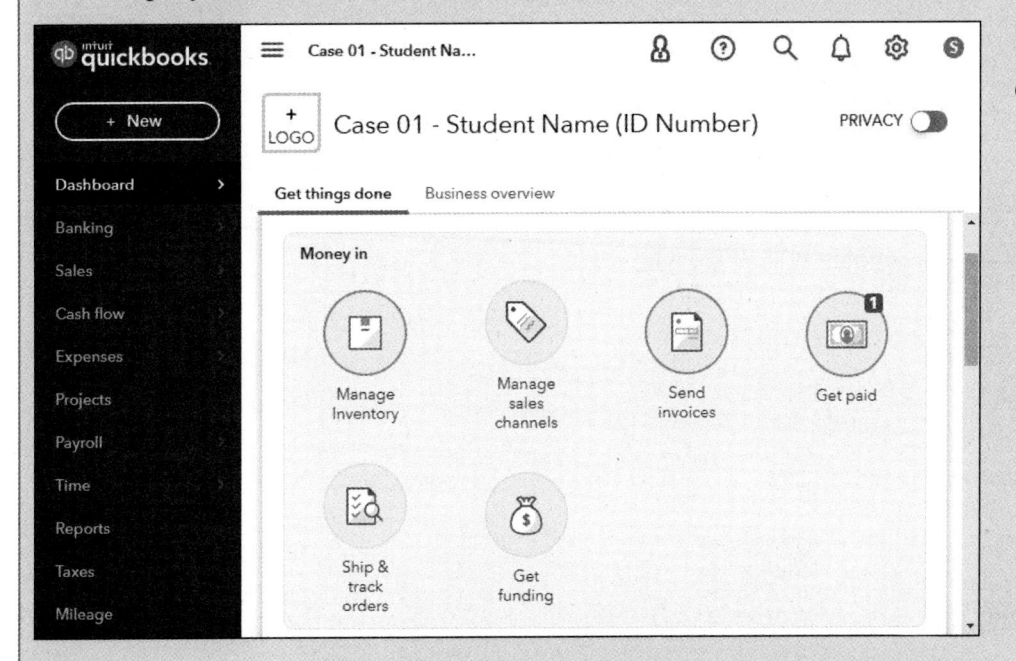

Figure 2.8

Company dashboard

15 Click the **Settings** icon to view the settings menu shown in Figure 2.9.

Figure 2.9
Settings menu

YOUR COMPANY	LISTS	TOOLS	PROFILE
Account and settings	All lists	Order checks	Feedback
Manage users	Products and services	Import data	Refer a friend
Custom form styles	Recurring transactions	Import desktop data	Privacy
Chart of accounts	Attachments	Export data	Switch company
QuickBooks labs	Custom fields	Reconcile	
	Tags	Budgeting	
		Audit log	
		SmartLook	

16 Click **Account and Settings** to view the Account and Settings section shown in Figure 2.10.

Figure 2.10
Account and Settings section

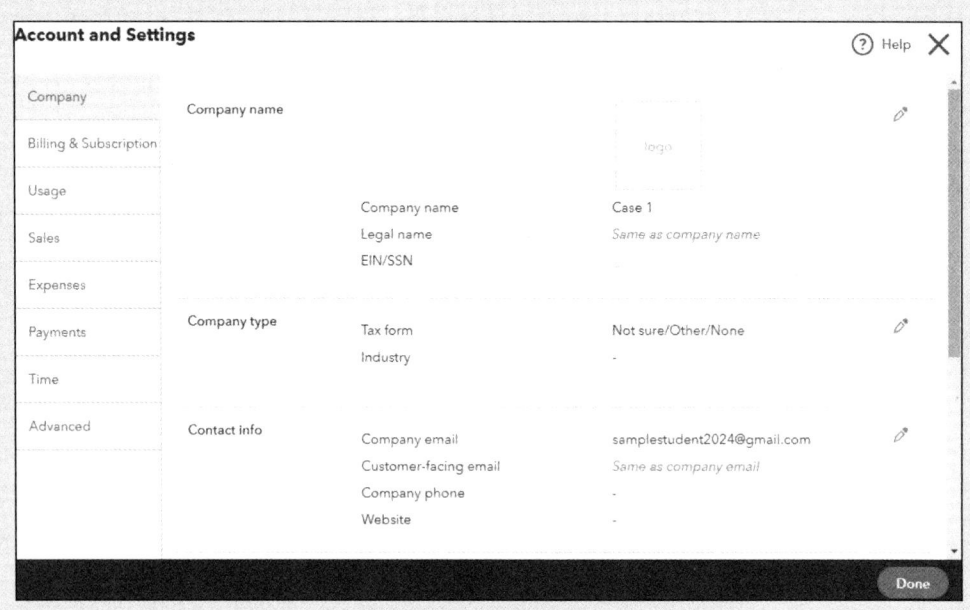

17 Click the **Company** tab and then click the **Pencil** icon in the Company name section of Account and Settings.

18 Confirm that **Case 01 - Student Name (ID Number)** replacing Student Name with your name and ID Number is in the Company Name text box and then place a check in the Same as company name check box as shown in Figure 2.11.

An Overview of QuickBooks Online **Chapter 2** 29

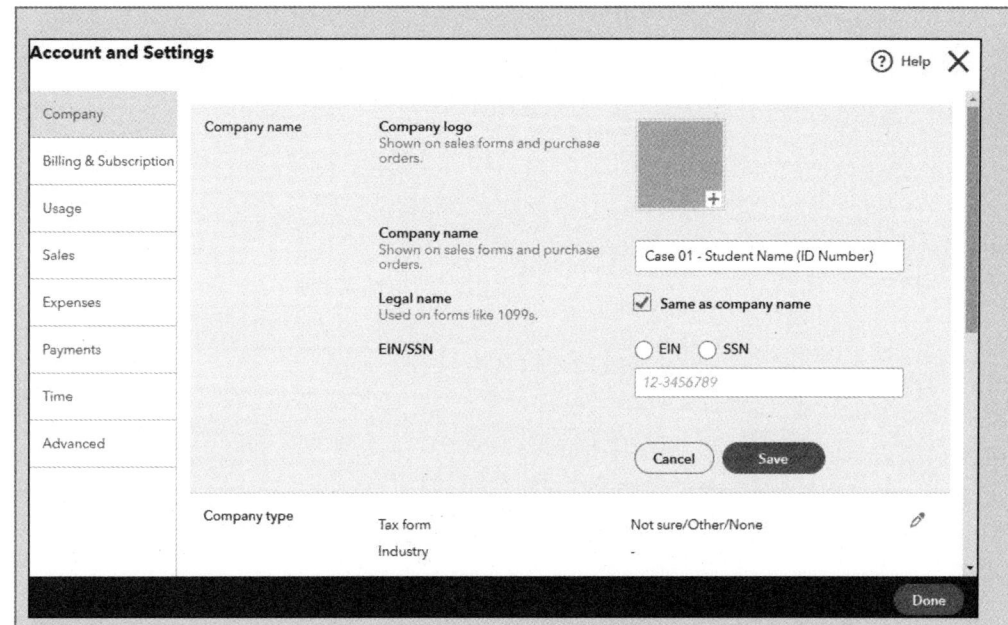

Figure 2.11

Changing your company name

19 Click **Save** to save your company name change.

20 Click the **Pencil** icon in the Company type section of Account and Settings

21 Confirm that Corporation is selected as the tax form as shown in Figure 2.12. The other options for Company type are shown. Depending on the case you're assigned, these may be more appropriate selections.

Figure 2.12

Choosing company type

22 Click **Save**.

23 Click the **Pencil** icon in the Address section of Account and Settings.

24 Type the address shown in Figure 2.13 into the Address section of Account and Settings. Remember that, depending on the case you're assigned, your case address may be different.

Figure 2.13

Company address

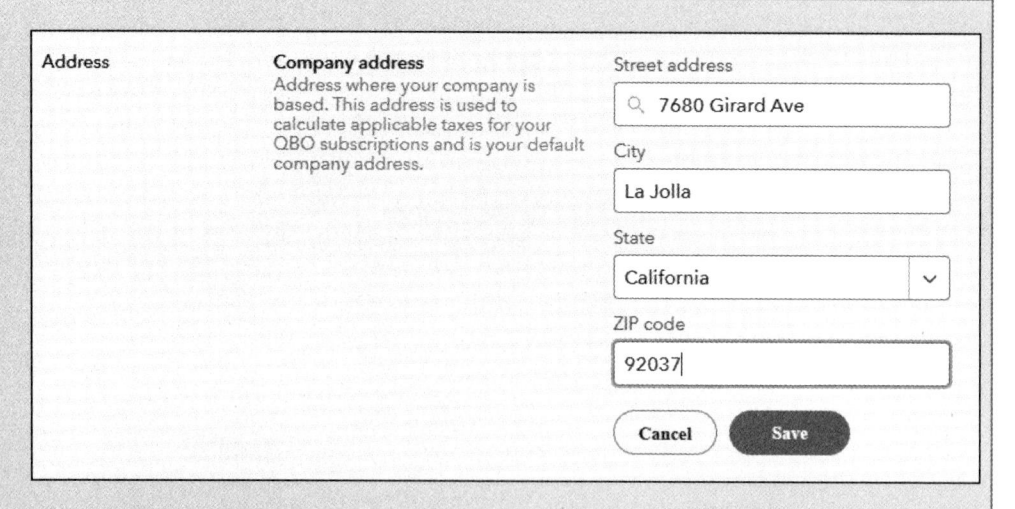

[Company address form showing: Street address: 7680 Girard Ave; City: La Jolla; State: California; ZIP code: 92037]

25 Click **Save**.

26 Click the **Sales** tab.

27 Make sure that the Preferred invoice terms are set to Net 30 in the Sales form content section and that Track inventory quantity on hand is On in the Products and services section.

28 Click **Done**.

29 Sign out of your QBO file by clicking on your account. In Figure 2.14, this is illustrated by clicking on the **S** in the upper right-hand corner of you QBO window and then clicking **Sign out**. Your window will look different.

Figure 2.14

Signing out of QBO

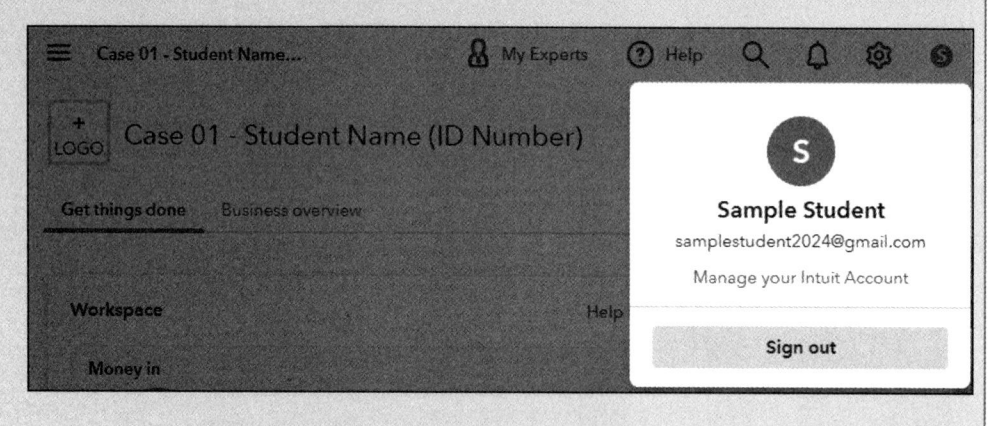

Navigating QBO

The Dashboard provides links to various tasks and resources. Clicking **Banking** in the navigation bar will let you set up a new checking account and view checking transactions. Clicking **Sales** in the navigation bar provides access to adding invoices and new customers, viewing existing balances, and highlighting overdue accounts. Clicking **Expenses** provides access to adding new expenses, new vendors, viewing existing balances, and highlighting overdue accounts. Clicking **Payroll** provides access to adding new employees and viewing payroll information. The Transactions and Reports links will be addressed later in this text.

First you'll need to login to your account and retrieve your QBO company.

Keep in mind that in this section, you'll be navigating QBO but not making any substantial changes to your Company. Modifications to your Company will occur in Chapter 3.

Navigate your browser to the Video Tutorials provided by Intuit (see website address specified in the Preface to this text) and then search on how to Navigate QuickBooks Online: Menus, Transactions, and Set Up

To login to the case you modified earlier in this chapter:

1. Type **https://qbo.intuit.com/** into your web browser.
2. Enter your User ID and password and then click **Sign In**.
3. Click **Skip for now** when asked to verify your number.
4. Click **Case 01 - Student Name** (Your window will include your name instead of Student Name) to view your QBO dashboard as shown in Figure 2.15.

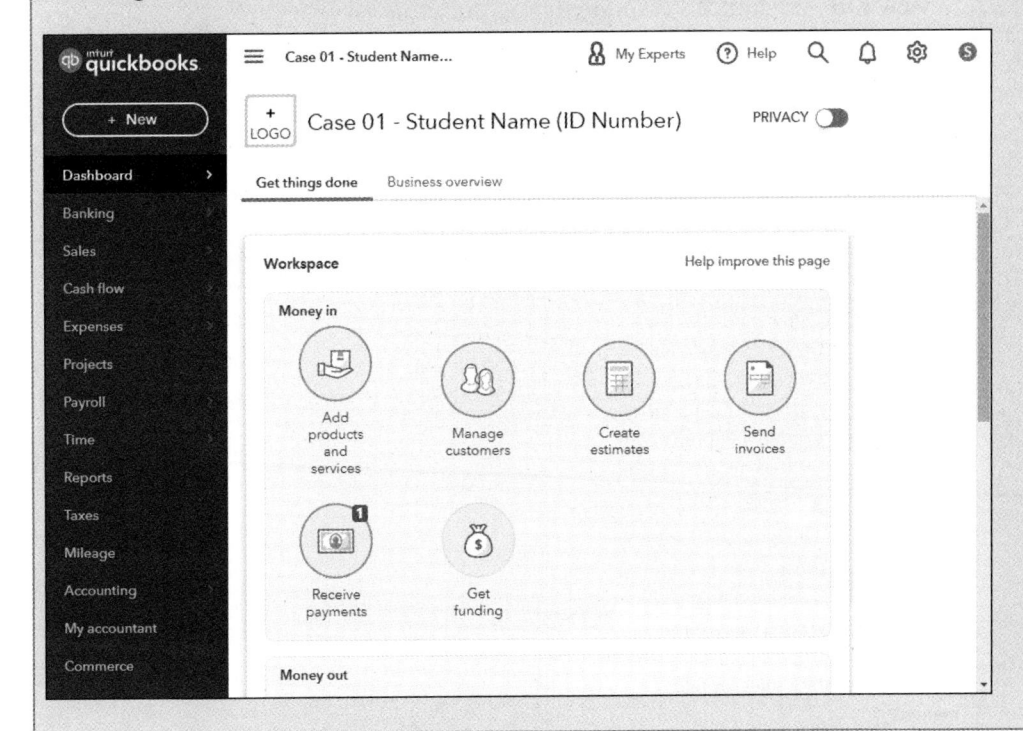

Figure 2.15

Changing your company name

Now that you're back into your QBO Company it's time to explore QBO's help features.

3. Then click **Add customer manually** to view Figure 2.20. As you have not yet entered any customers, QBO will ask you to add your first customer. You will do this later in Chapter 3. Remember QBO is an online application, and Intuit will change it often. Thus, the figures in this text may differ from what you see in QBO online.

Figure 2.20

Customer information window

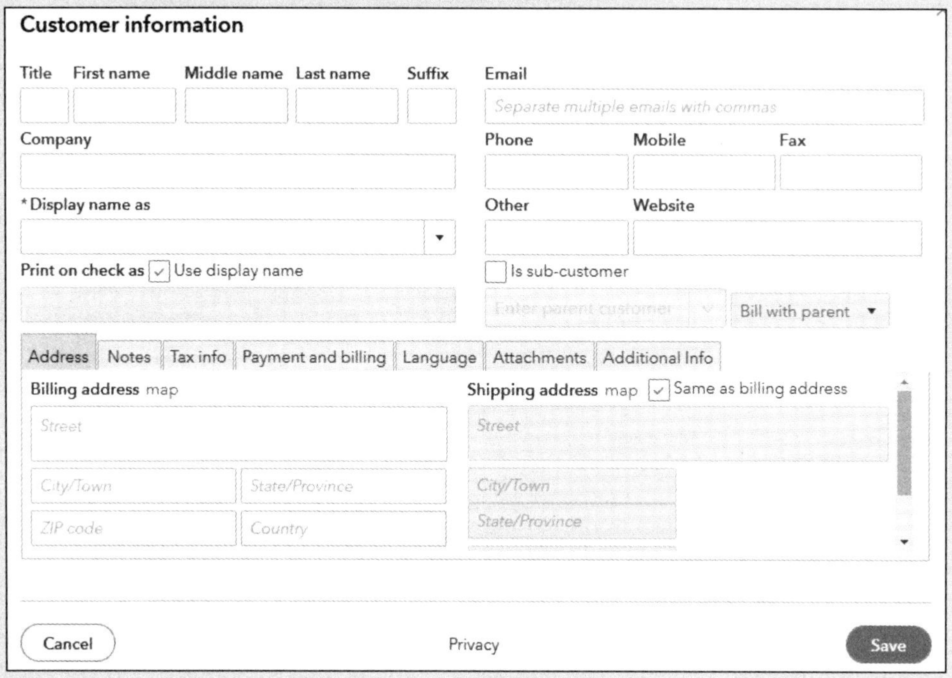

4. Click **Cancel** from the Customer information window, then click **Expenses** from the navigation bar, then click **Vendors**, and then click **Add vendor manually** to view Figure 2.21.

Figure 2.21

Vendor Information window

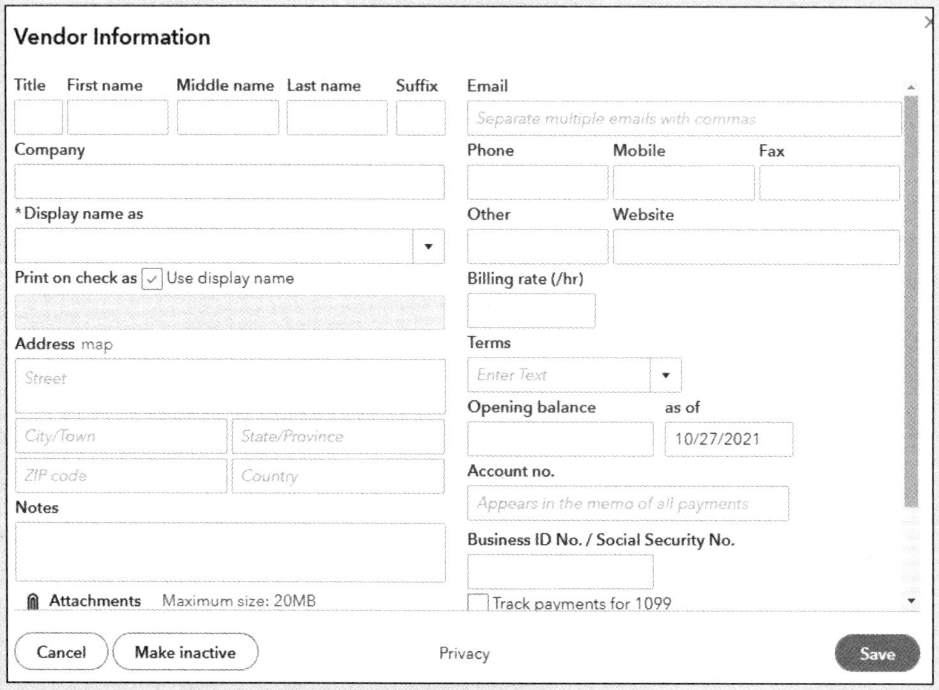

An Overview of QuickBooks Online **Chapter 2** **35**

5 Click **Cancel** from the Vendor Information window, then click **Payroll** from the navigation bar, and then click **Employees** to view Figure 2.22. In Chapter 3, you'll add employees by clicking **Add an employee** located at the bottom of the window shown. Once again in this chapter, we're just showing you how to navigate QBO.

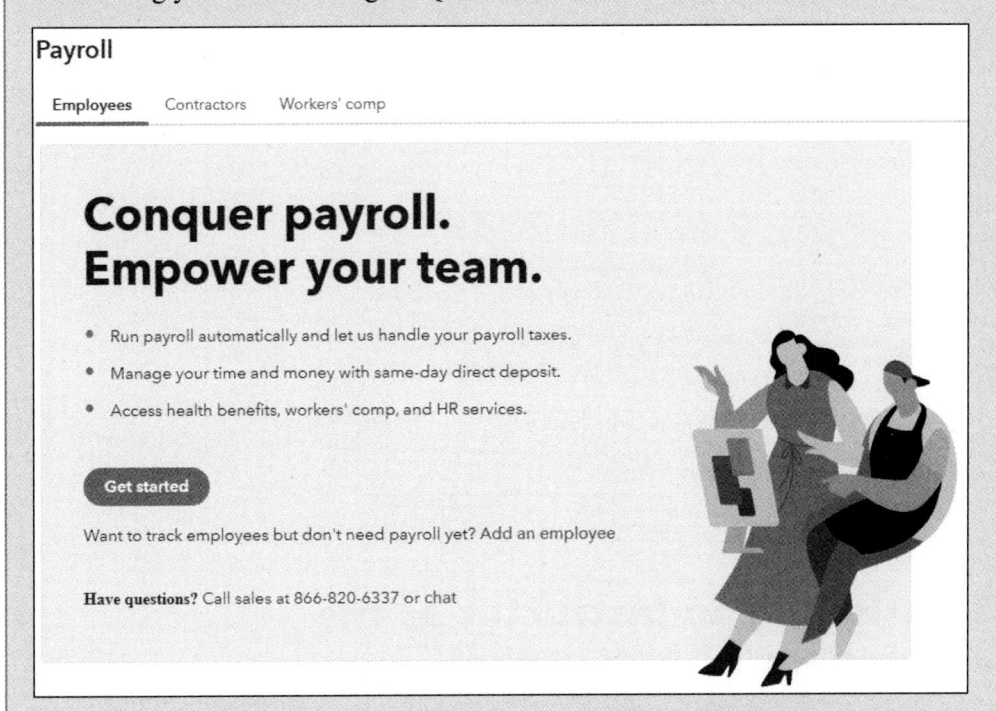

Figure 2.22

Getting started with payroll

6 Click the **Gear** icon located in the upper-right corner to view Figure 2.23. This menu gives you access to details about your company, lists (such as the chart of accounts, products and services, terms, etc.), tools (such as reconciling accounts and budgeting), and your profile, which will give you the ability to switch QBO companies.

Figure 2.23

Gear window

7 Click **Switch company** under the Profile heading to view Figure 2.24. Since you have only created one company, your window will only show your Case 1 file. However, if your instructor assigns you an additional case (they can assign you up to 4), more files will be shown such as you see in this figure. Click **Case 01 - Student Name** to return to your QBO company Dashboard.

Figure 2.24

Switching companies

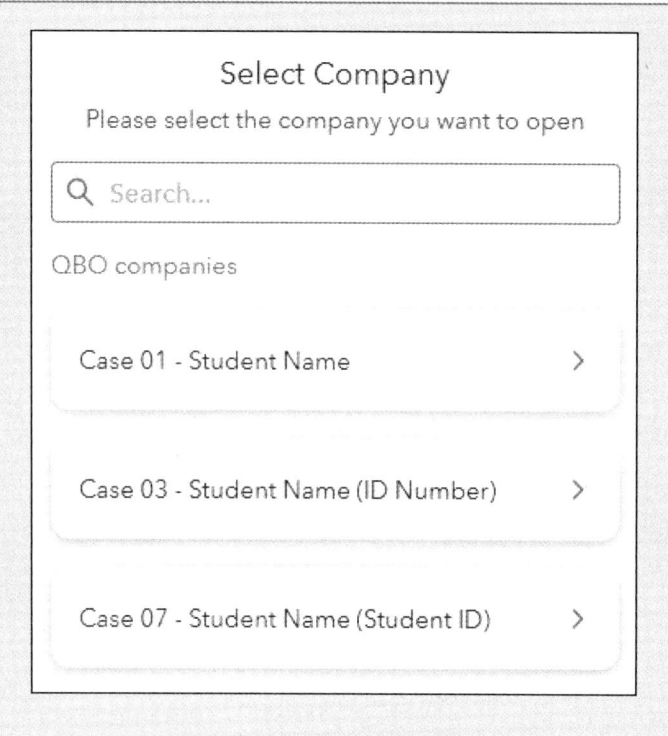

> **Select Company**
> Please select the company you want to open
>
> 🔍 Search...
>
> QBO companies
>
> Case 01 - Student Name >
>
> Case 03 - Student Name (ID Number) >
>
> Case 07 - Student Name (Student ID) >

"How to Give Your Accountant Access to Your QuickBooks"

Assigning an Instructor as the Company's "Accountant"

Your instructor may require you to assign them as your company's accountant. You do this so they, as your accountant, will always have access to your company files for grading and evaluation purposes. This will also assist the instructor in answering questions you may have about your company. The process of assigning an accountant to your company involves a brief interview in which you will provide your instructor's email address and name. Make sure you have that information before beginning this process. Your instructor will receive an email inviting them to be your accountant. Once the instructor accepts your invitation, they will have access to your company and the instructor's name will appear in the Accounting Firms section of the Manage Users page.

However, if your instructor is using the Intuit Educator Portal, you will not have to assign them as your accountant. Once they have assigned you a case, they will always be able to view your QBO file.

To assign an accountant to your company, do the following:

1. Click **My Accountant** from the navigation bar.
2. Type your instructor's email address in the space provided as shown in Figure 2.25.

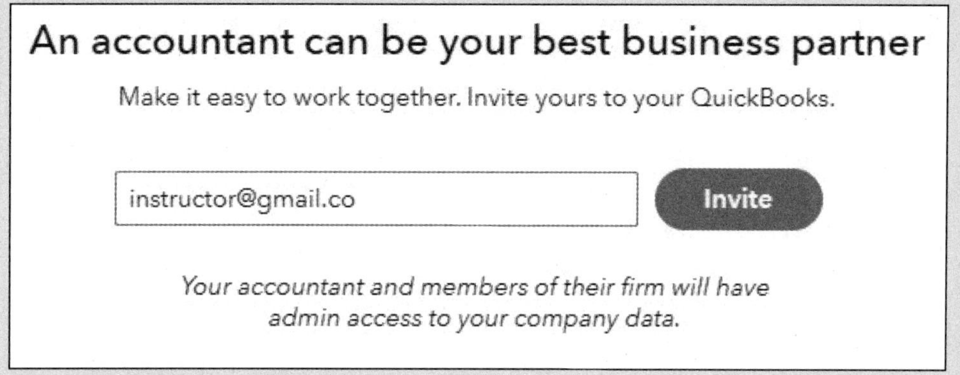

An Overview of QuickBooks Online **Chapter 2** **37**

> **An accountant can be your best business partner**
> Make it easy to work together. Invite yours to your QuickBooks.
>
> instructor@gmail.co   [Invite]
>
> *Your accountant and members of their firm will have admin access to your company data.*
>
> **3** Click the **Invite** button.
> **4** Once your instructor accepts your QuickBooks invitation, you'll be good to go.

Figure 2.25

Inviting your instructor to be your accountant

Video Tutorials for QuickBooks Online (Developed and Maintained by Intuit)

Intuit, the developer of QBO, has made available video tutorials on youtube.com. The tutorials are step-by-step videos to learn your way around QuickBooks. The videos are organized into the following categories:

- Get started
- Account management
- Banking
- Expenses and vendors
- QuickBooks Commerce
- Sales and customers
- Reports
- Taxes

Throughout this text, the author will reference videos in the appropriate chapters. To view all tutorials, navigate your browser to https://quickbooks.intuit.com/learn-support/en-us/tutorials?product=QuickBooks%20Online&tutorial=get-started.

To view two videos on QuickBooks Online, do the following:

1. Navigate your browser to the web address given earlier. (https://quickbooks.intuit.com/learn-support/en-us/tutorials?product=QuickBooks%20Online&tutorial=get-started) Your window should look like Figure 2.26.

Figure 2.26
Video tutorials for QBO

Video tutorials for QuickBooks Online
Watch step-by-step videos to learn your way around QuickBooks.

Account management | Banking | Expenses and vendors | Get started | Invoices and payments | Reports | Sales and customers | Taxes | View all help

2. Type **navigate menus** into the Search for anything text box and then press [**Enter**]. Your window should look like Figure 2.27.

Figure 2.27
Accessing a video tutorial on navigating QuickBooks

Search Results

All | Answered | Unanswered

All × Clear All

Navigate QuickBooks Online: Menus, Transactions & Set Up (3:53)

by QuickBooks • 👍 139 • ⏱ Updated August 27, 2021

https://www.youtube.com/watch?v=masTmBp4Sd8

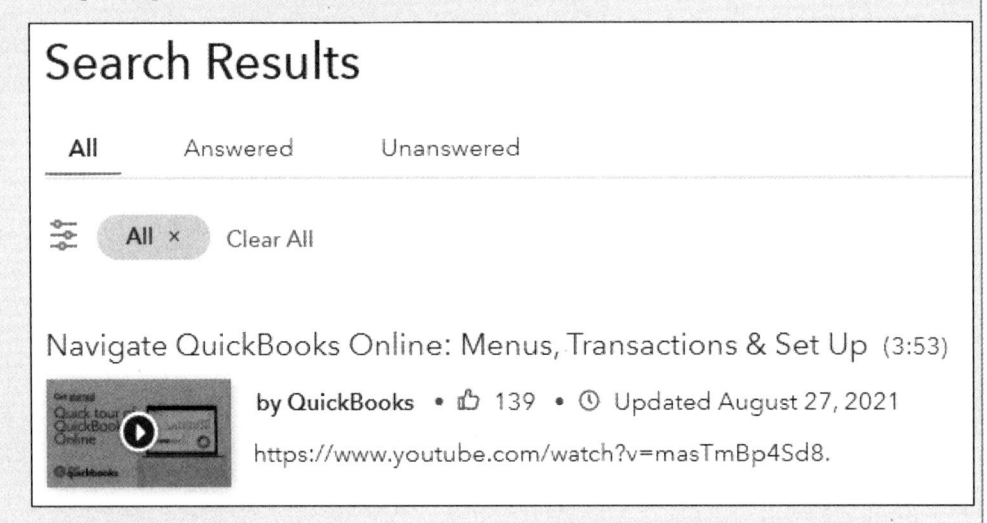

3. Click **Navigate QuickBooks Online: Menus, Transactions & Set Up** and then click the **Play** arrow (in the middle of the screen) to begin the video as shown in Figure 2.28.

Figure 2.28
Navigating QuickBooks Online video

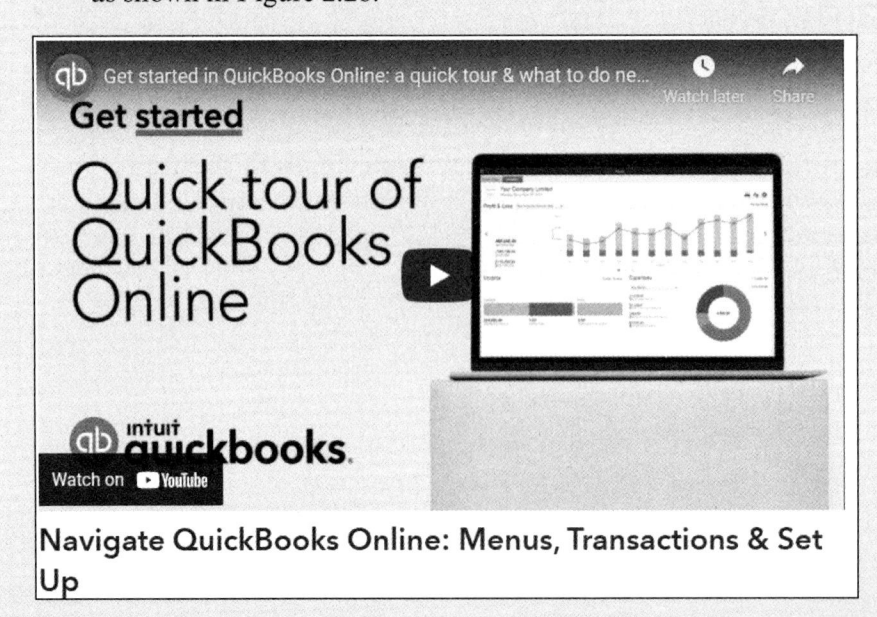

Get started in QuickBooks Online: a quick tour & what to do ne...

Get started

Quick tour of QuickBooks Online

intuit quickbooks

Watch on ▶ YouTube

Navigate QuickBooks Online: Menus, Transactions & Set Up

4 When you're done viewing the navigating video, return your browser to the previous page that lists the Getting Started videos.

5 Type **inventory** in the Search for anything text box and then press [Enter].

6 Click the text **Set up and track your inventory in QuickBooks Online,** then scroll down the page and then click the **Play** arrow (in the middle of the screen) to begin the video as shown in Figure 2.29.

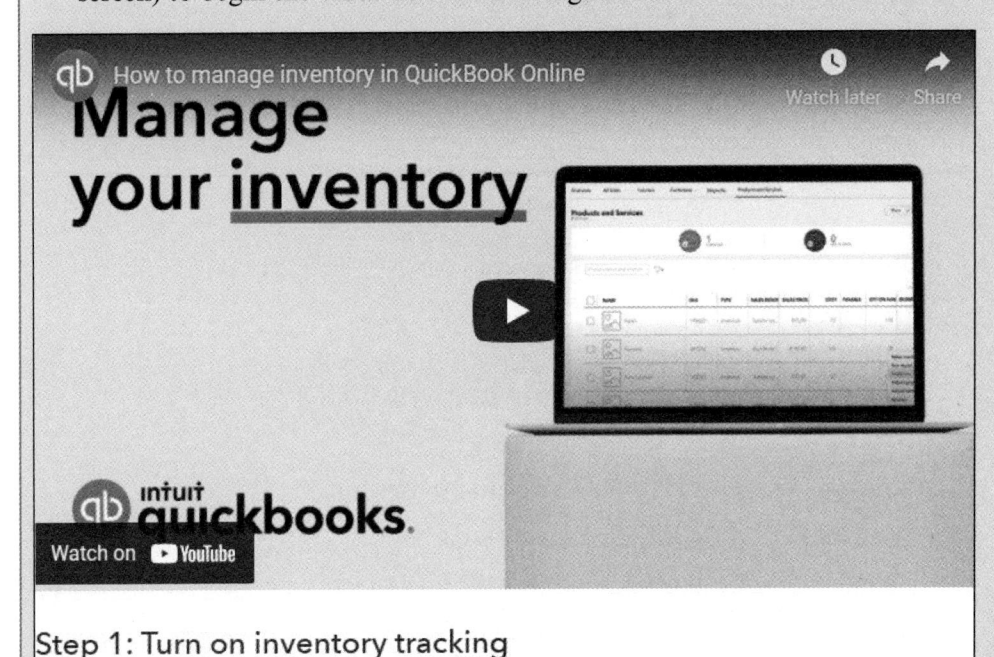

Figure 2.29

Managing inventory video

End Note

You have now been introduced to QBO, its basic features, and how it is similar to but not the same as QBDT. You logged into your Intuit account and provided basic information about your company and learned how to navigate around the QBO application. After assigning your instructor as your accountant, learning more about the help features in QBO, exploring Intuit's video tutorials in this chapter, and exploring the Sample Company in Chapter 1, you're ready to start entering your company's information into your QBO file in Chapter 3. Chapter 3 will demonstrate how to set up your company using the Sample Company. Then you will continue to set up your company by using the information provided at the end of Chapter 3 depending on what case your instructor has assigned.

practice

chapter 2

Chapter 2 Questions

1. How are QBO and QBDT different in the number of companies they can manage per license?
2. Does QBO work offline, without an Internet connection?
3. Do you need to back up QBO files?
4. How are QBO and QBDT similar?
5. What information do you need to supply to assign your instructor as the company's accountant?

Chapter 2 Matching

a. QBO _____ Click to access help
b. QBDT _____ Click to find past transactions
c. Gear icon _____ Click to access QBO employee information
d. Payroll _____ Online version of QuickBooks
e. Navigation bar _____ Click to add your instructor as your accountant
f. (+ New) icon _____ Provides links to QBO tasks and resources
g. Magnifying glass _____ Windows desktop version of QuickBooks
h. Help (?) icon _____ Click to add any transaction
i. Manage Users _____ Click to manage your subscription, users, and settings
j. Dashboard _____ On the left of the Dashboard, it shows a menu of items

Setting Up a New Company : Establishing a Chart of Accounts, Beginning Balances, Customers, Vendors, and Products/Services

chapter 3

Student Learning Outcomes

Upon completion of this chapter, the student will be able to do the following:

- Log into their account
- Change company settings
- Modify the chart of accounts; establish beginning balances; and create new customers, vendors, products, and services
- Close Opening Balance Equity and create a Balance Sheet
- Create, print, and export a Transaction Detail by Account report

Overview

You began this process in Chapter 2 when you created your account and provided basic information about your company, including the company name, address, industry, type, and so on. Now it's time to continue that process.

First off, however, you're going to revisit the Sample Company you worked on in Chapter 1. Each of the following chapters will work the same way. To begin, you will navigate your browser to the Intuit Sample Company. The text will demonstrate how to do certain tasks, such as modify defaults, add a new account, add a new transaction, and so on. These demonstrations will occur in the Sample Company. Remember, you can modify the Sample Company throughout each session, but once you close your browser window, QBO will not remember any of your activity in the Sample Company. When you navigate your browser back to the Sample Company, it will appear as it first did.

Each section of every chapter will begin with a demonstration using the Sample Company. That is followed by you logging back into QBO with the user name and password you created in Chapter 2 to complete an end-of-chapter case. In the case, you will be asked to perform tasks similar to those demonstrated in the Sample Company but now in your company. The tasks you accomplish on your company are permanent and will be there even after you close your QBO browser window. There is no Save File or Save File As command in QBO. Everything is saved for you.

42 Chapter 3 *Setting Up a New Company*

The dates used in this text for the Sample Company (Craig's Design and Landscaping Services) coincide with the dates this edition was written (November/December 2021/2022). When you access this Sample Company (e.g., in September of 2022), the transaction dates will be different. Thus the figures in this text and the instructions given specifying dates (like 9/30/21) will be different than what you see on your screen. The transactions themselves will be the same, but their corresponding dates will be different.

Company Settings

You can use this Sample Company to explore QBO as often as you would like. No matter what you do to modify this Sample Company, you will not be able to save it. When you leave and later return, it will look the same as it did initially.

To modify Sample Company settings, do the following:

1 Open your Internet browser.

2 Type **https://qbo.intuit.com/redir/testdrive** into your browser's address text box, and press [**Enter**] to view the Sample Company Dashboard.

3 From the Sample Company home page, click the **Gear** icon to manage your settings shown in Figure 3.1.

YOUR COMPANY	LISTS	TOOLS	PROFILE
Account and settings	All lists	Order checks	Feedback
Manage users	Products and services	Import data	Privacy
Custom form styles	Recurring transactions	Import desktop data	
Chart of accounts	Attachments	Export data	
QuickBooks labs	Custom fields	Reconcile	
	Tags	Budgeting	
		Audit log	
		SmartLook	
		Resolution center	

You're viewing QuickBooks in **Accountant view**. Learn more   Switch to Business view

Figure 3.1

Settings

4 Click **Account and settings**. The first screen is the Sample Company information shown in Figure 3.2. This is where you would change your company's name, tax form, industry, address etc. Scroll down this page to view information provided and then close this window.

Figure 3.2

Company settings

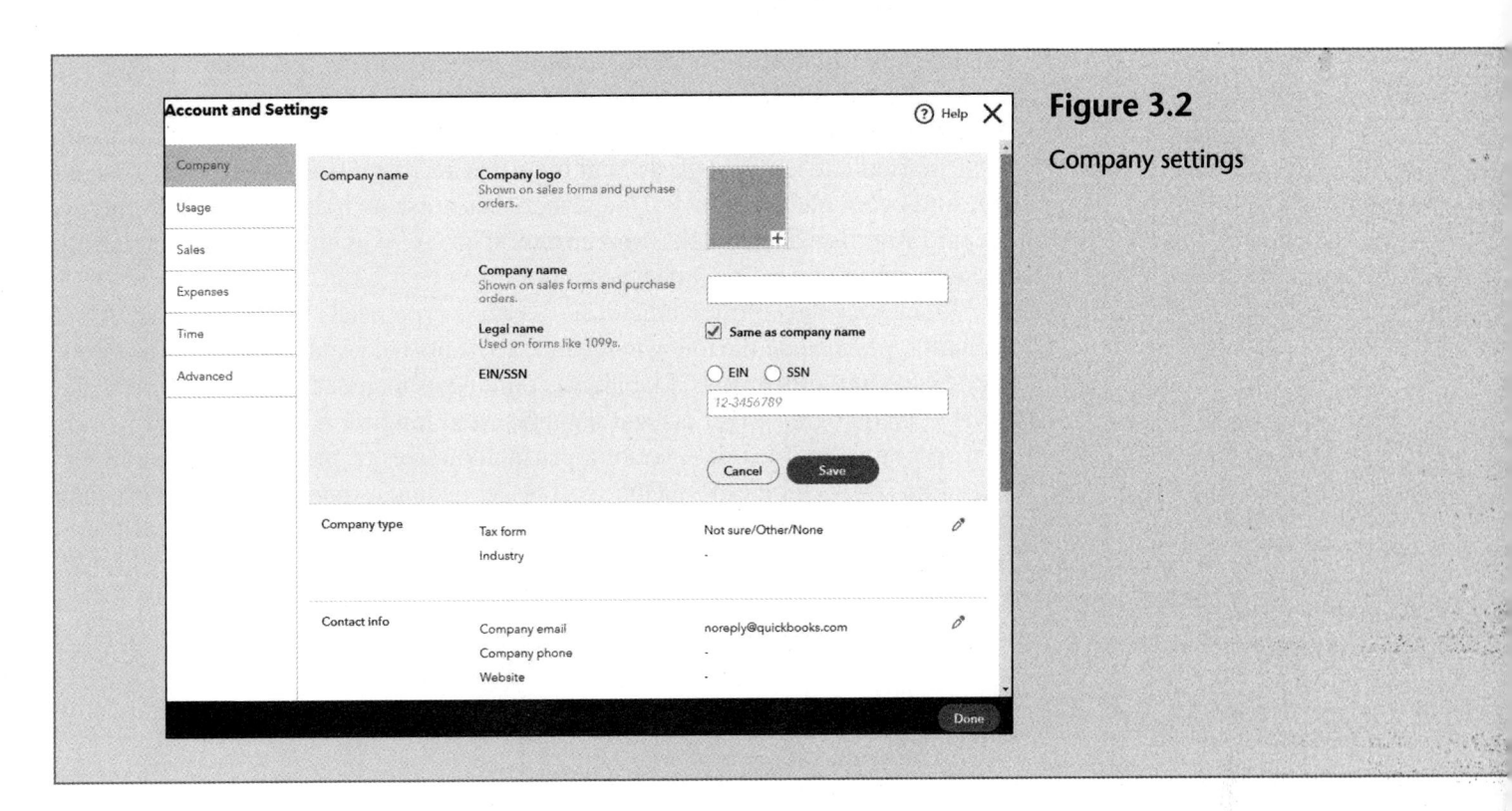

When you modify the settings of your company, you will visit this section of QBO to make changes and start by selecting the Pencil icon to edit each individual section. You reviewed the four sections of the Company settings window: Company, Sales, Expenses, and Advanced in Chapter 1. The most common changes to company settings involve turning on inventory, tracking of quantities on hand, tracking expenses by customer, making expenses and items billable, establishing default bill payment terms, using purchase orders, and tracking time.

Once you have modified the company settings, it is time to modify the chart of accounts.

Modify the Chart of Accounts and Establish Beginning Balances

You will continue your use of the Sample Company to learn the process of creating, modifying, and deleting accounts and of establishing beginning balances. If you are continuing from above, you will not need to open the Sample Company again. If not, follow the steps above to view the Sample Company. You should complete this entire section in one sitting so you do not lose your work. If you do leave and return, the cumulative balances will be inaccurate as your work will not have been saved while working in the Sample Company.

Creating accounts and related beginning balances only occurs when you are utilizing QBO for the first time and your business has been in operation for some time. The transition to QBO from a previous accounting system will indicate business events and balances that occurred prior to the first date of QBO use.

In this section, you will be adding new checking, inventory, prepaid rent, long-term debt, and common stock accounts to the Sample Company. You will also be establishing beginning balances for checking, accounts receivable, prepaid rent, inventory, and accounts payable. Every time you add a beginning

Navigate your browser to the Video Tutorials provided by Intuit (see website address specified in the Preface to this text) and then search on how to set up your chart of accounts.

balance, an equal and opposite amount is recorded to the Opening Balance Equity account (to keep debits and credits in balance).

QBO lets you establish a beginning amount for all of these accounts using basic journal entries. We will do that for some accounts, such as accounts receivable and accounts payable. For the other accounts, such as checking, inventory, prepaid rent, long-term debt, and common stock, you will set some beginning balances when you set up a new account.

When a new account is added, its account type needs to be specified. Asset account types include the following: bank, accounts receivable, other current assets, fixed assets, and other assets. Liability account types include the following: accounts payable, credit cards, other current liabilities, and long-term liabilities. Equity is its own account type. Income account types include sales of product income and services. Expense account types include cost of goods sold, expenses, and other expense. Every account needs to be assigned to one of these account types. This will dictate where the account appears in all reports, especially the income statement, balance sheet, and statement of cash flows. The detail type will further define where the account appears under its account type. Examples of bank account detail types include cash on hand, checking, money market, and savings.

To begin, let's add a new checking account with a beginning balance of $20,000.00.

To add a new checking account to the chart of accounts and establish a beginning balance, do the following:

1 Click the **Gear** icon and then click **Chart of Accounts**.

2 Click the **See your Chart of Accounts** button.

3 Click the **New** button in the upper-right corner of the chart of accounts.

4 Click anywhere in the Account Type text box, and select **Bank** as shown in Figure 3.3.

Figure 3.3

Account (adding a new bank account)

Setting Up a New Company **Chapter 3** **45**

5. Select **Checking** from the Detail Type list and type **Checking BOA** in the Name text box.

6. Select **Other**, then type **11/01/2021** in the Select a date text box, then type **20000** as the account balance, and then press **[Tab]** as shown in Figure 3.4. Remember the date you'll actually enter is the first of the month of the month and year you are actually working on QBO. For example, if you're viewing the Sample company in the month of December 2022, you would enter 12/01/2022. To enter the account balance, you'll need to scroll down the page to make the text box viewable.

Figure 3.4

Account (completing the addition of a new checking account)

7. Click the **Save and Close** button to view the modified chart of accounts shown in Figure 3.5, which now includes a new checking account with a balance of $20,000.00.

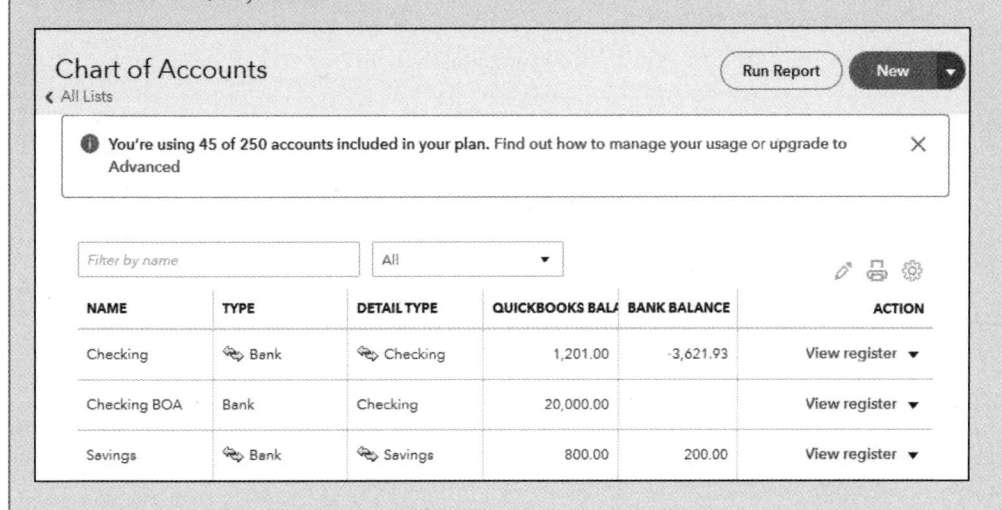

Figure 3.5

Chart of Accounts (modified with the new checking BOA account)

Navigate your browser to the Video Tutorials provided by Intuit (see website address specified in the Preface to this text) and then search on how top create an inventory product.

So far, we have added $20,000 to the assets to the Sample Company as of 11/1/21. The Opening Balance Equity account has also increased as the result of this adjustment. To continue, let's add a new product. In QBO, products are merchandise a company purchases from a vendor, maintains in inventory, and then sells to customers. Services are efforts made by a company to add value to a customer. In the Sample Company, an inventory account exists. If you create a new company, an inventory account may not exist. However, when you add a new product, a new inventory account, called inventory asset, will automatically be created.

To add a new product and service, do the following:

1. View the chart of accounts and note the Inventory Asset account with a QuickBooks balance of $596.25.
2. Click the **Gear** icon and click **Products and Services** from the Lists column.
3. Click **New**.
4. Select **Inventory** from the Product/Service information list.
5. Type **Stone Tile** as the new product in the Name text box.
6. Select **Landscaping** from the Category drop-down list.
7. Type **500** in the Initial quantity on hand text box and **11/01/2021** in the As of date text box.
8. Leave **Inventory Asset** as the Inventory asset account.
9. Type **Stone Tile** in the Description text box.
10. Type **2.50** in the Sales price/rate text box and **1.25** in the Cost text box.
11. Leave **Sales of Product Income** as the Income account and **Cost of Goods Sold** as the Expense account.
12. Select **Taxable - standard rate** from the Sales tax category text box drop-down list. Note it may already have been selected. Your window should look like Figure 3.6.

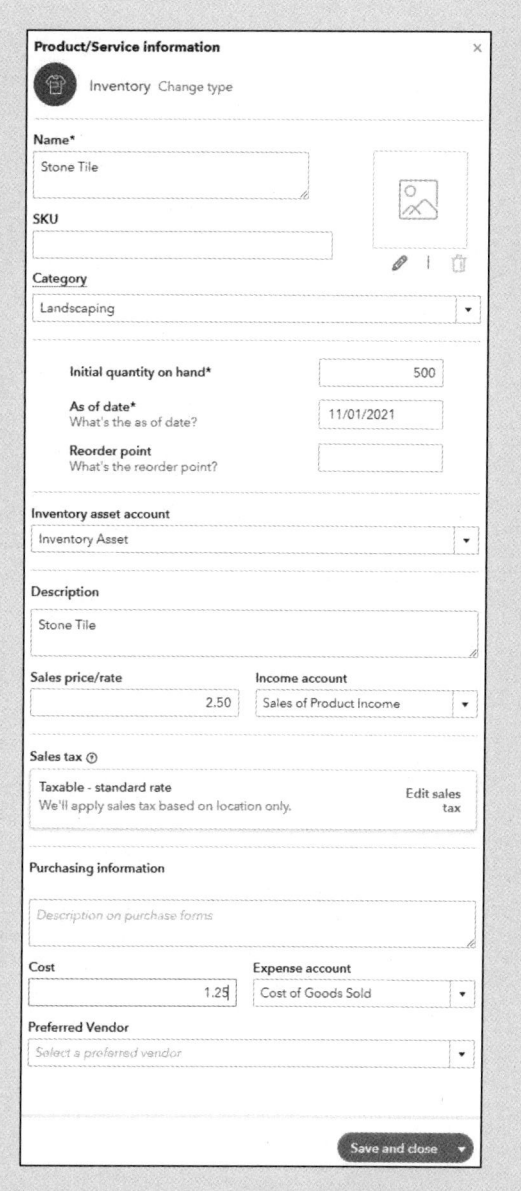

Figure 3.6

Product/Service information window

13 Click the down arrow in the Save and close button and then select **Save and New**.
14 Click on **Change type** next to the word Inventory at the top of the window. Click **Service**.
15 Type **Estimates** as the name of a new service.
16 Check the **I sell this product/service to my customers** check box and then uncheck the **I purchase this product/service from a vendor** check box.
17 Type **Estimates** as the Description on sales forms text box and then select **Design** from the Category drop-down list.
18 Type **50** in the Sales price/rate text box.
19 Click **Edit sales tax**, then click **Still don't see what you're looking for?**, then select **Nontaxable**.
20 Click **Done** and then click the **Save and Close** button.

21 Scroll down the list of products and services. Note the addition of the new Stone Tile product, with a quantity of 500, and the new Estimates service added.

22 Click the **Gear** icon and then **Chart of Accounts** and note the new balance in the Inventory Asset account of $1,221.25, which equals the previous balance of $596.25 plus the addition of $625.00 (500 units at the rate of $1.25).

So far, we have added a $20,625 (20,000.00 + 625.00) net increase to the assets to the Sample Company as of 11/1/21. The Opening Balance Equity account has increased as the result of this adjustment. To continue, let's add prepaid rent, long-term debt, and common stock accounts.

To add additional accounts, do the following:

1 Click the **New** button in the upper-right corner of the chart of accounts.

2 Click anywhere in the Account Type text box, and select **Other Current Assets**.

3 Select **Prepaid Expenses** as the Detail Type, and type **Prepaid Rent** as the name.

4 Select **Other**, then type **11/01/2021** in the Select a date text box, then type **4000** as the account balance, and then press [**Tab**].

5 Click the down arrow in the Save and Close button, and select **Save and New**.

6 Click anywhere in the Account Type text box, and select **Long-Term Liabilities**.

7 Select **Notes Payable** as the Detail Type, and type **Notes Payable Chase** as the name.

8 Select **Other**, then type **11/01/2021** in the Select a date text box, then type **9000** as the account balance, and then press [**Tab**].

9 Click **Save and New**.

10 Click anywhere in the Account Type text box, and select **Equity**.

11 Select **Common Stock** as the Detail Type, and type **Common Stock** as the name.

12 Select **Other**, then type **11/01/2021** in the Select a date text box, then type **1000** as the account balance, and then press [**Tab**].

13 Click the down arrow in the Save and New button, and select **Save and Close**.

14 Scroll down the chart of accounts. Note the addition of the new Prepaid Rent account with a balance of $4,000.00.

15 Continue scrolling down the chart of accounts. Note the addition of the new Notes Payable Chase account with a balance of $9,000.00.

16 Continue scrolling down the chart of accounts. Note the addition of the new Common Stock account with a balance of $1,000.00.

So far, we have added a $14,625 (20,000 + 625.00 + 4,000.00 − 9,000.00 − 1,000.00) net increase to the assets to the Sample Company as of 11/1/20. The Opening Balance Equity account is automatically increased as the result of this adjustment.

Lastly, we will set up beginning balances in accounts receivable and accounts payable by using journal entries and add a new customer and vendor at the same time. Journal entries are commonly used to adjust accounts. A customer is an entity to whom you sell products or provide a service. A vendor is an entity from whom you purchase products or services.

Navigate your browser to the Video Tutorials provided by Intuit (see website address specified in the Preface to this text) and then search on how to use journal entries.

To journalize accounts receivable and payable beginning balances, do the following:

1 Before you leave the chart of accounts, note the Opening Balance Equity account that has a balance of $5,287.50.

2 Click the [+ New] icon, and click on **Journal Entry** from the Other column.

3 Type **11/01/2021** in the Journal date text box.

4 Click in the **Account** column and then click the drop-down arrow.

5 Select **Accounts Receivable (A/R)** as the first account, and type **775** in the Debits column.

6 Click in the **Name** column, click the drop-down arrow, and select **+ Add new** to add a new customer related to this balance shown in Figure 3.7.

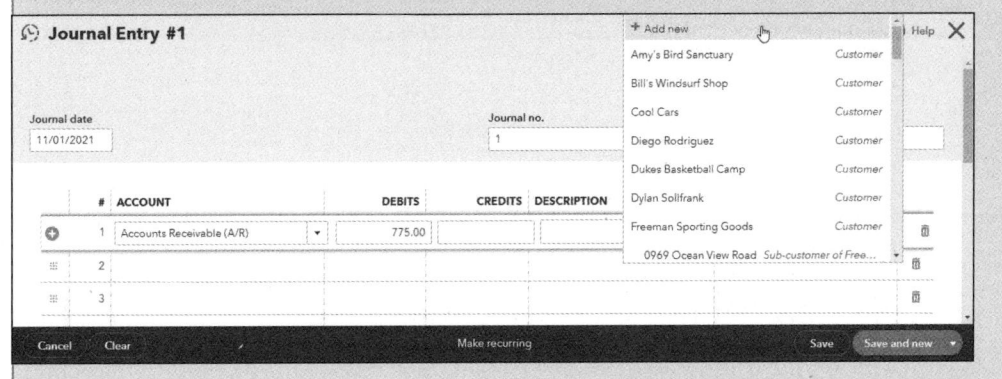

Figure 3.7

Accounts Receivable and Payable (journalizing beginning balances)

7 Type **Refugio** as the new customer shown in Figure 3.8.

Figure 3.8

New Name (adding a new customer name)

New Name

*Name

Refugio

Type

Customer ▼

+ Details   Save

8   Click **Save** in the New Name box.

9   Select **Accounts Payable (A/P)** as the second account, and type **500** in the Credits column.

10 Click in the **Name** column, click the drop-down arrow, and select **+ Add new** to add a new vendor.

11 Type **Rockster** as the Name, select **Vendor** as the Type and click **Save**.

12 Select **Opening Balance Equity** as the Account on line 3, and accept **275.00** in the Credits column. Your journal entry should look like Figure 3.9.

Figure 3.9

Journal Entry to set up A/R and A/P

Journal Entry #1

Journal date: 11/01/2021   Journal no.: 1

#	ACCOUNT	DEBITS	CREDITS	DESCRIPTION	NAME
1	Accounts Receivable (A/R)	775.00			Refugio
2	Accounts Payable (A/P)		500.00		Rockster
3	Opening Balance Equity		275.00		

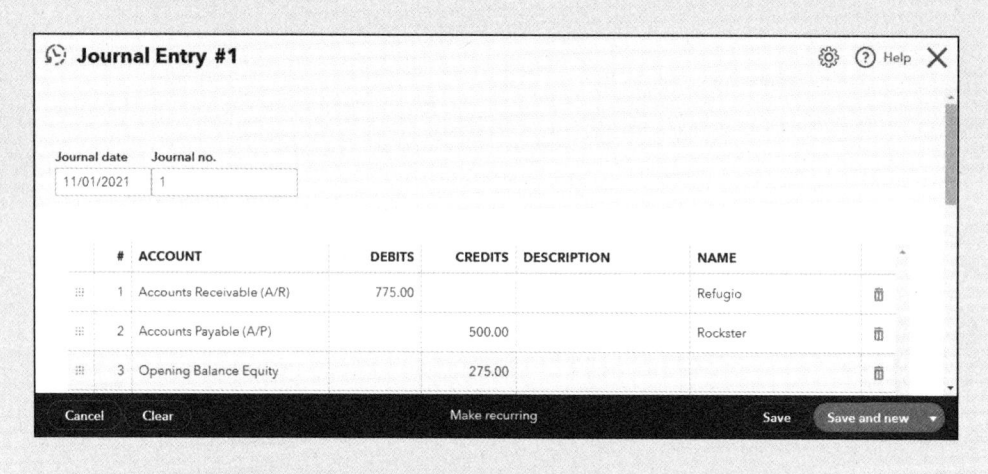

13 Click **Save and Close** to save your work.

14 Scroll down the chart of accounts, and note the Opening Balance Equity account, which now has a balance of $5,562.50 (5,287.50 + 775.00 − 500.00).

So far, we have added a $14,900 (20,000.00 + 625.00 + 4,000.00 − 9,000.00 − 1,000.00 + 775.00 − 500.00) net increase to the Sample Company as of 11/1/21. The Opening Balance Equity account has increased as the result of this adjustment. Additional adjustments were made when Intuit first set this company up. The balance as of 11/1/21 in the Opening Balance Equity account is $5,562.50.

Close Opening Balance Equity and Create a Balance Sheet

The final step in establishing beginning balances in QBO is to close out the Opening Balance Equity account as of 11/1/21 of $5,562.50. As we established a common stock account, the only account left in a corporation's equity accounts is retained earnings. Retained earnings are the earnings generated from prior years less dividends. You will need to create a trial balance, which lists the debit or credit balance in all accounts as of a specific date. Your instructor may ask you to customize, print, or export the trial balance to Excel, so you may do that as well.

To close opening balance equity and create, customize, save, print, and export a balance sheet, do the following:

1. Click the **+ New** icon, and click on **Journal Entry** from the Other column.
2. Type **11/01/2021** in the Journal date text box.
3. Select **Opening Balance Equity** as the first account, and type **5562.50** in the Debits column.
4. Select **Retained Earnings** as the second account, and type **5562.50** in the Credits column. Note: Retained Earnings was used since this company is a corporation. If this company was a sole proprietorship, you would use Owner's Equity. Your journal entry should look like Figure 3.10.

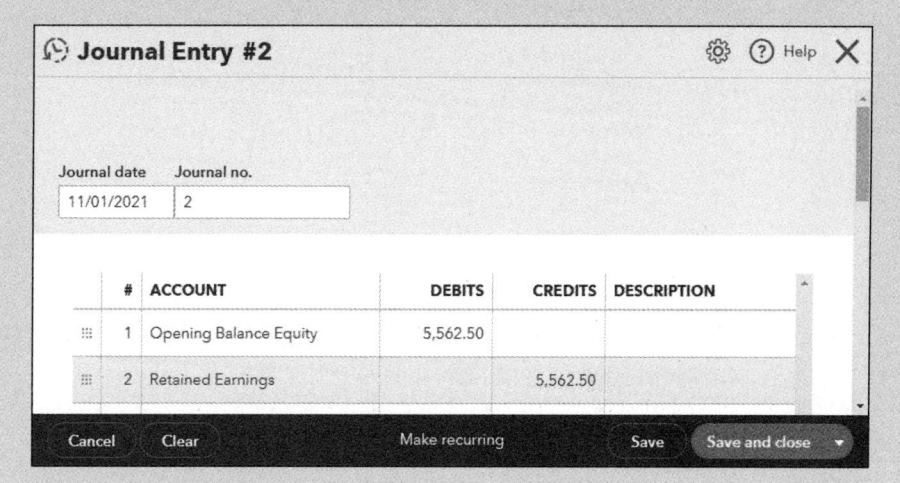

Figure 3.10

Journal Entry #2 (for closing Opening Balance Equity)

5. Click **Save and Close**.
6. Click **Reports** in the navigation bar.
7. Type **Balance Sheet** into the Find report by name search text box and then select **Balance Sheet** from the list provided from your search.
8. Scroll to the top of the Balance Sheet report and then select **Custom** from the drop-down list in the Report period text box.
9. Press **[Tab]** and then type your current system date in the from text box, and press **[Tab]**. (In this case, 11/1/2021.)
10. Type your current system date in the to text box, and press **[Tab]**.

VIDEO LINK

Navigate your browser to the Video Tutorials provided by Intuit (see website address specified in the Preface to this text) and then search on understanding the balance sheet.

52   **Chapter 3**   *Setting Up a New Company*

11 Click the **Run Report** button. Scroll to the top of the Balance Sheet report, and your screen should look similar to Figure 3.11 with different dates.

12 Click the **Printer** icon at the top of the report, and follow instructions to print your report as either a PDF file or a printed document and then close the Print window.

Figure 3.11

Balance Sheet (partial view as of 11/1/21)

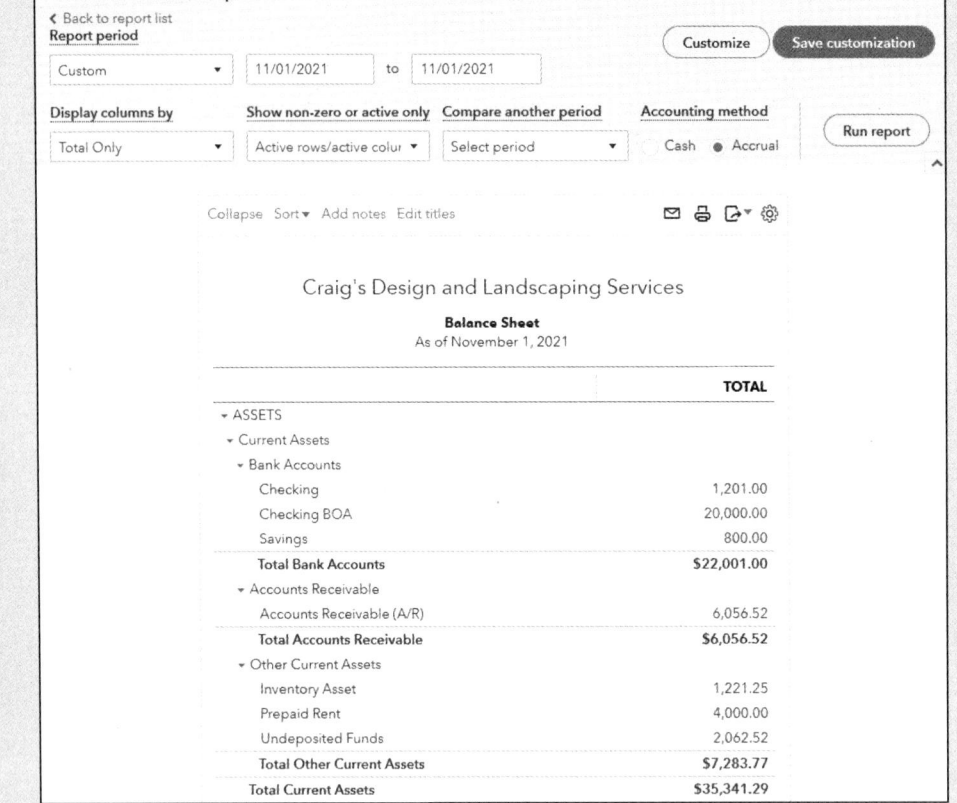

Balance Sheet Report

‹ Back to report list
Report period

| Custom | 11/01/2021 | to | 11/01/2021 |

Display columns by: Total Only
Show non-zero or active only: Active rows/active colur
Compare another period: Select period
Accounting method: Cash ● Accrual

[Customize] [Save customization] [Run report]

Collapse Sort▼ Add notes Edit titles

Craig's Design and Landscaping Services
Balance Sheet
As of November 1, 2021

	TOTAL
▼ ASSETS	
▼ Current Assets	
▼ Bank Accounts	
Checking	1,201.00
Checking BOA	20,000.00
Savings	800.00
Total Bank Accounts	**$22,001.00**
▼ Accounts Receivable	
Accounts Receivable (A/R)	6,056.52
Total Accounts Receivable	**$6,056.52**
▼ Other Current Assets	
Inventory Asset	1,221.25
Prepaid Rent	4,000.00
Undeposited Funds	2,062.52
Total Other Current Assets	**$7,283.77**
Total Current Assets	**$35,341.29**

VIDEO LINK

Navigate your browser to the Video Tutorials provided by Intuit (see website address specified in the Preface to this text) and then search on how to customize reports.

13 Click the **Save customization** button.

14 Type **Balance Sheet as of 11/1/2021** in the Custom report name text box as shown in Figure 3.12.

Setting Up a New Company **Chapter 3** 53

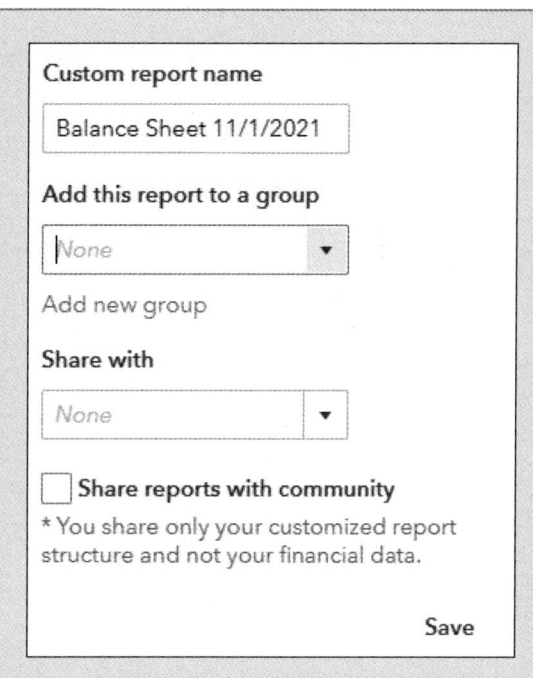

Figure 3.12

Save report customizations

15 Click **Save**.

16 Click the **Export** icon shown next to the Printer icon at the top of the report and then select **Export to Excel** from the drop-down list to begin the export to Excel process.

17 Click **Save** after you have navigated to a place on your computer to save this file.

18 Open Excel and then open the file you just saved.

19 After viewing your newly created Excel file, close Excel.

Navigate your browser to the Video Tutorials provided by Intuit (see website address specified in the Preface to this text) and then search on how to save customized reports.

Create, Print, and Export a Transaction Detail by Account

Often, you will want to investigate a detailed list of transactions you have recorded for a specific period. In your end-of-chapter cases, a usual explanation for an incorrect report is recording a transaction in the incorrect period. To explore this option, you will create a transaction detail by account report for a specific period. You can create such a report for a large period to see if your transactions were recorded in the proper period and to see where you may have entered a wrong amount or account.

To create, print, and export a transaction detail by account report for the period 1/1/10 to 12/31/25, do the following:

1 Click **Reports** from the navigation bar.

2 Type **Transaction** in the Find a report by name text box.

3 Select **Transaction Detail by Account**.

4 Scroll to the top of the report window and then select **Custom** from the Report period drop-down text box and then press [**Tab**].

5 Type **01/01/2010** in the text box and then press [**Tab**].

6 Type **12/31/2025** in the text box and then press [**Tab**].

7 Click **Run report**. Even though the transactions shown in this report should match yours, the dates will be different. The top of the report is shown in Figure 3.13.

Figure 3.13

Transaction Detail by Account Report (top section)

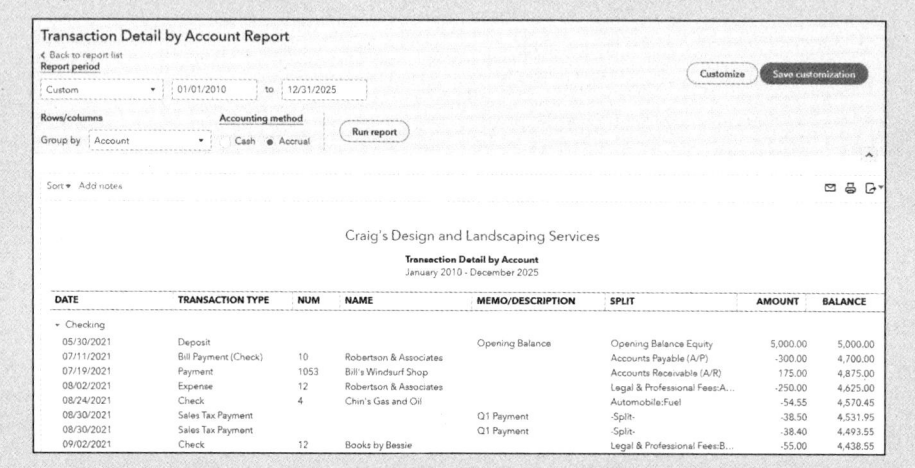

DATE	TRANSACTION TYPE	NUM	NAME	MEMO/DESCRIPTION	SPLIT	AMOUNT	BALANCE
▼ Checking							
05/30/2021	Deposit			Opening Balance	Opening Balance Equity	5,000.00	5,000.00
07/11/2021	Bill Payment (Check)	10	Robertson & Associates		Accounts Payable (A/P)	-300.00	4,700.00
07/19/2021	Payment	1053	Bill's Windsurf Shop		Accounts Receivable (A/R)	175.00	4,875.00
08/02/2021	Expense	12	Robertson & Associates		Legal & Professional Fees:A...	-250.00	4,625.00
08/24/2021	Check	4	Chin's Gas and Oil		Automobile:Fuel	-54.55	4,570.45
08/30/2021	Sales Tax Payment			Q1 Payment	-Split-	-38.50	4,531.95
08/30/2021	Sales Tax Payment			Q1 Payment	-Split-	-38.40	4,493.55
09/02/2021	Check	12	Books by Bessie		Legal & Professional Fees:B...	-55.00	4,438.55

8 Click **10** to view the Bill Payment (check) written to Robertson & Associates.

9 Close this window, scroll down the report, and investigate other transactions.

10 Scroll back to the top of this report, and click **Save customization**.

11 Click **Save**. Export this report like you exported the Balance Sheet earlier in this chapter.

12 Click the **Print** button to set this report up for printing; however, do not print this report as it is too long and unnecessary. Click **Cancel**.

13 Click the **Account** icon (in this case **C** for the owner Craig Carlson) and then click **Sign Out**. Note that once you sign out, all of your work on the Sample Company is gone. If you were to reopen the Sample Company, none of your changes made in this chapter would appear.

End Note

In this chapter, using the Sample Company you have modified company settings, added new accounts to the chart of accounts, and added beginning balances where appropriate. You have added customers, vendors, products, and services and closed the Opening Balance Equity account. You are ready to add operating activities like sales receipts, invoices, and cash receipts.

practice

Chapter 3 Questions

1. How do you access company settings?
2. When is it appropriate to add beginning balances to accounts?
3. What steps need to be followed to add an account to the chart of accounts?
4. When you add a beginning balance to an account, what other account is affected?
5. What information is required when adding a new product to QBO?
6. What additional information is required when you add beginning balance amounts to the accounts receivable account?
7. What additional information is required when you add beginning balance amounts to the accounts payable account?
8. Which additional account is used when you close Opening Balance Equity?
9. How do you access the Balance Sheet report?
10. How can you review a Transactions Report for any account when you are viewing the Balance Sheet?

Chapter 3 Matching

a. Transactions report	_____	Entity to whom you sell products/services
b. Trial balance	_____	Account used to offset beginning balance adjustments
c. Journal entry	_____	Merchandise a company purchases from a vendor
d. Opening Balance Equity	_____	Efforts made by a company to add value to a customer
e. Customer	_____	A listing of the debit or credit balances as of a specific date
f. Vendor	_____	Dictates where an account appears in all reports
g. Product	_____	Transactions for an account for a specified period
h. Service	_____	Entity from whom you purchase products/services
i. Account type	_____	Checking
j. Detailed type example	_____	Commonly used to adjust accounts

Chapter 3 Cases

The following cases require you to open the company you created in Chapter 2. Each of the following cases continues throughout the text in a sequential manner. For example, if you are assigned Case 01, you will use the file you modified in this chapter in all of the following chapters. Each of the following cases is similar in concepts assessed but differs in amounts and transactions. See the Preface to this text for a matrix of each student case and its attributes.

To reopen your company, do the following:

1. Open your Internet browser.
2. Type **https://qbo.intuit.com** into your browser's address text box.
3. Type your user ID and password into the text boxes as shown in Figure 3.14.

Figure 3.14
Sign In window (for logging in)

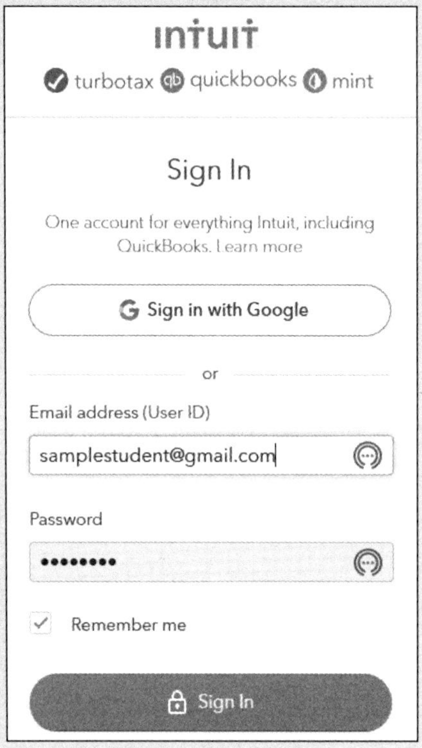

Case 1

Your company is a distributor of surfboards located in La Jolla, California. The company does not collect sales tax as all of its customers are resellers. Leave Industry text box blank. You began business in 2023 and want to use QBO starting January 1, 2024. Beginning balances as of 12/31/23 have been provided below.

You must make changes to your company. Based on what you learned in the text using the Sample Company, you are to make the following changes to the company you created in Chapter 2:

1. Modify settings as follows:
    a. Company
        i) Company name—Modify the company name to Case 01 – Student Name (ID Number) replacing Student Name with your name and ID Number with the number your instructor indicated.
        ii) Company type—Modify the Tax form by selecting **Form 1120** from the drop-down list of forms. Leave Industry text box blank and then click **Save**.
    b. Sales—Turn on – Track inventory quantity on hand. (This will automatically show items table on expense and purchase forms.)

c. Expenses
   i) Turn on – Track expenses and items by customer.
   ii) Turn on – Make expenses and items billable (no markup, track billable expenses and items as income in a single account, and no sales tax charged).
   iii) Default bill payment terms net 30.
   iv) Turn on – Use purchase orders (no custom fields).
d. Payments—No changes
e. Advanced
   i) Time tracking
      (1) Turn on – Add Service field to timesheets.
      (2) Turn on – Make Single-Time Activity Billable to Customer.

2 Create new accounts and related beginning balances as follows:

Account Type	Detail Type	Name	Balance	As of
Bank	Checking	Checking	25,000.00	12/31/23
Fixed Assets*	Furniture & Fixtures	Original cost	40,000.00	12/31/23
Fixed Assets*	Furniture & Fixtures	Depreciation	10,000.00	12/31/23
Long-Term Liabilities	Notes Payable	Notes Payable	60,000.00	12/31/23
Equity	Common Stock	Common Stock	1,000.00	12/31/23

*When entering a new fixed asset, place a check in the **Track depreciation of this asset** check box to reveal Original cost and Depreciation text boxes. Enter amounts from above as positive numbers.

3 Create two new products and one new service item as follows:

a. Products
   i) Name/Description – Rook 15, initial quantity 12/31/23 – 10, inventory asset account – Inventory Asset (this account will automatically be created in the chart of accounts when you add this product), price – $650, cost – $400, income account – Sales, expense account – Cost of Goods Sold
   ii) Name/Description – The Water Hog, track quantity, initial quantity 12/31/23 – 8, inventory asset account – Inventory Asset, price – $860, cost — $500, income account – Sales, expense account – Cost of Goods Sold

b. Service—Name/Description – Consulting, rate – $25, income account – Services. Click **+ Add new**, Account Type: Income, Detail Type: Service/Fee Income, Name: Services

c. Make changes to the following accounts via journal entry 1 as of 12/31/23 with an offset to Opening Balance Equity. Note: You'll have to add these accounts first.

Account	Amount	Name
Accounts Receivable	5,000.00	Blondie's Boards (new customer)
Prepaid Expenses	3,000.00	
Accounts Payable	4,500.00	Channel Islands (new vendor)

4   Close the Opening Balance Equity account to Retained Earnings via journal entry 2 as of 12/31/23.

5   Prepare and print a Trial Balance report as of 12/31/23, save it as a customized report named Trial Balance 12/31/17, and share it with all users. Click **Reports**, then scroll down the page to the For my accountant section, and click **Trial Balance**. Then select **Custom** as the report period and type **1/1/23** and **12/31/23** as the from–to dates. Your report should look like Figure 3.15.

6   If your trial balance differs from what is shown in Figure 3.15, do the following:

   a. Make sure all of your changes were dated 12/31/23.

   b. Click on the debit or credit balance to view a transactions report for each account, and investigate why your answer is different.

   c. Ask your instructor for assistance.

   d. Be sure your company matches the above as you will be adding additional business events in Chapter 4.

Figure 3.15

Trial Balance (as of 12/31/23)

Case 1
TRIAL BALANCE
As of December 31, 2023

	DEBIT	CREDIT
Checking	25,000.00	
Accounts Receivable	5,000.00	
Inventory Asset	8,000.00	
Prepaid Expenses	3,000.00	
Furniture & Fixtures:Depreciation		10,000.00
Furniture & Fixtures:Original cost	40,000.00	
Accounts Payable		4,500.00
Notes Payable		60,000.00
Common Stock		1,000.00
Opening Balance Equity		0.00
Retained Earnings		5,500.00
TOTAL	$81,000.00	$81,000.00

7   Export your Trial Balance report to Excel, and save it with the file name Student Name (replace with your name) Ch 03 Case 01 Trial Balance.xlsx.

8   Prepare and print a Transaction Detail by Account report for transactions between 1/1/24 and 12/31/24, save it as a customized report named Transaction Detail by Account, and share it with all users. If asked, indicate that your business is accrual based.

9   Use your Transaction Detail by Account report to locate any differences in your Trial Balance report created above.

   a. Make sure that all of your changes were dated 12/31/23.

   b. Click on the line that does not match to view the transaction for that account, and investigate why your answer differs.

c. Ask your instructor for assistance.

d. Be sure your company matches the above as you will be adding additional business events in Chapter 4.

10 Export your Transactions Detail by Account report to Excel, and save it with the file name Student Name (replace with your name) Ch 03 Case 01 Transaction Detail by Account.xlsx.

11 Sign out of your company.

Case 2

Your company is a distributor of remote control toys located in La Jolla, California. The company does not collect sales tax as all of its customers are resellers. You began business in 2024 and want to use QBO starting January 1, 2025. Beginning balances as of 12/31/24 have been provided below.

You must make changes to your company. Based on what you learned in the text using the Sample Company, you are to make the following changes to the company you created in Chapter 2:

1 Modify settings as follows:

a. Company—Company name – Modify the company name to Case 02 – Student Name (ID Number) replacing Student Name with your name and ID Number with the number your instructor indicated.

b. Sales—Turn on – Track quantity on hand. (This will automatically show items table on expense and purchase forms.)

c. Expenses
   i) Turn on – Track expenses and items by customer.
   ii) Turn on – Make expenses and items billable (no markup, track billable expenses and items as income in a single account, no sales tax charged).
   iii) Default bill payment terms net 30.
   iv) Turn on – Use purchase orders (no custom fields).

d. Payments—No changes

e. Advanced
   i) Time tracking
      (1) Turn on – Add Service field to timesheets.
      (2) Turn on – Make Single-Time Activity Billable to Customer.

2 Create new accounts and related beginning balances as follows:

Account Type	Detail Type	Name	Balance	As of
Bank	Checking	Checking	5,000.00	12/31/24
Fixed Assets*	Machinery & Equipment	Original cost	10,000.00	12/31/24
Fixed Assets*	Machinery & Equipment	Depreciation	1,000.00	12/31/24
Long-Term Liabilities	Notes Payable	Notes Payable	12,000.00	12/31/24
Equity	Common Stock	Common Stock	100.00	12/31/24

*When entering a new fixed asset, place a check in the **Track depreciation of this asset** check box to reveal Original cost and Depreciation text boxes. Enter amounts from above as positive numbers.

3   Create two new products and one new service item:
    a. Products
        i) Name/Description/Purchasing Information – Broon F830 Ride, initial quantity 12/31/24 – 4, inventory asset account – Inventory Asset. Note: This account will automatically be created in the chart of accounts when you add this product. Price – $1,500, cost – $800, income account – Sales, expense account – Cost of Goods Sold.
        ii) Name/Description/Purchasing Information – Sea Wind Carbon Sailboat, initial quantity 12/31/24 – 3, inventory asset account – Inventory Asset, price – $1,200, cost – $620, income account – Sales, expense account – Cost of Goods Sold.
    b. Service—Name/Description – Repairs, rate – $45, income account – Services. Click + **Add new** in the Income account text box, Account Type: Income, Detail Type: Service/Fee Income, Name: Services.
    c. Make changes to the following accounts via journal entry 1 as of 12/31/24 with an offset to Opening Balance Equity. Note: You'll have to add these accounts first.

Account	Amount	Name
Accounts Receivable	925.00	Benson's RC (new customer)
Prepaid Expenses	2,400.00	
Accounts Payable	1,900.00	Kyosho (new vendor)

4   Close the Opening Balance Equity account to Retained Earnings via journal entry 2 as of 12/31/24.

5   Prepare and print a Trial Balance report as of 12/31/24 (Click **Reports**, then scroll down the page to the For my accountant section, and click **Trial Balance**. Then select **Custom** as the report period and type **1/1/24** and **12/31/24** as the from–to dates.), save it as a customized report named Trial Balance 12/31/24, and share it with all users. Your report should look like Figure 3.16.

Figure 3.16
Trial Balance (as of 12/31/24)

Case 2
TRIAL BALANCE
As of December 31, 2024

	DEBIT	CREDIT
Checking	5,000.00	
Accounts Receivable	925.00	
Inventory Asset	5,060.00	
Prepaid Expenses	2,400.00	
Machinery & Equipment:Depreciation		1,000.00
Machinery & Equipment:Original cost	10,000.00	
Accounts Payable		1,900.00
Notes Payable		12,000.00
Common Stock		100.00
Opening Balance Equity		0.00
Retained Earnings		8,385.00
TOTAL	$23,385.00	$23,385.00

6. If your trial balance is different from what is shown in Figure 3.16, do the following:
   a. Make sure all of your changes were dated 12/31/24.
   b. Click on the debit or credit balance to view a transactions report for each account, and investigate why your answer is different.
   c. Ask your instructor for assistance.
   d. Be sure your company matches the above as you will be adding additional business events in Chapter 4.

7. Export your Trial Balance report to Excel, and save it with the file name Student Name (replace with your name) Ch 03 Case 02 Trial Balance.xlsx.

8. Prepare and print a Transaction Detail by Account report for all transactions between 1/1/10 and 12/31/28, save it as a customized report named Transaction Detail by Account, and share it with all users. If asked, indicate that your business is accrual based.

9. Use your Transaction Detail by Account report to locate any differences in your Trial Balance report created above.
   a. Make sure all of your changes were dated 12/31/24.
   b. Click on the line that does not match to view the transaction for that account, and investigate why your answer differs.
   c. Ask your instructor for assistance.
   d. Be sure your company matches the above as you will be adding additional business events in Chapter 4.

10. Export your Transactions Detail by Account report to Excel and save it with the file name Student Name (replace with your name) Ch 03 Case 02 Transaction Detail by Account.xlsx.

11. Sign out of your company.

Case 3

Your company sells and services cell phones. They are a sole proprietor located in La Jolla, California. The company does collect sales tax as all of its customers are consumers. (See Appendix 1 for directions on how to add a sales tax to a company file.) They began business in 2025 and want to use QBO starting January 1, 2026. Beginning balances as of 12/31/25 have been provided below.

You must make changes to your company. Based on what you learned in the text using the Sample Company, you are to make the following changes to the company you created in Chapter 2:

1. Modify settings as follows:
   a. Company—Company name – Modify the company name to Case 03 – Student Name (ID Number) replacing Student Name with your name and ID Number with the number your instructor indicated. Use 3990 La Jolla Shores Drive, La Jolla, CA 92037 as the company's address.
   b. SSN—Add 987-65-4321 as your business social security number as you are a sole proprietor.
   c. Sales—Make sure that Track inventory quantity on hand is on. (This will automatically show items table on expense and purchase forms.)

d. Expenses
   i) Turn on – Track expenses and items by customer.
   ii) Turn on – Make expenses and items billable (no markup, track billable expenses and items as income in a single account, and charge sales tax).
   iii) Set default bill payment terms to Due on receipt.
   iv) Turn on – Use purchase orders (no custom fields).
e. Payments—No changes
f. Time Time Sheet
   i) Turn on – Show service field to timesheets.
   ii) Turn on – Allow time to be billable.

2 Follow steps provided in Appendix 1 to add sales tax paid annually beginning 1/1/26.

3 Create new accounts and related beginning balances (Account Type, Detail Type, Name, Balance as of 12/31/25) as follows:

a. Bank, Checking, Checking, $12,000

b. Fixed Assets, Machinery & Equipment, Original cost, $15,000

Note: When entering a new fixed asset, place a check in the **Track depreciation of this asset** check box to reveal Original cost and Depreciation text boxes. Enter amounts from above as positive numbers.

Fixed Assets, Machinery & Equipment, Depreciation, $2,000

c. Long-Term Liabilities, Notes Payable, Notes Payable, $23,000

d. Equity, Owner's Equity, Owner's Equity, 0

4 Create two new products (Name/Description, initial quantity 12/31/25, inventory asset account, price, cost, income account, expense account):

a. Apple iPhone 7, 10, Inventory Asset, $750, $500. Note: This account will automatically be created in the chart of accounts when you add this product. Sales of Product Income, Cost of Goods Sold, taxable.

b. Pixel, 3, Inventory Asset, $650, $400, Sales of Product Income, Cost of Goods Sold, taxable.

5 Create two new service items (Name/Description, rate, income account):

a. Apple Repairs, $45, Services, not taxable. (Click + **Add new** in the Income account text box, Account Type: Income, Detail Type: Service/Fee Income, Name: Services.)

b. Pixel Repairs, $40, Services, not taxable.

6 Make changes to the following accounts via journal entry 1 as of 12/31/25 with an offset to Opening Balance Equity:

Account	Amount	Name
Accounts Receivable (A/R)	4,125.00	GHO Marketing (new customer)
Prepaid Expenses	2,750.00	
Accounts Payable (A/P)	5,000.00	Apple Inc. (new vendor)

7. Close the Opening Balance Equity account (which should have a balance of $10,075) to Owner's Equity via journal entry 2 as of 12/31/25. (Note: Use Owner's Equity as this company is a sole proprietorship. Retained Earnings would have been used if this company had been a corporation.)

8. Prepare and print a Trial Balance report as of 12/31/25, click the **Run report** button and then save it as a customized report named Trial Balance 12/31/25, and share it with all users. Click **Reports**, then scroll down the page to the For my accountant section, and click **Trial Balance**. Then select **Custom** as the report period and type **1/1/25** and **12/31/25** as the from–to dates. Your report should look like Figure 3.17.

Figure 3.17

Trial Balance

Case 03 - Student Name (ID Number)
Trial Balance
As of December 31, 2025

	DEBIT	CREDIT
Checking	12,000.00	
Accounts receivable (A/R)	4,125.00	
Inventory Asset	6,200.00	
Prepaid expenses	2,750.00	
Machinery & Equipment:Depreciation		2,000.00
Machinery & Equipment:Original cost	15,000.00	
Accounts Payable (A/P)		5,000.00
Notes Payable		23,000.00
Opening balance equity		0.00
Owner's Equity		10,075.00
TOTAL	$40,075.00	$40,075.00

9. If your trial balance differs from what is shown in Figure 3.17, do the following:
   a. Make sure all of your changes were dated 12/31/25.
   b. Click on the debit or credit balance to view a transactions report for each account, and investigate why your answer is different.
   c. Ask your instructor for assistance.
   d. Be sure your company matches the above as you will be adding additional business events in Chapter 4.

10. Export your Trial Balance report to Excel, and save it with the file name Student Name (replace with your name) Ch 03 Case 03 Trial Balance.xlsx.

11 Prepare and print a Transaction Detail by Account report for all transactions between 1/1/10 and 12/31/30, save it as a customized report named Transaction Detail by Account, and share it with all users. If asked, indicate that your business is accrual based.

12 Use your Transaction Detail by Account report to locate any differences in your Trial Balance report created above.
   a. Make sure all of your changes were dated 12/31/25.
   b. Click on the line that does not match to view the transaction for that account, and investigate why your answer differs.
   c. Ask your instructor for assistance.
   d. Be sure your company matches the above as you will be adding additional business events in Chapter 4.

13 Export your Transactions Detail by Account report to Excel and save it with the file name Student Name (replace with your name) Ch 03 Case 03 Transaction Detail by Account.xlsx.

14 Sign out of your company.

Case 4

Your company is a sports gym serving the Hollywood area in California. They sell month-to-month memberships to individuals and businesses as well as T-shirts, yoga pants, and other sports-related accessories. They began their business in 2020 and want to use QBO starting January 1, 2021. Beginning balances as of 12/31/20 have been provided below.

Based on what you learned in the text using the Sample Company, you are to make the following changes to the company you created in Chapter 2.

1 Modify settings as follows (click the **Gear** icon and then click **Account and Settings**):
   a. Company
      i) Name – Case 04 – Student Name (ID Number)
      ii) EIN – 98-9875461
      iii) Tax form – Form 1120
      iv) Industry – Fitness and Recreational Sports Centers
      v) Email – Your email address
      vi) Address – 6540 Sunset Blvd., Hollywood, CA 90028
   b. Sales (turn the following on, and all others turn off or leave off)
      i) Preferred invoice terms – Net 30
      ii) Custom transaction numbers
      iii) Show Product/Service column on sales form
      iv) Track quantity and price/rate
      v) Track inventory quantity on hand
      vi) Show aging table at the bottom of the statement
   c. Expenses (turn the following on, and all others turn off or leave off)
      i) Show items table on expense and purchase forms
      ii) Use purchase orders
   d. Payments—No changes
   e. Advanced—No changes

2 Add sales tax that is payable to the California State Board of Equalization. (Follow the steps provided in Appendix 1.)

3 Create new accounts and related beginning balances where appropriate. (Click the **Gear** icon and then click **Chart of Accounts**.)

   a. First account
      i) Account Type – Bank
      ii) Detail Type – Checking
      iii) Name – Checking
      iv) Balance as of 12/31/20 – $27,000

   b. Second account
      i) Account Type – Accounts Receivable (A/R)
      ii) Detail Type – Accounts Receivable (A/R)
      iii) Name – Accounts Receivable (A/R)
      iv) Balance as of 12/31/20 – n/a

   c. Third account
      i) Account Type – Other Current Assets
      ii) Detail Type – Prepaid Expenses
      iii) Name – Prepaid Expenses
      iv) Balance as of 12/31/20 – $12,000

   d. Fourth and fifth accounts (Note: When entering a new fixed asset, place a check in the **Track depreciation of this asset** check box to reveal Original cost and Depreciation text boxes. Enter both amounts as positive numbers.)
      i) Account Type – Fixed Asset
      ii) Detail Type – Fixed Asset Furniture
      iii) Name – Furniture
      iv) Original cost – $65,000 as of 12/31/20
      v) Depreciation – $10,000 as of 12/31/20

   e. Sixth and seventh accounts (see note above on depreciation)
      i) Account Type – Fixed Asset
      ii) Detail Type – Machinery & Equipment
      iii) Name – Machinery & Equipment
      iv) Original cost – $115,000 as of 12/31/20
      v) Depreciation – $6,500 as of 12/31/20

   f. Eighth account
      i) Account Type – Accounts Payable (A/P)
      ii) Detail Type – Accounts Payable (A/P)
      iii) Name – Accounts Payable (A/P)
      iv) Balance as of 12/31/20 – n/a

   g. Ninth account
      i) Account Type – Long-Term Liabilities
      ii) Detail Type – Notes Payable
      iii) Name – Notes Payable
      iv) Balance as of 12/31/20 – $82,000

Case 5

Your company is a software engineering firm in the state of Alabama. They develop training materials and computer workstations for government and commercial enterprises. In addition, they provide program support, training, and technical solutions. They want to use QBO starting January 1, 2022. Beginning balances as of 12/31/21 have been provided below.

Based on what you learned in the text using the Sample Company, you are to make the following changes to the company you created in Chapter 2.

1. Modify settings as follows (click the **Gear** icon and then click **Account and Settings**):

    a. Company
        i) Name – Case 05 – Student Name (ID Number)
        ii) SSN – 556-95-7847
        iii) Company type – Sole Proprietor
        iv) Tax form – Form 1040
        v) Industry – Software Publishing
        vi) Email – your email address
        vii) Address – 5100 Bradford Drive, Huntsville, AL 35805

    b. Sales (turn the following on, and all others turn off or leave off)
        i) Preferred invoice terms – Net 30
        ii) Custom transaction numbers
        iii) Show Product/Service column on sales form
        iv) Track quantity and price/rate
        v) Track inventory quantity on hand
        vi) Show aging table at bottom of statement

    c. Expenses (turn the following on, and all others turn off or leave off)
        i) Show items table on expense and purchase forms
        ii) Use purchase orders

    d. Payments—No changes

    e. Advanced—No changes

2. Add sales tax that is quarterly. (Follow the steps provided in Appendix 1.) Since this company is in Alabama, the instructions and Figure A.1 are different than what's listed for California. There are three agencies that receive tax payments: Alabama Department of Revenue; Alabama, Madison County; and Alabama, Huntsville. Select the filing frequency of quarterly in the three screens. Start date is 01/01/22.

3. Create new accounts and related beginning balances where appropriate (click the **Gear** icon and then click **Chart of Accounts**):

    a. First account
        i) Account Type – Bank
        ii) Detail Type – Checking
        iii) Name – Checking
        iv) Balance as of 12/31/21 – $30,000

b. Second account
   i) Account Type – Accounts Receivable (A/R)
   ii) Detail Type – Accounts Receivable (A/R)
   iii) Name – Accounts Receivable (A/R)
   iv) Balance as of 12/31/21 – n/a

c. Third account
   i) Account Type – Other Current Assets
   ii) Detail Type – Prepaid Expenses
   iii) Name – Prepaid Expenses
   iv) Balance as of 12/31/21 – $10,000

d. Fourth and fifth accounts (Note: When entering a new fixed asset, place a check in the **Track depreciation of this asset** check box to reveal Original cost and Depreciation text boxes. Enter both amounts as positive numbers.)
   i) Account Type – Fixed Assets
   ii) Detail Type – Fixed Asset Computers
   iii) Name – Fixed Asset Computers
   iv) Original cost – $250,000
   v) Depreciation – $25,000
   vi) Balance as of 12/31/21

e. Sixth and seventh account (see note above on depreciation)
   i) Account Type – Fixed Assets
   ii) Detail Type – Fixed Asset Furniture
   iii) Name – Fixed Asset Furniture
   iv) Original cost – $80,000
   v) Depreciation – $8,000
   vi) Balance as of 12/31/21

f. Eighth account
   i) Account Type – Accounts Payable (A/P)
   ii) Detail Type – Accounts Payable (A/P)
   iii) Name – Accounts Payable (A/P)
   iv) Balance as of 12/31/21 – n/a

g. Ninth account
   i) Account Type – Long-Term Liabilities
   ii) Detail Type – Notes Payable
   iii) Name – Notes Payable
   iv) Balance as of 12/31/21 – $45,000

h. Tenth account
   i) Account Type – Equity
   ii) Detail Type – Owner's Equity
   iii) Name – Owner's Equity
   iv) Balance as of 12/31/21 – $10,000

i. Eleventh account
   i) Account Type – Income
   ii) Detail Type – Service/Fee Income
   iii) Name – Consulting

4 Create two new inventory products as follows:
   a. First product
      i) Name – Training Materials – Volume 1
      ii) Initial quantity on hand – 20
      iii) As of date – 12/31/21
      iv) Inventory asset account – Inventory
      v) Description – Training Materials – Volume 1
      vi) Sales price/rate – $15,000
      vii) Income account – Sales
      viii) Taxable – standard rate
      ix) Purchasing information – Training Materials – Volume 1
      x) Cost – $8,000
      xi) Expense account – Cost of Goods Sold
   b. Second product
      i) Name – Training Materials – Volume 2
      ii) Initial quantity on hand – 30
      iii) As of date – 12/31/21
      iv) Inventory asset account – Inventory
      v) Description – Training Materials – Volume 2
      vi) Sales price/rate – $20,000
      vii) Income account – Sales
      viii) Taxable – standard rate
      ix) Purchasing information – Training Materials – Volume 2
      x) Cost – $10,000
      xi) Expense account – Cost of Goods Sold

5 Create two new service items as follows:
   a. First service
      i) Name – Program Support
      ii) Description – Yes you do sell this service to customers. "Program Support"
      iii) Sales price/rate – $300
      iv) Income account – Account Type: Income, Detail Type: Service/Fee Income, Name: Consulting Click **+ Add new** in the Income account text box, Account Type: Income, Detail Type: Service/Fee Income, Name: Consulting
      v) Nontaxable
      vi) Purchasing information – No you don't purchase this service from a vendor
   b. Second service
      i) Name – Technical Solutions
      ii) Description – Yes you do sell this service to customers. "Technical Solutions"
      iii) Sales price/rate – $400
      iv) Income account – Consulting
      v) Nontaxable
      vi) Purchase information – No you don't purchase this service from a vendor

6. Prepare journal entry 1 as of 12/31/21 with an offset to Opening Balance Equity to record the following beginning balances:

    a. Accounts Receivable (A/R) – Debit $150,000 – NASA (new customer)

    b. Accounts Payable (A/P) Credit $20,000 – Wild Research Inc. (new vendor)

    c. Notes Payable Credit $500,000 – Chase Bank (new vendor)

7. Prepare journal entry 2 as of 12/31/21 to close the Opening Balance Equity to Owner's Equity ($372,000).

8. Prepare and print a Trial Balance report with a custom reporting period of 1/1/21 to 12/31/21 and then save it as a customized report named Trial Balance 12/31/21. Your report should look like Figure 3.19.

Figure 3.19

Trial Balance

Case 05 - Student Name (ID Number)
TRIAL BALANCE
As of December 31, 2021

	DEBIT	CREDIT
Checking	30,000.00	
Accounts Receivable (A/R)	150,000.00	
Inventory	460,000.00	
Prepaid Expenses	10,000.00	
Fixed Asset Computers:Depreciation		25,000.00
Fixed Asset Computers:Original cost	250,000.00	
Fixed Asset Furniture:Depreciation		8,000.00
Fixed Asset Furniture:Original cost	80,000.00	
Accounts Payable (A/P)		20,000.00
Notes Payable		545,000.00
Opening Balance Equity		0.00
Owner's Equity		382,000.00
TOTAL	$980,000.00	$980,000.00

9. Prepare and print a Transaction Detail by Account report for all transactions between 1/1/10 and 12/31/23, and save it as a customized report named Transaction Detail by Account. If asked, indicate that your business is accrual based.

10. Use your Transaction Detail by Account report to locate any differences in your Trial Balance report created above.

    a. Make sure all your changes were dated 12/31/21.

    b. Click on the line that does not match to view the transaction for that account, and investigate why your answer differs.

    c. Ask your instructor for assistance.

    d. Be sure your company matches the above as you will be adding additional business events in Chapter 4.

Case 6

Your company is a Recreational Vehicle (RV) dealership in the state of Washington. They sell new RVs and related accessories to individuals and businesses. In addition, they repair and service RVs. They began business in 2021 and want to use QBO starting January 1, 2023. Beginning balances as of 12/31/22 have been provided below.

Based on what you learned in the text using the Sample Company, you are to make the following changes to the company you created in Chapter 2.

1. Modify settings as follows (click the **Gear** icon and then click **Account and Settings**):

    a. Company
        i) Name – Case 06 – Student Name (ID Number)
        ii) EIN – 99-9811161
        iii) Tax form – Form 1120
        iv) Industry – Automotive Dealers
        v) Email – your email address
        vi) Address – 4309 E Valley Hwy E, Sumner, WA 98390

    b. Sales (turn the following on, all others turn off or leave off)
        i) Preferred invoice terms – Net 30
        ii) Custom transaction numbers
        iii) Show Product/Service column on sales form
        iv) Track quantity and price/rate
        v) Track inventory quantity on hand
        vi) Show aging table at bottom of statement

    c. Expenses (turn the following on, all others turn off or leave off)
        i) Show items table on expense and purchase forms
        ii) Use purchase orders

    d. Payments—No changes

    e. Advanced—No changes

2. Add sales tax that is payable to the Washington State Department of Revenue (follow the steps provided in Appendix 1).

3. Create new accounts and related beginning balances where appropriate (click the **Gear** icon and then click **Chart of Accounts**):

    a. First account
        i) Account Type – Bank
        ii) Detail Type – Checking
        iii) Name – Checking
        iv) Balance as of 12/31/22 – $50,000

    b. Second account
        i) Account Type – Accounts Receivable (A/R)
        ii) Detail Type – Accounts Receivable (A/R)
        iii) Name – Accounts Receivable (A/R)
        iv) Balance as of 12/31/22 – n/a

c. Third account
   i) Account Type – Other Current Assets
   ii) Detail Type – Loans to Officers
   iii) Name – Loans to Officers
   iv) Balance as of 12/31/22 – $15,000

d. Fourth and fifth accounts (Note: When entering a new fixed asset, place a check in the **Track depreciation of this asset** check box to reveal Original cost and Depreciation text boxes. Enter both amounts from above as positive numbers.)
   i) Account Type – Fixed Asset
   ii) Detail Type – Buildings
   iii) Name – Buildings
   iv) Original cost $150,000
   v) Depreciation $15,000
   vi) Balance as of 12/31/22

e. Sixth and seventh account (see note above)
   i) Account Type – Fixed Asset
   ii) Detail Type – Machinery & Equipment
   iii) Name – Machinery & Equipment
   iv) Original cost $100,000
   v) Depreciation $10,000
   vi) Balance as of 12/31/22

f. Eighth account
   i) Account Type – Accounts Payable (A/P)
   ii) Detail Type – Accounts Payable (A/P)
   iii) Name – Accounts Payable (A/P)
   iv) Balance as of 12/31/22 – n/a

g. Ninth account
   i) Account Type – Long-Term Liabilities
   ii) Detail Type – Notes Payable
   iii) Name – Notes Payable
   iv) Balance as of 12/31/22 – n/a

h. Tenth account
   i) Account Type – Equity
   ii) Detail Type – Common Stock
   iii) Name – Common Stock
   iv) Balance as of 12/31/22 – n/a

i. Eleventh account
   i) Account Type – Equity
   ii) Detail Type – Paid-In Capital or Surplus
   iii) Name – Paid-In Capital
   iv) Balance as of 12/31/22 – n/a

4. Create two new Inventory products as follows:
   a. First product
      i) Name – 2022 Winnebago Revel 44E
      ii) Initial quantity on hand – 2

iii) As of date – 12/31/22
iv) Inventory asset account – Inventory Asset
v) Description – 2022 Winnebago Revel 44E
vi) Sales price/rate – $150,000
vii) Income account – Sales of Product Income
viii) Sales Tax Category – Taxable-Standard rate
ix) Purchasing information – 2022 Winnebago Revel 44E
x) Cost – $120,000
xi) Expense account – Cost of Goods Sold

b. Second product
i) Name – 2022 Winnebago View 24G
ii) Initial quantity on hand – 3
iii) As of date – 12/31/22
iv) Inventory asset account – Inventory Asset
v) Description – 2022 Winnebago View 24G
vi) Sales price/rate – $140,000
vii) Income account – Sales of Product Income
viii) Sales Tax Category – Taxable-Standard rate
ix) Purchasing information – 2022 Winnebago View 24G
x) Cost – $112,000
xi) Expense account – Cost of Goods Sold

5 Create two new service items as follows:

a. First service
i) Name – Lube, Oil, Filter
ii) Description – Yes you do sell this service to customers. "Lube, Oil, Filter"
iii) Sales price/rate – $300
iv) Income account – Sales
v) Sales Tax Category – Nontaxable
vi) Purchasing information – No you don't purchase this service from a vendor

b. Second service
i) Name – Transmission Service
ii) Description – Yes you do sell this service to customers. "Transmission Service"
iii) Sales price/rate – $350
iv) Income account – Sales
v) Sales Tax Category – Nontaxable
vi) Purchasing information – No you don't purchase this service from a vendor

6 Prepare journal entry 1 as of 12/31/22 with an offset to Opening Balance Equity to record the following beginning balances:

a. Accounts Receivable (A/R) – Debit $10,000 – Sam Ski (new customer)

b. Accounts Payable (A/P) Credit $464,000 – Winnebago (new vendor)

c. Notes Payable Credit $100,000 – Chase Bank (new vendor)

d. Common Stock Credit $1,000

e. Paid-In Capital Credit $250,000

   f. Opening Balance Equity Debit $805,000

7 Prepare journal entry 2 as of 12/31/22 to close the Opening Balance Equity to Retained Earnings ($61,000).

8 Prepare and print a Trial Balance report with a custom reporting period of 1/1/22 to 12/31/22 and then save it as a customized report named Trial Balance 12/31/22. Your report should look like Figure 3.20.

Figure 3.20

Trial Balance

Case 06 - Student Name (ID Number)

TRIAL BALANCE
As of December 31, 2022

	DEBIT	CREDIT
Checking	50,000.00	
Accounts Receivable (A/R)	10,000.00	
Inventory Asset	576,000.00	
Loans To Officers	15,000.00	
Buildings:Depreciation		15,000.00
Buildings:Original cost	150,000.00	
Machinery & Equipment:Depreciation		10,000.00
Machinery & Equipment:Original cost	100,000.00	
Accounts Payable (A/P)		464,000.00
Notes Payable		100,000.00
Common Stock		1,000.00
Opening Balance Equity		0.00
Paid-In Capital		250,000.00
Retained Earnings		61,000.00
TOTAL	$901,000.00	$901,000.00

9 Prepare and print a Transaction Detail by Account report for all transactions between 1/1/10 and 12/31/25 and then save it as a customized report named Transaction Detail by Account. If asked, indicate that your business is accrual based.

10 Use your Transaction Detail by Account report to locate any differences in your Trial Balance report created above.

   a. Make sure all your changes were dated 12/31/22.

   b. Click on the line that does not match to view the transaction for that account and investigate why your answer differs.

   c. Ask your instructor for assistance.

   d. Be sure your company matches the above as you will be adding additional business events in Chapter 4.

Chapter 4

Recording Operating Activities: Sales and Cash Receipts

Student Learning Outcomes

Upon completion of this chapter, the student will be able to do the following:

- Create a new service, product, and customer
- Record a sales receipt
- Record an invoice for services rendered on account
- Record an invoice for products sold on account
- Record cash receipts (payments received on account)
- Deposit payments received on account
- Prepare a Transaction Detail by Account report

Overview

Intuit has provided a Sample Company online to provide new users a test-drive of its QBO product. In this chapter, you will open this Sample Company and practice various features of QBO. You will be recording operating activities, such as adding new services, new products, new customers, new sales receipts, new invoices, and new cash receipts to the Sample Company file. Remember, if you stop in the middle of this work, none of your work will be saved. So, when you return, the same Sample Company, without your work, will appear. At the end of chapter, you will perform the same tasks completed on the Sample Company on your Student Company. That work of course will be saved. Your system date will differ from the date shown under the company name QBO. Transaction dates on your screen may also differ from the figures shown throughout this text.

Services, Products, and Customers

In this section, you will add new services, products, and customers. To add new services and products, you will access the Product and Services section using the Gear icon. To add customers, you will use the Customers menu item in the navigation bar.

To add new services, products, and customers to the Sample Company, do the following:

1 Open your Internet browser.

2 Type **https://qbo.intuit.com/redir/testdrive** into your browser's address text box, and then press [**Enter**] to view the Sample Company Dashboard. If asked, provide security information before proceeding.

   Your system date will differ from the date shown under the company name in the following figure. Transaction dates on your screen may also differ from the figures shown throughout this text.

3 Click the **Gear** icon, and click **Products and Services** as shown in Figure 4.1.

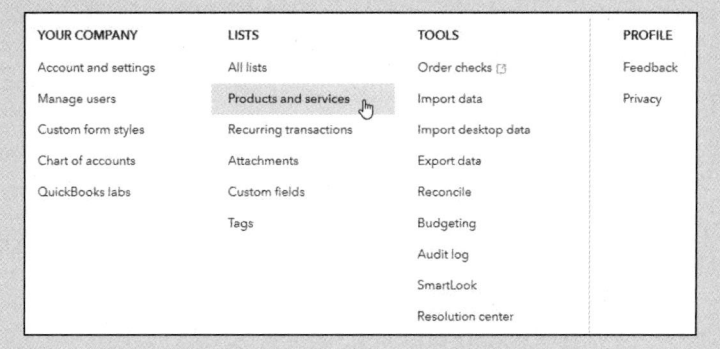

Figure 4.1

List of Products and Services

4 Click **New** in the upper-right corner of the Products and Services list.
5 Click **Service**.
6 Type **Rose Consulting** in the Name text box and the Description text boxes.
7 Select **Landscaping** from the Category drop-down text box, then check the I sell this product/service to my customers check box, and then type **45** in the Sales price/rate text box.
8 Scroll down the window and accept Services as the Income account and then click **Edit sales tax**, then click **Still don't see what you're looking for?**, then select **Nontaxable,** and then click **Done**. Your window should now look like Figure 4.2.

Navigate your browser to the Video Tutorials provided by Intuit (see website address specified in the Preface to this text) and then search on How to Set Up Service Items.

Figure 4.2

Adding a new service (partial view)

78 **Chapter 4** *Recording Operating Activities: Sales and Cash Receipts*

9. Click on the drop-down arrow to the right of the Save and Close button, and select **Save and New**.
10. Click **Change type** and then select **Inventory**.
11. Type **Roses** in the Name text box and then click the drop-down arrow in the Category text box and select **Landscaping**.
12. Type **0** in the Initial Quantity On Hand text box and type today's date in the As Of Date text box.
13. Select **Inventory Asset** as the Inventory asset account.
14. Type **Roses** in the Description and in Purchasing information text boxes.
15. Type **25** in the Sales price/rate text box and **15** in the Cost text box.
16. Select **Sales of Product Income** from the Income account drop-down list and **Cost of Goods Sold** from the Expense account drop-down list.
17. Click **Edit sales tax**, then click **Still don't see what you're looking for?**, then select **Taxable - standard rate**, and then click **Done**. A partial view of the Product or Service Information window should look like Figure 4.3. Note that the Sample Company had already set up Sales Taxes. To learn more about setting up Sales Taxes read Appendix 1—Sales Taxes.

Navigate your browser to the Video Tutorials provided by Intuit (see website address specified in the Preface to this text) and then search on How to Create an Inventory Product.

Figure 4.3

Adding a new product (partial view)

Navigate your browser to the Video Tutorials provided by Intuit (see website address specified in the Preface to this text) and then search on How to Set Up Sales Tax.

Initial quantity on hand*	0
As of date* What's the as of date?	02/03/2022
Reorder point What's the reorder point?	
Inventory asset account	Inventory Asset
Description	Roses
Sales price/rate	25
Income account	Sales of Product Income
Sales tax	Taxable - standard rate — We'll apply sales tax based on location only. Edit sales tax
Purchasing information	Roses
Cost	15
Expense account	Cost of Goods Sold
Preferred Vendor	Select a preferred vendor

18 Click on the drop-down arrow to the right of the **Save and new button**, and select **Save and close**.

19 Scroll down the revised list of Products and Services to see the service and product you entered as shown in Figure 4.4.

NAME ▲	SKU	TYPE	SALES DES	SALES PRIC	COST	TAXABLE	QTY ON HA	REORDER P	ACTION
Rose Consulting		Service	Rose C...	45					Edit ▼
Roses		Inventory	Roses	25	15	✓	0		Edit ▼
Sod		Service	Sod			✓			Edit ▼

Figure 4.4

Updated list of Products and Services (partial view)

20 Click **Sales** from the navigation bar, then click **Customers**, and then click the **New customer** button.

21 Type **Roxy Corporation** in the Company text box.

22 Type **James** in the First name text box and **Roxy** in the Last name text box.

23 Select the **Address** tab, and type **101 Ocean View, La Jolla, CA, 92130** in the appropriate text boxes. Select **Roxy Corporation** from the Display name as drop-down text box. Click **Save** and then click **Edit** to view the data you just entered. A partial view of the Customer information window is shown in Figure 4.5.

Navigate your browser to the Video Tutorials provided by Intuit (see website address specified in the Preface to this text) and then search on How to Manage Customers.

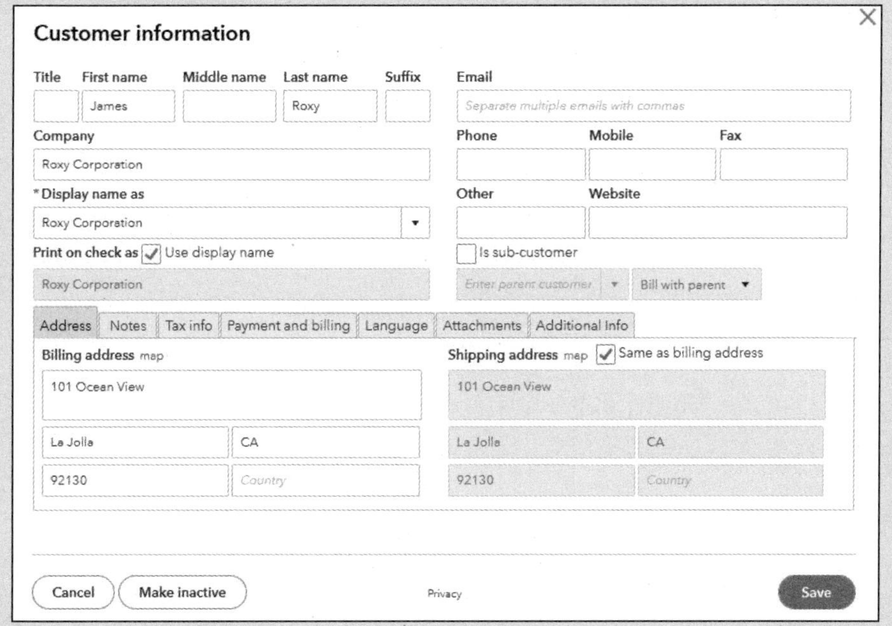

Figure 4.5

Customer information window (partial view)

24 Select the **Payment and billing** tab, and select **Net 30** from the Terms text box.

25 The Roxy Corporation customer window appears as shown in Figure 4.6.

Figure 4.6

Roxy Corporation customer window

26 Click **Save**.

You have now added a new service, a new product, and a new customer. Next up, adding sales receipts to record cash sales and invoices to record credit sales.

Sales Receipts and Invoices

A business uses sales receipts to record sales transactions on a daily basis when payment is received at the same time as a product or service is delivered. Sales invoices are used to record sales transactions when customers are granted credit terms and given some time to pay after a product or service is delivered. In either case, sales are recorded when the product is sold or service is rendered.

Navigate your browser to the Video Tutorials provided by Intuit (see website address specified in the Preface to this text) and then search on Sales Receipt versus Invoice.

To add sales receipts and invoices to the Sample Company, do the following:

1 Continue from where you left off. If you closed the Sample Company, follow the steps at the beginning of this chapter to reopen it. Keep in mind that if you close the Sample Company, all of your work thus far in this chapter is lost as it has reset itself.

2 Click the *+ New* icon, and select **Sales Receipt** as shown in Figure 4.7.

Figure 4.7

Create window (adding a sales receipt)

Navigate your browser to the Video Tutorials provided by Intuit (see website address specified in the Preface to this text) and then search on How to Record a Sales Receipt.

Recording Operating Activities: Sales and Cash Receipts **Chapter 4** 81

3 Select **Bill's Windsurf Shop** from the Choose a customer drop-down list in the upper-left corner of the Sales Receipt window.

4 Your computer's system date has been entered as the Sales Receipt date.

5 Select **Check** from the drop-down list of Payment methods.

6 Select **Undeposited Funds** from the Deposit to drop-down text box. The check will be recorded in the Undeposited Funds account as deposits for this company are made every other day.

7 On line 1 of the sales receipt, select **Pump P461-17** in the Product/Service column.

8 Type **2** in the QTY (Quantity) column.

9 On line 2 of the sales receipt, select **Rock Fountain R154-88** in the Product/Service column.

10 Type **2** in the QTY (Quantity) column and then press [**Tab**]. The sales receipt should look like Figure 4.8.

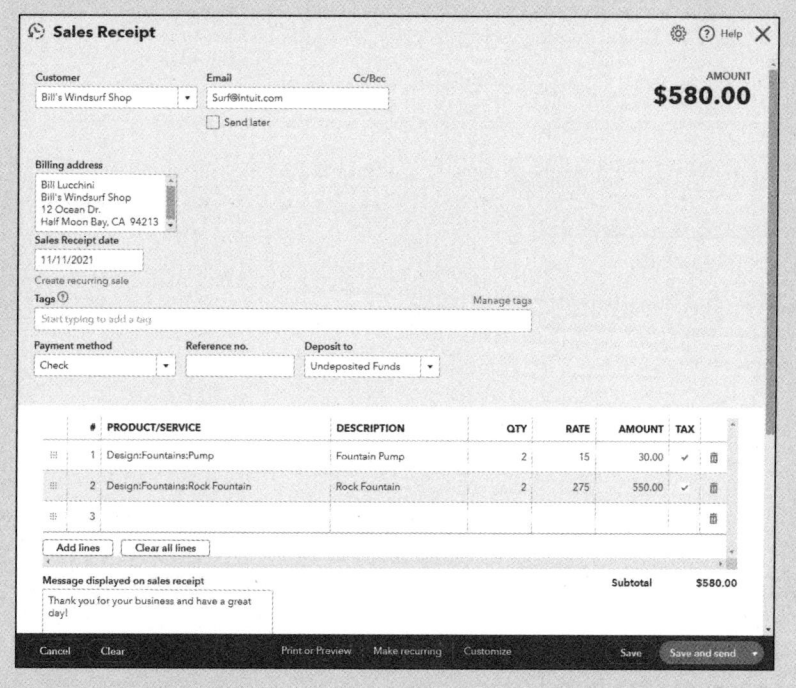

Figure 4.8

Sales Receipt before Sales Tax (partial view)

11 Scroll down the sales receipt, and select **California 8%** from the drop-down list in the Select a sales tax rate text box. The lower half of your sales receipt should look like Figure 4.9 with the $46.40 tax amount added.

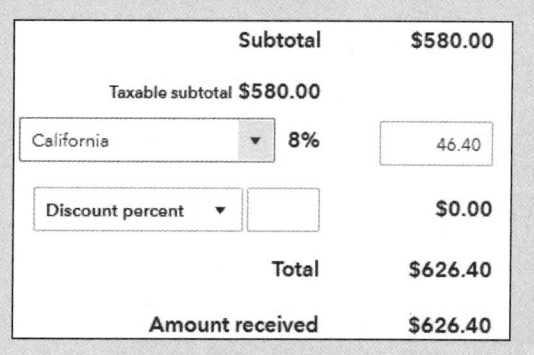

Figure 4.9

Sales Receipt after Sales Tax (partial view)

12. Click **Save and close**.
13. Click **Sales** and then click **Customers** from the navigation bar, and click **Bill's Windsurf Shop**. A listing of recent transactions affecting that customer is shown, including the recently recorded sales receipt, in Figure 4.10.

Figure 4.10

Bill's Windsurf Shop (recent transactions)

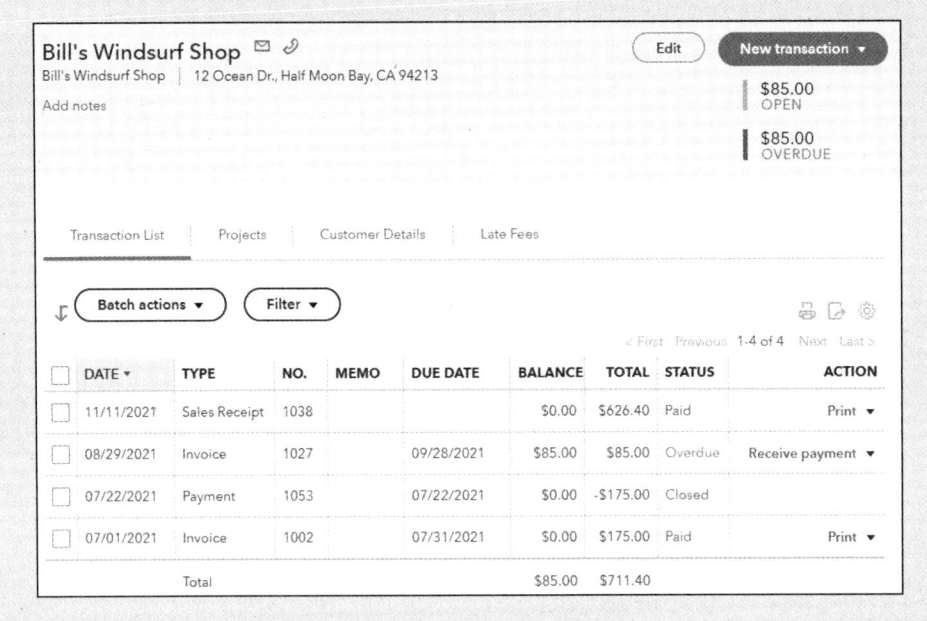

DATE	TYPE	NO.	MEMO	DUE DATE	BALANCE	TOTAL	STATUS	ACTION
11/11/2021	Sales Receipt	1038			$0.00	$626.40	Paid	Print
08/29/2021	Invoice	1027		09/28/2021	$85.00	$85.00	Overdue	Receive payment
07/22/2021	Payment	1053		07/22/2021	$0.00	-$175.00	Closed	
07/01/2021	Invoice	1002		07/31/2021	$0.00	$175.00	Paid	Print
	Total				$85.00	$711.40		

14. Click the **+ New** icon, and select **Invoice** as shown in Figure 4.11.

Figure 4.11

Adding an invoice

CUSTOMERS
- Invoice
- Receive payment
- Estimate
- Credit memo
- Sales receipt
- Refund receipt
- Delayed credit
- Delayed charge

Navigate your browser to the Video Tutorials provided by Intuit (see website address specified in the Preface to this text) and then search on How to Record Invoices.

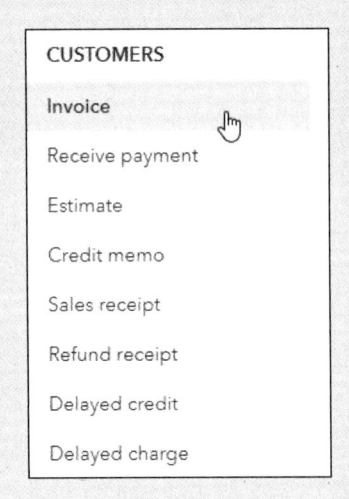

15. Select **Cool Cars** from the Choose a customer drop-down list in the upper-left corner of the Invoice window.
16. Your computer's system date has been entered as the Invoice date, and the default terms for this customer are in the appropriate text boxes.
17. On line 1 of the invoice, select **Trimming** as the service provided.
18. Type **5** as the quantity.
19. On line 2 of the invoice, select **Pest Control** as the service provided.
20. Type **3** as the quantity and then press [**Tab**]. The invoice should look like Figure 4.12.

Recording Operating Activities: Sales and Cash Receipts Chapter 4 83

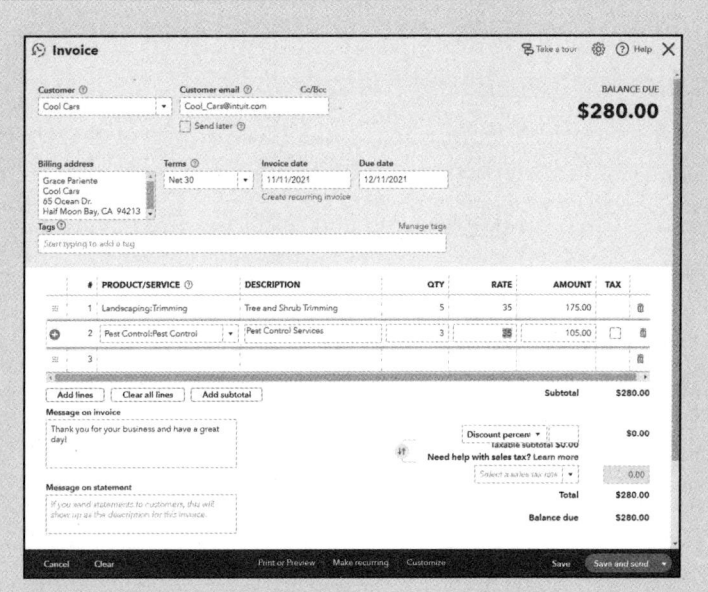

Figure 4.12

Invoice (partial view)

21. Scroll down the invoice and select **California 8%** from the Select a sales tax rate text box. Even though a rate is selected, no sales tax is applied. Both services are not taxable, and thus, no sales tax is added.

22. Click **Save and Close**.

23. Click **Sales** and then select **Customers** menu item from the navigation bar and then click **Cool Cars**. A listing of recent transactions affecting that customer is shown, including the recorded invoice, in Figure 4.13.

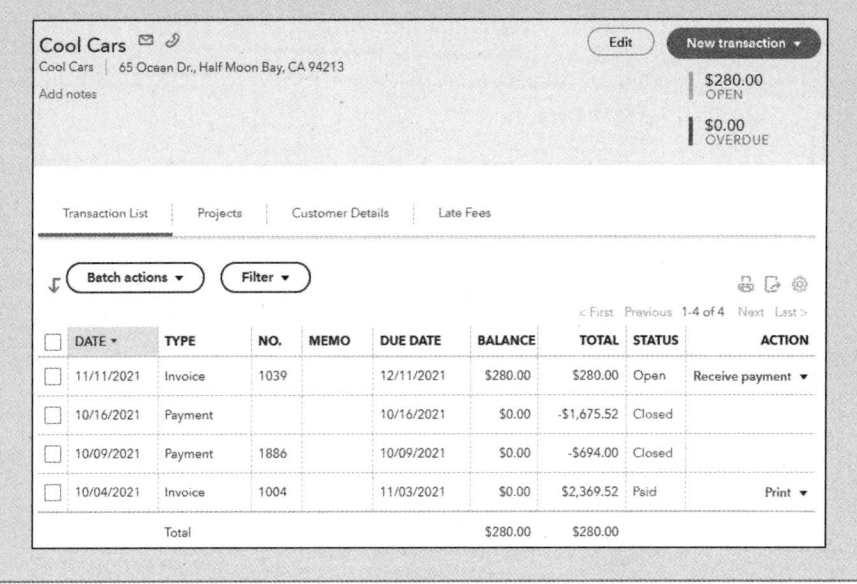

Figure 4.13

Cool Cars (recent transactions)

Cash Receipts

In QBO, the concept of cash receipts is referred to as receiving payments. Thus, to record the receipt of payment from a customer, you can use the Receive Payment item in the Create menu to record the transaction, or you can use Receive Payment from the Action column in a customer's list of transactions. Once a payment is received, it must be deposited into your bank account. This is a separate but important process in QBO.

To record the receipt of a payment to the Sample Company from a customer, do the following:

1. Continue from where you left off. If you closed the Sample Company, follow the steps at the beginning of this chapter to reopen it.
2. Click the **+ New** icon, and select **Receive Payment** as shown in Figure 4.14.

Figure 4.14

Receive Payment (recording the receipt of a customer payment)

Navigate your browser to the Video Tutorials provided by Intuit (see website address specified in the Preface to this text) and then search on How to Record the Receipt of Payment on an Invoice.

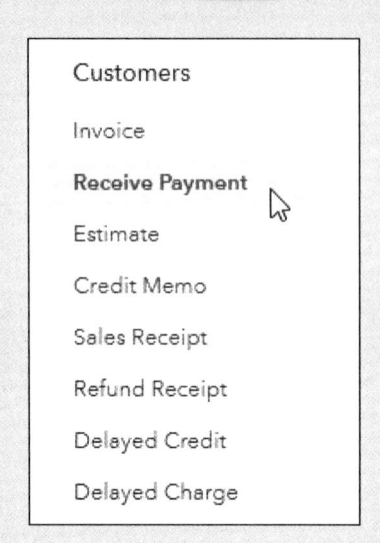

3. Select **Jeff's Jalopies** from the Choose a customer drop-down list in the upper-left corner of the Receive Payment window.
4. Your computer's system date has been entered as the Payment date.
5. Select **Check** as the Payment method. Select **Undeposited Funds** from the Deposit to text box.
6. Place a check in the Invoice # 1022 check box as shown in Figure 4.15. (Do not click Save.)

Figure 4.15

Receive Payment window

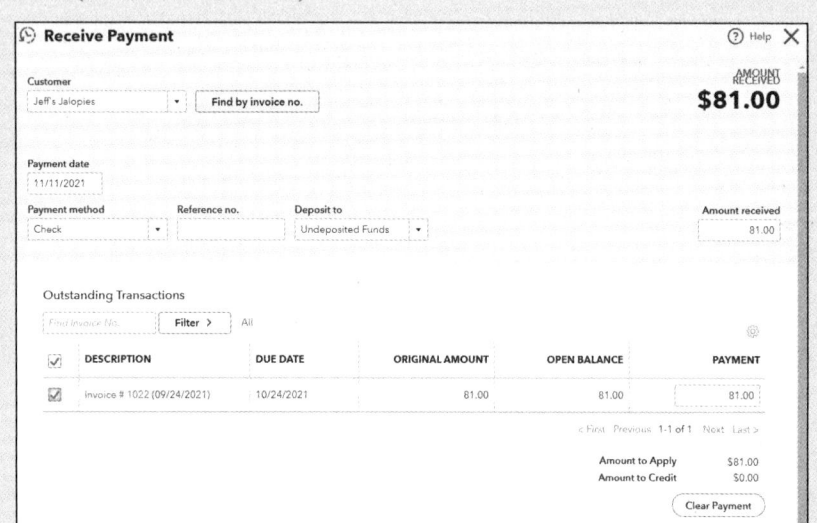

7. Click **Cancel** so you can explore the other means of recording this transaction. Click **Yes** when asked if you want to leave without saving.

8   Click **Sales**, then click **Customers** from the navigation bar, and click **Jeff's Jalopies**. A listing of recent transactions affecting that customer is shown, including invoice # 1022, in Figure 4.16.

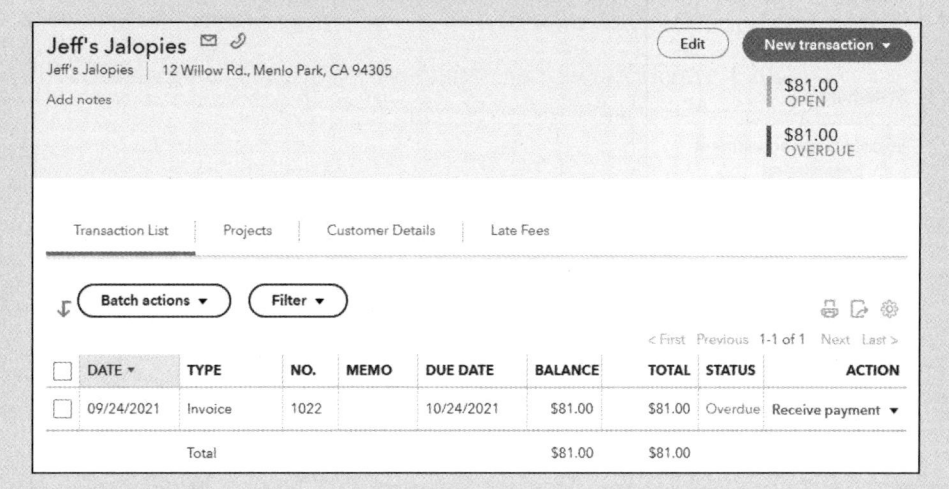

Figure 4.16

Jeff's Jalopies (recent transactions)

9   Click **Receive payment** in the Action column next to invoice # 1022.

10 The same Receive Payment window you saw earlier reappears. Thus, you have two ways of accessing and recording the receipt of payments from a customer. Enter the same information you did earlier as shown in Figure 4.15, and click **Save and Close**.

11 In the Jeff's Jalopies window, the transactions and payment are shown, and the balance is $0.00 as shown in Figure 4.17.

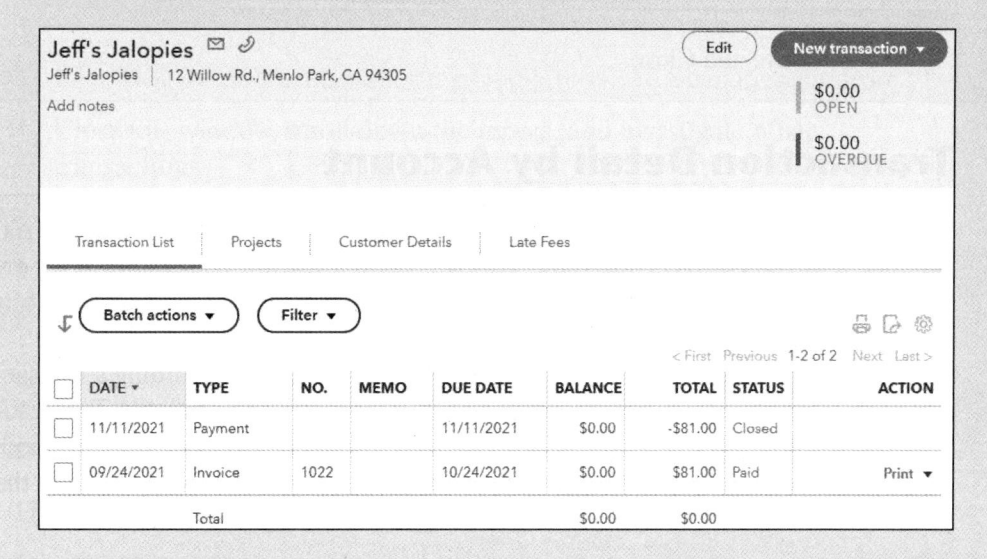

Figure 4.17

Jeff's Jalopies window (recent transactions after payment)

12 Click the (+ New) icon, and select **Bank deposit** from the Other column as shown in Figure 4.18.

practice

Chapter 4 Questions

1. What steps need to be followed to add a new product or service?
2. What steps need to be followed to record a new sales receipt?
3. What steps need to be followed to record a new invoice?
4. What steps need to be followed to record a new payment from a customer?
5. What steps need to be followed to record a new deposit to the bank?
6. What are the differences between adding a new product and adding a new service?
7. What is the difference between a sales receipt and a sales invoice?

Chapter 4 Matching

a. Invoice	_____	A service in the Sample Company
b. Sales receipt	_____	Providing the bank a payment from a customer
c. Product	_____	Used when recording a sale on account
d. Service	_____	Used to add invoices, sales receipts, or bank deposits
e. [+ New] icon	_____	A customer in the Sample Company
f. Payment from a customer	_____	Quantities of this are not tracked
g. Deposit	_____	Used when cash is collected at the time of a sale
h. Pest control	_____	Cash receipts received from a sale
i. Roses	_____	Quantities of this are tracked
j. Cool Cars	_____	A product that is added in the Sample Company

Chapter 4 Cases

The following cases require you to open the company you updated in Chapter 3. Each of the following cases continues throughout the text in a sequential manner. For example, if you are assigned Case 01, you will use the file you modified in this chapter in all of the following chapters. Each of the following cases is similar in concepts assessed but differs in amounts and transactions. See the Preface to this text for a matrix of each student case and its attributes.

To reopen your company, do the following:

1. Open your Internet browser.
2. Type **https://qbo.intuit.com** into your browser's address text box.
3. Type your user ID and password into the text boxes as you have done before.

Case 1

Add some operating activities (sales and cash receipts) to your company. Based on what you learned in the text using the Sample Company, you are to make the following changes to the Case 1 company you modified in Chapter 3:

1. Add a new customer – Name: Sarah Hay, Company: Hey Hays Surf, Display name as: Sarah Hay, Address: 230 Beach Way, La Jolla, CA, 92039.

2. Add a new service – Tune-Up, rate: $85.00, income account: Services.

3. Add a new product – Fred Rubble, initial quantity on hand: 0, as of date: 1/1/24, Inventory asset account: Inventory Asset, price: $950.00, cost: $600.00, income account: Sales, expense account: Cost of Goods Sold.

4. Record a new sales receipt on 1/3/24 – Customer: Blondie's Boards, payment method: Check, reference no.: 893, deposit to: Undeposited Funds (add this new current asset account), product: Rook 15, quantity: 2.

5. Record a new invoice on 1/4/24 – Customer: Sarah Hay, terms: Net 30, service: Tune-Up, quantity: 2, product: The Water Hog, quantity: 1.

6. Record a new cash payment received on 1/5/24 – Customer: Blondie's Boards, payment method: Check, reference no.: 984, deposit to: Undeposited Funds, amount received: $5,000.00. (Be sure to place a check in the Journal Entry #1 check box.)

7. Record a deposit made on 1/8/24 to the checking account – Received from: Blondie's Boards, amount received: $1,300.00, related to: Sales Receipt.

8. Prepare a Trial Balance report with a From date of 1/1/24 and a To date of 1/31/24, save it as a customized report named Trial Balance 1/31/24, and share it with all users. Your report should look like Figure 4.22. If asked, indicate that your business is accrual based.

Figure 4.22

Trial Balance (as of 1/31/24)

Case 1
TRIAL BALANCE
As of January 31, 2024

	DEBIT	CREDIT
Checking	26,300.00	
Accounts Receivable	1,030.00	
Inventory Asset	6,700.00	
Prepaid Expenses	3,000.00	
Undeposited Funds	5,000.00	
Furniture & Fixtures:Depreciation		10,000.00
Furniture & Fixtures:Original cost	40,000.00	
Accounts Payable		4,500.00
Notes Payable		60,000.00
Common Stock		1,000.00
Opening Balance Equity		0.00
Retained Earnings		5,500.00
Sales		2,160.00
Services		170.00
Cost of Goods Sold	1,300.00	
TOTAL	**$83,330.00**	**$83,330.00**

9. If your trial balance differs from what is shown in Figure 4.22, do the following:

   a. Make sure that all of your changes were dated in January 2024.

   b. Click on the debit or credit balance to view a transactions report for each account, and investigate why your answer differs.

   c. Ask your instructor for assistance.

   d. Be sure your company matches the above as you will be adding additional business events in Chapter 5.

10. Export your Trial Balance report to Excel, and save it with the file name Student Name (replace with your name) Ch 04 Case 01 Trial Balance.xlsx.

11. Open and print the custom report you created in the Chapter 3 called Transaction Detail by Account.

12. Use your Transaction Detail by Account report to locate any differences in your Trial Balance report created above.

    a. Make sure all of your changes were dated in January 2024.

    b. Click on the line that does not match to view the transaction for that account, and investigate why your answer differs.

    c. Ask your instructor for assistance.

    d. Be sure your company matches the above as you will be adding additional business events in Chapter 5.

13 Export your Transactions Detail by Account report to Excel and save it with the file name Student Name (replace with your name) Ch 04 Case 01 Transaction Detail by Account.xlsx.

14 Sign out of your company.

Case 2

Add some operating activities (sales and cash receipts) to your company. Based on what you learned in the text using the Sample Company, you are to make the following changes to the Case 2 company you modified in Chapter 3:

1 Add a new customer – Hagen's Toys, 3983 Torrey Pines, La Jolla, CA, 92039.

2 Add a new service – Custom Painting, rate: $45.00, income account: Services.

3 Add two new products – GO Aircraft Radio, initial quantity on hand: 0, as of date: 1/1/25, Inventory asset account: Inventory Asset, price: $4,999.00, cost: $2,500.00, income account: Sales, expense account: Cost of Goods Sold and Taylor 22cc, initial quantity on hand: 0, as of date: 1/1/25, Inventory asset account: Inventory Asset, price: $2,999.00, cost: $1,500.00, income account: Sales, expense account: Cost of Goods Sold.

4 Record a new sales receipt on 1/3/25 – Customer: Benson's RC, payment method: Credit Card, reference no.: 16756, deposit to: Undeposited Funds, product: Broon F830 Ride, quantity: 3.

5 Record a new invoice on 1/4/25 – Customer: Hagen's Toys, terms: Net 30, service: Custom Painting, quantity: 5, product: Seawind Carbon Sailboat, quantity: 1.

6 Record a new cash payment received on 1/7/25 – Customer: Benson's RC, payment method: Check, reference no.: 9847, deposit to: Undeposited Funds, amount received: $925.00. (Be sure to place a check in the Journal Entry #1 check box.)

7 Record a deposit made on 1/7/25 to the checking account – Received from: Benson's RC, amount received: $4,500.00, related to: Sales Receipt.

8 Prepare a Trial Balance report with a From date of 1/1/25 and a To date of 1/31/25, save it as a customized report named Trial Balance 1/31/25, and share it with all users. Your report should look like Figure 4.23. If asked, indicate that your business is accrual based.

Figure 4.23

Trial Balance (as of 1/31/25)

Case 2
TRIAL BALANCE
As of January 31, 2025

	DEBIT	CREDIT
Checking	9,500.00	
Accounts Receivable	1,425.00	
Inventory Asset	2,040.00	
Prepaid Expenses	2,400.00	
Undeposited Funds	925.00	
Machinery & Equipment:Depreciation		1,000.00
Machinery & Equipment:Original cost	10,000.00	
Accounts Payable		1,900.00
Notes Payable		12,000.00
Common Stock		100.00
Opening Balance Equity		0.00
Retained Earnings		8,385.00
Sales		5,700.00
Services		225.00
Cost of Goods Sold	3,020.00	
TOTAL	$29,310.00	$29,310.00

9   If your trial balance differs from what is shown in Figure 4.23, do the following:

   a.   Make sure that all of your changes were dated in January 2025.

   b.   Click on the debit or credit balance to view a transactions report for each account, and investigate why your answer differs.

   c.   Ask your instructor for assistance.

   d.   Be sure your company matches the above as you will be adding additional business events in Chapter 5.

10   Export your Trial Balance report to Excel, and save it with the file name Student Name (replace with your name) Ch 04 Case 02 Trial Balance.xlsx.

11   Open and print the custom report you created in Chapter 3, which is called Transaction Detail by Account.

12   Use your Transaction Detail by Account report to locate any differences in your Trial Balance report created above.

   a.   Make sure that all of your changes were dated in January 2025.

   b.   Click on the line that does not match to view the transaction for that account, and investigate why your answer differs.

   c.   Ask your instructor for assistance.

   d.   Be sure your company matches the above as you will be adding additional business events in Chapter 5.

13 Export your Transactions Detail by Account report to Excel, and save it with the file name Student Name (replace with your name) Ch 04 Case 02 Transaction Detail by Account.xlsx.

14 Sign out of your company.

Case 3

Now it's time for you to add some operating activities (sales and cash receipts) to your company. Based on what you learned in the text using the Sample Company, you are to make the following changes to the Case 3 company you modified in Chapter 3:

1 Add a new customer – Surfer Sales, 3983 Torrey Pines, La Jolla, CA, 92039.

2 Add a new service – Phone Consulting, rate: $35.00, income account: Services, not taxable.

3 Add two new products – Apple iPhone 6s, initial quantity on hand: 0, inventory asset account: Inventory Asset, price: $549.00, cost: $349.00, income account: Sales of Product Income, expense account: Cost of Goods Sold, taxable and Apple iPhone 7 Plus, initial quantity on hand: 0, inventory asset account: Inventory Asset, price: $800, cost: $600.00, income account: Sales of Product Income, expense account: Cost of Goods Sold, taxable. Use 12/31/25 for the as of date.

4 Record a new sales receipt on 1/3/26 – customer: Surfer Sales, payment method: Credit Card, reference no.: 16756, deposit to: Payments to deposit product: Apple iPhone 7, quantity: 6, and 3 hours of Phone Consulting. Click **See the math** to update amounts.

5 Record a new invoice on 1/6/26 – customer: GHO Marketing, terms: Net 30, 3 hours of Apple Repairs, product: Apple iPhone 7, quantity: 3. Click **See the math** to update amounts.

6 Record a new cash payment received on 1/7/26 – customer: GHO Marketing, payment method: Check, reference no.: 9847, deposit to: Payments to deposit, amount received: $4,125.00. (Be sure to place a check in the Journal Entry #1 check box.)

7 Record a deposit made on 1/9/26 to the checking account of $9,078.75, which was received from Surfer Sales, amount $4,953.75, and related to Sales Receipt and GHO Marketing, amount $4,125.00, related to Payment.

8 Prepare a Trial Balance report with a From date of 1/1/26 and a To date of 1/31/26 and then save it as a customized report named Trial Balance 1/31/26 and share it with all users. Your report should look like Figure 4.24.

Figure 4.24

Trial Balance as of 1/31/26

Case 03 - Student Name (ID Number)

Trial Balance
As of January 31, 2026

	DEBIT	CREDIT
Checking	21,078.75	
Accounts receivable (A/R)	2,559.38	
Inventory Asset	1,700.00	
Payments to deposit	0.00	
Prepaid expenses	2,750.00	
Machinery & Equipment:Depreciation		2,000.00
Machinery & Equipment:Original cost	15,000.00	
Accounts Payable (A/P)		5,000.00
California Department of Tax and Fee Administration ...		523.13
Notes Payable		23,000.00
Opening balance equity		0.00
Owner's Equity		10,075.00
Sales of Product Income		6,750.00
Services		240.00
Cost of goods sold	4,500.00	
TOTAL	**$47,588.13**	**$47,588.13**

9. If your trial balance is different than Figure 4.24, do the following:
    a. Make sure that all of your changes were dated in January 2026.
    b. Click on the debit or credit balance to view a transactions report for each account, and investigate why your answer is different.
    c. Ask your instructor for assistance.
    d. Be sure your company matches the above as you will be adding additional business events in Chapter 5.

10. Export your Trial Balance report to Excel, and save it with the file name Student Name (replace with your name) Ch 04 Case 03 Trial Balance.xlsx.

11. Open and print the custom report you created in Chapter 3, which is called Transaction Detail by Account.

12. Use your Transaction Detail by Account report to locate any differences in your Trial Balance report created above.
    a. Make sure that all of your changes were dated in January 2026.
    b. Click on the line that doesn't match to view the transaction for that account, and investigate why your answer is different.
    c. Ask your instructor for assistance.
    d. Be sure your company matches the above as you will be adding additional business events in Chapter 5.

13 Export your Transactions Detail by Account report to MS Excel and save it with the file name Student Name (replace with your name) Ch 04 Case 03 Transaction Detail by Account.xlsx.

14 Sign out of your company.

Case 4

Now it's time for you to add some operating activities (sales and cash receipts) to your company. Based on what you learned in the text using the Sample Company, you are to make the following changes to the Case 4 company you modified in Chapter 3:

1 Add two new accounts.

   a. First account

      i) Account Type – Other Current Assets

      ii) Detail Type/Name – Undeposited Funds

   b. Second account

      i) Account Type – Expenses

      ii) Detail Type – Other Business Expenses

      iii) Name – Laundry Service

2 Add three new customers.

   a. Flyer Corporation, 32 Wilshire Blvd., Hollywood, CA 90028, terms: Net 30

   b. ABC Studios, 2300 W Riverside Dr., Burbank, CA 91506, terms: Net 30

   c. Sam Shepard, 10 Hollywood Blvd., Hollywood, CA 90028, terms: Due on receipt

3 Modify an existing customer (use Help to learn how to do this).

   a. Company – Disney

   b. Address – 500 South Buena Vista Street, Burbank, CA 91505, terms: Net 30

4 Add three new vendors.

   a. Bowflex Inc., 3393 Main St., Vancouver, WA 98607, terms: Net 30

   b. NordicTrack Inc., 23 First St., Logan, UT 84321, terms: Net 30

   c. Laundry Service, 432 Sunset Blvd., Hollywood, CA, 90028, terms: Due on receipt

5. Modify an existing vendor (use Help to learn how to do this).
   a. Company – Precor
   b. Address – 20031 142nd Avenue NE, Woodinville, WA 98072, terms: Net 30

6. Create a new service item as follows:
   a. Name/Description – Monthly Fee – Corporate Membership 50 Employees
   b. Description – Yes you do sell this service to customers
   c. Sales price/rate – $6,000
   d. Income account – Sales
   e. Is taxable – No
   f. Purchasing information – No you don't purchase this service from a vendor

7. Modify two existing service items (use Help to learn how to do this).
   a. Old Name/Description – Monthly Fee – New Name/Description – Monthly Fee – Individual
   b. Old Name/Description – Training – New Name/Description – Training – Individual

8. Add two new products.
   a. First product
      i) Name – Bowflex Dumbbells
      ii) Initial quantity on hand – 0
      iii) As of date – 12/31/20
      iv) Inventory asset account – Inventory Asset
      v) Description – Bowflex Dumbbells
      vi) Sales price/rate – $249
      vii) Income account – Sales of Product Income
      viii) Is taxable – Yes
      ix) Purchasing information – Bowflex Dumbbells
      x) Cost – $200
      xi) Expense account – Cost of Goods Sold
   b. Second product
      i) Name – Power Block Elite Dumbbells
      ii) Initial quantity on hand – 0
      iii) As of date – 12/31/20
      iv) Inventory asset account – Inventory Asset
      v) Description – Power Block Elite Dumbbells
      vi) Sales price/rate – $299
      vii) Income account – Sales of Product Income

viii) Is taxable – Yes

ix) Purchasing information – Power Block Elite Dumbbells

x) Cost – $199

xi) Expense account – Cost of Goods Sold

9 Record a new sales receipt to Sam Shepard on 1/5/21 for 6 months of Monthly Fee – Individual, 10 hours of Training – Individual, 1 T-shirt, and 1 pair of Yoga pants. Total $1,726.65 (including sales tax) received via check number 6571 and deposited to the Undeposited Funds account.

10 Record a new ABC Studios invoice 1002 on 1/6/21 for 1 Monthly Fee – Corporate Membership 50 Employees and 50 T-shirts for a total amount of $7,368.75 (including sales tax).

11 Record a new Flyer Corporation invoice 1003 on 1/6/21 for 1 Monthly Fee – Corporate Membership 50 Employees and 50 hours of Training – Individual and 50 pairs of Yoga pants for a total amount of $12,213.75 (including sales tax).

12 Record a partial cash payment of $6,000.00 received on 1/14/21 from Disney using check 9744 recorded to the Undeposited Funds account. (Be sure to place a check in the Journal Entry #1 check box.)

13 Record a bank deposit of $7,726.65 made on 1/15/21 from Disney and Sam Shepard.

14 Prepare and print a Trial Balance report with a custom reporting period of 1/1/21 to 1/31/21, and then save it as a customized report named Trial Balance 1/31/21. Your report should look like Figure 4.25.

Case 4 Student Name (Student ID)

TRIAL BALANCE
As of January 31, 2021

	DEBIT	CREDIT
Checking	34,726.65	
Accounts Receivable (A/R)	22,082.50	
Inventory Asset	3,868.00	
Prepaid Expenses	12,000.00	
Undeposited Funds	0.00	
Furniture:Depreciation		10,000.00
Furniture:Original cost	65,000.00	
Machinery & Equipment:Depreciation		6,500.00
Machinery & Equipment:Original cost	115,000.00	
Accounts Payable (A/P)		18,000.00
California State Board of Equalization Payable		339.15
Notes Payable		82,000.00
Common Stock		1,000.00
Opening Balance Equity		0.00
Retained Earnings		115,500.00
Sales		17,400.00
Sales of Product Income		3,570.00
Cost of Goods Sold	1,632.00	
TOTAL	$254,309.15	$254,309.15

Figure 4.25

Trial Balance as of 1/31/21

15 Prepare and print a Transaction Detail by Account report for all transactions between 1/1/10 and 12/31/22, and save it as a customized report named Transaction Detail by Account. If asked, indicate that your business is accrual based.

16 Use your Transaction Detail by Account report to locate any differences in your Trial Balance report created above.

    a. Make sure all your changes were dated in January 2021.

    b. Click on the line that does not match to view the transaction for that account, and investigate why your answer differs.

    c. Ask your instructor for assistance.

    d. Be sure your company matches the above as you will be adding additional business events in Chapter 5.

Case 5

Now it's time for you to add some operating activities (sales and cash receipts) to your company. Based on using what you learned in the text using the Sample Company, you are to make the following changes to the Case 4 company you modified in Chapter 3:

1 Add three new accounts.

    a. First account
        i) Account Type – Other Current Assets
        ii) Detail Type/Name – Undeposited Funds

    b. Second account
        i) Account Type – Expenses
        ii) Detail Type – Equipment Rental
        iii) Name – Equipment Rental

    c. Third account
        i) Account Type – Expenses
        ii) Detail Type – Legal & Professional Fees
        iii) Name – Recruiting

2 Add two new customers.

    a. US Department of Defense, 25203 Baneberry, San Antonio, TX, 78260, terms: Net 15

    b. Boeing, 3365 160th Ave SE 3307, Bellevue, WA, 98008, terms: Net 30

3 Modify an existing customer (use help to learn how to do this).

    a. Company – Boeing

    b. Address – 4800 Oak Grove Dr, Pasadena, CA, 91109, terms: Net 30

4 Add three new vendors.

    a. United Rentals, 376 Dan Tibbs Rd, Huntsville, AL 35806, terms: Net 30

    b. Indeed, 6433 Champion Grandview Way, Austin, TX, 78750, terms: Net 30

    c. HP Computers, 1501 Page Mill Rd, Palo Alto, CA, 94020, terms: Net 30

5. Modify an existing vendor (use Help to learn how to do this).
   a. Company – Chase Bank
   b. Address – 416 West Jefferson, Louisville, KY, 40202, terms: Due on receipt

6. Create a new service item as follows:
   a. Name/Description – Consulting
   b. Description – You sell this product/service to my customers
   c. Sales price/rate – $350
   d. Income account – Consulting
   e. Nontaxable
   f. Purchasing information – No you don't purchase this service from a vendor

7. Modify two existing service items (use Help to learn how to do this).
   a. Old name/Description – Technical Solutions – New name/Description – Technical Solutions – Commercial
   b. Old name/Description – Program Support – New name/Description – Program Support – Government

8. Add two new inventory products.
   a. First product
      i) Name – Computer Workstation 100
      ii) Initial quantity on hand – 0
      iii) As of date – 12/31/21
      iv) Inventory asset account – Inventory
      v) Description – Computer Workstation 100
      vi) Sales price/rate – $15,000
      vii) Income account – Sales
      viii) Taxable – standard rate
      ix) Purchasing Information – Computer Workstation 100
      x) Cost – $7,000
      xi) Expense account – Cost of Goods Sold
   b. Second product
      i) Name – Computer Workstation 500
      ii) Initial quantity on hand – 0
      iii) As of date – 12/31/21
      iv) Inventory asset account – Inventory
      v) Description – Computer Workstation 500
      vi) Sales price/rate – $35,000
      vii) Income account – Sales
      viii) Taxable – standard rate
      ix) Purchasing Information – Computer Workstation 500
      x) Cost – $17,000
      xi) Expense account – Cost of Goods Sold

9. Record a new sales receipt 1001 to a new customer Blue Origin on 1/4/22 for 50 hours of consulting and received payment via check number 1687 and deposited to the Undeposited Funds account.

10. Record a new invoice 1002 on 1/6/22 to the US Department of Defense for 100 hours of Program Support – Government. If asked, select **I'll create invoice for my accounting, but won't send any**. If asked how I want to get paid, select **Check**.

11. Record a new invoice 1003 on 1/7/22 to Boeing for 80 hours of Technical Solutions – Commercial and 1 Training Materials – Volume 1 for a total invoice of $48,350.00 including sales tax. Click **See the math** to update amounts.

12. Record a cash payment of $70,000.00 received on 1/10/22 from NASA using check 18842 recorded to the Undeposited Funds account. Select **Journal Entry #1** in Outstanding Transactions section.

13. Record a bank deposit of $87,500.00 made on 1/12/22 from Blue Origin and NASA.

14. Prepare and print a Trial Balance report with a custom reporting period of 1/1/22 to 1/31/22 and then save it as a customized report named Trial Balance 1/31/22. Your report should look like Figure 4.26.

Figure 4.26

Trial Balance

Case 05 - Student Name (ID Number)
TRIAL BALANCE
As of January 31, 2022

	DEBIT	CREDIT
Checking	117,500.00	
Accounts Receivable (A/R)	158,350.00	
Inventory	452,000.00	
Prepaid Expenses	10,000.00	
Undeposited Funds	0.00	
Fixed Asset Computers:Depreciation		25,000.00
Fixed Asset Computers:Original cost	250,000.00	
Fixed Asset Furniture:Depreciation		8,000.00
Fixed Asset Furniture:Original cost	80,000.00	
Accounts Payable (A/P)		20,000.00
Alabama Department of Revenue Payable		600.00
Alabama, Huntsville Payable		675.00
Alabama, Madison County Payable		75.00
Notes Payable		545,000.00
Opening Balance Equity		0.00
Owner's Equity		382,000.00
Consulting		79,500.00
Sales		15,000.00
Cost of Goods Sold	8,000.00	
TOTAL	$1,075,850.00	$1,075,850.00

15. Open and print your previously saved report Transaction Detail by Account.

16. Use your Transaction Detail by Account report to locate any differences in your Trial Balance report created above.

    a. Make sure all your changes were dated in January 2022.

    b. Click on the line that does not match to view the transaction for that account, and investigate why your answer differs.

    c. Ask your instructor for assistance.

    d. Be sure your company matches the above as you will be adding additional business events in Chapter 5.

Case 6

Now it's time for you to add some operating activities (sales and cash receipts) to your company. Based on using what you learned in the text using the Sample Company, you are to make the following changes to the Case 6 company you modified in Chapter 3:

1. Add two new accounts.
    a. First account
        i) Account Type – Other Current Assets
        ii) Detail Type/Name – Prepaid Expenses
    b. Second account
        i) Account Type – Other Current Assets
        ii) Detail Type – Inventory
        iii) Name – Inventory Parts

2. Change the name of expense account Repairs & Maintenance to Repairs.

3. Add two new customers.
    a. Ebony Williams, 4101 S Sheridan Ave., Tacoma, WA, 98418, terms: Net 30
    b. Deja Smith, 4648 N Defiance St., Tacoma, WA, 98407, terms: Net 30

4. Modify an existing customer.
    a. Company – Sam Ski
    b. Address – 5633 89th Ave SE, Mercer Island, WA, 98040, terms: Net 30

5. Add two new vendors.
    a. Airstream, Inc., 419 West Pike Street, Jackson Center, OH 45334, terms: Net 30
    b. Thor Motor Coach, 701 County Road 15 Elkhart, Indiana 46516, terms: Net 30

6. Modify an existing vendor.
    a. Company – Winnebago (change Company and Display name to Winnebago, Inc.)
    b. Address – 605 West Crystal Lake Road, Forest City, IA, 50436, terms: Net 30

7. Create two new service items as follows:
    a. First service
        i) Name – Basic 6,000-mile service
        ii) Description – Yes you do sell this service to customers
        iii) Sales price/rate – $450
        iv) Income account – Sales
        v) Sales Tax Category – Nontaxable
        vi) Purchasing information – No you don't purchase this service from a vendor

b. Second service
   i) Name – Roof inspection and repair
   ii) Description – Yes you do sell this service to customers
   iii) Sales price/rate – $500
   iv) Income account – Sales
   v) Sales Tax Category – Nontaxable
   vi) Purchasing information – No you don't purchase this service from a vendor

c. Third service
   i) Name – Sewer system inspection and repair
   ii) Description – Yes you do sell this service to customers
   iii) Sales price/rate – $600
   iv) Income account – Sales
   v) Sales Tax Category – Nontaxable
   vi) Purchasing information – No you don't purchase this service from a vendor

8 Add two new inventory products.
   a. First product
      i) Name – 2023 Thor Motor Coach Palazzo 33.2
      ii) Inventory asset account – Inventory Asset
      iii) Description – 2023 Thor Motor Coach Palazzo 33.2
      iv) Sales price/rate – $180,000
      v) Income account – Sales of Product Income
      vi) Sales Tax Category – Taxable - Standard rate
      vii) Purchasing information – 2023 Thor Motor Coach Palazzo 33.2
      viii) Cost – $144,000
      ix) Expense account – Cost of Goods Sold
      x) Preferred Vendor – Thor Motor Coach
      xi) Initial quantity on hand – 0
      xii) As of date – 12/31/22

   b. Second product
      i) Name – 2023 Airstream Flying Cloud 27FB TWIN
      ii) Inventory asset account – Inventory Asset
      iii) Description – 2023 Airstream Flying Cloud 27FB TWIN
      iv) Sales price/rate – $99,000
      v) Income account – Sales of Product Income
      vi) Sales Tax Category – Taxable - Standard rate
      vii) Purchasing information – 2023 Airstream Flying Cloud 27FB TWIN
      viii) Cost – $80,000
      ix) Expense account – Cost of Goods Sold
      x) Preferred Vendor – Airstream, Inc.
      xi) Initial quantity on hand – 0
      xii) As of date – 12/31/22

9 Record a new sales receipt 1001 on 01/05/23 to a new customer Donald Biden for the sale of a 2022 Winnebago Revel 44E for $150,000 plus sales tax of $13,950 with payment method credit card for a total of $163,950.

10 Record a new invoice 1002 on 01/09/23 to Deja Smith for the sale of a 2022 Winnebago View 24G for $140,000 plus sales tax of $13,020 on account for a total of $153,020.

11 Record a new cash payment received on 1/11/23 – Customer: Sam Ski, payment method: Check, deposit to: Undeposited Funds, amount received: $10,000.

12 Record a deposit made on 1/12/23 to the checking account of $10,000 which was received from: Sam Ski.

13 Prepare and print a Trial Balance report with a custom reporting period of 1/1/23 to 1/31/23 and then save it as a customized report named Trial Balance 1/31/23. Your report should look like Figure 4.27.

Figure 4.27

Trial Balance

Case 06 - Student Name (ID Number)
TRIAL BALANCE
As of January 31, 2023

	DEBIT	CREDIT
Checking	223,950.00	
Accounts Receivable (A/R)	153,020.00	
Inventory Asset	344,000.00	
Loans To Officers	15,000.00	
Undeposited Funds	0.00	
Buildings:Depreciation		15,000.00
Buildings:Original cost	150,000.00	
Machinery & Equipment:Depreciation		10,000.00
Machinery & Equipment:Original cost	100,000.00	
Accounts Payable (A/P)		464,000.00
Washington State Department of Revenue Payable		26,970.00
Notes Payable		100,000.00
Common Stock		1,000.00
Opening Balance Equity		0.00
Paid-In Capital		250,000.00
Retained Earnings		61,000.00
Sales of Product Income		290,000.00
Cost of Goods Sold	232,000.00	
TOTAL	$1,217,970.00	$1,217,970.00

14 Prepare and print a Transaction Detail by Account report for all dates, and then save it as a customized report named Transaction Detail by Account All Dates. If asked, indicate that your business is accrual based.

15 Use your Transaction Detail by Account report to locate any differences in your Trial Balance report created above.

   a. Make sure all your changes were dated in January 2023.

   b. Click on the line that does not match to view the transaction for that account and investigate why your answer differs.

   c. Ask your instructor for assistance.

   d. Be sure your company matches the above as you will be adding additional business events in Chapter 5.

chapter 5
Recording Operating Activities: Purchases and Cash Payments

Student Learning Outcomes

Upon completion of this chapter, the student will be able to do the following:

- Create a vendor
- Record a purchase order
- Record a bill for the receipt of products/services on account
- Record the payment of bills
- Record credit card charges
- Record checks
- Prepare a Trial Balance and drill down to a transaction report for an account

Overview

Intuit has provided a Sample Company online to provide new users a test-drive of its QBO product. In this chapter, you will open this Sample Company and practice various features of QBO. You will be recording operating activities such as adding vendors, purchase orders, bills, bill payments, credit card charges, and checks to the Sample Company file. Remember, if you stop in the middle of this work, none of your work will be saved. So, when you return, the same Sample Company, without your work, will appear. In the end of chapter work, you will be asked to perform the same tasks completed on the Sample Company on your Student Company. That work, of course, will be saved. Your system date will differ from the date shown under the company name QBO. Transaction dates on your screen may also differ from the figures shown throughout this text.

Vendors

In this section, you will be adding new vendors. Recall that vendors are your company's suppliers of products and services. To add vendors, you will use the Vendors menu item in the navigation bar.

Navigate your browser to the Video Tutorials provided by Intuit (see website address specified in the Preface to this text) and then search on How to Manage Vendors.

Recording Operating Activities: Purchases and Cash Payments **Chapter 5** 105

To add new vendors to the Sample Company, do the following:

1. Open your Internet browser.
2. Type **https://qbo.intuit.com/redir/testdrive** into your browser's address text box, and then press [**Enter**] to view the Sample Company Dashboard.
3. Click **Expenses**, then click **Vendors** in the navigation bar, and then click the **New Vendor** button.
4. Type **Valley Rock** in the Company text box.
5. Type the address **290 Central Ave., Middletown, CA, 94482** in the appropriate text boxes.
6. Select **Net 30** from the Terms text box. A Vendor Information window is shown in Figure 5.1.

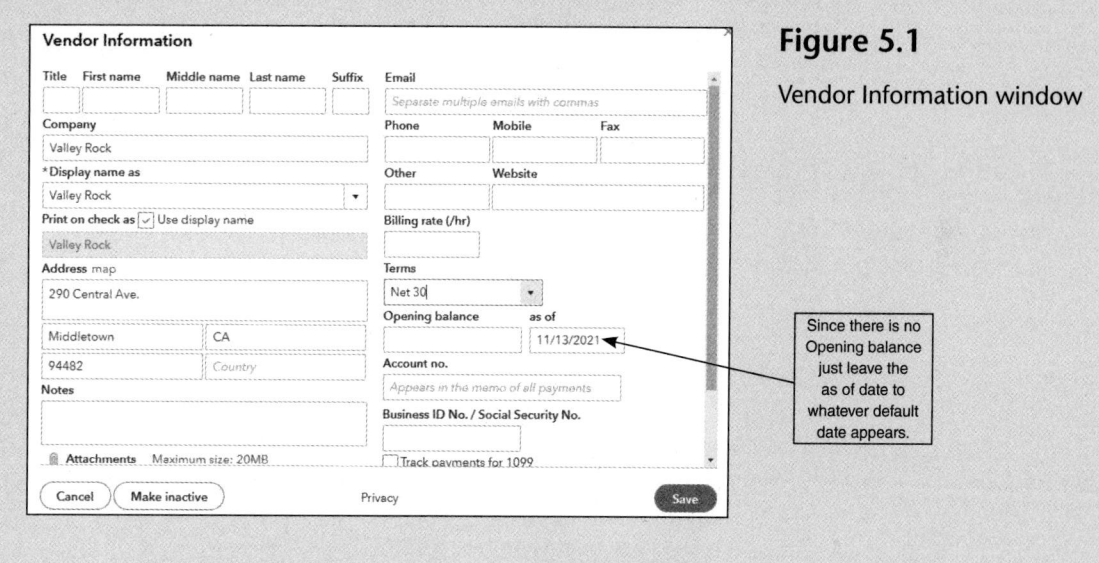

Figure 5.1

Vendor Information window

Since there is no Opening balance just leave the as of date to whatever default date appears.

7. Click **Save**.

You have added a new vendor. If you need to edit a vendor's information just click **Expenses**, then **Vendors**, then click on a vendor, then click **Edit**. Update the vendor information, then click **Save**. Next up is adding purchase orders.

Purchase Orders

A business uses purchase orders to formally order products or services from its vendors. Purchase orders are also used as a reference and control for products received. During the creation of a purchase order, you can create a new product. Purchase orders can be for inventory or for products ordered for a specific customer.

Navigate your browser to the Video Tutorials provided by Intuit (see website address specified in the Preface to this text) and then search on How to Enter Purchase Orders.

To add two purchase orders and new product to the Sample Company, do the following:

1. Continue from where you left off above.
2. Click the [+ New] icon, and select **Purchase order** as shown in Figure 5.2. **Trouble?** If you receive an error message indicating that purchase orders are turned off, click **Settings** in the error text box, then turn purchase orders on, then click **Save**.

106　Chapter 5　　*Recording Operating Activities: Purchases and Cash Payments*

Figure 5.2

+ New window (adding a purchase order)

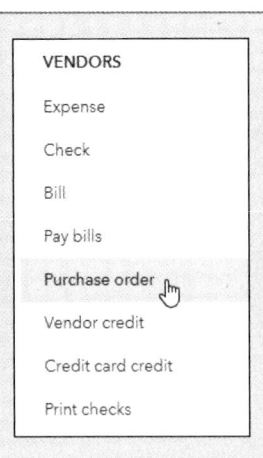

```
VENDORS
Expense
Check
Bill
Pay bills
Purchase order
Vendor credit
Credit card credit
Print checks
```

3. Select **Valley Rock** from the Vendor drop-down list in the upper-left corner of the Purchase Order window.

4. Your computer's system date has been entered as the Purchase Order date.

5. Click in the **Product/Service** column on line 1 of the purchase order's Item details section, and select **Add new** as shown in Figure 5.3.

Figure 5.3

Purchase Order (adding a new product)

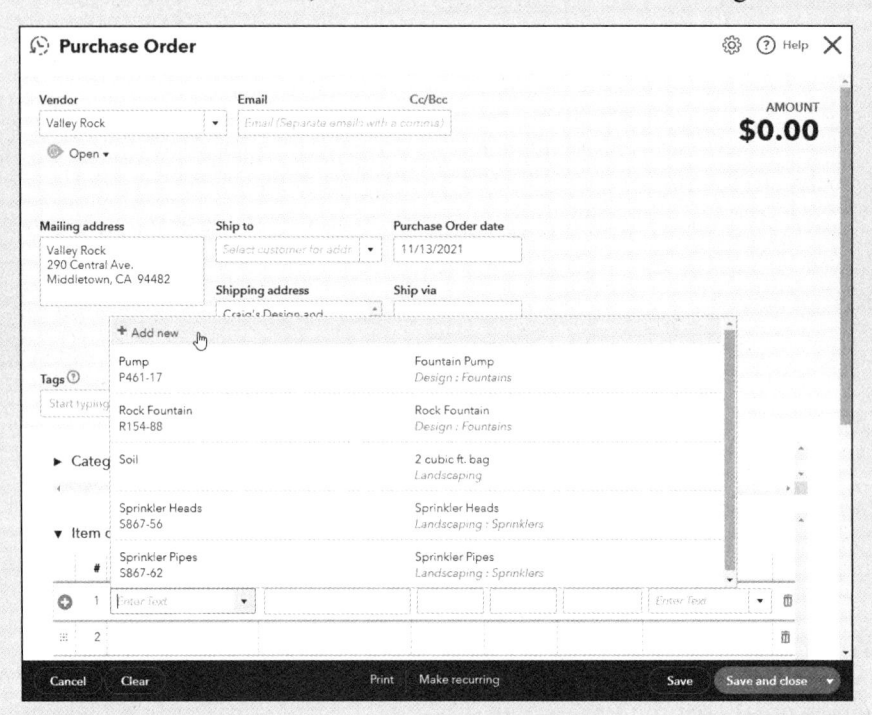

6. Create a new product, as you have done before—product type: Inventory, Name and Description: Landscape Rock, initial quantity on hand: **0**, As of date: your system date, Category: Landscaping, inventory asset account: Inventory Asset, Sales price/rate: 75, cost: 50, income account: Sales of Product Income, expense account: Cost of Goods Sold, Sales tax category: Taxable - standard rate. Click **Save and Close**.

7. Type **100** in the QTY column. Leave the Customer field blank as this order is for inventory. Your completed purchase order should look like Figure 5.4.

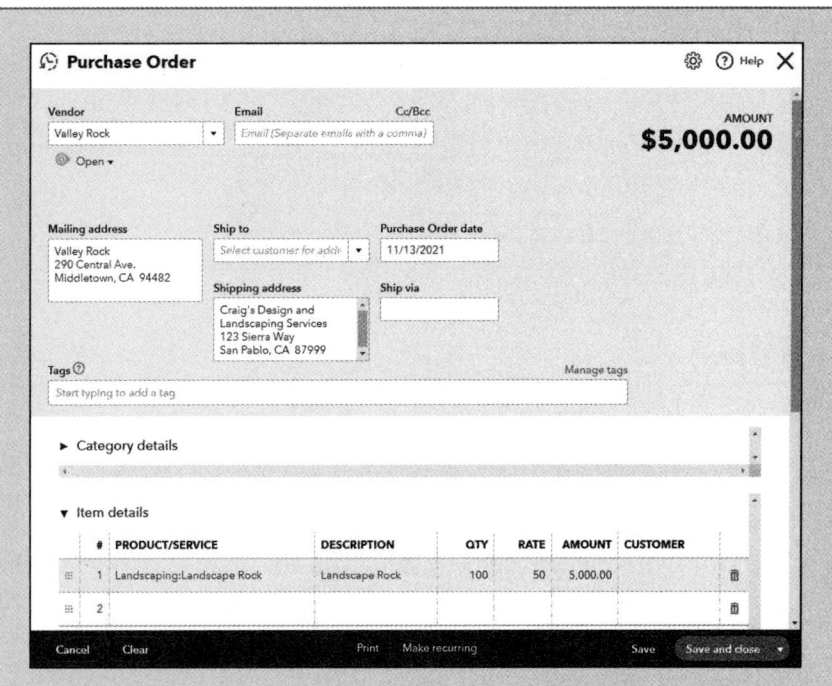

Figure 5.4

Purchase Order (for Valley Rock)

8 Click **Save and New**.

9 Select **Hicks Hardware** from the Vendor drop-down list in the upper-left corner of the Purchase Order window. Accept your current system date as the Purchase Order date.

10 The Item details section of the purchase order is filled out with information from the last purchase order completed for this vendor. Leave all lines of the Product/Service column as it is.

11 Click on **25** (the QTY amount for item #3). Note that when you select the existing QTY value, QBO displays the quantity of that item on hand. In this case, 31 as shown in Figure 5.5.

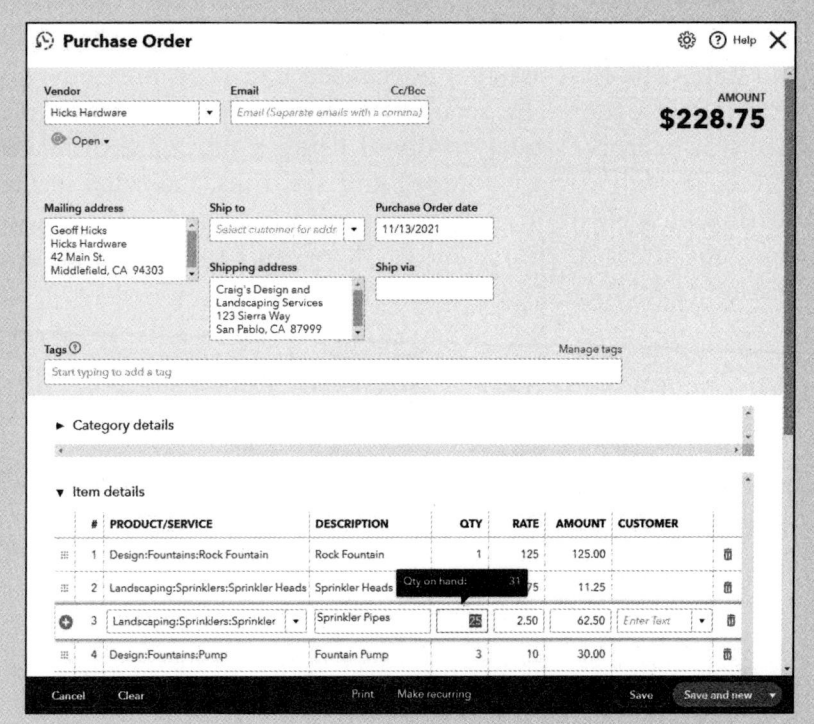

Figure 5.5

Purchase Order (to Hicks Hardware)

12 Now change the amounts in the QTY column as follows: Rock Fountain **3**, Sprinkler Heads **20**, Sprinkler Pipes **30**, and Pump **4**.

13 Select **Kookies by Kathy** in the Customer column for all four items. Your total purchase order amount should be $505.

14 Click **Save and Close**.

Navigate your browser to the Video Tutorials provided by Intuit (see website address specified in the Preface to this text) and then search on How to Enter Bills.

Bills

In the previous chapter, you created invoices to customers for products or services rendered. That invoice served as a bill to that customer signifying a sales transaction for you and a bill to them. Likewise, when you enter into a business transaction, such as purchasing a product or service from a vendor, you expect them to send you an invoice. In QBO, the invoice you receive from a vendor is called a bill. Bills are recorded in QBO to signify the receipt of a product or service and a related liability, usually accounts payable. The inventory account is affected when the bill represents a product being delivered.

In QBO, the terms of those bills could be one of the following: due on receipt, net 10, net 15, net 30, or net 60. The net reference means the bill is due to be paid within a specified number of days, for example, 10, 15, 30, or 60 days. Other terms, for example, 2/10 net 30, provide for a 2% discount on the invoice if paid within 10 days; otherwise, a payment is required within 30 days. Even though you can set up such terms to appear on invoices to customers and bills from vendors, QBO does not calculate them automatically. To simplify your learning of QBO, discounts have not been implemented in this text.

In this section, you will focus on recording a bill for the receipt of services and products on account, meaning you will have been given terms (usually net 30), so you will not have to pay the bill for 30 days after the bill date. The first product purchased had been previously ordered using a purchase order. The second product ordered is a new product, which had not been previously ordered using a purchase order. Both of these purchases will affect inventory and are, thus, recorded in the Items detail section of a bill. The third transaction is a service that was rendered and does not affect inventory and is, therefore, recorded in the Account details section of a bill.

To record a bill from a vendor for the receipt of products/services on account, do the following:

1 Continue from where you left off.

2 Click the [+ New] icon, and click **Bill** in the Vendors column as shown in Figure 5.6.

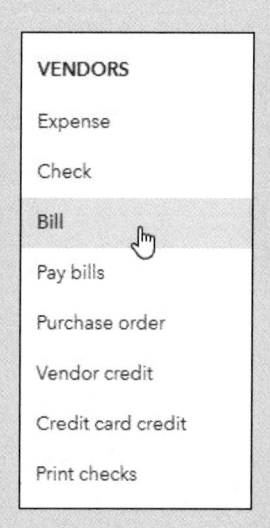

Recording Operating Activities: Purchases and Cash Payments **Chapter 5** **109**

Figure 5.6

+ New window (entering bills)

3 Select **Tim Phillip Masonry** from the Vendor drop-down list.

4 Select **Net 30** from the drop-down list of Terms. Accept your current system date as the Bill date.

5 Collapse the Category details section of the bill by clicking on the arrow next to Category details.

6 Expand the Item details section of the bill by clicking on the arrow next to Item details.

7 Click **Add all** in the Add to Bill section, which identifies an open purchase order #1002 from this vendor located on the right of the bill as shown in Figure 5.7.

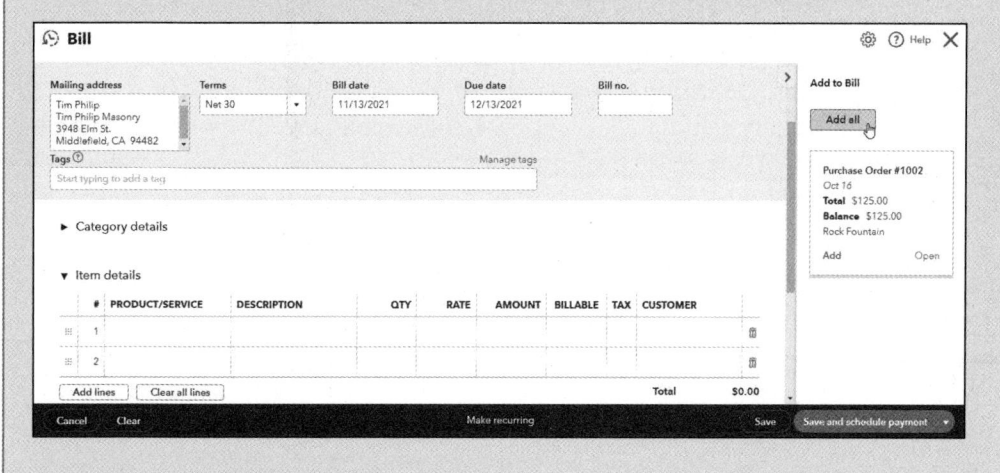

Figure 5.7

Bill (adding purchase order information)

8   The bill now contains information from purchase order #1002 as shown in Figure 5.8. **Trouble?** If information provided in the Product/Service column (or any other column) is cut off or not visible, simply place your cursor between column titles and drag to the left or right to decrease or increase the column width.

Figure 5.8

Bill (after purchase order information is added)

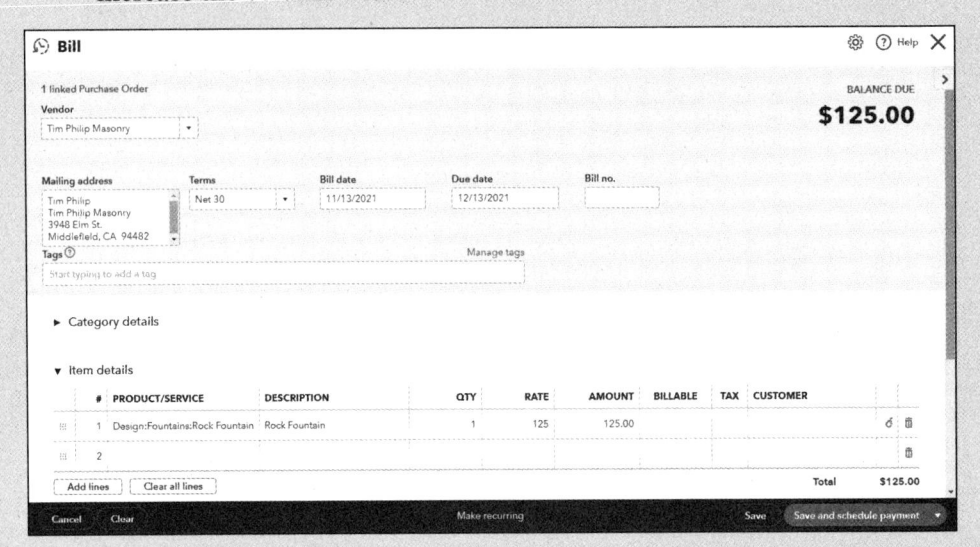

9   Click **Save and new**.

10 Select **Tania's Nursery** from the Vendor drop-down list.

11 Select **Net 30** from the drop-down list of Terms. Accept your current system date as the Bill date.

12 Select **Add new** on line 1 of the bill in the Product/Service column of the Item details section. **Trouble?** If instead of seeing a Product/Service column you see a Category column, you are in the Category details section instead of the Item details section (a common mistake).

13 Add a new product as you have done before—product type: **Inventory**, Name and Description: **Lavender**, initial quantity on hand: **0**, As of date: your system date, Category: **Landscaping**, inventory asset account: **Inventory Asset**, Sales price/rate: **15**, cost: **10**, income account: **Sales of Product Income**, expense account: **Cost of Goods Sold**, Sales tax: Taxable - standard rate. Click **Save and Close** in the Product/Service Information window.

14 Type **100** on line 1 of the bill in the QTY column.

15 Click **Save and New**.

16 Select **Computers by Jenni** from the Vendor drop-down list.

17 Select **Net 30** from the drop-down list of Terms. Accept your current system date as the Bill date.

18 Expand the Category details section of the bill by clicking on the arrow next to Category details.

19 Collapse the Item details section of the bill by clicking on the arrow next to Item details.

20 Select **Equipment Rental** on line 1 of the bill in the Category column.

21 Type **1200** on line 1 of the bill in the Amount column and then press **[Tab]**. Your window should look like Figure 5.9.

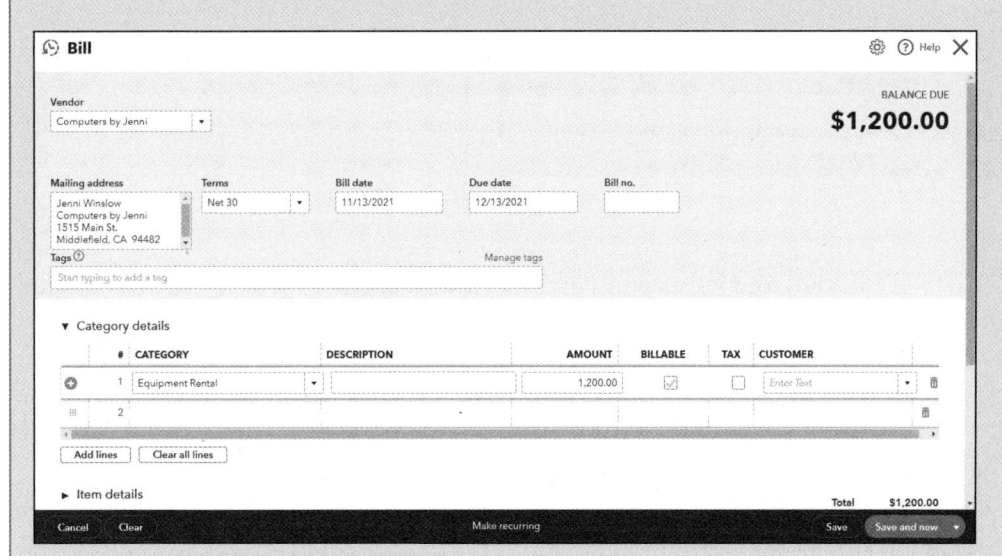

Figure 5.9

Bill (for services)

22 Click **Save and new**.

23 Select **Brosnahan Insurance Agency** from the Choose a vendor drop-down list.

24 Accept **Net 10** from the drop-down list of Terms.

25 The bill information is filled in automatically based on the last bill entered for this vendor.

26 Select **Prepaid Expenses** on line 1 of the bill in the Category column replacing Insurance.

27 Type **1800** on line 1 of the bill in the Amount column replacing the existing amount and then press **[Tab]**. Your window should look like Figure 5.10.

Figure 5.10

Bill for Prepaid Expenses (recording)

28 Click **Save and Close**.

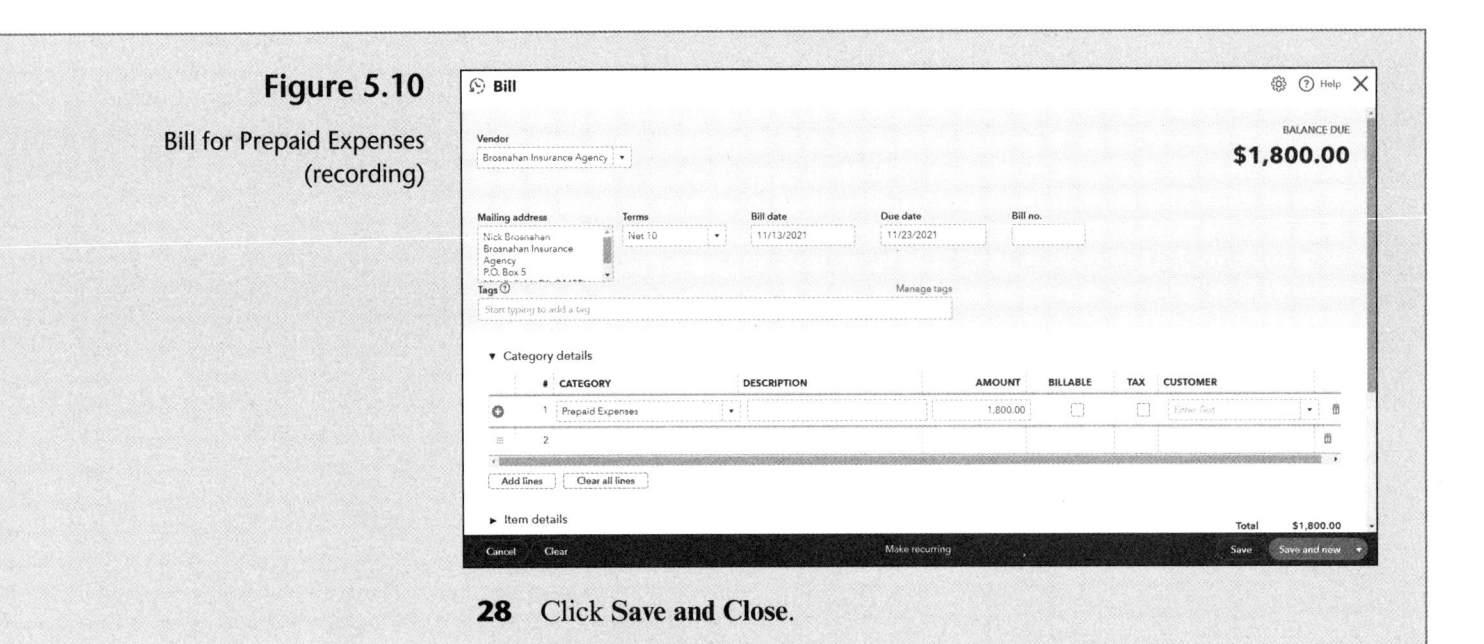

All bills entered increased an asset or an expense account. Inventory purchases were all recorded in the Item details section and increased the quantity of those products (as long as they were originally set up as "tracked" products). Equipment rental was recorded as an expense and the prepaid insurance was recorded as an asset (Prepaid Expenses). All bills increased the accounts payable liability account.

Payment of Bills, Use of a Credit Card, Payments for Items Other Than Bills

Navigate your browser to the Video Tutorials provided by Intuit (see website address specified in the Preface to this text) and then search on How to Record Bill Payments.

In this section, you will focus on recording the payment of a bill for the receipt of services and/or products on account, recording credit card charges, or recording the payment by check for other items.

To pay bills, do the following:

1. Continue from where you left off.
2. Click the (+ New) icon, and click **Pay bills** in the Vendors column as shown in Figure 5.11.

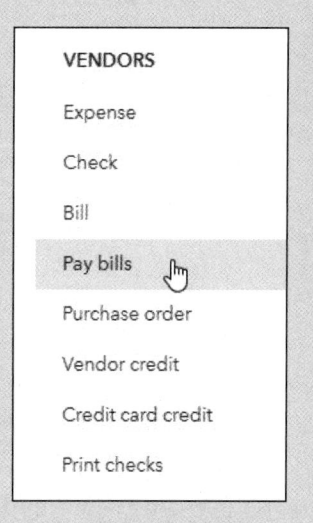

Figure 5.11

+ New window (paying bills)

3. A listing of possible bills that can be paid appears. In the Pay Bills window, select **Mastercard** from the drop-down list in the Payment account box. Click the **Payee** column title to sort the listing by payee alphabetically. Your screen should look like Figure 5.12.

Figure 5.12

Bills to pay

4. Click and hold your mouse between the Payee and Ref No. columns and drag to the right to increase the width of the Payee column.

5. Click and hold your mouse between the Ref No. and Due Date columns and drag to the left to decrease the width of the Ref No. column.

6. Click the **Due Date** column to sort bills by due date, and then click in the check box of payees PG&E, Norton Lumber and Building Materials, Robertson & Associates, and Brosnahan Insurance Agency. Remember your dates will be different than shown in the figures. Note that each of those payees has a red icon indicating that the due date has been exceeded as shown in Figure 5.13.

Figure 5.13

Bills to pay (selecting)

	Pay Bills					? Help ✕
Payment account: Mastercard Balance $157.72		Payment date: 11/13/2021				TOTAL PAYMENT AMOUNT **$847.67**
Filter > Last 365 Days						9 open bills, 4 overdue
	PAYEE	REF NO.	DUE DATE ▲	OPEN BALANCE	CREDIT APPLIED	PAYMENT TOTAL
✓	PG&E		10/03/2021	$86.44	Not available	86.44
✓	Norton Lumber and Building Ma...		10/18/2021	$205.00	Not available	205.00
✓	Robertson & Associates		10/18/2021	$315.00	Not available	315.00
✓	Brosnahan Insurance Agency		10/21/2021	$241.23	Not available	241.23
Cancel						Schedule payments online ▼

7 Click **Save and close**.

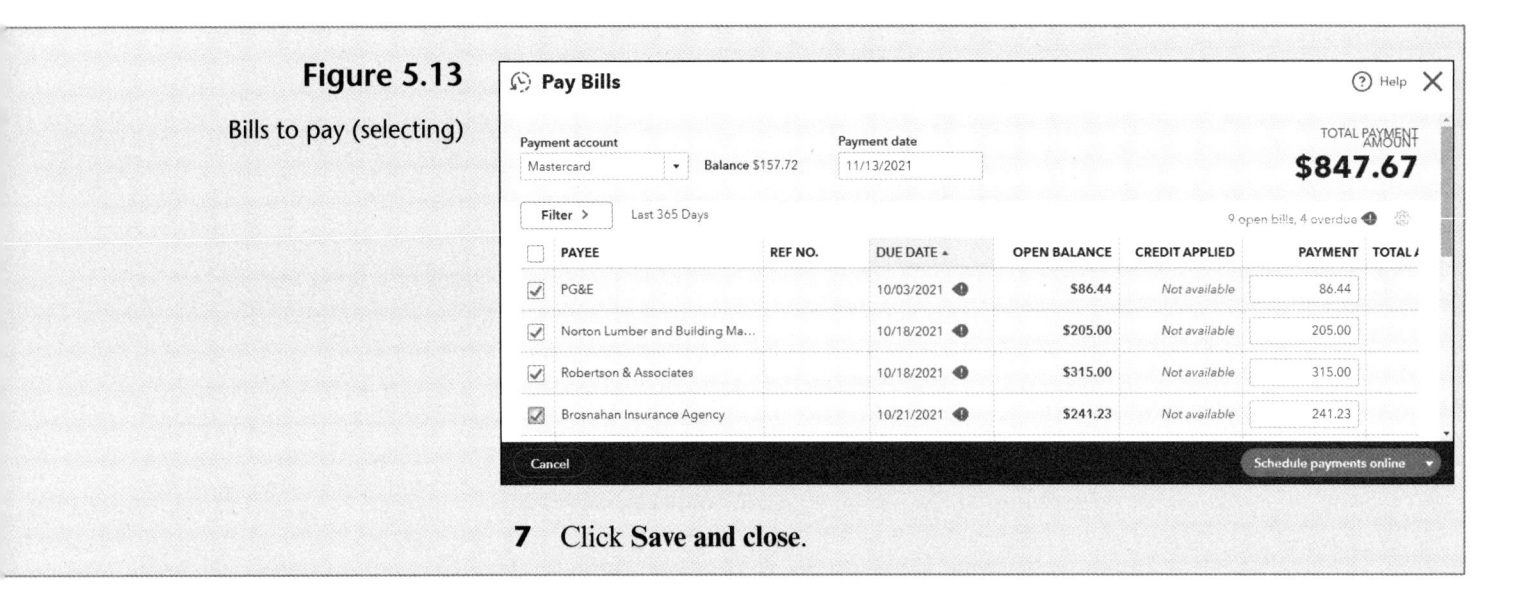

You have now paid bills for products/services received for which you received a bill. However, often you will pay for a product/service or another expense for which you have not received a bill. Often, these are vendors who give you no terms and require you to pay immediately. These terms are called *due on receipt*. For example, a credit card charge for fuel or a check for supplies. To record these transactions, you will use either the Expense task or the Check task after clicking the [+ New] icon. For ease of use, you will be directed to use the Expense task for all credit card transactions and the Check task for all checking account payments even though the Expense task can be used for either credit card charges or check payments.

To record a credit card or check payment, do the following:

1 Click the [+ New] icon.

2 Click **Expense** under the Vendors column.

3 Select **Chin's Gas and Oil** from the drop-down list in the Payee text box.

4 Select **Mastercard** from the drop-down list in the Payment account text box.

5 Accept **Automobile:Fuel** in the row 1 of Category column, then type **85** as the amount replacing the existing 52.56, and then press [**Tab**]. Your window should look like Figure 5.14.

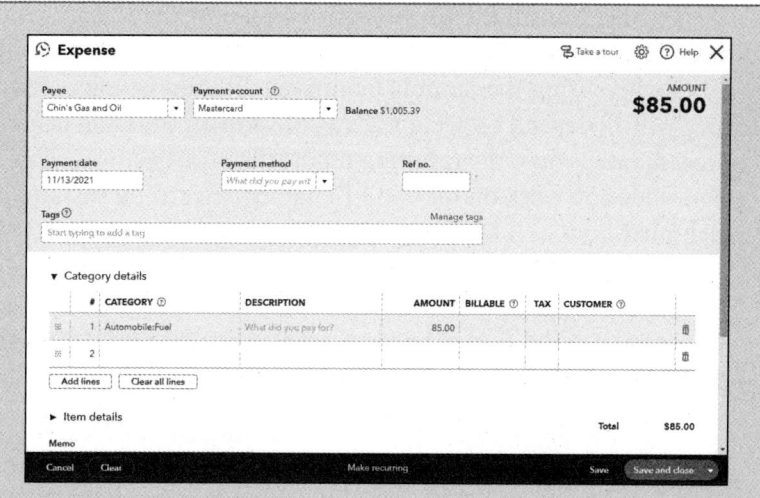

Figure 5.14

Credit card charge

6. Click **Save and close**.
7. Click the [+ New] icon.
8. Click **Check** under the Vendors column.
9. Select **Cal Telephone** from the drop-down list in the Payee text box.
10. Select **Checking** from the drop-down list in the Bank Account text box (it should already be selected).
11. Type **77** in the Check no. text box.
12. Type **Utilities:Telephone** in the row 1 of Category column, and type **325** as the amount and then press [**Tab**] as shown in Figure 5.15.

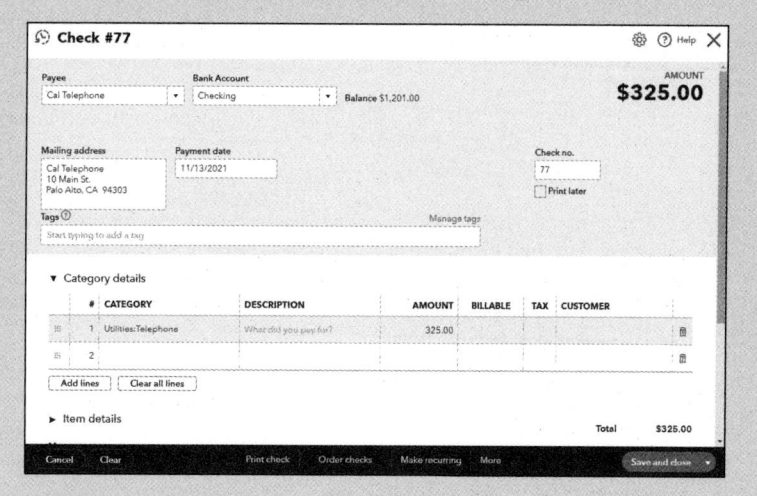

Figure 5.15

Check #77 (payment)

13. Click **Save and close**.

Trial Balance

The work you completed in this chapter had an effect on the company's trial balance. You decided to create a Trial Balance report and investigate the checking, inventory asset, and accounts payable accounts. In the process, you realized that purchase orders do not affect a company's accounts until products are received or services are rendered.

Trouble? Recall the previous discussion of dates and amounts when using the Sample Company. Dates in the text figures will be different than what you see in QBO when using the Sample Company. Ending balances may also be different as they will all depend on what actual date you are entering transactions. Focus on the process rather than the resulting report dates or balances. This will not be the situation when you work on the end-of-chapter cases as those dates have been specifically identified.

To create a trial balance and investigate some account activity, do the following:

1 Click **Reports**, type **Trial Balance** into the Find report by name text box, and press **[Enter]**. Scroll to the top of the report. The upper portion of that report is shown in Figure 5.16.

Figure 5.16

Trial Balance (upper portion)

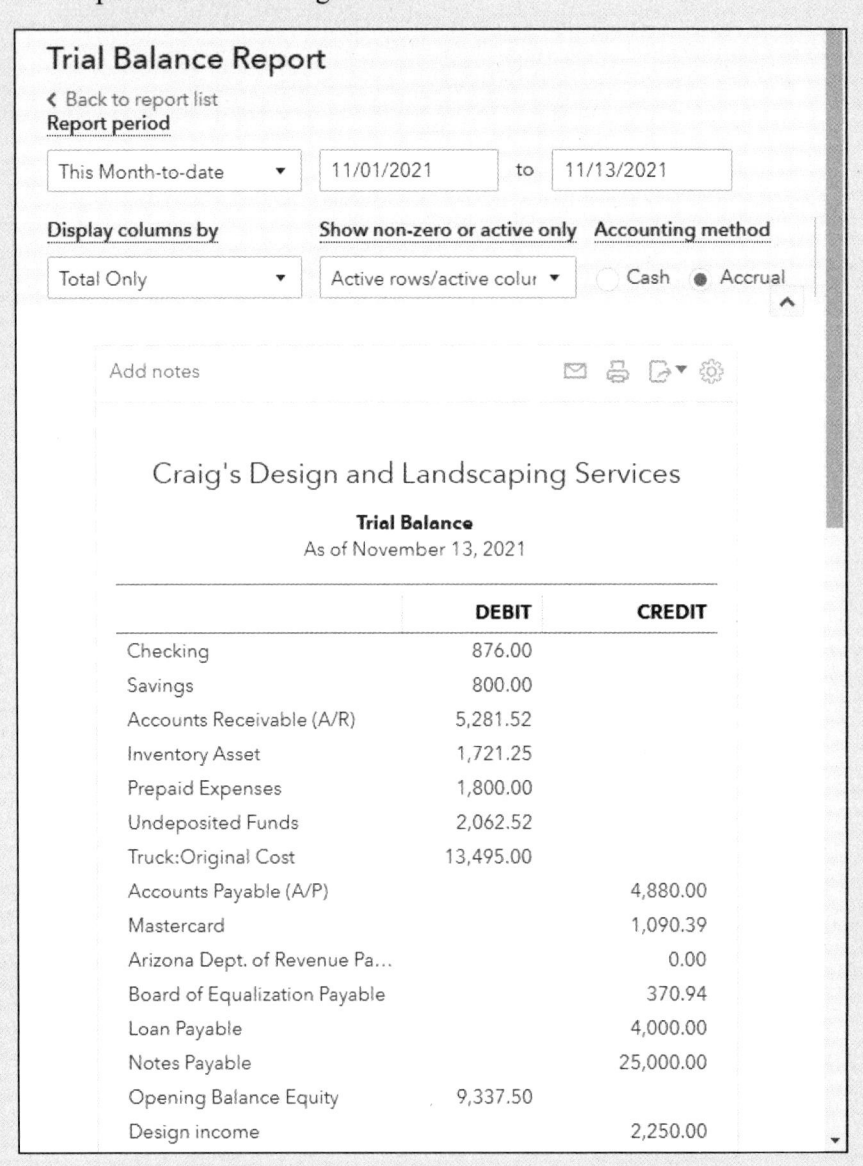

Trial Balance Report

‹ Back to report list
Report period

This Month-to-date ▼   11/01/2021   to   11/13/2021

Display columns by   **Show non-zero or active only**   **Accounting method**

Total Only ▼   Active rows/active colur ▼   ○ Cash ● Accrual

Add notes

Craig's Design and Landscaping Services

Trial Balance
As of November 13, 2021

	DEBIT	CREDIT
Checking	876.00	
Savings	800.00	
Accounts Receivable (A/R)	5,281.52	
Inventory Asset	1,721.25	
Prepaid Expenses	1,800.00	
Undeposited Funds	2,062.52	
Truck:Original Cost	13,495.00	
Accounts Payable (A/P)		4,880.00
Mastercard		1,090.39
Arizona Dept. of Revenue Pa…		0.00
Board of Equalization Payable		370.94
Loan Payable		4,000.00
Notes Payable		25,000.00
Opening Balance Equity	9,337.50	
Design income		2,250.00

2 Click the Checking account balance of **876.00** to produce a Transaction Report for the Checking Account. See Figure 5.17. Note again that your checking account balance may be different.

Recording Operating Activities: Purchases and Cash Payments — Chapter 5 — 117

Figure 5.17

Transaction Report (for the Checking account)

DATE	TRANSACTION TYPE	NUM	NAME	MEMO/DESCRIPTION	ACCOUNT	SPLIT	AMOUNT	BALANCE
▼ Checking								
Beginning Balance								2,101.00
11/01/2021	Credit Card Credit				Checking	Mastercard	-900.00	1,201.00
11/13/2021	Check	77	Cal Telephone		Checking	Utilities:Telephone	-325.00	876.00
Total for Checking							$ -1,225.00	
TOTAL							$ -1,225.00	

Craig's Design and Landscaping Services — Transaction Report — November 1-13, 2021

3 Click the **Printer** icon to print this report.

4 Click **Back to report summary**.

5 Click the Inventory Asset account balance of **1,721.25** to produce a Transaction Report for the Inventory Asset account. The two bills for product purchases you recorded earlier in this chapter are shown in Figure 5.18.

Figure 5.18

Transaction Report (for the Inventory Asset account)

DATE	TRANSACTION TYPE	NUM	NAME	MEMO/DESCRIPTION	ACCOUNT	SPLIT	AMOUNT	BALANCE
▼ Inventory Asset								
Beginning Balance								596.25
11/13/2021	Bill		Tim Philip Masonry	Rock Fountain	Inventory Asset	Accounts Payable (A/P)	125.00	721.25
11/13/2021	Inventory Starting Value	START		Lavender - Opening invento...	Inventory Asset	Opening Balance Equity	0.00	721.25
11/13/2021	Inventory Starting Value	START		Landscape Rock - Opening i...	Inventory Asset	Opening Balance Equity	0.00	721.25
11/13/2021	Bill		Tania's Nursery	Lavender	Inventory Asset	Accounts Payable (A/P)	1,000.00	1,721.25
Total for Inventory Asset							$1,125.00	
TOTAL							$1,125.00	

6 Click the **Printer** icon to print this report.

7 Click **Back to report summary**.

8 Click the Accounts Payable (A/P) account balance of **4,880.00** to produce a Transaction Report for the Accounts Payable (A/P) account. The bills for product and service purchases and the bill payments you recorded earlier in this chapter are shown in Figure 5.19.

Figure 5.19

Transaction Report (for the Accounts Payable account)

DATE	TRANSACTION TYPE	NUM	NAME	MEMO/DESCRIPTION	ACCOUNT	SPLIT	AMOUNT	BALANCE
▼ Accounts Payable (A/P)								
Beginning Balance								1,602.67
11/13/2021	Bill		Tim Philip Masonry		Accounts Payable (A/P)	Inventory Asset	125.00	1,727.67
11/13/2021	Bill		Tania's Nursery		Accounts Payable (A/P)	Inventory Asset	1,000.00	2,727.67
11/13/2021	Bill		Computers by Jenni		Accounts Payable (A/P)	Equipment Rental	1,200.00	3,927.67
11/13/2021	Bill Payment (Credit Card)		Brosnahan Insurance Agency		Accounts Payable (A/P)	Mastercard	-241.23	3,686.44
11/13/2021	Bill Payment (Credit Card)		PG&E		Accounts Payable (A/P)	Mastercard	-86.44	3,600.00
11/13/2021	Bill Payment (Credit Card)		Norton Lumber and Buildin...		Accounts Payable (A/P)	Mastercard	-205.00	3,395.00
11/13/2021	Bill Payment (Credit Card)		Robertson & Associates		Accounts Payable (A/P)	Mastercard	-315.00	3,080.00
11/13/2021	Bill		Brosnahan Insurance Agency		Accounts Payable (A/P)	Prepaid Expenses	1,800.00	4,880.00
Total for Accounts Payable (A/P)							$3,277.33	
TOTAL							$3,277.33	

9 Click the **Printer** icon to print this report.
10 Click **Back to report summary**.
11 Sign out of QBO.

End Note

In this chapter, you added a vendor, a product, purchase orders, bills, payment of bills, a credit card purchase, and a check payment. You also produced a trial balance and drilled down through that trial balance to see the effect the bills and payment of bills affected accounts. In the next chapter, you will work with investing and financing activities.

Chapter 5 Questions

1. Why does a business use purchase orders?
2. Describe the steps to create a new product from within a purchase order.
3. What happens when you create a new purchase order to a vendor from whom you recently placed a different purchase order?
4. What accounts are affected when a bill from a vendor supplying you products is recorded?
5. What appears when you click **Pay bills** after clicking the ⊕ New icon?
6. Describe the process for increasing or decreasing the width of a column in the listing of bills to pay.
7. What are the steps to record a credit card charge?
8. What are the steps to record a check written to pay something other than bills?
9. What are the steps to view a transaction report for the checking account from a trial balance?
10. What are the steps to view a transaction report for the inventory account from a trial balance?

Chapter 5 Matching

a. Purchase order　　　_____　　Purchases that affect inventory are recorded here
b. Due on receipt　　　_____　　An invoice sent by a vendor to a customer
c. Bill　　　　　　　　_____　　Purchases that don't affect inventory are recorded here
d. Net 30　　　　　　　_____　　Task used to record checks in the checking account
e. Item detail section　 _____　　Suppliers of products and services
f. Category detail section _____　A formal means to order products from vendors
g. Pay Bills　　　　　　_____　　Pay a bill within 30 days after the bill date
h. Check　　　　　　　_____　　Task used to record credit card charges
i. Expense　　　　　　_____　　Terms that provide no credit
j. Vendor　　　　　　　_____　　Paying vendors who have billed you

Chapter 5 Cases

The following cases require you to open the company you updated in Chapter 4. Each of the following cases continues throughout the text in a sequential manner. For example, if you are assigned Case 01, you will use the file you modified in this chapter in all of the following chapters. Each of the following cases is similar in concepts assessed but differs in amounts and transactions. See the Preface to this text for a matrix of each student case and its attributes.

> **To reopen your company, do the following:**
>
> 1 Open your Internet browser.
>
> 2 Type **https://qbo.intuit.com** into your browser's address text box.
>
> 3 Type your user ID and password into the text boxes as you have done before.

Case 1

Add some operating activities (purchases, credit card charges, and cash payments) to your company.

Based on what you learned in the text using the Sample Company, you are to make the following changes to the Case 1 company you modified in Chapter 4:

1 Add a new vendor – Stewart Surfboards, 2102 S El Camino Real, San Clemente, CA 92672, terms: net 30.

2 Add a new vendor – Village Travel, 100 S El Camino Real, San Clemente, CA 92672, terms: due on receipt.

3 Add a new vendor – Office Depot, 101 Main St., San Diego, CA 92600, terms: due on receipt.

4 Add a new account – account type: Credit Card, detail type: Credit Card, name: VISA.

5 Add a new account – account type: Other Current Assets, detail type: Other Current Assets, name: Supplies Asset.

6 Add a new tracked product – Name/description: California Nose Rider, initial quantity on hand: 0, As of date: 01/02/24, inventory asset account: Inventory Asset, price: 3,200.00, cost: 1,700.00, income account: Sales, expense account: Cost of Goods Sold.

7 Add a new tracked product – Name/description: 808, initial quantity on hand: 0, As of date: 01/02/24, inventory asset account: Inventory Asset, price: 2,700.00, cost: 1,500.00, income account: Sales, expense account: Cost of Goods Sold.

8 Record a new purchase order for products on 1/2/24 – Vendor: Channel Islands, product 1: Fred Rubble, QTY: 5, product 2: Rook 15, QTY: 4, product 3: The Water Hog, QTY: 1.

9 Record a new purchase order for products on 1/3/24 – Vendor: Stewart Surfboards, product 1: 808, QTY: 2, product 2: California Nose Rider, QTY: 1.

10 Record a new bill based on a purchase order #1001 on 1/5/24 – Vendor: Channel Islands, terms: Net 15. All items ordered were received.

11 Record a new bill without a purchase order on 1/8/24 – New vendor: San Diego Gas & Electric, terms: Net 15, category: Utilities, amount: 145.00.

12 Record a new bill without a purchase order on 1/9/24 – New vendor: Prime Properties, terms: Net 15, category 1: Rent or Lease, amount: 2,500.00, category 2: Prepaid Expenses, amount: 5,000.00.

13 Pay all bills due to Channel Islands on 1/19/24 using the checking account and starting with check no. 1001.

14 Record a credit card charge on 1/10/24 – vendor: Village Travel, using credit card: VISA, category: Travel, amount: 1,800.00.

15 Record check on 1/11/24 – no.: 1002, vendor: Office Depot, amount: 375.00, account: Supplies Asset.

16 Open your previously customized report named Trial Balance 1/31/24. If a cash or accrual message appears, just close the message. Your report should look like Figure 5.20.

Case 1
TRIAL BALANCE
As of January 31, 2024

	DEBIT	CREDIT
Checking	16,325.00	
Accounts Receivable	1,030.00	
Inventory Asset	11,800.00	
Prepaid Expenses	8,000.00	
Supplies Asset	375.00	
Undeposited Funds	5,000.00	
Furniture & Fixtures:Depreciation		10,000.00
Furniture & Fixtures:Original cost	40,000.00	
Accounts Payable		7,645.00
VISA		1,800.00
Notes Payable		60,000.00
Common Stock		1,000.00
Opening Balance Equity		0.00
Retained Earnings		5,500.00
Sales		2,160.00
Services		170.00
Cost of Goods Sold	1,300.00	
Rent or Lease	2,500.00	
Travel	1,800.00	
Utilities	145.00	
TOTAL	**$88,275.00**	**$88,275.00**

Figure 5.20

Trial Balance (as of 1/31/24)

17 Create and print a Transaction Report for the Checking account as you did earlier in the chapter.

18 Create and print a Transaction Report for the Inventory Asset account as you did earlier in the chapter.

19 Create and print a Transaction Report for the Accounts Payable (A/P) account as you did earlier in the chapter.

20 If your trial balance differs from what is shown in Figure 5.20, do the following:

   a. Make sure all of your changes were dated in January 2024.

   b. View the Transaction Reports you just created to locate any errors.

   c. Ask your instructor for assistance.

   d. Be sure your company matches the above as you will be adding additional business events in Chapter 6.

21 Export your Trial Balance report to Excel, and save it with the file name Student Name (replace with your name) Ch 05 Case 01 Trial Balance.xlsx.

22 Open and print the custom report you created in the last chapter called Transaction Detail by Account.

23 Export your Transactions Detail by Account report to Excel, and save it with the file name Student Name (replace with your name) Ch 05 Case 01 Transaction Detail by Account.xlsx.

24 Sign out of your company.

Case 2

Add some operating activities (purchases, credit card charges, and cash payments) to your company.

Based on what you learned in the text using the Sample Company, you are to make the following changes to the Case 2 company you modified in Chapter 4:

1 Add a new vendor – E-flite, 700 Annapolis Ln N Suite #175, Plymouth, MN, 55447, terms: net 15.

2 Add a new vendor – Village Steak House, 100 S El Camino Real, San Clemente, CA 92672, terms: due on receipt.

3 Add a new vendor – Staples, 101 Main St., San Diego, CA 92600, terms: due on receipt.

4 Add a new account – account type: Credit Card, detail type: Credit Card, name: AMEX.

5 Add a new account – account type: Other Current Assets, detail type: Other Current Assets, name: Supplies Asset.

6 Add a new product – name/description: Sport Cub S, initial quantity on hand: 0, As of date: 01/02/25, inventory asset account: Inventory Asset, price: 600.00, cost: 479.00, income account: Sales, expense account: Cost of Goods Sold.

7 Add a new product – name/description: Mystique RES, initial quantity on hand: 0, As of date: 01/02/25, inventory asset account: Inventory Asset, price: 450.00, cost: 325.00, income account: Sales, expense account: Cost of Goods Sold.

8 Record a new purchase order for products on 1/2/25 – vendor: E-flite, product 1: Sport Cub S, QTY: 5, product 2: Mystique RES, QTY: 3.

9. Record a new purchase order for products on 1/3/25 – vendor: Kyosho, product 1: Broon F830 Ride, QTY: 4, product 2: GO Aircraft Radio, QTY: 2, product 3: Seawind Carbon Sailboat, QTY: 1.

10. Record a new bill based on a purchase order #1001 on 1/7/25 – vendor: E-flite, terms: Net 15. All items ordered were received.

11. Record a new bill without a purchase order on 1/8/25 – new vendor: San Diego News-Press, terms: Net 15, category: Advertising, amount: 500.00. Note: If your chart of accounts contains Advertising and Marketing, then change the account to read Advertising only.

12. Record a new bill without a purchase order on 1/10/25 – new vendor: Gomez Insurance, terms: Net 15, category 1: Insurance, amount: 400.00, category 2: Prepaid Expenses, amount: 4,400.00.

13. Pay bill due to Kyosho on 1/18/25 using the checking account and starting with check no. 1001.

14. Record a credit card charge on 1/11/25 – vendor: Village Steak House, using credit card: AMEX, category: Meals and Entertainment, amount: 240.00.

15. Record check on 1/14/25 – no.: 1002, vendor: Staples, amount: 450.00, account: Supplies Asset.

16. Open your previously customized report named Trial Balance 1/31/25. Your report should look like Figure 5.21.

Figure 5.21

Trial Balance (as of 1/31/25)

Case 2
TRIAL BALANCE
As of January 31, 2025

	DEBIT	CREDIT
Checking	7,150.00	
Accounts Receivable	1,425.00	
Inventory Asset	5,410.00	
Prepaid Expenses	6,800.00	
Supplies Asset	450.00	
Undeposited Funds	925.00	
Machinery & Equipment:Depreciation		1,000.00
Machinery & Equipment:Original cost	10,000.00	
Accounts Payable		8,670.00
AMEX		240.00
Notes Payable		12,000.00
Common Stock		100.00
Opening Balance Equity		0.00
Retained Earnings		8,385.00
Sales		5,700.00
Services		225.00
Cost of Goods Sold	3,020.00	
Advertising	500.00	
Insurance	400.00	
Meals and Entertainment	240.00	
TOTAL	**$36,320.00**	**$36,320.00**

17 Create and print a Transaction Report for the Checking account as you did earlier in the chapter.

18 Create and print a Transaction Report for the Inventory Asset account as you did earlier in the chapter.

19 Create and print a Transaction Report for the Accounts Payable (A/P) account as you did earlier in the chapter.

20 If your trial balance differs from what is shown in Figure 5.21, do the following:

   a. Make sure that all of your changes were dated in January 2025.

   b. View the Transaction Reports you created to locate any errors.

   c. Ask your instructor for assistance.

   d. Be sure your company matches the above as you will be adding additional business events in Chapter 6.

21 Export your Trial Balance report to Excel, and save it with the file name Student Name (replace with your name) Ch 05 Case 02 Trial Balance.xlsx.

22 Open and print the custom report you created in the last chapter called Transaction Detail by Account.

23 Export your Transactions Detail by Account report to Excel, and save it with the file name Student Name (replace with your name) Ch 05 Case 02 Transaction Detail by Account.xlsx.

24 Sign out of your company.

Case 3

Now it's time for you to add some operating activities (purchases, credit card charges, and cash payments) to your company.

Based on what you learned in the text using the Sample Company, you are to make the following changes to the Case 3 company you modified in Chapter 4:

1 Add a new vendor – Google, Inc., 1600 Amphitheatre Parkway, Mountain View, CA 94043, terms: Net 15.

2 Add a new vendor – Samsung, Inc., 105 Challenger Rd., Ridgefield Park, NJ 07660, terms: Net 15.

3 Add a new vendor – Staples, Inc., 101 Main St., San Diego, CA 92600, terms: Net 30.

4 Modify Apple Inc. (existing Vendor) – Name should be Apple Computer, Inc., address: 1 Infinite Loop Cupertino, CA 95014, terms: Net 15.

5 Add a new account – account type: Credit Card, detail type: Credit Card, name: AMEX.

6 Add a new account – account type: Other Current Assets, detail type: Other Current Assets, name: Supplies Asset.

7. Add a new product – Name/Description & Purchasing information: Samsung Galaxy 8, initial quantity on hand: 0, inventory asset account: Inventory Asset, Sales price: 450.00, cost: 350.00, income account: Sales of Product Income, expense account: Cost of Goods Sold. (Use 01/06/2026 as the "as of date.") Sales tax: Taxable - standard rate.

8. Add a new product – Name/Description & Purchasing information: Samsung Note, initial quantity on hand: 0, inventory asset account: Inventory Asset, Sales price: 850.00, cost: 650.00, income account: Sales of Product Income, expense account: Cost of Goods Sold. (Use 01/06/2026 as the "as of date.") Sales tax: Taxable - standard rate.

9. Record a new purchase order (1001) for products on 1/6/26 – vendor: Google, Inc., Pixel, QTY: 10.

10. Record a new purchase order (1002) for products on 1/7/26 – vendor: Samsung, Inc., product 1: Samsung Galaxy 8, QTY: 5, product 2: Samsung Note, QTY: 8.

11. Record a new bill based on a purchase order #1001 dated 1/6/26 – vendor: Google, Inc., terms: Net 15. All items ordered were received on 1/10/26 (the bill date).

12. Record a new bill without a purchase order on 1/8/26 – new vendor: News-Press, terms: Net 15, category: Advertising & Marketing, amount: 1,300.00.

13. Record a new bill without a purchase order on 1/10/26 – new vendor: Hathaway Insurance, terms: Net 15, category 1: Insurance, amount: 300.00, category 2: Prepaid expenses, amount: 3,300.00.

14. Pay bill due to Apple Computer, Inc. on 1/18/26 using the checking account and starting with check no. 321.

15. Record a credit card charge on 1/11/26 – new vendor: Village Steak House, using credit card: AMEX, category: Meals, amount: 123.00.

16. Record check on 1/14/26 – no.: 322, vendor: Staples, amount: 327.00, category: Supplies Asset.

17. Open and print your previously customized report named Trial Balance 1/31/26. Your report should look like Figure 5.22.

Figure 5.22

Trial Balance as of 1/31/26

Case 03 - Student Name (ID Number)

Trial Balance
As of January 31, 2026

	DEBIT	CREDIT
Checking	15,751.75	
Accounts receivable (A/R)	2,559.38	
Inventory Asset	5,700.00	
Payments to deposit	0.00	
Prepaid expenses	6,050.00	
Supplies Asset	327.00	
Machinery & Equipment:Depreciation		2,000.00
Machinery & Equipment:Original cost	15,000.00	
Accounts Payable (A/P)		8,900.00
AMEX		123.00
California Department of Tax and Fee Administration ...		523.13
Notes Payable		23,000.00
Opening balance equity		0.00
Owner's Equity		10,075.00
Sales of Product Income		6,750.00
Services		240.00
Cost of goods sold	4,500.00	
Advertising & marketing	1,300.00	
Insurance	300.00	
Meals	123.00	
TOTAL	**$51,611.13**	**$51,611.13**

18 Create and print a Transaction Report for the Checking account like you did in the chapter.

19 Create and print a Transaction Report for the Accounts Receivable (A/R) account.

20 Create and print a Transaction Report for the Inventory Asset account like you did in the chapter.

21 Create and print a Transaction Report for the Accounts Payable (A/P) account like you did in the chapter.

22 If your trial balance is different than Figure 5.22, do the following:

   a. Make sure that all of your changes were dated in January 2026.

   b. View the Transaction Reports you just created to locate any errors.

   c. Ask your instructor for assistance.

   d. Be sure your company matches the above as you will be adding additional business events in Chapter 6.

23 Export your Trial Balance report to Excel, and save it with the file name Student Name (replace with your name) Ch 05 Case 03 Trial Balance.xlsx.

24 Open and print the custom report you created in the last chapter called Transaction Detail by Account.

25 Export your Transactions Detail by Account report to Excel, and save it with the file name Student Name (replace with your name) Ch 05 Case 03 Transaction Detail by Account.xlsx.

26 Sign out of your company.

Case 4

Now it's time for you to add some operating activities (purchases and cash payments) to your company.

Based on what you learned in the text using the Sample Company, you are to make the following changes to the Case 4 company you modified in Chapter 4:

1 Add a new vendor – GEICO Insurance, 335 Park Ave., Los Angeles, CA 90034, terms: Net 15.

2 Add a new account – Account Type: Other Current Assets, Detail Type: Other Current Assets, name: Supplies.

3 Add a new account – Account Type: Credit Card, Detail Type: Credit Card, name: VISA.

4 Add a new service – Name/Description information: Towel Service, Sales price/rate: 20.00, income account: Sales, Is taxable: No.

5 Record sales receipt 1004 to a new customer: Enterprise Inc., on 1/4/21 for 5 Monthly Fee – Corporate Membership 50 Employees and 50 Towel Service. Check no. 9847 was received and immediately deposited to the company's checking account in the amount of $31,000.

6 Record a new purchase order (1001) for products on 1/7/21 – vendor: Bowflex, product: Bowflex Dumbbells, QTY: 25.

7 Record a new purchase order (1002) for products on 1/8/21 – vendor: Precor, product: Power Block Elite Dumbbells, QTY: 15.

8 Record a new bill based on a purchase order #1001 dated 1/15/21 – vendor: Bowflex, terms: Net 15. All items ordered were received on 1/15/21 (the bill date).

9 Record a new bill without a purchase order on 1/16/21 – new vendor: Supreme Marketing, terms: Net 15, category: Advertising & Marketing, amount: $1,800.00.

10 Record a new bill without a purchase order on 1/18/21 – vendor: Laundry Service, terms: Net 15, category: Supplies, amount: $1,400.00.

11 Pay bills due to Precor and Laundry Service on 1/18/21 using the checking account and starting with check no. 25498.

12 Record credit card charge on 1/20/21 – vendor: GEICO Insurance, using credit card: VISA, category: Insurance, amount: $2,400.00.

13 Record check on 1/21/21 – check no.: 25500, vendor: NordicTrack, amount: $750.00, category: Repairs & Maintenance.

14 Prepare and print the Trial Balance 1/31/21 report you saved previously. Your report should look like Figure 5.23.

7   Add a new product.

    a. Name – Trailer Cover

    b. Inventory asset account – Inventory Parts

    c. Description – Trailer Cover

    d. Sales price/rate – $500

    e. Income account – Sales of Product Income

    f. Sales tax category – Taxable - standard rate

    g. Purchasing information – Trailer Cover

    h. Cost – $400

    i. Expense account – Cost of Goods Sold

    j. Preferred Vendor – National Covers

    k. Initial quantity on hand – 0

    l. As of date – 12/31/22

8   Record a new purchase order (1001) for two trailers on 1/7/23 – vendor: Airstream, Inc., product 1: 2023 Airstream Flying Cloud 27FB TWIN, QTY:1, product 2: 2023 Airstream Globetrotter 30RB, QTY: 1.

9   Record a new purchase order (1002) for inventory parts on 1/8/23 – vendor: National Covers, product 1: RV Cover, QTY: 5, product 2: Trailer Cover, QTY: 4.

10 Record a new bill based on a purchase order #1001 dated 1/13/23 – vendor: Airstream, Inc., terms: Net 30. All items ordered were received on 1/13/23 (the bill date).

11 Record a new bill without a purchase order on 1/16/23 – new vendor: Pacific Marketing, terms: Net 15, account: Advertising & Marketing, amount: $8,000.

12 Record a new bill without a purchase order on 1/17/23 – vendor: State Farm Insurance, terms: Net 15, account: Prepaid Expenses, amount: $18,000.

13 Paid $150,000 on bill due to Winnebago, Inc. on 1/18/23 using the checking account and starting Check no. 589.

14 Record expense on 1/19/23 – new vendor: Elite Events, using credit card: AMEX, account: Advertising & Marketing, amount: $6,000.

15 Record check on 1/19/23, Check no.: 590, new vendor: Jay's Detail, amount: $1,800, account: Contractors.

16 Record a new bill based on a purchase order #1002 dated 1/8/23 – vendor: National Covers, terms: Net 30. All items ordered were received on 1/20/23 (the bill date).

17 Prepare and print the Trial Balance 1/31/23 report you saved previously. Your report should look like Figure 5.25.

Figure 5.25

Trial Balance as of 1/31/23

Case 06 - Student Name (ID Number)
TRIAL BALANCE
As of January 31, 2023

	DEBIT	CREDIT
Checking	72,150.00	
Accounts Receivable (A/R)	153,020.00	
Inventory Asset	524,000.00	
Inventory Parts	4,000.00	
Loans To Officers	15,000.00	
Prepaid Expenses	18,000.00	
Undeposited Funds	0.00	
Buildings:Depreciation		15,000.00
Buildings:Original cost	150,000.00	
Machinery & Equipment:Depreciation		10,000.00
Machinery & Equipment:Original cost	100,000.00	
Accounts Payable (A/P)		524,000.00
AMEX		6,000.00
Washington State Department of Revenue Payable		26,970.00
Notes Payable		100,000.00
Common Stock		1,000.00
Opening Balance Equity		0.00
Paid-In Capital		250,000.00
Retained Earnings		61,000.00
Sales of Product Income		290,000.00
Cost of Goods Sold	232,000.00	
Advertising & Marketing	14,000.00	
Contractors	1,800.00	
TOTAL	$1,283,970.00	$1,283,970.00

18 Investigate differences between your trial balance and the trial balance shown above.

19 If necessary, prepare and print the Transaction Detail by Account report for all dates you saved previously to investigate identified differences.

    a. Make sure all your changes were dated in January 2023.

    b. Click on the line that does not match to view the transaction for that account, and investigate why your answer differs.

    c. Ask your instructor for assistance.

    d. Be sure your company matches the above as you will be adding additional business events in Chapter 6.

chapter 6

Recording Investing and Financing Activities

Student Learning Outcomes

Upon completion of this chapter, the student will be able to do the following:

- Record the acquisition of a fixed asset
- Record the acquisition of a long-term investment
- Record the sale of common stock
- Record the payment of a dividend
- Record a long-term borrowing (long-term debt)
- Record payment on long-term borrowing (long-term debt)
- Record the acquisition of a fixed asset by taking on new debt

Overview

Intuit has provided a Sample Company online to provide new users a test-drive of its QBO product. In this chapter, you will open this Sample Company and practice various features of QBO. You will be recording investing activities such as acquiring a long-term investment and a fixed asset to the Sample Company file. In addition, you will be recording financing activities, such as selling common stock, paying a dividend, borrowing on a long-term basis, and making payments on long-term debt to the Sample Company file. Lastly, you will be recording an investing activity, acquiring a new fixed asset, and a financing activity by borrowing funds to purchase the fixed asset. Remember, if you stop in the middle of this work, none of your work will be saved. So when you return, the same Sample Company, without your work, will appear. In some parts of the chapter, you'll be asked to sign out of the Sample Company and sign back in so the Sample Company is reset to its original state. In the end of chapter work, you will be asked to perform the same tasks completed on the Sample Company on your Student Company. That work, of course, will be saved.

Fixed Assets

In this section, you will be recording the acquisition of fixed assets. Fixed assets are long-term tangible property that a firm owns and uses in the production of its income and is not expected to be consumed or converted into cash any sooner than at least one year's time. Normally, a fixed asset's cost is depreciated over time as a means of allocating its cost over its useful life. The depreciation is recorded to a depreciation expense account and added to an accumulated depreciation (contra-asset) account. That process will be explained in the chapter on adjusting entries.

To add an asset, you will use the Check task accessed by clicking the [+ New] icon. Alternatively, you could purchase new fixed assets with using a credit card or take on new debt. The Sample Company had a fixed asset account for trucks, which you'll use to record the purchase of a truck. If you were to purchase some other type of fixed asset, equipment for example, you would need to create a new fixed asset account named Equipment and two additional subaccounts to the Equipment account: Original Cost and Accumulated Depreciation.

To record the purchase of a new truck and new equipment in the Sample Company, do the following:

1 Open your Internet browser.

2 Type **https://qbo.intuit.com/redir/testdrive** into your browser's address text box and then press [**Enter**] to view the Sample Company Dashboard.

3 Click the [+ New] icon and then click **Check**.

4 Select + **Add new** from the drop-down list in the Choose a payee text box.

5 Type **Sunset Auto** in the Name text box, select **Vendor** as the Type, and click **Save**.

6 Accept the given Payment date and Check no. provided by QBO.

7 Type **Truck:Original Cost** in the Category column of line 1.

8 Type **2500** in the Amount column of line 1 and then press [**Tab**]. Your screen should look like Figure 6.1.

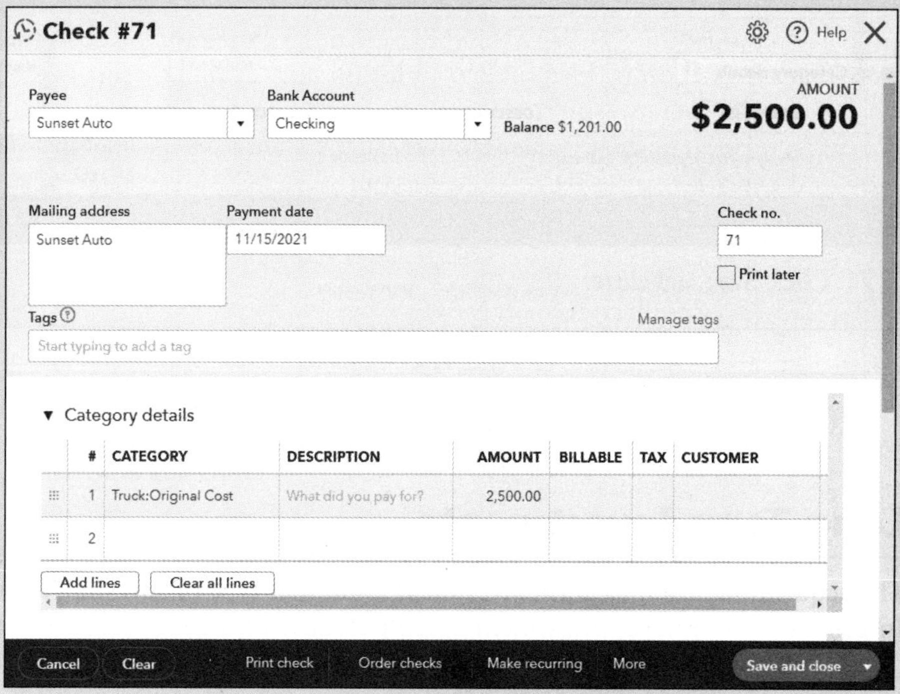

Figure 6.1

Purchase of truck

Equity Transactions (Common Stock, Dividends, Owner Investments, and Owner Withdrawals)

In a corporation, the sale of common stock and the payment of cash dividends to shareholders are two common financing activities. Common stock is a stockholders' equity account. Dividends are a distribution of earnings to shareholders and are accounted for as a reduction in retained earnings. Both of these are cash activities in that the sale of stock results in a cash receipt (you will account for it as a bank deposit), whereas the payment of a cash dividend results in a cash payment. Two previous payments from customers appear when you attempt to record a bank deposit from the issuance of stock. These payments have been received but not recorded. Ignore those for now. To simplify this transaction, we will assume that the common stock is no-par common stock, and thus, no additional paid-in capital exists. Also, we'll assume that the declaration, record, and payment dates are all the same.

In a sole proprietorship, there is no common stock or dividends. Instead, there are owner investments and owner withdrawals. Owner investments are recorded by entering a bank deposit to the Owner's Equity account. Owner withdrawals are recorded by entering a check to the Owner's Equity account. Since the Sample Company is a corporation, an example of these transactions is not provided.

To record the sale of stock and payment of cash dividends in the Sample Company, do the following:

1. Follow the steps to reopen the Sample Company found at the beginning of this chapter.
2. Click the [+ New] icon and then select **Bank Deposit**.
3. Select + **Add new** from the drop-down list in the Received From column of line 1 in the Add funds to this deposit section. The Add funds to this deposit section is below the Select the payments included in this deposit section so you may have to scroll down the page to find it.
4. Type **WB Investments** in the Name text box, select **Vendor** in the Type box, and click **Save**.
5. Accept the given date provided by QBO.
6. Select + **Add new** from the drop-down list in the Account column of line 1.
7. Select **Equity** from the drop-down list in the Account Type text box.
8. Select **Common Stock** from the drop-down list in the Detail Type text box.
9. Accept **Common Stock** in the Name text box, and click **Save and Close**.
10. Select **Check** as the Payment Method.
11. Type **10000** in the Amount column of line 1, and press [**Tab**]. Your screen should look like Figure 6.4.

Recording Investing and Financing Activities **Chapter 6** 139

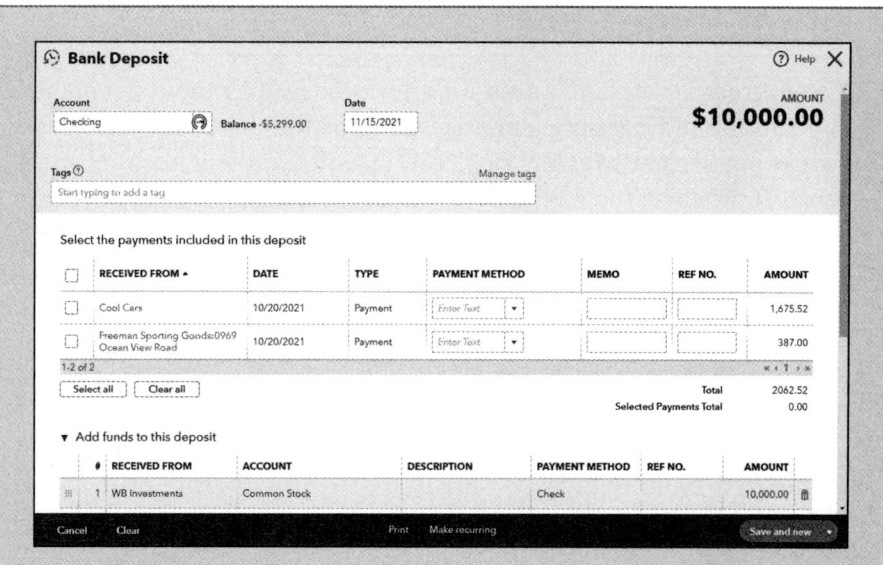

Figure 6.4

Recording the deposit of funds from the sale of common stock

12. Click **Save and close**.
13. Click the **+ New** icon, and select **Check**.
14. Select **+ Add new** from the drop-down list in the Choose a payee text box.
15. Type **Shareholders** in the Name text box, select **Vendor** in the Type box, and click **Save**.
16. Accept the given Payment date and Check no. provided by QBO.
17. Select **Retained Earnings** from the drop-down list in the Category column of line 1.
18. Type **1250** in the Amount column of line 1, and press **[Tab]**. Your screen should look like Figure 6.5. Note that your check number may be different than shown below.

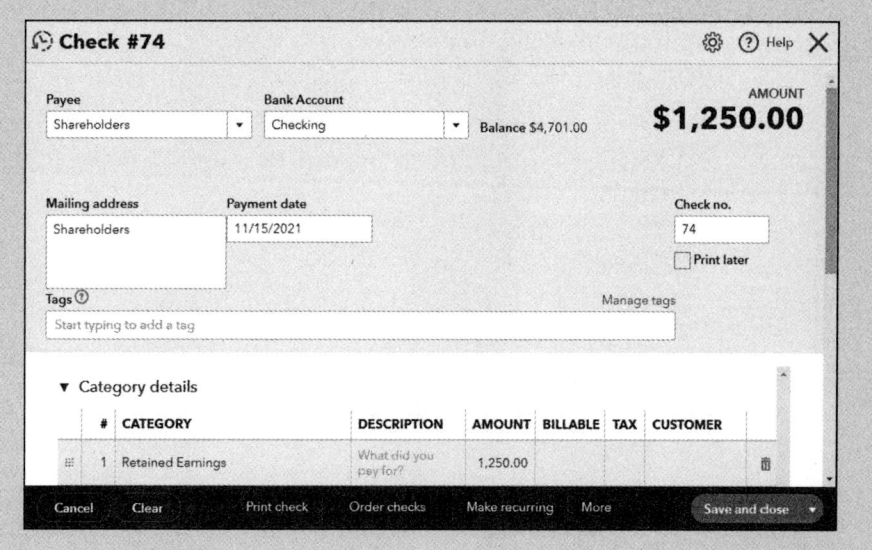

Figure 6.5

Payment of dividends

19. Click **Save and close**.
20. Do not sign out of the Sample Company.

Long-Term Debt

The borrowing of funds on a long-term basis and the repayment of debt are two additional financing activities. Both of these are cash activities in that the borrowing of funds results in a cash receipt (you will account for it as a bank deposit), whereas the payment of the debt results in a cash payment. There are two previous payments from customers that appear when you attempt to record a bank deposit from the borrowing of funds. These payments have been received but not recorded. You'll ignore those for now. This company decided to take the funds from the stock sale recorded above and the new borrowings below to pay off the old long-term debt with interest.

To record the receipt of funds from borrowing and the payment of long-term debt in the Sample Company, do the following:

1. Continue from where you left off. If you closed the Sample Company, follow the steps to reopen it found at the beginning of this chapter.

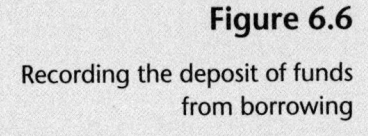

2. Click the **+ New** icon and then select **Bank Deposit**.

3. Select **+ Add new** from the drop-down list in the Received From column of line 1 in the Add funds to this deposit section.

4. Type **Bank of La Jolla** in the Name text box, select **Vendor** in the Type box, and click **Save**.

5. Accept the given date provided by QBO.

6. Select **Notes Payable** from the drop-down list in Account column of line 1.

7. Select **Check** from the drop-down list in the Payment Method column of line 1.

8. Type **15000** in the Amount column of line 1, and press [**Tab**]. Your screen should look like Figure 6.6.

Figure 6.6

Recording the deposit of funds from borrowing

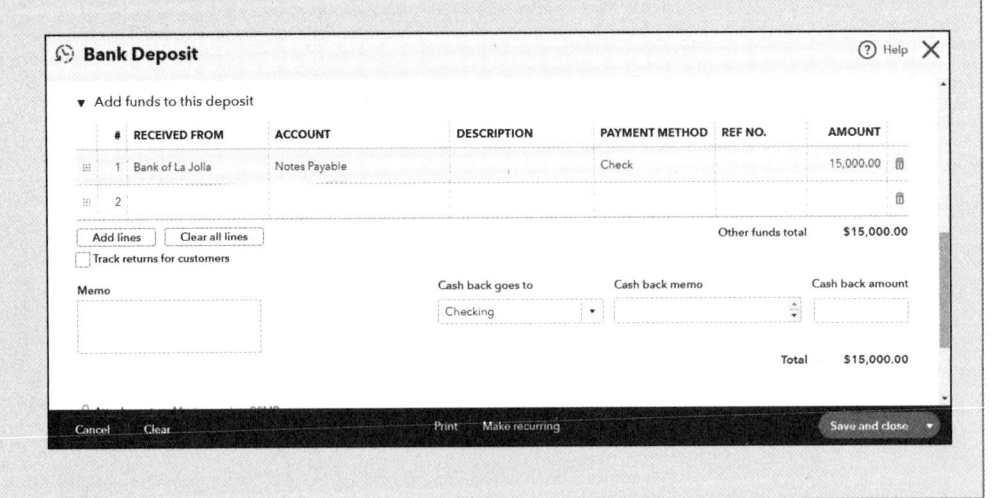

9. Click **Save and close**.
10. Click the [+ New] icon, and select **Check**.
11. Select **+ Add new** from the drop-down list in the Choose a payee text box.
12. Type **Bank of San Diego** in the Name text box, select **Vendor** in the Type box, and click **Save**.
13. Accept the given Payment date and Check no. provided by QBO.
14. Select **Notes Payable** from the drop-down list in the Category column of line 1.
15. Type **25000** in the Amount column of line 1 and then press [**Tab**].
16. Select **+ Add new** from the drop-down list in the Account column of line 2.
17. Select **Expenses** from the drop-down list in the Account Type text box.
18. Select **Interest Paid** from the drop-down list in the Detail Type text box.
19. Type **Interest Expense** in the Name text box, and click **Save and Close**.
20. Type **1000** in the Amount column of line 2, and press [**Tab**]. Your screen should look like Figure 6.7. Note that your check number may be different than shown below.

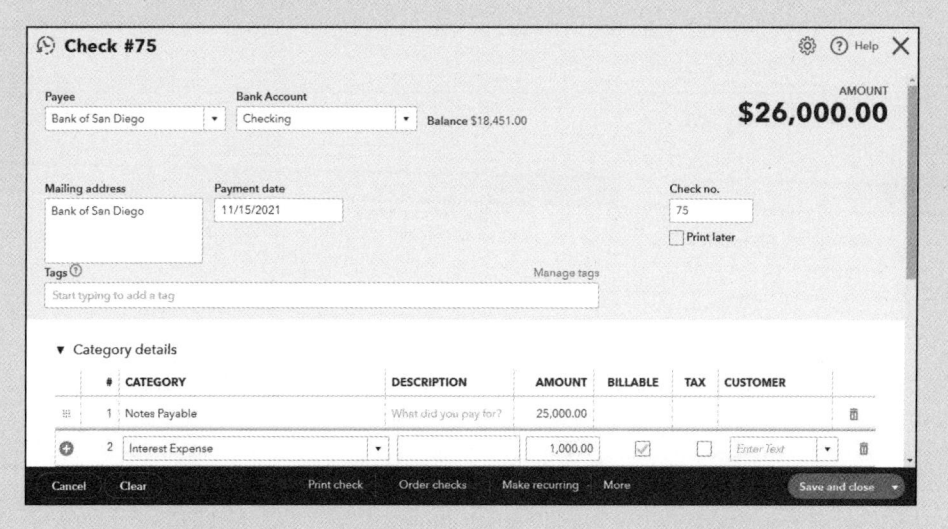

Figure 6.7

Repayment of long-term debt with interest

21. Click **Save and close**. If a warning message appears indicating a duplicate check number, just click **Yes**.
22. Do not sign out of the Sample Company.

Acquisition of a Fixed Asset in Exchange for Long-Term Debt

You completed the process for recording an investing activity (purchase of a fixed asset) and a financing activity (borrowing on a long-term basis). Both of these transactions were recorded by affecting the checking account (cash).

Occasionally, a company acquires a fixed asset by issuing long-term debt, for example, purchasing another truck in exchange for a note payable. This cannot be recorded using the checking account since no funds were exchanged. Instead, you will use the journal entry process to record the fixed asset acquisition and the long-term debt borrowing.

To record the purchase of a fixed asset by issuing debt, do the following:

1 Continue from where you left off. If you closed the Sample Company, follow the steps to reopen it found at the beginning of this chapter.
2 Click the **+ New** icon, and select **Journal Entry**.
3 Accept the Journal date and Journal no. provided by QBO.
4 Select **Truck:Original Cost** from the drop-down list in the Account column of line 1.
5 Type **3400** in the Debits column of line 1.
6 Select **Notes Payable** from the drop-down list in the Account column of line 2.
7 Accept **3,400.00** in the Credits column of line 2, and press [**Tab**] to view the journal entry as shown in Figure 6.8.

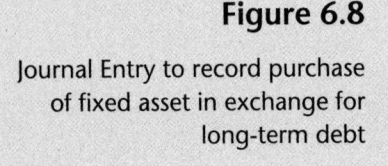

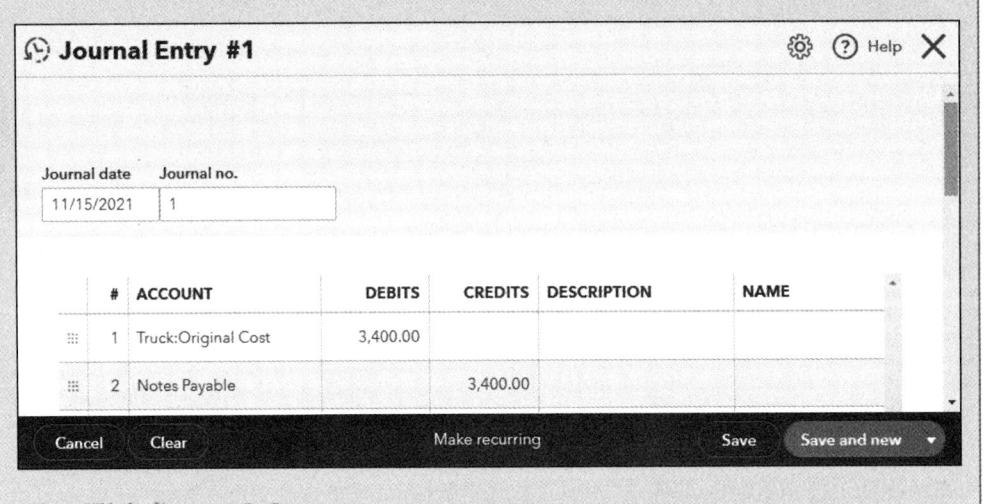

Figure 6.8

Journal Entry to record purchase of fixed asset in exchange for long-term debt

#	ACCOUNT	DEBITS	CREDITS	DESCRIPTION	NAME
1	Truck:Original Cost	3,400.00			
2	Notes Payable		3,400.00		

Journal date: 11/15/2021   Journal no.: 1

8 Click **Save and close**.
9 Sign out of the Sample Company.

End Note

In this chapter, you recorded investing activities: the acquisition of fixed assets and of long-term investments, the sale of common stocks, the payment of a dividend, the borrowing and payment of long-term debt, and the acquisition of fixed assets by taking on new debt. In the next chapter, you will work with payroll.

practice

Chapter 6 Questions

1. What are the steps to record the acquisition of a fixed asset using a check?
2. What are the steps to record the acquisition of a fixed asset for a note payable?
3. What are the steps to record the sale of common stock?
4. What are the steps to record the payment of dividends?
5. What are the steps to record borrowing on a note payable?

Chapter 6 Matching

a. Operating activity	_____	Long-term tangible property that a firm owns
b. Investing activity	_____	Distribution of earnings to shareholders
c. Financing activity	_____	A stockholders' equity account
d. Fixed assets	_____	Used to record purchase of a fixed asset for a note
e. Long-term investment	_____	A five-year note payable
f. Common stock	_____	Sales receipt
g. Dividends	_____	A financial instrument that matures in more than one year
h. Long-term debt	_____	Used to record amounts received from a note payable
i. Bank deposit	_____	Sale of common stock
j. Journal entry	_____	Purchase of common stock

Chapter 6 Cases

The following cases require you to open the company you updated in Chapter 5. Each of the following cases is continued throughout the text in a sequential manner. For example, if you are assigned Case 01, you will use the file you modified in this chapter in all following chapters. Each of the following cases is similar in concepts assessed but differs in amounts and transactions.

To reopen your company, do the following:

1. Open your Internet browser.
2. Type **https://qbo.intuit.com** into your browser's address text box.
3. Type your user ID and password into the text boxes as you have done before.

Case 1

Now add some investing and financing activities to your company.

Based on what you learned in the text using the Sample Company, you are to make the following changes to the Case 1 company you modified in Chapter 5:

1. Create a new fixed asset account with an account type: Fixed Asset, detail type: Machinery & Equipment, name: Equipment. Track depreciation of this asset.

2. Create a new asset account with an account type: Other Assets, detail type: Other Long-Term Assets, name: Investments.

3. Record the purchase of a new computer on 1/10/24 from Office Depot, check: 1003, amount: $1,375, category: Equipment:Original Cost.

4. Record a long-term investment on 1/11/24 to Etrade (a new vendor), check: 1004, amount: $4,000, category: Investments.

5. Record the sale of common stock on 1/12/24 to Shareholders (a new vendor), deposit amount: $20,000, account: Common Stock payment method: Check.

6. Record the payment of dividends to Shareholders on 1/15/24, check: 1005, in the amount of $500.

7. Record the deposit of funds from a new note payable signed on 1/16/24 with Bank of CA (a new vendor) in the amount of $65,000 payment method: Check.

8. Record the payment to Rabo Bank (a new vendor) to retire an existing note payable on 1/16/24 of $60,000 with interest of $600 using check 1006.

9. Record the purchase of an additional computer on 1/17/24 from Office Depot in exchange for a note payable of $1,800, account: Equipment:Original Cost.

10. Change the name of account Interest Paid to Interest Expense, then open your previously customized report named Trial Balance 1/31/24. Your report should look like Figure 6.9.

11. Create and print a Transaction Report for the Checking account.

12. Create and print a Transaction Report for the Equipment:Original Cost account.

13. Create and print a Transaction Report for the Notes Payable account.

14. Create and print a Transaction Report for the Common Stock account.

15. If your trial balance differs from Figure 6.9, do the following:
    a. Make sure that all of your changes were dated in January 2024.
    b. View the Transaction Reports you just created to locate any errors.
    c. Ask your instructor for assistance.
    d. Be sure your company matches the above as you will be adding additional business events in Chapter 7.

Figure 6.9

Trial Balance as of 1/31/24

Case 1
TRIAL BALANCE
As of January 31, 2024

	DEBIT	CREDIT
Checking	34,850.00	
Accounts Receivable	1,030.00	
Inventory Asset	11,800.00	
Prepaid Expenses	8,000.00	
Supplies Asset	375.00	
Undeposited Funds	5,000.00	
Equipment:Original Cost	3,175.00	
Furniture & Fixtures:Depreciation		10,000.00
Furniture & Fixtures:Original cost	40,000.00	
Investments	4,000.00	
Accounts Payable		7,645.00
VISA		1,800.00
Notes Payable		66,800.00
Common Stock		21,000.00
Opening Balance Equity		0.00
Retained Earnings		5,000.00
Sales		2,160.00
Services		170.00
Cost of Goods Sold	1,300.00	
Interest Expense	600.00	
Rent or Lease	2,500.00	
Travel	1,800.00	
Utilities	145.00	
TOTAL	**$114,575.00**	**$114,575.00**

16 Export your Trial Balance report to Excel, and save it with the file name Student Name (replace with your name) Ch 06 Case 01 Trial Balance.xlsx.

17 Open and print the custom report you created in the last chapter called Transaction Detail by Account.

18 Export your Transactions Detail by Account report to Excel, and save it with the file name Student Name (replace with your name) Ch 06 Case 01 Transaction Detail by Account.xlsx.

19 Sign out of your company.

Case 2

Now add some investing and financing activities to your company.

Based on what you learned in the text using the Sample Company, you are to make the following changes to the Case 2 company you modified in Chapter 5:

1 Create a new fixed asset account with an account type: Fixed Asset, detail type: Furniture & Fixtures, name: Furniture. Track depreciation of this asset.

2 Create a new asset account with an account type: Other Assets, detail type: Other Long-Term Assets, name: Investments.

3. Record the purchase of new furniture on 1/11/25 from Staples, check: 1003, amount: $2,250, category: Furniture:Original Cost.

4. Record a long-term investment on 1/11/25 to Raymond James (a new vendor), check: 1004, amount: $3,200, category: Investments.

5. Record the sale of common stock on 1/14/25 to Shareholders (a new vendor), deposit amount: $25,000, account: Common Stock, payment method: Check.

6. Record the payment of dividends to Shareholders on 1/15/25, check: 1005, amount: $800, category: Retained Earnings.

7. Record the deposit of funds from a new note payable signed on 1/16/25 with Bank of TJ (a new vendor) in the amount of $25,000, payment method: Check.

8. Record the payment to Community Bank (a new vendor) to retire an existing note payable on 1/16/25 of $12,000 with interest of $300 using check 1006.

9. Record the purchase of additional furniture from Staples on 1/17/25 in exchange for a note payable of $2,625, account: Furniture:Original Cost.

10. Change the name of account Interest Paid to Interest Expense, then open your previously customized report named Trial Balance 1/31/25. Your report should look like Figure 6.10.

Figure 6.10

Trial Balance as of 1/31/25

Case 2
TRIAL BALANCE
As of January 31, 2025

	DEBIT	CREDIT
Checking	38,600.00	
Accounts Receivable	1,425.00	
Inventory Asset	5,410.00	
Prepaid Expenses	6,800.00	
Supplies Asset	450.00	
Undeposited Funds	925.00	
Furniture:Original Cost	4,875.00	
Machinery & Equipment:Depreciation		1,000.00
Machinery & Equipment:Original cost	10,000.00	
Investments	3,200.00	
Accounts Payable		8,670.00
AMEX		240.00
Notes Payable		27,625.00
Common Stock		25,100.00
Opening Balance Equity		0.00
Retained Earnings		7,585.00
Sales		5,700.00
Services		225.00
Cost of Goods Sold	3,020.00	
Advertising	500.00	
Insurance	400.00	
Interest Expense	300.00	
Meals and Entertainment	240.00	
TOTAL	$76,145.00	$76,145.00

11 Create and print a Transaction Report for the Checking account.

12 Create and print a Transaction Report for the Furniture:Original Cost account.

13 Create and print a Transaction Report for the Notes Payable account.

14 Create and print a Transaction Report for the Common Stock account.

15 If your trial balance differs from Figure 6.10, do the following:

   a. Make sure that all of your changes were dated in January 2025.

   b. View the Transaction Reports you created to locate any errors.

   c. Ask your instructor for assistance.

   d. Be sure your company matches the above as you will be adding additional business events in Chapter 7.

16 Export your Trial Balance report to Excel, and save it with the file name Student Name (replace with your name) Ch 06 Case 02 Trial Balance.xlsx.

17 Open and print the custom report you created in the last chapter called Transaction Detail by Account.

18 Export your Transactions Detail by Account report to Excel, and save it with the file name Student Name (replace with your name) Ch 06 Case 02 Transaction Detail by Account.xlsx.

19 Sign out of your company.

Case 3

Now it's time for you to add some investing and financing activities to your company.

Based on what you learned in the text using the Sample Company, you are to make the following changes to the Case 3 company you modified in Chapter 5:

1 Open your chart of accounts. Create a new fixed asset account with an account type: Fixed Asset, detail type: Fixed Asset Computers, name: Computers. Track depreciation of this asset.

2 Create a new asset account with a category type: Other Assets, detail type: Other Long-Term Assets, name: Investments.

3 Open your chart of accounts and confirm that it contains an equity account with an account type: Equity, detail type: Owner's Equity, and name: Owner's Equity.

4 Record the purchase of a new computer on 1/12/26 from Staples, Inc., check: 323, amount: $3,000, category: Computers: Original Cost.

5 Record a long-term investment on 1/13/26 to E-Trade (a new vendor), check: 324, amount: $5,700, category: Investments.

6 Record an owner's contribution on 1/14/26 to Owners (a new vendor) after receiving a check that was immediately deposited in the amount: $40,000 to account: Owner's Equity.

7 Record the deposit of funds from a new note payable signed on 1/16/26 with Chase Bank (a new vendor) in the amount of $32,000.

8 Record the payment to Rabobank (a new vendor) to retire an existing note payable on 1/17/26 of $23,000 with interest of $300 using check 325 for a total of $23,300.

9 Record the purchase of machinery and equipment from Leeds, Inc., (a new vendor) on 1/17/26 in exchange for a note payable of $31,800.

10 Open and print your previously customized report named Trial Balance 1/31/26. Your report should look like Figure 6.11.

Figure 6.11

Trial Balance as of 1/31/26

Case 03 - Student Name (ID Number)

Trial Balance
As of January 31, 2026

	DEBIT	CREDIT
Checking	55,751.75	
Accounts receivable (A/R)	2,559.38	
Inventory Asset	5,700.00	
Payments to deposit	0.00	
Prepaid expenses	6,050.00	
Supplies Asset	327.00	
Computers:Original cost	3,000.00	
Machinery & Equipment:Depreciation		2,000.00
Machinery & Equipment:Original cost	46,800.00	
Investments	5,700.00	
Accounts Payable (A/P)		8,900.00
AMEX		123.00
California Department of Tax and Fee Administratio…		523.13
Notes Payable		63,800.00
Opening balance equity		0.00
Owner's Equity		50,075.00
Sales of Product Income		6,750.00
Services		240.00
Cost of goods sold	4,500.00	
Advertising & marketing	1,300.00	
Insurance	300.00	
Interest paid	300.00	
Meals	123.00	
TOTAL	$132,411.13	$132,411.13

11 Create and print a Transaction Report for the Checking account.

12 Create and print a Transaction Report for the Computers:Original Cost account.

13 Create and print a Transaction Report for the Notes Payable account.

14 Create and print a Transaction Report for the Owner's Equity account.

15. If your trial balance is different than Figure 6.11, do the following:
    a. Make sure that all of your changes were dated in January 2026.
    b. View the Transaction Reports you just created to locate any errors.
    c. Ask your instructor for assistance.
    d. Be sure your company matches the above as you will be adding additional business events in Chapter 7.
16. Export your Trial Balance report to Excel, and save it with the file name Student Name (replace with your name) Ch 06 Case 03 Trial Balance.xlsx.
17. Open and print the custom report you created in the last chapter called Transaction Detail by Account.
18. Export your Transactions Detail by Account report to Excel, and save it with the file name Student Name (replace with your name) Ch 06 Case 03 Transaction Detail by Account.xlsx.
19. Sign out of your company.

Case 4

Now it's time for you to add some investing and financing activities to your company.

Based on what you learned in the text using the Sample Company, you are to make the following changes to the Case 4 company you modified in Chapter 5:

1. Create a new fixed asset account with an account type: Fixed Asset, detail type: Buildings, name: Buildings. Track depreciation of this asset.
2. Create a new asset account with an account type: Other Assets, detail type: Other Long-Term Assets, name: Investments.
3. Change the name of the Interest Paid expense account to Interest Expense.
4. Record the signing of a new 8%, 24-month note payable on 1/01/21 with Coast Bank (a new vendor) in the amount of $18,000. A check was received from Coast Bank and immediately deposited.
5. Record the purchase of a new building on 1/23/21 from ABC Holdings (a new vendor), check: 25501, amount: $35,000.
6. Record the purchase of a long-term investment on 1/25/21 from Barber Investments, Inc. (a new vendor), check: 25502, amount: $8,000.
7. Record the sale of common stock on 1/26/21 to Shareholders (a new vendor) receiving a $10,000 check that was immediately deposited.

8. Record the purchase of furniture from Pacific Furniture (a new vendor) on 1/27/21 in exchange for a note payable of $6,000.

9. Record the payment of principle ($694) and interest ($120) to Coast Bank on the $18,000 note payable on 1/31/21 with check 25503.

10. Record the payment of $1,000 in dividends to Shareholders on 1/31/21, check: 25504.

11. Prepare and print the Trial Balance 1/31/21 report you saved previously. Your report should look like Figure 6.12.

Figure 6.12

Trial Balance as of 1/31/21

Case 4 Student Name (Student ID)

TRIAL BALANCE
As of January 31, 2021

	DEBIT	CREDIT
Checking	28,762.65	
Accounts Receivable (A/R)	22,082.50	
Inventory Asset	8,868.00	
Prepaid Expenses	12,000.00	
Supplies	1,400.00	
Undeposited Funds	0.00	
Buildings:Original cost	35,000.00	
Furniture:Depreciation		10,000.00
Furniture:Original cost	71,000.00	
Machinery & Equipment:Depreciation		6,500.00
Machinery & Equipment:Original cost	115,000.00	
Investments	8,000.00	
Accounts Payable (A/P)		6,800.00
VISA		2,400.00
California State Board of Equalization Payable		339.15
Notes Payable		105,306.00
Common Stock		11,000.00
Opening Balance Equity		0.00
Retained Earnings		114,500.00
Sales		48,400.00
Sales of Product Income		3,570.00
Cost of Goods Sold	1,632.00	
Advertising & Marketing	1,800.00	
Insurance	2,400.00	
Interest Expense	120.00	
Repairs & Maintenance	750.00	
TOTAL	**$308,815.15**	**$308,815.15**

12. Investigate differences between your trial balance and the trial balance shown above.

13 If necessary, prepare and print the Transaction Detail by Account report you saved previously to investigate identified differences.

   a. Make sure all your changes were dated in January 2021.
   b. Click on the line that does not match to view the transaction for that account, and investigate why your answer differs.
   c. Ask your instructor for assistance.
   d. Be sure your company matches the above as you will be adding additional business events in Chapter 7.

Case 5

Now it's time for you to add some investing and financing activities to your company.

Based on what you learned in the text using the Sample Company, you are to make the following changes to the Case 5 company you modified in Chapter 5:

1 Create a new fixed asset account with an account type: Fixed Assets, detail type: Fixed Asset Copiers, name: Fixed Asset Copiers. Track depreciation of this asset.

2 Create a new asset account with an account type: Other Assets, detail type: Other Long-Term Assets, name: Investments.

3 Create an expense account with an account type: Expenses, detail type: Interest Paid, name: Interest Expense.

4 Record the signing of a new 6%, 36-month note payable on 1/01/22 with Gold Coast Bank (a new vendor) in the amount of $25,000. A check was received from Gold Coast Bank and immediately deposited.

5 Record the purchase of a new copier on 1/03/22 from Coastal Copy (a new vendor), check: 3008, amount: $25,000.

6 Record the purchase of a long-term investment on 1/25/22 from Fleet Investments, Inc. (a new vendor), check: 3009, amount: $50,000.

7 Record the additional investment as a deposit on 1/26/22 from Owners (a new vendor) receiving a $80,000 check that was immediately deposited as an increase in Owner's Equity.

8 Record the purchase of computers (fixed asset) from Acme Equipment on 1/3/22 in exchange for a note payable to Acme Equipment of $30,000.

9 Record the payment of $20,907 (principal $18,182 and interest $2,725) to Chase Bank on a note payable on 1/31/22 with check 3010.

10 Record the payment of $761 (principal $636 and interest $125) to Gold Coast Bank on a note payable on 1/31/22 with check 3011.

11 Record the payment of $913 (principal $763 and interest $150) to Acme Equipment on a note payable on 1/31/22 with check 3012.

12 Record the payment of $5,000 in withdrawals (use Owner's Equity category) to Owners on 1/31/22, check: 3013.

13. Record a new invoice 1005 on 1/31/22 to a new customer Northrup (Net 15 terms) for 30 Computer Workstation 100 items for a total invoice of $490,500 including sales tax. (Be sure to click **See the math**.)

14. Prepare and print the Trial Balance 1/31/22 report you saved previously. Your report should look like Figure 6.13.

Figure 6.13

Trial Balance as of 1/31/22

TRIAL BALANCE
As of January 31, 2022

	DEBIT	CREDIT
Checking	256,419.00	
Accounts Receivable (A/R)	648,850.00	
Inventory	512,000.00	
Prepaid Expenses	22,000.00	
Undeposited Funds	0.00	
Fixed Asset Computers:Depreciation		25,000.00
Fixed Asset Computers:Original cost	280,000.00	
Fixed Asset Copiers:Original cost	25,000.00	
Fixed Asset Furniture:Depreciation		8,000.00
Fixed Asset Furniture:Original cost	80,000.00	
Investments	50,000.00	
Accounts Payable (A/P)		362,000.00
AMEX		6,300.00
Alabama Department of Revenue Payable		24,600.00
Alabama, Huntsville Payable		27,675.00
Alabama, Madison County Payable		3,075.00
Notes Payable		580,419.00
Opening Balance Equity		0.00
Owner's Equity		457,000.00
Consulting		79,500.00
Sales		615,000.00
Training		3,500.00
Cost of Goods Sold	298,000.00	
Advertising & Marketing	3,000.00	
Equipment Rental	7,500.00	
Interest Expense	3,000.00	
Recruiting	6,300.00	
TOTAL	**$2,192,069.00**	**$2,192,069.00**

15. Investigate differences between your trial balance and the trial balance shown above.

16. If necessary, prepare and print the Transaction Detail by Account report you saved previously to investigate identified differences.

    a. Make sure all your changes were dated in January 2022.

    b. Click on the line that does not match to view the transaction for that account, and investigate why your answer differs.

    c. Ask your instructor for assistance.

    d. Be sure your company matches the above as you will be adding additional business events in Chapter 7.

Case 6

Now it's time for you to add some investing and financing activities to your company.

Based on what you learned in the text using the Sample Company, you are to make the following changes to the Case 6 company you modified in Chapter 5:

1. Create a new fixed asset account with an account type: Fixed Asset, detail type: Fixed Asset Computers, name: Computers. Track depreciation of this asset.
2. Change the name of the Interest Paid category to Interest Expense using the Chart of Accounts edit feature.
3. Record the signing of a new 4%, 36-month note payable on 1/01/23 with Seattle Bank (a new vendor) in the amount of $20,000. This was an addition to the existing $100,000 note payable that existed on 12/31/22. A check was received from Seattle Bank and immediately deposited.
4. Record the purchase of a new computer on 1/23/23 from Best Buy (a new vendor), check: 591, amount: $8,000.
5. Record the purchase of a long-term investment on 1/25/23 from McConnel Investments, Inc. (a new vendor), check: 592, amount: $12,000.
6. Record the sale of common stock on 1/26/23 to Shareholders (a new vendor) receiving a $10,000 check that was immediately deposited ($100 common stock $9,900 Paid-In Capital).
7. Record the purchase of machinery & equipment from GM (a new vendor) on 1/27/23 in exchange for a note payable of $12,000.
8. Record the payment of $3,542.88 (principle $3,142.88 and interest $400.00) to Seattle Bank on the $120,000 note payable on 1/31/23 with check 593.
9. Record the payment of $500 in dividends to Shareholders on 1/31/23, check: 594 (remember to use Retained Earnings to record dividends).
10. Prepare and print the Trial Balance 1/31/23 report you saved previously. Your report should look like Figure 6.14.

Figure 6.14

Trial Balance as of 1/31/23

Case 06 - Student Name (ID Number)

TRIAL BALANCE
As of January 31, 2023

	DEBIT	CREDIT
Checking	78,107.12	
Accounts Receivable (A/R)	153,020.00	
Inventory Asset	524,000.00	
Inventory Parts	4,000.00	
Investments	12,000.00	
Loans To Officers	15,000.00	
Prepaid Expenses	18,000.00	
Undeposited Funds	0.00	
Buildings:Depreciation		15,000.00
Buildings:Original cost	150,000.00	
Computers	8,000.00	
Machinery & Equipment	12,000.00	
Machinery & Equipment:Depreciation		10,000.00
Machinery & Equipment:Original cost	100,000.00	
Accounts Payable (A/P)		524,000.00
AMEX		6,000.00
Washington State Department of Revenue Payable		26,970.00
Notes Payable		128,857.12
Common Stock		1,100.00
Opening Balance Equity		0.00
Paid-In Capital		259,900.00
Retained Earnings		60,500.00
Sales of Product Income		290,000.00
Cost of Goods Sold	232,000.00	
Advertising & Marketing	14,000.00	
Contractors	1,800.00	
Interest Expense	400.00	
TOTAL	$1,322,327.12	$1,322,327.12

11 Investigate differences between your trial balance and the trial balance shown above.

12 Prepare and print the Transaction Detail by Account report for all dates you saved previously to investigate identified differences.

    a. Make sure all your changes were dated in January 2023.

    b. Click on the line that does not match to view the transaction for that account, and investigate why your answer differs.

    c. Ask your instructor for assistance.

    d. Be sure your company matches the above as you will be adding additional business events in Chapter 7.

Chapter 7

Recording Payroll

Student Learning Outcomes

Upon completion of this chapter, the student will be able to do the following:

- Add a new employee
- Add payroll-related general ledger accounts
- Pay employees and record payroll expenses and liabilities

Overview

Intuit has provided a Sample Company online to let new users test-drive its QBO product. In this chapter, you will open this Sample Company and practice payroll activities in QBO. QBO Payroll is an add-on feature to QBO. You can use a trial version of QBO Payroll, but it only lasts for 30 days. Even though the payroll features available through QBO Payroll are extensive and helpful, they focus on real companies and real-time frames. Thus, this chapter will focus on the creation of new employees, general ledger accounts, and payment to employees without the use of QBO Payroll.

Remember, if you stop in the middle of this work, none of your work will be saved. So, when you return, the same Sample Company, without your work, will appear. In some parts of the chapter, you will be asked to sign out of the Sample Company and sign back in so the Sample Company is reset to its original state. In the end of chapter work, you will be asked to perform the same tasks completed on the Sample Company on your Student Company. That work, of course, will be saved.

Employees

In this section, you will be adding a new employee to QBO.

To add a new employee to the Sample Company, do the following:

1. Open your Internet browser.
2. Type **https://qbo.intuit.com/redir/testdrive** into your browser's address text box, and press [**Enter**] to view the Sample Company Dashboard.
3. Click **Payroll** and then click **Employees** from the navigation bar.
4. Click the **Add an employee** button.
5. Click the **Not right now** button when asked to Turn payroll on.
6. Type **May West** as the employee's name and provide the following address information: **2393 Ridge Place #3, Rancho Mar, CA, 93154**. Type **178** as the Employee ID No. Your screen should look like Figure 7.1.

Figure 7.1

Employee Information (adding a new employee)

7. Click **Save**.
8. Your Employees window should now reflect three employees as shown in Figure 7.2.

Figure 7.2

Employees

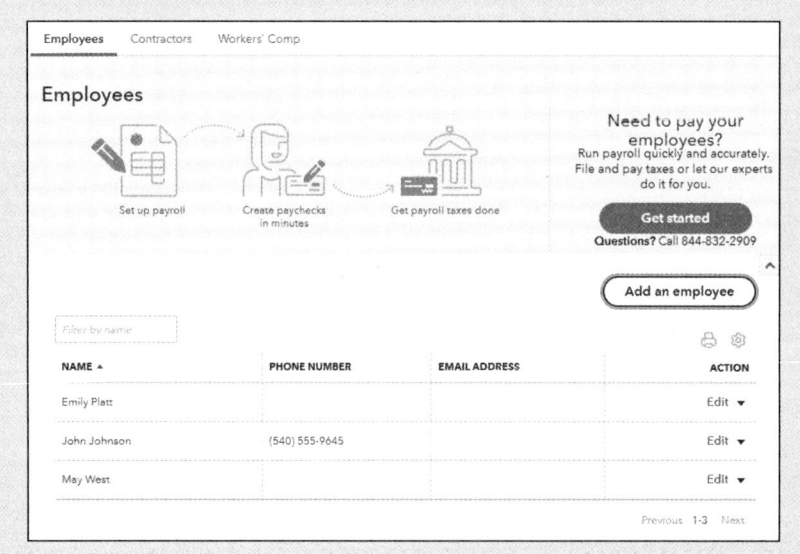

Payroll Accounts

Once again, if you were using QuickBooks Payroll Online, general ledger accounts to capture payroll information would be created for you in the setup process. However, since you are not using QuickBooks Payroll Online, you will have to create them on your own. To keep things simple, you can create the minimum two new accounts for payroll: Payroll (expense) and Payroll Tax Payable (liability).

An employer agrees to pay its employees a salary per month or an hourly rate. In either case, for the agreed upon salary or hourly rate times hours worked, amounts are recorded to the Payroll (expense) account. Depending on the state, employees are often required to have an estimated amount of federal and state income taxes withheld from their paychecks by their employers. In addition, employers must withhold social security (6.2%) and Medicare (1.45%) taxes. Amounts withheld from employees will be recorded in the Payroll Tax Payable (liability) account until remitted to the U.S. Treasury and state government entities. Employers must match those amounts for social security (6.2%) and Medicare (1.45%) taxes. These matching costs will be recorded as additional Payroll expense.

To add payroll-related accounts to the Sample Company, do the following:

1. Continue from where you left off. If you closed the Sample Company, follow the steps to reopen it found at the beginning of this chapter.
2. Click the **Gear** icon and then click **Chart of Accounts**.
3. Click **See your Chart of Accounts** and then click **New**.
4. Select **Expenses** from the drop-down list in the Account Type text box.
5. Select **Payroll Expenses** from the drop-down list in the Detail Type text box.
6. Type **Payroll** in the Name text box replacing Payroll Expenses as shown in Figure 7.3.

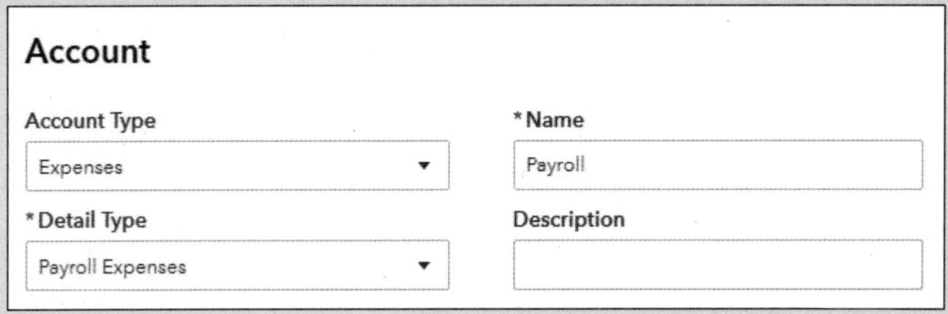

Figure 7.3

Account (adding a new payroll account)

7. Click **Save and New**.
8. Select **Other Current Liabilities** from the drop-down list in the Account Type text box.

> 9 Select **Payroll Tax Payable** from the drop-down list in the Detail Type text box.
>
> 10 Accept **Payroll Tax Payable** in the Name text box.
>
> 11 Click **Save and Close**.

You have added two payroll-related general ledger accounts.

Pay Employees

The payment of employees requires gathering information from each employee that helps determine withholding amounts and payroll expenses. The federal and state governments provide formulas and/or tables to help employers calculate these amounts. In this text, you will be provided these amounts. Additional taxes, such as training, unemployment, and so on, are ignored for this illustration. Since payroll is a recurring event, it will help to make these checks recur, which can be edited for each payroll for changes in hours worked where applicable. In this example, payroll is paid semimonthly.

See Figure 7.4 for a payroll for your Sample Company.

Figure 7.4
Semimonthly payroll information

Pay/Tax/Withholding	Emily	John	May	Total
Hours if applicable	n/a	80	60	
Annual salary or hourly rate	$ 60,000	$ 18.00	$ 18.00	
Gross pay	2,500.00	1,440.00	1,080.00	5,020.00
Federal withholding	342.50	197.28	147.96	687.74
Social security employee (6.2%)	155.00	89.28	66.96	311.24
Medicare employee (1.45%)	36.25	20.88	15.66	72.79
Employee withholding	**533.75**	**307.44**	**230.58**	**1,071.77**
Social security employer (6.2%)	155.00	89.28	66.96	311.24
Medicare company employer (1.45%)	36.25	20.88	15.66	72.79
Employer payroll tax expense	**191.25**	**110.16**	**82.62**	**384.03**
Net Check amount	1,966.25	1,132.56	849.42	3,948.23

To record the payment of employees in the Sample Company, do the following:

1 Continue from where you left off.

2 Click the [+ New] icon, and select **Check**.

3 Select **Emily Platt** from the drop-down list in the **Payee** text box. (Note: Employees are located at the bottom of the list.)

4 Accept the given date and check number QBO provides.

5 Select **Payroll** from the drop-down list in Category column of line 1.

6   Type **2500** in the Amount column of line 1, and press [**Tab**] once.

7   Select **Payroll Tax Payable** from the drop-down list in Category column of line 2.

8   Type **−533.75** in the Amount column of line 1, and press [**Tab**] once. (Be sure to enter this amount as a negative number.)

9   Select **Payroll** from the drop-down list in Category column of line 3.

10 Type **191.25** in the Amount column of line 3, and press [**Tab**] once.

11 Select **Payroll Tax Payable** from the drop-down list in Category column of line 4.

12 Type **−191.25** in the Amount column of line 4, and press [**Tab**] once. (Be sure to enter this amount as a negative number.) Your screen should look like Figure 7.5.

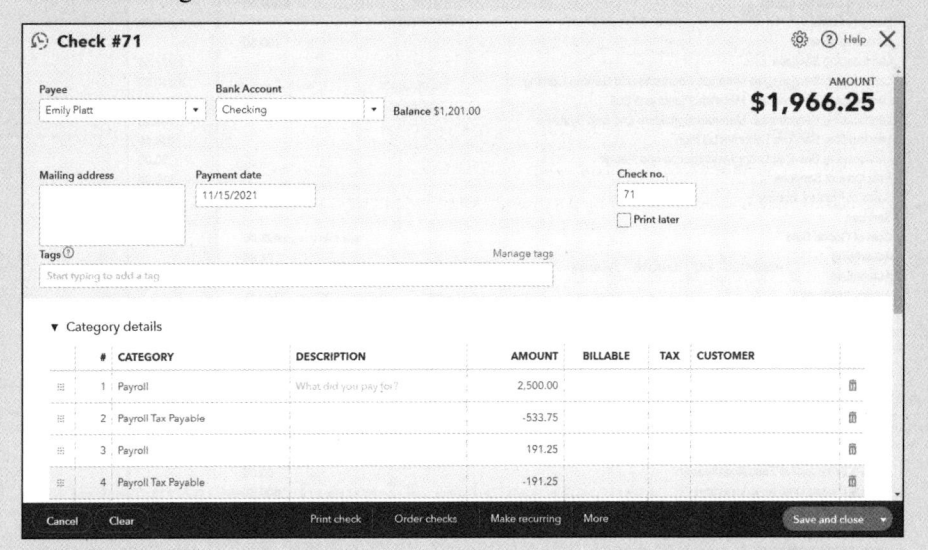

Figure 7.5

Check #71 (paycheck for Emily Platt)

13 Click **Make recurring** located at the bottom of the screen.

14 Select **Unscheduled** from the drop-down list in the Type text box.

15 Click **Save template**.

16 Click the **Gear** icon.

17 Select **Recurring Transactions** located in the List column.

18 Click **Use** located in the Action column of the Emily Platt row. The check window will appear again completed like that shown in Figure 7.5.

19 Make sure the date is correct and then click **Save and New**.

20 Enter payroll information found in Figure 7.4 for John and May in the same way as you entered payroll information for Emily above. Be sure to make each of these unscheduled recurring events.

21 After entering the last check to record payroll above, click **Save and Close**.

22 Click **Reports** from the navigation bar.

162   Chapter 7   *Recording Payroll*

30 Click **Use** on the May West template to view a new payroll check for May.

31 Add 14 days to the Payment date text box representing the next semimonthly period. In this example, the new date is 11/29/2021; of course, yours will differ.

32 Payroll information for this next semimonthly period is shown in Figure 7.10. Note that the hours worked are different, and John received an increase in his hourly rate.

Figure 7.10

Semimonthly payroll information

Pay/Tax/Withholding	Emily	John	May	Total
Hours if applicable	n/a	75	63	
Annual salary or hourly rate	$ 60,000	$ 20.00	$ 18.00	
Gross pay	2,500.00	1,500.00	1,134.00	5,134.00
Federal withholding	342.50	205.50	155.36	703.36
Social security employee (6.2%)	155.00	93.00	70.31	318.31
Medicare employee (1.45%)	36.25	21.75	16.44	74.44
Employee withholding	533.75	320.25	242.11	1,096.11
Social security employer (6.2%)	155.00	93.00	70.31	318.31
Medicare company employer (1.45%)	36.25	21.75	16.44	74.44
Employer payroll tax expense	191.25	114.75	86.75	392.75
Net Check amount	1,966.25	1,179.75	891.89	4,037.89

33 Type **1134** in the Amount column on line 1.

34 Type **−242.11** in the Amount column on line 2.

35 Type **86.75** in the Amount column on line 3.

36 Type **−86.75** in the Amount column on line 4. Your screen should now look like Figure 7.11.

Figure 7.11

Check #74 (May West payroll check)

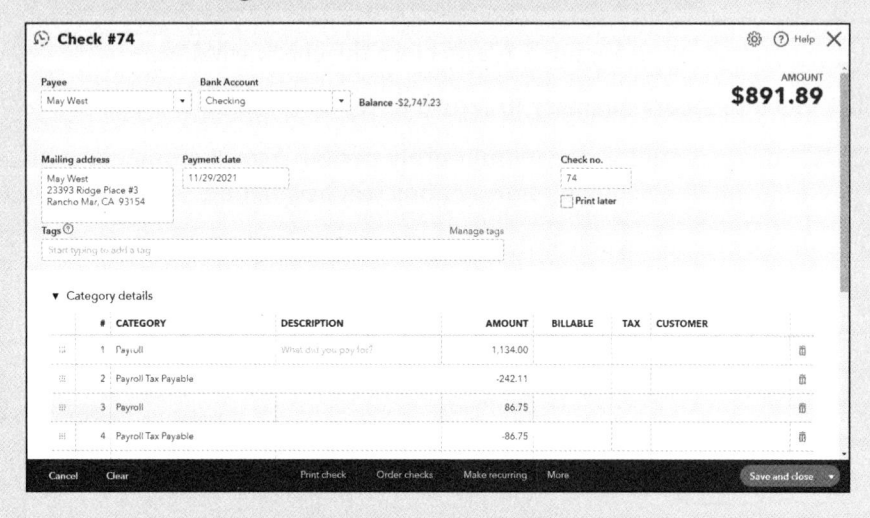

37 Click **Save and close**.

38 Use the same process (clicking **Use** from the Recurring Transactions list) for John and Emily to record their paychecks based on the new information shown in Figure 7.10. (Since Emily is salaried, her information remains the same each pay period, so nothing needs to be changed from the recurring transaction information provided.) Click **Yes** to accept a duplicate check number if QBO identifies that the check number you are proposing has been used.

39 Click **Reports** from the navigation bar.

40 Type **Trial Balance** in the Find report by name search box, and press [**Enter**].

41 Scroll to the top of the Trial Balance report. Change the from date to the beginning of the month and the to date to the end of the month in which you recorded the most recent payroll transactions. In our case, that would have been from 11/1/21 to 11/30/21. Your dates will be different. When changed, click **Run report** to see a partial view of the trial balance as shown in Figure 7.12.

Figure 7.12

Trial Balance

Craig's Design and Landscaping Services
Trial Balance
As of November 30, 2021

	DEBIT	CREDIT
Checking		6,785.12
Savings	800.00	
Accounts Receivable (A/R)	5,281.52	
Inventory Asset	596.25	
Undeposited Funds	2,062.52	
Truck:Original Cost	13,495.00	
Accounts Payable (A/P)		1,602.67
Mastercard		157.72
Arizona Dept. of Revenue Payable		0.00
Board of Equalization Payable		370.94
Loan Payable		4,000.00
Payroll Tax Payable		2,944.66
Notes Payable		25,000.00
Opening Balance Equity	9,337.50	
Design income		2,250.00
Discounts given	89.50	
Landscaping Services		1,477.50
Landscaping Services:Job Materials:Fountains and Garden Lighting		2,246.50
Landscaping Services:Job Materials:Plants and Soil		2,351.97
Landscaping Services:Job Materials:Sprinklers and Drip Systems		138.00
Landscaping Services:Labor:Installation		250.00
Landscaping Services:Labor:Maintenance and Repair		50.00
Pest Control Services		110.00
Sales of Product Income		912.75
Services		503.55
Cost of Goods Sold	405.00	
Advertising	74.86	
Automobile	113.96	
Automobile:Fuel	349.41	
Equipment Rental	112.00	
Insurance	241.23	
Job Expenses	155.07	
Job Expenses:Job Materials:Decks and Patios	234.04	
Job Expenses:Job Materials:Plants and Soil	353.12	
Job Expenses:Job Materials:Sprinklers and Drip Systems	215.66	
Legal & Professional Fees	75.00	
Legal & Professional Fees:Accounting	640.00	
Legal & Professional Fees:Bookkeeper	55.00	
Legal & Professional Fees:Lawyer	400.00	
Maintenance and Repair	185.00	
Maintenance and Repair:Equipment Repairs	755.00	
Meals and Entertainment	28.49	
Office Expenses	18.08	
Payroll	10,930.78	

Accrual Basis Monday, November 15, 2021 09:44 AM GMT-08:00 1/2

Craig's Design and Landscaping Services
Trial Balance
As of November 30, 2021

	DEBIT	CREDIT
Rent or Lease	900.00	
Utilities:Gas and Electric	200.53	
Utilities:Telephone	130.86	
Miscellaneous	2,916.00	
TOTAL	**$51,151.38**	**$51,151.38**

42 Click the **6,785.12** amount on the Checking line to view a transaction report for the checking account as shown in Figure 7.13.

Figure 7.13

Transaction Report (checking account)

DATE	TRANSACTION TYPE	NUM	NAME	MEMO/DESCRIPTION	ACCOUNT	SPLIT	AMOUNT	BALANCE
Checking								
Beginning Balance								2,101.00
11/03/2021	Credit Card Credit				Checking	Mastercard	-900.00	1,201.00
11/15/2021	Check	72	John Johnson		Checking	-Split-	-1,132.56	68.44
11/15/2021	Check	71	Emily Platt		Checking	-Split-	-1,966.25	-1,897.81
11/15/2021	Check	73	May West		Checking	-Split-	-849.42	-2,747.23
11/29/2021	Check	76	Emily Platt		Checking	-Split-	-1,966.25	-4,713.48
11/29/2021	Check	75	John Johnson		Checking	-Split-	-1,179.75	-5,893.23
11/29/2021	Check	74	May West		Checking	-Split-	-891.89	-6,785.12
Total for Checking							**$ -8,886.12**	
TOTAL							**$ -8,886.12**	

Craig's Design and Landscaping Services — Transaction Report — November 2021

43. Match your screen with Figure 7.13, which may be in a different order than yours. It will show different dates. In this figure, only one payroll occurred so far in November. If you completed both payrolls in one month, then your figure will reflect more transactions. Take note of any differences.

44. Click any payroll-related transaction if you want to drill down to the payroll check you recorded to see if you can fix any differences noted.

45. Fix any errors you discover.

46. Sign out of this Sample Company.

You have recorded two semimonthly payroll checks for the Sample Company. Keep in mind that since you are not using QuickBooks Payroll Online, there are no employee records of earnings or taxes.

End Note

In this chapter, you added a new employee, a new payroll (expense) account, and a new payroll tax payable (liability) account and paid employees. In the next chapter, you will work with budgets and bank reconciliations.

practice

Chapter 7 Questions

1. What are the steps to create a new employee?
2. What are the steps to create a new account?
3. What are the two minimum accounts needed to account for payroll?
4. What types of costs are included in the Payroll (expense) account?
5. What types of costs are included in the Payroll Tax Payable (liability) account?

Chapter 7 Matching

a. 6.2% _____ Account used to record the liability for Federal income tax withheld
b. 1.45% _____ An add-on feature to QBO
c. Payroll _____ Rate used to calculate an employee's Medicare tax
d. Payroll tax payable _____ Hours worked times hourly rate
e. QBO Payroll _____ Use to more efficiently record periodic payroll
f. Gross pay _____ Payroll tax payable
g. Recurring transactions _____ Accessed by clicking an amount on the trial balance
h. Transaction report _____ One type of recurring event
i. Unscheduled _____ Account used to record all payroll expenses
j. Record as negative amounts _____ Rate used to calculate an employee's social security tax

Chapter 7 Cases

The following cases require you to open the company you updated in Chapter 6. Each of the following cases continues throughout the text in a sequential manner. For example, if you are assigned Case 01, you will use the file you modified in this chapter in all following chapters. Each of the following cases is similar in concepts assessed but differs in amounts and transactions.

To reopen your company, do the following:

1. Open your Internet browser.
2. Type **https://qbo.intuit.com** into your browser's address text box.
3. Type your user ID and password into the text boxes as you have done before.

Case 1

Now add some payroll activities to your company. Do not install QBO Payroll. Based on what you learned in the text using the Sample Company, you are to make the following changes to the Case 1 company you modified in Chapter 6:

1. Add two new accounts like you did in the chapter: Payroll (expense) and Payroll Tax Payable (liability).
2. Add a new employee: Ben Franklin, 32 Ocean View Lane, La Jolla, CA, 92037, employee ID number: 556-12-3467.
3. Add a second employee: Betsy Ross, 2323 1st Street, La Jolla, CA, 92037, employee ID number: 458-87-1974.
4. Payroll is paid twice a month on the 17th and the last day of each month.
5. Record payroll (as you did in the chapter) for 1/17/24 based on the information shown in Figure 7.14. After recording each employee's check, be sure to designate it as a recurring transaction.

Figure 7.14

Payroll information (for 1/17/24)

Pay/Tax/Withholding	Ben	Betsy	Total
Hours if applicable	n/a	73	
Annual salary or hourly rate	$ 95,000	$ 21.50	
Gross pay	3,958.33	1,569.50	5,527.83
Federal withholding	542.29	215.02	757.31
Social security employee (6.2%)	245.42	97.31	342.73
Medicare employee (1.45%)	57.40	22.76	80.16
Employee withholding	845.11	335.09	1,180.20
Social security employer (6.2%)	245.42	97.31	342.73
Medicare company employer (1.45%)	57.40	22.76	80.16
Employer payroll tax expense	302.82	120.07	422.89
Net Check amount	3,113.22	1,234.41	4,347.63

6. Use the recurring transactions template you created above to help you record payroll (as you did in the chapter) for 1/31/24 based on the information shown in Figure 7.15.

Figure 7.15

Payroll information (for 1/31/24)

Pay/Tax/Withholding	Ben	Betsy	Total
Hours if applicable	n/a	68	
Annual salary or hourly rate	$ 95,000	$ 21.50	
Gross pay	**3,958.33**	**1,462.00**	**5,420.33**
Federal withholding	542.29	200.29	742.58
Social security employee (6.2%)	245.42	90.64	336.06
Medicare employee (1.45%)	57.40	21.20	78.60
Employee withholding	**845.11**	**312.13**	**1,157.24**
Social security employer (6.2%)	245.42	90.64	336.06
Medicare company employer (1.45%)	57.40	21.20	78.60
Employer payroll tax expense	**302.82**	**111.84**	**414.66**
Net Check amount	3,113.22	1,149.87	4,263.09

7 Open your previously customized report named Trial Balance 1/31/24. Your report should look like Figure 7.16.

Figure 7.16

Trial Balance (as of 1/31/24)

	DEBIT	CREDIT
Checking	26,239.28	
Accounts Receivable	1,030.00	
Inventory Asset	11,800.00	
Prepaid Expenses	8,000.00	
Supplies Asset	375.00	
Undeposited Funds	5,000.00	
Equipment:Original Cost	3,175.00	
Furniture & Fixtures:Depreciation		10,000.00
Furniture & Fixtures:Original cost	40,000.00	
Investments	4,000.00	
Accounts Payable		7,645.00
Visa		1,800.00
Payroll Tax Payable		3,174.99
Notes Payable		66,800.00
Common Stock		21,000.00
Opening Balance Equity		0.00
Retained Earnings		5,000.00
Sales		2,160.00
Services		170.00
Cost of Goods Sold	1,300.00	
Interest Expense	600.00	
Payroll	11,785.71	
Rent or Lease	2,500.00	
Travel	1,800.00	
Utilities	145.00	
TOTAL	**$117,749.99**	**$117,749.99**

8. Create and print a Transaction Report for the Checking account.
9. Create and print a Transaction Report for the Payroll Tax Payable account.
10. If your trial balance differs from the one in Figure 7.16, do the following:
    a. Make sure all of your changes were dated in January 2024.
    b. View the Transaction Reports you created to locate any errors.
    c. Ask your instructor for assistance.
    d. Be sure your company matches the above as you will be adding additional business events in Chapter 8.
11. Export your Trial Balance report to Excel, and save it with the file name Student Name (replace with your name) Ch 07 Case 01 Trial Balance.xlsx.
12. Open and print the custom report you created in the last chapter called Transaction Detail by Account.
13. Export your Transactions Detail by Account report to Excel, and save it with the file name Student Name (replace with your name) Ch 07 Case 01 Transaction Detail by Account.xlsx.
14. Sign out of your company.

Case 2

Now add some payroll activities to your company. Do not install QBO Payroll. Based on what you learned in the text using the Sample Company, you are to make the following changes to the Case 2 company you modified in Chapter 6:

1. Add two new accounts like you did in the chapter: Payroll (expense) and Payroll Tax Payable (liability).
2. Add a new employee: Frank Benjamin, 32 Ocean View Lane, La Jolla, CA, 92037, employee ID number: 556-12-3467.
3. Add a second employee: Sara Juarez, 2323 1st Street, La Jolla, CA, 92037, employee ID number: 458-87-1974.
4. Payroll is paid twice a month on the 16th and the last day of each month.
5. Record payroll (like you did in the chapter) for 1/16/25 based on the information shown in Figure 7.17. After recording each employee's check, be sure to designate it as a recurring transaction.

Recording Payroll **Chapter 7** 169

Pay/Tax/Withholding	Frank	Sara	Total
Hours if applicable	n/a	71	
Annual salary or hourly rate	$ 72,000	$ 18.75	
Gross pay	**3,000.00**	**1,331.25**	**4,331.25**
Federal withholding	411.00	182.38	593.38
Social security employee (6.2%)	186.00	82.54	268.54
Medicare employee (1.45%)	43.50	19.30	62.80
Employee withholding	**640.50**	**284.22**	**924.72**
Social security employer (6.2%)	186.00	82.54	268.54
Medicare company employer (1.45%)	43.50	19.30	62.80
Employer payroll tax expense	**229.50**	**101.84**	**331.34**
Net Check amount	2,359.50	1,047.03	3,406.53

Figure 7.17

Payroll information (for 1/16/25)

6 Use the recurring transactions template you created above to help you record payroll (as you did in the chapter) for 1/31/25 based on the information shown in Figure 7.18.

Pay/Tax/Withholding	Frank	Sara	Total
Hours if applicable	n/a	66	
Annual salary or hourly rate	$ 72,000	$ 18.75	
Gross pay	**3,000.00**	**1,237.50**	**4,237.50**
Federal withholding	411.00	169.54	580.54
Social security employee (6.2%)	186.00	76.73	262.73
Medicare employee (1.45%)	43.50	17.94	61.44
Employee withholding	**640.50**	**264.21**	**904.71**
Social security employer (6.2%)	186.00	76.73	262.73
Medicare company employer (1.45%)	43.50	17.94	61.44
Employer payroll tax expense	**229.50**	**94.67**	**324.17**
Net Check amount	2,359.50	973.29	3,332.79

Figure 7.18

Payroll information (for 1/31/25)

7   Open your previously customized report named Trial Balance 1/31/25. Your report should look like Figure 7.19.

Figure 7.19

Trial Balance (as of 1/31/25)

Case 2
TRIAL BALANCE
As of January 31, 2025

	DEBIT	CREDIT
Checking	31,860.68	
Accounts Receivable	1,425.00	
Inventory Asset	5,410.00	
Prepaid Expenses	6,800.00	
Supplies Asset	450.00	
Undeposited Funds	925.00	
Furniture:Original Cost	4,875.00	
Machinery & Equipment:Depreciation		1,000.00
Machinery & Equipment:Original cost	10,000.00	
Investments	3,200.00	
Accounts Payable		8,670.00
AMEX		240.00
Payroll Tax Payable		2,484.94
Notes Payable		27,625.00
Common Stock		25,100.00
Opening Balance Equity		0.00
Retained Earnings		7,585.00
Sales		5,700.00
Services		225.00
Cost of Goods Sold	3,020.00	
Advertising	500.00	
Insurance	400.00	
Interest Expense	300.00	
Meals and Entertainment	240.00	
Payroll	9,224.26	
TOTAL	**$78,629.94**	**$78,629.94**

8   Create and print a Transaction Report for the Checking account.

9   Create and print a Transaction Report for the Payroll Tax Payable account.

10 If your trial balance differs from the one in Figure 7.19, do the following:

   a. Make sure all of your changes were dated in January 2025.

   b. View the Transaction Reports you created to locate any errors.

   c. Ask your instructor for assistance.

   d. Be sure your company matches the above as you will be adding additional business events in Chapter 8.

11 Export your Trial Balance report to Excel, and save it with the file name Student Name (replace with your name) Ch 07 Case 02 Trial Balance.xlsx.

12 Open and print the custom report you created in the last chapter called Transaction Detail by Account.

13 Export your Transactions Detail by Account report to Excel, and save it with the file name Student Name (replace with your name) Ch 07 Case 02 Transaction Detail by Account.xlsx.

14 Sign out of your company.

Case 3

Now add some payroll activities to your company. Do not install QBO Payroll. Based on what you learned in the text using the Sample Company, you are to make the following changes to the Case 3 company you modified in Chapter 6:

1 If necessary, add two new accounts like you did in the chapter: Payroll (expense) and Payroll Tax Payable (liability).

2 Add a new employee: Kira Jennings, 32 Ocean View Lane, La Jolla, CA, 92037, employee ID number: 556-33-3467.

3 Add a second employee: Jedi Vu, 2323 1st Street, La Jolla, CA, 92037, employee ID number: 458-22-1974.

4 Payroll is paid twice a month on the 16th and the last day of each month.

5 Record payroll (like you did in the chapter) for 1/16/26 based on the information shown in Figure 7.20 using checks 326 and 327. Be sure to designate both as a recurring transaction.

Pay/Tax/Withholding	Kira	Jedi	Total
Hours if applicable	n/a	70	
Annual salary or hourly rate	$ 48,000	$ 17.00	
Gross pay	**2,000.00**	**1,190.00**	**3,190.00**
Federal withholding	274.00	163.03	437.03
Social security employee (6.2%)	124.00	73.78	197.78
Medicare employee (1.45%)	29.00	17.26	46.26
Employee withholding	**427.00**	**254.07**	**681.07**
Social security employer (6.2%)	124.00	73.78	197.78
Medicare company employer (1.45%)	29.00	17.26	46.26
Employer payroll tax expense	**153.00**	**91.04**	**244.04**
Net Check amount	1,573.00	935.93	2,508.93

Figure 7.20

Payroll information for 1/16/26

6 Use the recurring transactions template you created above to help you record payroll (like you did in the chapter) for 1/31/26 based on the information shown in Figure 7.21 using checks 328 and 329.

Figure 7.21

Payroll information for 1/31/26

Pay/Tax/Withholding	Kira	Jedi	Total
Hours if applicable	n/a	75	
Annual salary or hourly rate	$ 48,000	$ 17.00	
Gross pay	**2,000.00**	**1,275.00**	**3,275.00**
Federal withholding	274.00	174.68	448.68
Social security employee (6.2%)	124.00	79.05	203.05
Medicare employee (1.45%)	29.00	18.49	47.49
Employee withholding	**427.00**	**272.22**	**699.22**
Social security employer (6.2%)	124.00	79.05	203.05
Medicare company employer (1.45%)	29.00	18.49	47.49
Employer payroll tax expense	**153.00**	**97.54**	**250.54**
Net Check amount	1,573.00	1,002.78	2,575.78

7 Open your previously customized report named Trial Balance 1/31/26. Your report should look like Figure 7.22.

Figure 7.22

Trial Balance as of 1/31/26

Case 03 - Student Name (ID Number)
Trial Balance
As of January 31, 2026

	DEBIT	CREDIT
Checking	50,667.04	
Accounts receivable (A/R)	2,559.38	
Inventory Asset	5,700.00	
Payments to deposit	0.00	
Prepaid expenses	6,050.00	
Supplies Asset	327.00	
Computers:Original cost	3,000.00	
Machinery & Equipment:Depreciation		2,000.00
Machinery & Equipment:Original cost	46,800.00	
Investments	5,700.00	
Accounts Payable (A/P)		8,900.00
AMEX		123.00
California Department of Tax and Fe…		523.13
Payroll Tax Payable		1,874.87
Notes Payable		63,800.00
Opening balance equity		0.00
Owner's Equity		50,075.00
Sales of Product Income		6,750.00
Services		240.00
Cost of goods sold	4,500.00	
Advertising & marketing	1,300.00	
Insurance	300.00	
Interest paid	300.00	
Meals	123.00	
Payroll	6,959.58	
TOTAL	**$134,286.00**	**$134,286.00**

8 Create and print a Transaction Report for the Checking account.

9 Create and print a Transaction Report for the Payroll Tax Payable account.

10 If your trial balance is different than Figure 7.22, do the following:
   a. Make sure that all of your changes were dated in January 2026.
   b. View the Transaction Reports you just created to locate any errors.
   c. Ask your instructor for assistance.
   d. Be sure your company matches the above as you will be adding additional business events in Chapter 8.

11 Export your Trial Balance report to Excel, and save it with the file name Student Name (replace with your name) Ch 07 Case 03 Trial Balance.xlsx.

12 Open and print the customized report you created in the last chapter called Transaction Detail by Account.

13 Export your Transactions Detail by Account report to Excel, and save it with the file name Student Name (replace with your name) Ch 07 Case 03 Transaction Detail by Account.xlsx.

14 Sign out of your company.

Case 4

Now add some payroll activities to your company. Do not install QBO Payroll. Based on what you learned in the text using the Sample Company, you are to make the following changes to the Case 4 company you modified in Chapter 6:

1 Add two new accounts like you did in the chapter: Payroll (expense) and Payroll Tax Payable (liability).

2 Add a new employee: Graham O'Leary.

3 Add additional employees: Allegra Munoz and Beckett Yamamomo.

4 Payroll is paid twice a month on the 15th and the last day of each month.

5 Record payroll (like you did in the chapter) for 1/15/21 based on the information shown in Figure 7.23. After recording each employee's check, be sure to designate it as a recurring transaction.

Figure 7.23

Payroll information for 1/15/21

Pay/Tax/Withholding	Graham	Allegra	Beckett	Total
Hours if applicable	n/a	75	83	
Annual salary or hourly rate	$ 75,000	$ 25.00	$ 22.00	
Gross pay	3,125.00	1,875.00	1,826.00	6,826.00
Federal withholding	428.13	256.88	250.16	935.16
Social security employee (6.2%)	193.75	116.25	113.21	423.21
Medicare employee (1.45%)	45.31	27.19	26.48	98.98
Employee withholding	667.19	400.31	389.85	1,457.35
Social security employer (6.2%)	193.75	116.25	113.21	423.21
Medicare company employer (1.45%)	45.34	27.19	26.48	99.01
Employer payroll tax expense	239.09	143.44	139.69	522.22
Net Check amount	2,457.81	1,474.68	1,436.15	5,368.64

6 Use the recurring transactions template you created above to help you record payroll (as you did in the chapter) for 1/31/21 based on the information shown in Figure 7.24.

Pay/Tax/Withholding	Graham	Allegra	Beckett	Total
Hours if applicable	n/a	70	88	
Annual salary or hourly rate	$ 75,000	$ 25.00	$ 22.00	
Gross pay	**3,125.00**	**1,750.00**	**1,936.00**	**6,811.00**
Federal withholding	428.13	239.75	265.23	933.11
Social security employee (6.2%)	193.75	108.50	120.03	422.28
Medicare employee (1.45%)	45.31	25.38	28.07	98.76
Employee withholding	**667.19**	**373.63**	**413.34**	**1,454.15**
Social security employer (6.2%)	193.75	108.50	120.03	422.28
Medicare company employer (1.45%)	45.34	25.38	28.07	98.79
Employer payroll tax expense	**239.09**	**133.88**	**148.10**	**521.07**
Net Check amount	2,457.81	1,376.37	1,522.67	5,356.85

Figure 7.24

Payroll information for 1/31/21

7 Prepare and print the Trial Balance 1/31/21 report you saved previously. Your report should look like Figure 7.25.

Figure 7.25

Trial Balance as of 1/31/21

Case 4 Student Name (Student ID)

TRIAL BALANCE
As of January 31, 2021

	DEBIT	CREDIT
Checking	18,037.16	
Accounts Receivable (A/R)	22,082.50	
Inventory Asset	8,868.00	
Prepaid Expenses	12,000.00	
Supplies	1,400.00	
Undeposited Funds	0.00	
Buildings:Original cost	35,000.00	
Furniture:Depreciation		10,000.00
Furniture:Original cost	71,000.00	
Machinery & Equipment:Depreciation		6,500.00
Machinery & Equipment:Original cost	115,000.00	
Investments	8,000.00	
Accounts Payable (A/P)		6,800.00
VISA		2,400.00
California State Board of Equalization ...		339.15
Payroll Tax Payable		3,954.80
Notes Payable		105,306.00
Common Stock		11,000.00
Opening Balance Equity		0.00
Retained Earnings		114,500.00
Sales		48,400.00
Sales of Product Income		3,570.00
Cost of Goods Sold	1,632.00	
Advertising & Marketing	1,800.00	
Insurance	2,400.00	
Interest Expense	120.00	
Payroll	14,680.29	
Repairs & Maintenance	750.00	
TOTAL	$312,769.95	$312,769.95

8 Investigate differences between your trial balance and the trial balance shown above.

9 If necessary, prepare and print the Transaction Detail by Account report you saved previously to investigate identified differences.

   a. Make sure all your changes were dated in January 2021.

   b. Click on the line that does not match to view the transaction for that account, and investigate why your answer differs.

   c. Ask your instructor for assistance.

   d. Be sure your company matches the above as you will be adding additional business events in Chapter 8.

Case 5

Now add some payroll activities to your company. Do not install QBO Payroll. Based on what you learned in the text using the Sample Company, you are to make the following changes to the Case 5 company you modified in Chapter 6:

1 Add two new accounts like you did in the chapter: Payroll (expense) and Payroll Tax Payable (liability).

2 Add a new employee: Jamal Hope.

3 Add a second employee: Rebecca Fairly.

4 Add a third employee: Sarah Lockwood.

5 Payroll is paid twice a month on the 15th and the last day of each month.

6 Record payroll (like you did in the chapter) for 1/15/22 based on the information shown in Figure 7.26. After recording each employee's check, be sure to designate it as a recurring transaction.

Pay/Tax/Withholding	Jamal	Rebecca	Sarah	Total
Hours if applicable	n/a	n/a	80	
Annual salary or hourly rate	$ 125,000	$ 100,000	$ 40.00	
Gross pay	5,208.33	4,166.67	3,200.00	12,575.00
Federal withholding	713.54	570.83	438.40	1,722.78
Social security employee (6.2%)	322.92	258.33	198.40	779.65
Medicare employee (1.45%)	75.52	60.42	46.40	182.34
Employee withholding	1,111.98	889.58	683.20	2,684.76
Social security employer (6.2%)	322.92	258.33	198.40	779.65
Medicare company employer (1.45%)	75.55	60.45	46.40	182.40
Employer payroll tax expense	398.47	318.78	244.80	962.05
Net Check amount	4,096.35	3,277.09	2,516.80	9,890.24

Figure 7.26

Payroll information for 1/15/22

7 Use the recurring transactions template you created above to help you record payroll (as you did in the chapter) for 1/31/22 based on the information shown in Figure 7.27. You may enter payroll for employees in any order; just keep in mind that your check numbers may not match the Transactions Detail by Account report.

Figure 7.27

Payroll information for 1/31/22

Pay/Tax/Withholding	Jamal	Rebecca	Sarah	Total
Hours if applicable	n/a	n/a	75	
Annual salary or hourly rate	$ 125,000	$ 100,000	$ 40.00	
Gross pay	**5,208.33**	**4,166.67**	**3,000.00**	**12,375.00**
Federal withholding	713.54	570.83	411.00	1,695.38
Social security employee (6.2%)	322.92	258.33	186.00	767.25
Medicare employee (1.45%)	75.52	60.42	43.50	179.44
Employee withholding	**1,111.98**	**889.58**	**640.50**	**2,642.06**
Social security employer (6.2%)	322.92	258.33	186.00	767.25
Medicare company employer (1.45%)	75.55	60.45	43.50	179.50
Employer payroll tax expense	**398.47**	**318.78**	**229.50**	**946.75**
Net Check amount	4,096.35	3,277.09	2,359.50	9,732.94

8 Prepare and print the Trial Balance 1/31/22 report you saved previously. Your report should look like Figure 7.28.

Figure 7.28

Trial Balance as of 1/31/22

TRIAL BALANCE
As of January 31, 2022

	DEBIT	CREDIT
Checking	236,795.82	
Accounts Receivable (A/R)	648,850.00	
Inventory	512,000.00	
Prepaid Expenses	22,000.00	
Undeposited Funds	0.00	
Fixed Asset Computers:Depreciation		25,000.00
Fixed Asset Computers:Original cost	280,000.00	
Fixed Asset Copiers:Original cost	25,000.00	
Fixed Asset Furniture:Depreciation		8,000.00
Fixed Asset Furniture:Original cost	80,000.00	
Investments	50,000.00	
Accounts Payable (A/P)		362,000.00
AMEX		6,300.00
Alabama Department of Revenue Payable		24,600.00
Alabama, Huntsville Payable		27,675.00
Alabama, Madison County Payable		3,075.00
Payroll Tax Payable		7,235.62
Notes Payable		580,419.00
Opening Balance Equity		0.00
Owner's Equity		457,000.00
Consulting		79,500.00
Sales		615,000.00
Training		3,500.00
Cost of Goods Sold	298,000.00	
Advertising & Marketing	3,000.00	
Equipment Rental	7,500.00	
Interest Expense	3,000.00	
Payroll	26,858.80	
Recruiting	6,300.00	
TOTAL	**$2,199,304.62**	**$2,199,304.62**

9. Investigate differences between your trial balance and the trial balance shown above.

10. If necessary, prepare and print the Transaction Detail by Account report you saved previously to investigate identified differences.

    a. Make sure all your changes were dated in January 2022.

    b. Click on the line that does not match to view the transaction for that account, and investigate why your answer differs.

    c. Ask your instructor for assistance.

    d. Be sure your company matches the above as you will be adding additional business events in Chapter 8.

Case 6

Now add some payroll activities to your company. Do not install QBO Payroll. Based on what you learned in the text using the Sample Company, you are to make the following changes to the Case 6 company you modified in Chapter 6:

1. Add two new accounts like you did in the chapter: Payroll (expense) and Payroll Tax Payable (liability).

2. Add new employees:

    a. Oliver Peters, 4737 Forest Ave SE, Mercer Island, WA, 98040, employee ID number: 1347.

    b. Rhett Brady, 1706 9th Ave SE, Puyallup, WA, 98372, employee ID number: 1348.

    c. Emelia Carlstrom, 518 Guptil Ave, Sumer, WA, 98390, employee ID number: 1349.

3. Payroll is paid twice a month on the 15th and the last day of each month.

4. Record payroll (like you did in the chapter) for 1/15/23 based on the information shown in Figure 7.29 using checks 595, 596, and 597. After recording each employee's check, be sure to designate it as a recurring transaction.

Pay/Tax/Withholding	Oliver	Rhett	Emelia
Hours if applicable	n/a	n/a	80
Annual salary or hourly rate	$ 85,000	$ 60,000	$ 35.00
Gross pay	**3,541.67**	**2,500.00**	**2,800.00**
Federal withholding	485.22	342.50	383.60
Social security employee (6.2%)	219.58	155.00	173.60
Medicare employee (1.45%)	51.35	36.25	40.60
Employee withholding	**756.15**	**533.75**	**597.80**
Social security employer (6.2%)	219.59	155.00	173.60
Medicare company employer (1.45%)	51.38	36.28	40.60
Employer payroll tax expense	**270.97**	**191.28**	**214.20**
Net Check amount	2,785.52	1,966.25	2,202.20

Figure 7.29

Payroll information for 1/15/23

180 Chapter 7 *Recording Payroll*

5. Use the recurring transactions templates you created above to help you record payroll (as you did in the chapter) for 1/31/23 based on the information shown in Figure 7.30 using checks 598, 599, and 600.

Figure 7.30

Payroll information for 1/31/23

Pay/Tax/Withholding	Oliver	Rhett	Emelia
Hours if applicable	n/a	n/a	75
Annual salary or hourly rate	$ 85,000	$ 60,000	$ 35.00
Gross pay	**3,541.67**	**2,500.00**	**2,625.00**
Federal withholding	485.22	342.50	359.63
Social security employee (6.2%)	219.58	155.00	162.75
Medicare employee (1.45%)	51.35	36.25	38.06
Employee withholding	**756.15**	**533.75**	**560.44**
Social security employer (6.2%)	219.59	155.00	162.75
Medicare company employer (1.45%)	51.38	36.28	38.06
Employer payroll tax expense	**270.97**	**191.28**	**200.81**
Net Check amount	2,785.52	1,966.25	2,064.56

6. Prepare and print the Trial Balance 1/31/23 report you saved previously. Your report should look like Figure 7.31.

Figure 7.31

Trial Balance as of 1/31/23

Case 06 - Student Name (ID Number)
TRIAL BALANCE
As of January 31, 2023

	DEBIT	CREDIT
Checking	64,336.82	
Accounts Receivable (A/R)	153,020.00	
Inventory Asset	524,000.00	
Inventory Parts	4,000.00	
Investments	12,000.00	
Loans To Officers	15,000.00	
Prepaid Expenses	18,000.00	
Undeposited Funds	0.00	
Buildings:Depreciation		15,000.00
Buildings:Original cost	150,000.00	
Computers	8,000.00	
Machinery & Equipment	12,000.00	
Machinery & Equipment:Depreciation		10,000.00
Machinery & Equipment:Original cost	100,000.00	
Accounts Payable (A/P)		524,000.00
AMEX		6,000.00
Payroll Tax Payable		5,077.55
Washington State Department of Revenue Payable		26,970.00
Notes Payable		128,857.12
Common Stock		1,100.00
Opening Balance Equity		0.00
Paid-In Capital		259,900.00
Retained Earnings		60,500.00
Sales of Product Income		290,000.00
Cost of Goods Sold	232,000.00	
Advertising & Marketing	14,000.00	
Contractors	1,800.00	
Interest Expense	400.00	
Payroll	18,847.85	
TOTAL	$1,327,404.67	$1,327,404.67

7 Investigate differences between your trial balance and the trial balance shown above.

8 If necessary, prepare and print the Transaction Detail by Account report you saved previously to investigate identified differences.

   a. Make sure all your changes were dated in January 2023.

   b. Click on the line that does not match to view the transaction for that account and investigate why your answer differs.

   c. Ask your instructor for assistance.

   d. Be sure your company matches the above as you will be adding additional business events in Chapter 8.

Chapter 8

Establishing Budgets and Preparing Bank Reconciliations

Student Learning Outcomes

Upon completion of this chapter, the student will be able to do the following:

- Add budget amounts to create a budget
- Create Profit and Loss budget reports
- Reconcile a checking account and print a reconciliation report

Overview

Intuit has provided a Sample Company online to provide new users a test-drive of its QBO product. In this chapter, you will open this Sample Company and practice budget activities in QBO and reconcile a bank account. Budgets and bank reconciliations provide internal control over business activities. Significant deviations between actual and budget amounts could identify and help resolve problems. Unexplained differences identified in bank reconciliations can point to possible fraud or incompetency issues.

Remember, if you stop in the middle of this work, none of your work will be saved. So, when you return, the same Sample Company, without your work, will appear. In some parts of the chapter, you will be asked to sign out of the Sample Company and then sign back in so the Sample Company is reset to its original state. In the end of chapter work, you will be asked to perform the same tasks completed on the Sample Company on your Student Company. That work, of course, will be saved.

Budget Creation

In this section, you will be establishing a Profit and Loss budget in QBO, which tracks amounts in income and expense accounts. QBO will interview you to determine budget amounts. You will be creating your budget from scratch since you have no historical amounts in QBO.

Establishing Budgets and Preparing Bank Reconciliations **Chapter 8** 183

To create a Profit and Loss budget for the Sample Company, do the following:

1. Open your Internet browser.
2. Type **https://qbo.intuit.com/redir/testdrive** into your browser's address text box, and press [**Enter**] to view the Sample Company Dashboard.
3. Click the **Gear** icon, and select **Budgeting** as shown in Figure 8.1.

Figure 8.1

Budgeting window (accessing the budgeting process)

4. Click **Add budget**.
5. Leave the default fiscal year provided, and type **Budget 1** as the Budget name. (The default fiscal year will change based on the date you opened the Sample Company. Thus, the dates in your QBO will not match the dates shown in the text figures for the Sample Company.)
6. Click **Next**.
7. Click in the **Design income** account, which will activate the Edit—Design income section of the worksheet.
8. Type **3000** in the Jan text box, and then place your cursor over the Copy Across button as shown in Figure 8.2.

Figure 8.2

Profit and Loss (budget worksheet)

184 Chapter 8 *Establishing Budgets and Preparing Bank Reconciliations*

9. Click the **Copy Across** button to view Figure 8.3.

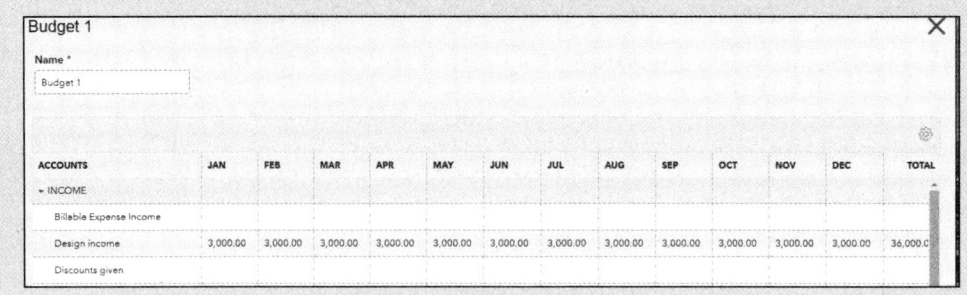

Figure 8.3

Profit and Loss (design income budget amounts)

ACCOUNTS	JAN	FEB	MAR	APR	MAY	JUN	JUL	AUG	SEP	OCT	NOV	DEC	TOTAL
▼ INCOME													
Billable Expense Income													
Design income	3,000.00	3,000.00	3,000.00	3,000.00	3,000.00	3,000.00	3,000.00	3,000.00	3,000.00	3,000.00	3,000.00	3,000.00	36,000.0
Discounts given													

10. Add additional monthly amounts in the January column for Income accounts as follows: Fountains and Garden Lighting 2000, Plants and Soil 2000, Sprinklers and Drip Systems 500, Installation 300, Maintenance and Repair 50, Pest Control Services 100, Sales of Product Income 1000, and Services 400. Copy across each amount entered above for the entire year and then click **Save**.

11. Click the **Gear** icon in the budget window then select **Year** to view by year. Place a check in the **Hide blank rows** check box and then place a check in the **Compact** check box under Display density. Your newly entered amounts are shown in Figure 8.4.

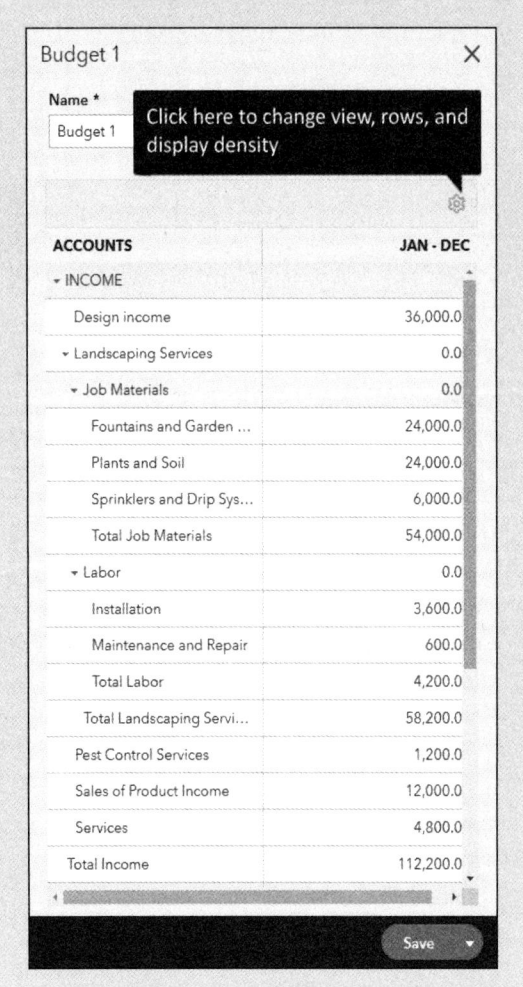

Figure 8.4

Profit and Loss (budget worksheet partial view)

ACCOUNTS	JAN - DEC
▼ INCOME	
Design income	36,000.0
▼ Landscaping Services	0.0
▼ Job Materials	0.0
Fountains and Garden ...	24,000.0
Plants and Soil	24,000.0
Sprinklers and Drip Sys...	6,000.0
Total Job Materials	54,000.0
▼ Labor	0.0
Installation	3,600.0
Maintenance and Repair	600.0
Total Labor	4,200.0
Total Landscaping Servi...	58,200.0
Pest Control Services	1,200.0
Sales of Product Income	12,000.0
Services	4,800.0
Total Income	112,200.0

Establishing Budgets and Preparing Bank Reconciliations **Chapter 8** 185

12 Click the **Gear** icon again and then click **Month** to change the view by to Month and uncheck the **Hide blank rows** checkbox.

13 Scroll down the budget worksheet, and add additional January amounts for cost of goods sold: 400, advertising: 100, automobile: 500, equipment rental: 100, insurance: 250, job expenses: 1000, legal and professional fees: 950, maintenance and repair: 900, rent or lease: 800, utilities: 500, and miscellaneous: 3000. Copy across each amount entered for the entire year. Click the **Gear** icon in the budget window then select **Year** to view by year. Place a check in the **Hide blank rows** check box.

14 Click **Save and close**.

You have entered budgeted amounts and stored them in QBO. Now, view budget reports.

Budget Reports

QBO has two basic budget-related reports: Budget Overview and Budget vs. Actual. The overview report only lists budget data. The Budget vs. Actual lists budget data compared to actual transactions inputted into QBO.

To view budget reports in the Sample Company, do the following:

1 Continue from where you left off.

2 Click the **Reports**, and type **Budget** in the Find report by name text box.

3 Select **Budget Overview**, click **Customize**, click **Rows/Columns**, select **Accounts vs. Total** from the Show Grid drop-down list, and then click **Run report**. Now click **Collapse** to view the collapsed Budget Overview report for the year as shown in Figure 8.5.

4 Click **Customize** to modify the Budget Overview report.

5 Change the From: and To: dates to the current month and year. (In this case, the new From: is 10/1/2021 and the new To: is 10/31/2021. If your current system date, today's date, is, for example, 10/8/2022, you would change the From: to 10/1/2022 and the To: to 10/31/2022.)

Figure 8.5

Budget Overview (collapsed report)

Craig's Design and Landscaping Services
Budget Overview: Budget 1 - FY21 P&L
January - December 2021

	TOTAL
▼ Income	
Design income	36,000.00
Landscaping Services	58,200.00
Pest Control Services	1,200.00
Sales of Product Income	12,000.00
Services	4,800.00
Total Income	**$112,200.00**
▼ Cost of Goods Sold	
Cost of Goods Sold	4,800.00
Total Cost of Goods Sold	**$4,800.00**
GROSS PROFIT	**$107,400.00**
▼ Expenses	
Advertising	1,200.00
Automobile	6,000.00
Equipment Rental	1,200.00
Insurance	3,000.00
Job Expenses	12,000.00
Legal & Professional Fees	11,400.00
Maintenance and Repair	10,800.00
Rent or Lease	9,600.00
Utilities	6,000.00
Total Expenses	**$61,200.00**
NET OPERATING INCOME	**$46,200.00**
▼ Other Expenses	
Miscellaneous	36,000.00
Total Other Expenses	**$36,000.00**
NET OTHER INCOME	**$ -36,000.00**
NET INCOME	**$10,200.00**

6. Check the **Without cents** check box as shown in Figure 8.6.

Figure 8.6

Customizing Budget Overview

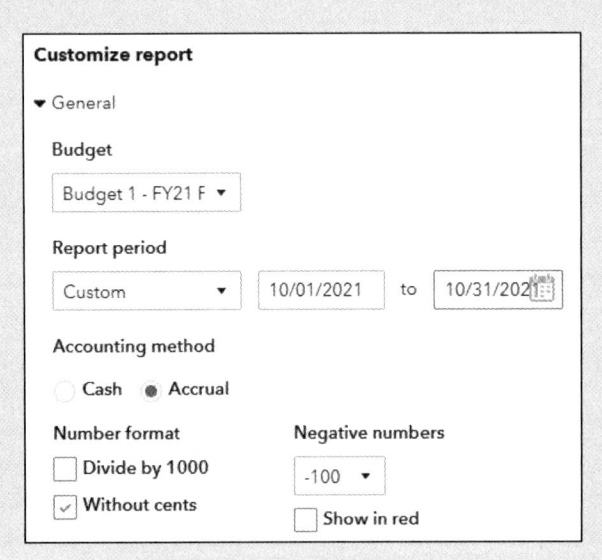

Customize report

▼ General

Budget

[Budget 1 - FY21 F ▼]

Report period

[Custom ▼] [10/01/2021] to [10/31/2021]

Accounting method

○ Cash ● Accrual

Number format   Negative numbers

☐ Divide by 1000   [-100 ▼]

☑ Without cents   ☐ Show in red

7. Click **Run report** to view the customized Budget Overview report as shown in Figure 8.7.

Figure 8.7

Budget Overview (customized report)

Craig's Design and Landscaping Services
Budget Overview: Budget 1 - FY21 P&L
October 2021

	TOTAL
▼ Income	
Design income	3,000
Landscaping Services	4,850
Pest Control Services	100
Sales of Product Income	1,000
Services	400
Total Income	**$9,350**
▼ Cost of Goods Sold	
Cost of Goods Sold	400
Total Cost of Goods Sold	**$400**
GROSS PROFIT	$8,950
▼ Expenses	
Advertising	100
Automobile	500
Equipment Rental	100
Insurance	250
Job Expenses	1,000
Legal & Professional Fees	950
Maintenance and Repair	900
Rent or Lease	800
Utilities	500
Total Expenses	**$5,100**
NET OPERATING INCOME	$3,850
▼ Other Expenses	
Miscellaneous	3,000
Total Other Expenses	**$3,000**
NET OTHER INCOME	$ -3,000
NET INCOME	$850

8   Click **Save customization**, type **Budget Overview** in the Custom report name text box, and then click **Save**.

9   Click **Reports**, once again type **Budget** into the Find report by name text box, and then select **Budget vs. Actuals** from the list of recommended reports.

10   Click **Collapse**.

11   Click **Customize** to modify the Budget vs. Actuals report.

12   Change the From: and To: dates to the first and last days of the prior month. (In this case, the new From: is 10/01/2021 and the new To: is 10/31/2021. If your current system date, today's date, is, for example, 11/8/2022, you would change the From: to 10/01/2022 and the To: to 10/31/2022.)

13   Click **Rows/Columns**, select **Accounts vs. Total** in the drop-down list in the Show Grid text box, and then check the **Without cents** check box as shown in Figure 8.8.

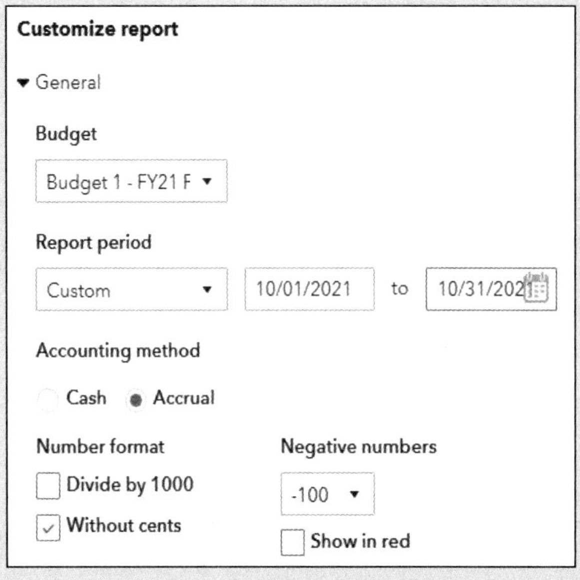

Figure 8.8

Customizing Budget vs. Actuals

Customize report

▼ General

Budget

[Budget 1 - FY21 F ▼]

Report period

[Custom ▼] [10/01/2021] to [10/31/2021]

Accounting method

○ Cash   ● Accrual

Number format   Negative numbers

☐ Divide by 1000   [-100 ▼]
☑ Without cents   ☐ Show in red

14 Click **Run report**. A partial view of the customized Budget vs. Actuals report is shown in Figure 8.9. Note: Your budget amounts should match this figure but your actual amounts will be different since the actual data changes based on when you are using the Sample Company.

Figure 8.9

Budget vs. Actual report

Craig's Design and Landscaping Services
Budget vs. Actuals: Budget 1 - FY21 P&L
October 2021

	ACTUAL	BUDGET	OVER BUDGET	% OF BUDGET
▼ Income				
Design income	1,275	3,000	-1,725	43.00 %
Discounts given	-90		-90	
Landscaping Services	4,300	4,850	-550	89.00 %
Pest Control Services	-30	100	-130	-30.00 %
Sales of Product Income	913	1,000	-87	91.00 %
Services	504	400	104	126.00 %
Total Income	**$6,872**	**$9,350**	**$ -2,478**	**73.00 %**
▼ Cost of Goods Sold				
Cost of Goods Sold	405	400	5	101.00 %
Total Cost of Goods Sold	**$405**	**$400**	**$5**	**101.00 %**
GROSS PROFIT	$6,467	$8,950	$ -2,483	72.00 %
▼ Expenses				
Advertising	75	100	-25	75.00 %
Automobile	293	500	-207	59.00 %
Equipment Rental	112	100	12	112.00 %
Insurance	241	250	-9	96.00 %
Job Expenses	603	1,000	-397	60.00 %
Legal & Professional Fees	565	950	-385	59.00 %
Maintenance and Repair	940	900	40	104.00 %
Meals and Entertainment	28		28	
Office Expenses	18		18	
Rent or Lease	900	800	100	113.00 %
Utilities	188	500	-312	38.00 %
Total Expenses	**$3,964**	**$5,100**	**$ -1,136**	**78.00 %**
NET OPERATING INCOME	$2,503	$3,850	$ -1,347	65.00 %
▼ Other Expenses				
Miscellaneous	2,666	3,000	-334	89.00 %
Total Other Expenses	**$2,666**	**$3,000**	**$ -334**	**89.00 %**
NET OTHER INCOME	$ -2,666	$ -3,000	$334	89.00 %
NET INCOME	$ -163	$850	$ -1,013	-19.00 %

15 Click **Save customization**, type **Budget vs. Actuals** in the Custom report name text box, and then click **Save**.

16 Sign out of the Sample Company.

Bank Reconciliation

Good internal control requires frequent reconciliations between bank records and a company's records of cash receipts and payments completed by someone other than the accountant or bookkeeper who is responsible for maintaining accounting records. The process involves comparing items that appear in the checking account with those items appearing on the bank statement. Deposits that appear in the checking account but do not appear on the bank statement are referred to as deposits in transit. Checks that appear in the checking account but do not appear on the bank statement are referred to as outstanding checks. They usually appear as checks on the next bank statement.

In QBO, if you discover a deposit recorded by the bank but not recorded in the checking account (determined to be an error in the checking account), you should correct the checking account by recording the deposit. Likewise, if you discover a check recorded by the bank but not recorded in the checking account (determined to be an error in the checking account), you should correct the checking account by recording the check. In the following example, neither was identified.

To create reconciliation for the Sample Company, do the following:

1 Open your Internet browser.

2 Type **https://qbo.intuit.com/redir/testdrive** into your browser's address text box, and press [**Enter**] to view the Sample Company Dashboard.

3 Click the **Gear** icon, and select **Reconcile** as shown in Figure 8.10.

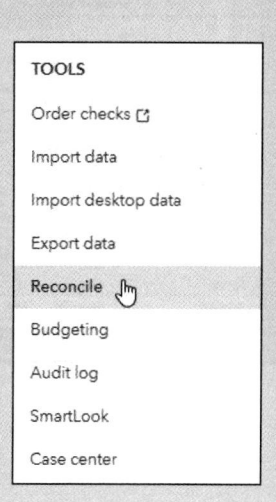

Figure 8.10

Reconciliation process (access)

Case 1

Now it is time to create a budget and reconcile a bank account. Based on what you learned in the text using the Sample Company, you are to make the following changes to the Case 1 company you modified in Chapter 7:

1. Add an invoice on 1/30/24 to customer: Blondie's Boards, terms: Net 30, for 4 Fred Rubbles, 7 Water Hogs, and 8 Rook 15 surfboards.

2. Add an invoice on 1/31/24 to a new customer: Surf Rider Foundation, terms: Net 30, for 100 hours of consulting.

3. Create a new budget titled "Budget 1." Be sure to select FY 2024 (Jan 2024–Dec 2024) from the Fiscal Year drop-down list in the new budget window. Enter the following budgeted amounts: sales: 40000, services: 3000, cost of goods sold: 23500, interest expense: 600, payroll: 12000, rent or lease: 2500, travel: 500, and utilities: 200. Amounts provided should be input for each month of 2024.

4. Create and customize, save customization as Budget Overview Budget 1, print, and export to Excel a Budget Overview report for the month of January 2024. Your report should look like Figure 8.16.

Figure 8.16

Budget Overview (January 2024)

Case 1
BUDGET OVERVIEW: BUDGET 1 - FY24 P&L
January 2024

	TOTAL
Income	
Sales	40,000.00
Services	3,000.00
Total Income	**$43,000.00**
Cost of Goods Sold	
Cost of Goods Sold	23,500.00
Total Cost of Goods Sold	**$23,500.00**
Gross Profit	**$19,500.00**
Expenses	
Interest Expense	600.00
Payroll	12,000.00
Rent or Lease	2,500.00
Travel	500.00
Utilities	200.00
Total Expenses	**$15,800.00**
Net Operating Income	**$3,700.00**
Net Income	**$3,700.00**

5. Create and customize, save customization as Budget vs. Actual Budget 1, print, and export to Excel a Budget vs. Actuals report for the month of January 2024. Your report should look like Figure 8.17.

Figure 8.17

Budget vs. Actuals (January 2024)

Case 1
BUDGET VS. ACTUALS: BUDGET 1 - FY24 P&L
January 2024

	ACTUAL	BUDGET	OVER BUDGET	% OF BUDGET
Income				
Sales	17,180.00	40,000.00	-22,820.00	42.95 %
Services	2,670.00	3,000.00	-330.00	89.00 %
Total Income	**$19,850.00**	**$43,000.00**	**$ -23,150.00**	**46.16 %**
Cost of Goods Sold				
Cost of Goods Sold	10,400.00	23,500.00	-13,100.00	44.26 %
Total Cost of Goods Sold	**$10,400.00**	**$23,500.00**	**$ -13,100.00**	**44.26 %**
Gross Profit	**$9,450.00**	**$19,500.00**	**$ -10,050.00**	**48.46 %**
Expenses				
Interest Expense	600.00	600.00	0.00	100.00 %
Payroll	11,785.71	12,000.00	-214.29	98.21 %
Rent or Lease	2,500.00	2,500.00	0.00	100.00 %
Travel	1,800.00	500.00	1,300.00	360.00 %
Utilities	145.00	200.00	-55.00	72.50 %
Total Expenses	**$16,830.71**	**$15,800.00**	**$1,030.71**	**106.52 %**
Net Operating Income	**$ -7,380.71**	**$3,700.00**	**$ -11,080.71**	**-199.48 %**
Net Income	**$ -7,380.71**	**$3,700.00**	**$ -11,080.71**	**-199.48 %**

6 Open and print the custom report you created in the last chapter called Transaction Detail by Account.

7 Export your Transactions Detail by Account report to Excel, and save it with the file name Student Name (replace with your name) Ch 08 Case 01 Transaction Detail by Account.xlsx.

8 Reconcile your company's checking account. No service charges were incurred or interest earned. The ending bank statement balance on 1/31/24 was $29,202.37.

9 After a review of the company's most recent bank statement and a comparison with the company's checking account, you discover some checks and payments recorded in the checking account that did not appear on the bank statement. Place a check next to all checks and payments *except* for check 1009 to Ben Franklin for 3,113.22 and check 1010 to Betsy Ross for 1,149.87, neither of which had cleared the bank.

10 After a review of the company's most recent bank statement and a comparison with the company's checking account, you discover some deposits and other credits recorded in the checking account that did not appear on the bank statement. Place a check next to all deposits and other credits *except* for a deposit on 1/8/24 from Blondie's Boards for 1,300, which had not cleared the bank.

11 Print the resulting Reconciliation Report. Select **All dates** from the Report Period drop-down text box, then click **2024**, and then click **View Report** on the statement ending date 01/31/24 line.

12 Sign out of your company.

Case 2

Now it is time to create a budget and reconcile a bank account. Based on what you learned in the text using the Sample Company, you are to make the following changes to the Case 2 company you modified in Chapter 7:

1. Add an invoice on 1/30/25 to customer: Hagen's Toys, terms: Net 30, for 100 hours of custom painting.

2. Add an invoice on 1/31/25 to a new customer: Zack's RC, terms: Net 30, for 2 Sea Wind Carbon Sailboats and 2 Mystique RES.

3. Create a new budget titled "Budget 1." Be sure to select FY 2025 (Jan 2025–Dec 2025) from the Fiscal Year drop-down list in the new budget window. Enter the following budgeted amounts: sales: 10,000, services: 4,000, cost of goods sold: 5,000, advertising: 500, insurance: 425, interest expense: 300, meals and entertainment: 250, and payroll: 9,000. Amounts provided should be input for each month of 2025.

4. Create and customize, save customization as Budget Overview Budget 1, print, and export to Excel a Budget Overview report for the month of January 2025. Your report should look like Figure 8.18.

Figure 8.18

Budget Overview (January 2025)

Case 2
BUDGET OVERVIEW: BUDGET 1 - FY25 P&L
January 2025

	TOTAL
Income	
Sales	10,000.00
Services	4,000.00
Total Income	**$14,000.00**
Cost of Goods Sold	
Cost of Goods Sold	5,000.00
Total Cost of Goods Sold	**$5,000.00**
Gross Profit	**$9,000.00**
Expenses	
Advertising	500.00
Insurance	425.00
Interest Expense	300.00
Meals and Entertainment	250.00
Payroll	9,000.00
Total Expenses	**$10,475.00**
Net Operating Income	**$ -1,475.00**
Net Income	**$ -1,475.00**

5. Create and customize, save customization as Budget vs. Actuals Budget 1, print, and export to Excel a Budget vs. Actuals report for the month of January 2025. Your report should look like Figure 8.19.

Figure 8.19

Budget vs. Actuals (January 2025)

Case 2
BUDGET VS. ACTUALS: BUDGET 1 - FY25 P&L
January 2025

	ACTUAL	BUDGET	OVER BUDGET	% OF BUDGET
Income				
Sales	9,000.00	10,000.00	-1,000.00	90.00 %
Services	4,725.00	4,000.00	725.00	118.13 %
Total Income	**$13,725.00**	**$14,000.00**	**$ -275.00**	**98.04 %**
Cost of Goods Sold				
Cost of Goods Sold	4,910.00	5,000.00	-90.00	98.20 %
Total Cost of Goods Sold	**$4,910.00**	**$5,000.00**	**$ -90.00**	**98.20 %**
Gross Profit	**$8,815.00**	**$9,000.00**	**$ -185.00**	**97.94 %**
Expenses				
Advertising	500.00	500.00	0.00	100.00 %
Insurance	400.00	425.00	-25.00	94.12 %
Interest Expense	300.00	300.00	0.00	100.00 %
Meals and Entertainment	240.00	250.00	-10.00	96.00 %
Payroll	9,224.26	9,000.00	224.26	102.49 %
Total Expenses	**$10,664.26**	**$10,475.00**	**$189.26**	**101.81 %**
Net Operating Income	**$ -1,849.26**	**$ -1,475.00**	**$ -374.26**	**125.37 %**
Net Income	**$ -1,849.26**	**$ -1,475.00**	**$ -374.26**	**125.37 %**

6 Open and print the custom report you created in the last chapter called Transaction Detail by Account.

7 Export your Transactions Detail by Account report to Excel, and save it with the file name Student Name (replace with your name) Ch 08 Case 02 Transaction Detail by Account.xlsx.

8 Reconcile your company's checking account. No service charges were incurred or interest earned. The ending bank statement balance on 1/31/25 was $30,693.47.

9 After a review of the company's most recent bank statement and a comparison with the company's checking account, you discover some checks and payments recorded in the checking account that did not appear on the bank statement. Place a check next to all checks and payments *except* for check 1009 to Frank Benjamin for 2,359.50 and check 1010 to Sara Juarez for 973.29, neither of which had cleared the bank.

10 After a review of the company's most recent bank statement and a comparison with the company's checking account, you discover a deposit and other credit recorded in the checking account that did not appear on the bank statement. Place a check next to all deposits and other credits *except* for a deposit on 1/7/25 from Benson's RC for 4,500, which had not cleared the bank.

11 Print the resulting Reconciliation Report. Select **All dates** from the Report Period drop-down text box, then click **2025**, and then click **View Report** on the statement ending date 01/31/25 line.

12 Sign out of your company.

Case 3

Now it is time to create a budget and reconcile a bank account. Based on what you learned in the text using the Sample Company, you are to make the following changes to the Case 3 company you modified in Chapter 7:

1. Add the following bill and product received from Samsung, Inc. on 1/30/26, terms: Net 15, received 5 Samsung Galaxy 8 and 8 Samsung Note phones.

2. Add an invoice on 1/30/26 to a new taxable customer: Diamond Girl, Inc., terms: Net 30, for 4 Samsung Galaxy 8 and 5 Samsung Note phones and 6 hours of Phone Consulting. Click **See the math** to update sales tax amounts.

3. Add a payment received from GHO Marketing on 1/31/26 for $2,559.38, which was deposited the same day into the checking account.

4. Create a new budget titled "Budget 1." Be sure to select FY 2026 (Jan 2026–Dec 2026) from the Fiscal Year drop-down list in the new budget window. Enter the following budgeted amounts: sales of product income: 20,000, services: 1,000, cost of goods sold: 10,000, advertising & marketing: 1,000, insurance: 500, interest paid: 350, meals: 250, and payroll: 7,000. Amounts provided should be input for each month of 2026.

5. Create a Budget Overview report for January 2026. Customize your report to show accounts vs. totals. Save customization as Budget Overview. Your report should look like Figure 8.20.

Figure 8.20

Budget Overview (January 2026)

Case 03 - Student Name (ID Number)
Budget Overview: Budget 1 - FY26 P&L
January 2026

	TOTAL
▼ Income	
Sales of Product Income	20,000.00
Services	1,000.00
Total Income	**$21,000.00**
▼ Cost of Goods Sold	
Cost of goods sold	10,000.00
Total Cost of Goods Sold	**$10,000.00**
GROSS PROFIT	$11,000.00
▼ Expenses	
Advertising & marketing	1,000.00
Insurance	500.00
Interest paid	350.00
Meals	250.00
Payroll	7,000.00
Total Expenses	**$9,100.00**
NET OPERATING INCOME	$1,900.00
NET INCOME	$1,900.00

6 Create a Budget vs. Actuals report for the month of January 2026. Customize and save your report to show accounts vs. totals without cents. Your report should look like Figure 8.21.

Case 03 - Student Name (ID Number)
Budget vs. Actuals: Budget 1 - FY26 P&L
January 2026

	ACTUAL	BUDGET	OVER BUDGET	% OF BUDGET
▼ Income				
Sales of Product Income	12,800	20,000	-7,200	64.00 %
Services	450	1,000	-550	45.00 %
Total Income	**$13,250**	**$21,000**	**$ -7,750**	**63.00 %**
▼ Cost of Goods Sold				
Cost of goods sold	9,150	10,000	-850	92.00 %
Total Cost of Goods Sold	**$9,150**	**$10,000**	**$ -850**	**92.00 %**
GROSS PROFIT	**$4,100**	**$11,000**	**$ -6,900**	**37.00 %**
▼ Expenses				
Advertising & marketing	1,300	1,000	300	130.00 %
Insurance	300	500	-200	60.00 %
Interest paid	300	350	-50	86.00 %
Meals	123	250	-127	49.00 %
Payroll	6,960	7,000	-40	99.00 %
Total Expenses	**$8,983**	**$9,100**	**$ -117**	**99.00 %**
NET OPERATING INCOME	$ -4,883	$1,900	$ -6,783	-257.00 %
NET INCOME	$ -4,883	$1,900	$ -6,783	-257.00 %

Figure 8.21

Budget vs. Actuals for January 2026

7 Reconcile your company's checking account. No service charges were incurred or interest earned. The ending bank statement balance on 1/31/26 was $51,669.82.

8 After a review of the company's most recent statement and a comparison with the company's checking account, you note that one check and one deposit that were recorded in the checking account did not appear on the bank statement. Place a check next to all checks and payments *except* for check 329 to Jedi Vu for 1,002.78 and the deposit from GHO Marketing for 2,559.38, which had not cleared the bank.

9 Print the resulting Reconciliation Report after hiding additional information.

10 Sign out of your company.

Case 4

Now it is time to create a budget and reconcile a bank account. Based on what you learned in the text using the Sample Company, you are to make the following changes to the Case 4 company you modified in Chapter 7:

1. Create a new budget titled "Budget 1." Be sure to select FY 2021 (Jan 2021–Dec 2021) from the Fiscal Year drop-down list in the new budget window. Enter the following budgeted amounts for 2021: sales: 50,000, sales of product income: 4,000, cost of goods sold: 1,500, advertising & marketing: 2,400, insurance: 2,000, interest expense: 300, payroll: 15,000, and repairs & maintenance: $500. Amounts provided should be input for each month of 2021.

2. Create, customize (save customization as Budget Overview), and print a Budget Overview report for the month of January 2021 without cents showing accounts vs. totals. Your report should look like Figure 8.22.

Figure 8.22

Budget Overview for January 2021

Case 04 - Student Name (ID Number)

BUDGET OVERVIEW: BUDGET 1 - FY21 P&L

January 2021

	TOTAL
▼ Income	
Sales	50,000
Sales of Product Income	4,000
Total Income	**$54,000**
▼ Cost of Goods Sold	
Cost of Goods Sold	1,500
Total Cost of Goods Sold	**$1,500**
GROSS PROFIT	$52,500
▼ Expenses	
Advertising & Marketing	2,400
Insurance	2,000
Interest Expense	300
Payroll	15,000
Repairs & Maintenance	500
Total Expenses	**$20,200**
NET OPERATING INCOME	$32,300
NET INCOME	$32,300

3. Create, customize (save customization as Budget vs. Actuals), and print a Budget vs. Actuals report for the month of January 2021 without cents showing accounts vs. totals. Your report should look like Figure 8.23.

Figure 8.23

Budget vs. Actuals for January 2021

Case 04 - Student Name (ID Number)

BUDGET VS. ACTUALS: BUDGET 1 - FY21 P&L
January 2021

	ACTUAL	BUDGET	OVER BUDGET	% OF BUDGET
▼ Income				
Sales	48,400	50,000	-1,600	97.00 %
Sales of Product Income	3,570	4,000	-430	89.00 %
Total Income	**$51,970**	**$54,000**	**$ -2,030**	**96.00 %**
▼ Cost of Goods Sold				
Cost of Goods Sold	1,632	1,500	132	109.00 %
Total Cost of Goods Sold	**$1,632**	**$1,500**	**$132**	**109.00 %**
GROSS PROFIT	$50,338	$52,500	$ -2,162	96.00 %
▼ Expenses				
Advertising & Marketing	1,800	2,400	-600	75.00 %
Insurance	2,400	2,000	400	120.00 %
Interest Expense	120	300	-180	40.00 %
Payroll	14,680	15,000	-320	98.00 %
Repairs & Maintenance	750	500	250	150.00 %
Total Expenses	**$19,750**	**$20,200**	**$ -450**	**98.00 %**
NET OPERATING INCOME	$30,588	$32,300	$ -1,712	95.00 %
NET INCOME	$30,588	$32,300	$ -1,712	95.00 %

4. Reconcile your company's checking account. No service charges were incurred or interest earned. The ending bank statement balance on 1/31/21 was $10,936.19.

5. After a review of the company's most recent statement and a comparison with the company's checking account, you note that a $10,000 deposit on 1/26/21 and checks 25509 and 25510 (for $1,376.37 and $1,522.66 respectfully) had not cleared the bank.

6. Print the resulting Reconciliation Report. Select **All dates** from the Report Period drop-down text box, then click **2021**, and then click **View Report** on the statement ending date 01/31/21 line.

7. Sign out of your company.

Case 5

Now it is time to create a budget and reconcile a bank account. Based on what you learned in the text using the Sample Company, you are to make the following changes to the Case 5 company you modified in Chapter 7:

1. Create a new budget titled "Budget 1." Be sure to select FY 2022 (Jan 2022–Dec 2022) from the Fiscal Year drop-down list in the new budget window. Enter the following budgeted amounts for January 2022: consulting: 75,000, sales: 500,000, training: 4,000, cost of goods sold: 250,000, advertising & marketing: 3,500, equipment rental: 8,000, insurance: 6,000, interest expense: 4,000, payroll: 30,000, recruiting: 4,000, and repairs & maintenance: $2,500. Amounts provided should be copied for each month of 2022.

2. Create, customize (save customization as Budget Overview), and print a Budget Overview report for the month of January 2022 without cents showing accounts vs. totals. Your report should look like Figure 8.24.

Figure 8.24

Budget Overview for January 2022

Case 05 - Student Name (ID Number)

BUDGET OVERVIEW: BUDGET 1 - FY22 P&L

January 2022

	TOTAL
▼ Income	
Consulting	75,000
Sales	500,000
Training	4,000
Total Income	**$579,000**
▼ Cost of Goods Sold	
Cost of Goods Sold	250,000
Total Cost of Goods Sold	**$250,000**
GROSS PROFIT	$329,000
▼ Expenses	
Advertising & Marketing	3,500
Equipment Rental	8,000
Insurance	6,000
Interest Expense	4,000
Payroll	30,000
Recruiting	4,000
Repairs & Maintenance	2,500
Total Expenses	**$58,000**
NET OPERATING INCOME	$271,000
NET INCOME	$271,000

3. Create, customize (save customization as Budget vs. Actuals), and print a Budget vs. Actuals report for the month of January 2022 without cents showing accounts vs. totals. Your report should look like Figure 8.25.

4. Reconcile your company's checking account. No service charges were incurred or interest earned. The ending bank statement balance on 1/31/22 was $194,109.76.

5. After a review of the company's most recent statement and a comparison with the company's checking account, you note that a $80,000 deposit on 1/26/22 and all checks written on 1/31/22 had not cleared the bank.

Figure 8.25

Budget vs. Actuals for January 2022

Case 05 - Student Name (ID Number)
BUDGET VS. ACTUALS: BUDGET 1 - FY22 P&L
January 2022

	ACTUAL	BUDGET	OVER BUDGET	% OF BUDGET
Income				
Consulting	79,500	75,000	4,500	106.00 %
Sales	615,000	500,000	115,000	123.00 %
Training	3,500	4,000	-500	88.00 %
Total Income	**$698,000**	**$579,000**	**$119,000**	**121.00 %**
Cost of Goods Sold				
Cost of Goods Sold	298,000	250,000	48,000	119.00 %
Total Cost of Goods Sold	**$298,000**	**$250,000**	**$48,000**	**119.00 %**
GROSS PROFIT	**$400,000**	**$329,000**	**$71,000**	**122.00 %**
Expenses				
Advertising & Marketing	3,000	3,500	-500	86.00 %
Equipment Rental	7,500	8,000	-500	94.00 %
Insurance		6,000	-6,000	
Interest Expense	3,000	4,000	-1,000	75.00 %
Payroll	26,859	30,000	-3,141	90.00 %
Recruiting	6,300	4,000	2,300	158.00 %
Repairs & Maintenance		2,500	-2,500	
Total Expenses	**$46,659**	**$58,000**	**$ -11,341**	**80.00 %**
NET OPERATING INCOME	**$353,341**	**$271,000**	**$82,341**	**130.00 %**
NET INCOME	**$353,341**	**$271,000**	**$82,341**	**130.00 %**

6 Print the resulting Reconciliation Report. Select **All dates** from the Report Period drop-down text box, then click **2022**, and then click **View Report** on the statement ending date 01/31/22 line. A partial view of that report should look like Figure 8.26.

Figure 8.26

Bank Reconciliation as of 1/31/22 (partial view)

Case 05 - Student Name (ID Number)
Checking, Period Ending 01/31/2022

RECONCILIATION REPORT

Any changes made to transactions after this date aren't included in this report.

Summary	USD
Statement beginning balance	30,000.00
Checks and payments cleared (8)	-115,390.24
Deposits and other credits cleared (3)	279,500.00
Statement ending balance	194,109.76
Uncleared transactions as of 01/31/2022	42,686.06
Register balance as of 01/31/2022	236,795.82

7 Sign out of your company.

Case 6

Now it is time to create a budget and reconcile a bank account. Based on what you learned in the text using the Sample Company, you are to make the following changes to the Case 6 company you modified in Chapter 7:

1. Create a new budget titled "Budget 1." Be sure to select FY 2023 (Jan 2023–Dec 2023) from the Fiscal Year drop-down list in the new budget window. Enter the following budgeted amounts for 2023: sales: 10,000, sales of product income: 300,000, cost of goods sold: 230,000, advertising & marketing: 15,000, contractors: 2,000, insurance: 3,000, interest expense: 500, payroll: 20,000, repairs: 500, and depreciation: 1,000. Amounts provided should be input for each month of 2023.

2. Create, customize (save customization as Budget Overview), and print a Budget Overview report for the month of January 2023 without cents showing accounts vs. totals. Your report should look like Figure 8.27

Figure 8.27

Budget Overview for January 2023

Case 06 - Student Name (ID Number)

BUDGET OVERVIEW: BUDGET 1 - FY23 P&L

January 2023

	TOTAL
▼ Income	
Sales	10,000
Sales of Product Income	300,000
Total Income	**$310,000**
▼ Cost of Goods Sold	
Cost of Goods Sold	230,000
Total Cost of Goods Sold	**$230,000**
GROSS PROFIT	$80,000
▼ Expenses	
Advertising & Marketing	15,000
Contractors	2,000
Insurance	3,000
Interest Expense	500
Payroll	20,000
Repairs	500
Total Expenses	**$41,000**
NET OPERATING INCOME	$39,000
▼ Other Expenses	
Depreciation	1,000
Total Other Expenses	**$1,000**
NET OTHER INCOME	$ -1,000
NET INCOME	$38,000

3   Create, customize (save customization as Budget vs. Actuals), and print a Budget vs. Actuals report for the month of January 2023 without cents showing accounts vs. totals. Your report should look like Figure 8.28.

Figure 8.28

Budget vs. Actuals for January 2023

Case 06 - Student Name (ID Number)
BUDGET VS. ACTUALS: BUDGET 1 - FY23 P&L
January 2023

	TOTAL			
	ACTUAL	BUDGET	OVER BUDGET	% OF BUDGET
▼ Income				
Sales		10,000	-10,000	
Sales of Product Income	290,000	300,000	-10,000	97.00 %
Total Income	**$290,000**	**$310,000**	**$ -20,000**	**94.00 %**
▼ Cost of Goods Sold				
Cost of Goods Sold	232,000	230,000	2,000	101.00 %
Total Cost of Goods Sold	**$232,000**	**$230,000**	**$2,000**	**101.00 %**
GROSS PROFIT	$58,000	$80,000	$ -22,000	73.00 %
▼ Expenses				
Advertising & Marketing	14,000	15,000	-1,000	93.00 %
Contractors	1,800	2,000	-200	90.00 %
Insurance		3,000	-3,000	
Interest Expense	400	500	-100	80.00 %
Payroll	18,848	20,000	-1,152	94.00 %
Repairs		500	-500	
Total Expenses	**$35,048**	**$41,000**	**$ -5,952**	**85.00 %**
NET OPERATING INCOME	$22,952	$39,000	$ -16,048	59.00 %
▼ Other Expenses				
Depreciation		1,000	-1,000	
Total Other Expenses	**$0**	**$1,000**	**$ -1,000**	**0%**
NET OTHER INCOME	$0	$ -1,000	$1,000	0.00 %
NET INCOME	$22,952	$38,000	$ -15,048	60.00 %

4   Reconcile your company's checking account. No service charges were incurred or interest earned. The ending bank statement balance on 1/31/23 was $65,196.03.

5   After a review of the company's most recent statement and a comparison with the company's checking account, you note that a $10,000 deposit on 1/26/23 and checks 593, 594, 598, 599, and 600 had not cleared the bank.

6   Print the resulting Reconciliation Report.

7   Sign out of your company.

Chapter 9

Analysis and Recording of Adjusting Entries

Student Learning Outcomes

Upon completion of this chapter, the student will be able to do the following:

- Prepare an unadjusted trial balance
- Make adjusting entries for the following:
  - Prepaid expenses
  - Accrued expenses
  - Unearned revenue
  - Accrued revenue
  - Depreciation

Overview

Intuit has provided a Sample Company online to let new users test-drive its QBO product. In this chapter, you will open this Sample Company and practice adjusting entry activities in QBO. Prior to the creation of periodic financial statements, generally accepted accounting principles (GAAP) require that accounting records be adjusted to reflect accrual accounting. This process insures revenues are recorded in the period in which they are earned and that expenses are recorded in the period in which they were consumed. In the process, expenses will be matched in the same period to the revenues generated from incurring those expenses.

There are five types of adjusting entries. Expenses paid, prior to being consumed, should be deferred (supplies, rent, insurance, etc.) and recorded as assets (supplies asset, prepaid rent, prepaid insurance, etc.) until they are consumed. To defer is to postpone. Expenses incurred prior to being paid (payroll, rent, utilities, etc.) must be recorded and accrued as a liability. To accrue is to increase. Revenue collected prior to being earned must be deferred (sales, services, etc.) and recorded as liabilities (unearned revenue, etc.) until they are earned. Revenues earned prior to being collected (sales and services, etc.) must be recorded and accrued as a receivable. Lastly, fixed assets (buildings, furniture, equipment, vehicles, etc.) must be depreciated over their useful life to match costs with revenues.

Remember, if you stop in the middle of this work, none of your work will be saved. So, when you return, the same Sample Company, without your work, will appear. In some parts of the chapter, you will be asked to sign out of the Sample Company and sign back in so the Sample Company is reset to its original state. In the end of chapter work, you will be asked to perform the same tasks completed on the Sample Company on your Student Company. That work, of course, will be saved.

Trial Balance

In this section, you will create a trial balance (before adjusting entries), which must be analyzed in light of end of the period business events to determine the required adjusting entries.

> **To create a trial balance for the Sample Company, do the following:**
>
> 1 Open your Internet browser.
>
> 2 Type **https://qbo.intuit.com/redir/testdrive** into your browser's address text box and then press [**Enter**] to view the Sample Company Dashboard.
>
> 3 Click **Reports** from the navigation bar.
>
> 4 Type **Trial Balance** in the Find report by name search box and then select **Trial Balance** from the drop-down list provided.
>
> 5 Change the From: date to the first of the previous month and the To: date to the last day of the previous month (in this case, 10/01/2021 and 10/31/2021; your date will be different as will your amounts), and then click **Run Report** to see a partial view of the trial balance as shown in Figure 9.1.

Figure 9.1

Trial Balance report (partial view)

Craig's Design and Landscaping Services
Trial Balance
As of October 31, 2021

	DEBIT	CREDIT
Checking	2,101.00	
Savings	800.00	
Accounts Receivable (A/R)	5,281.52	
Inventory Asset	596.25	
Undeposited Funds	2,062.52	
Truck:Original Cost	13,495.00	
Accounts Payable (A/P)		1,602.67
Mastercard		1,003.73
Arizona Dept. of Revenue Payable		0.00
Board of Equalization Payable		370.94
Loan Payable		4,000.00
Notes Payable		25,000.00
Opening Balance Equity	9,337.50	
Design income		2,250.00
Discounts given	89.50	
Landscaping Services		1,477.50
Landscaping Services:Job Materials:Fountains and G...		2,246.50
Landscaping Services:Job Materials:Plants and Soil		2,351.97
Landscaping Services:Job Materials:Sprinklers and D...		138.00
Landscaping Services:Labor:Installation		250.00
Landscaping Services:Labor:Maintenance and Repair		50.00
Pest Control Services		110.00
Sales of Product Income		912.75
Services		503.55

Adjusting Journal Entries: Prepaid Expenses

Further investigation of this trial balance and period end business activities indicates that $500 of supplies were recorded as a miscellaneous expense but should have been deferred as a supplies asset until consumed in some future period. Thus, an adjusting entry is necessary.

To record an adjusting entry for supplies in the Sample Company, do the following:

1. Continue from where you left off. If you closed the Sample Company, follow the steps to reopen it found at the beginning of this chapter.
2. Click the **+ New** icon and then click **Journal Entry**.
3. Type the last day of the previous month into the Journal date text box (in this case, 10/31/2021).
4. Type **Supplies Asset** on line 1 of the Account column, and click **+ Add Supplies Asset** as shown in Figure 9.2. (This is another way to add a new account in QBO.)

Figure 9.2

Journal entry (adding a new account)

Journal date	Journal no.
10/31/2021	1

#	ACCOUNT	DEBITS	CREDITS	DESCRIPTION
1	Supplies Asset			
2	+ Add Supplies Asset			

5. Select **Other Current Assets** from the drop-down list in the Account Type text box.
6. Select **Other Current Assets** from the drop-down list in the Detail Type text box.
7. Click **Save and close**.
8. Type **500** into the Debits column of line 1.
9. Select **Miscellaneous** from the drop-down list in line 2 of the Accounts column.
10. Accept **500** into the Credits column of line 2 and then press **[Tab]** to view the journal entry as shown in Figure 9.3.

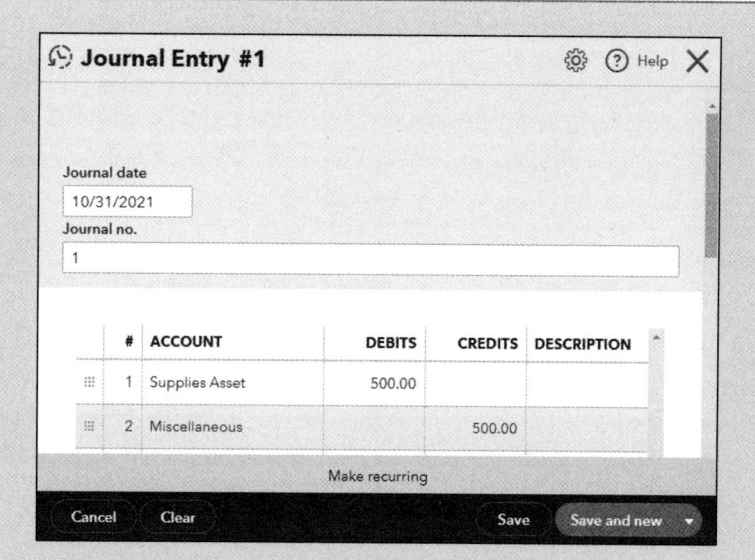

Analysis and Recording of Adjusting Entries **Chapter 9** 209

Figure 9.3

Journal Entry #1 (to defer supplies)

Journal Entry #1

Journal date: 10/31/2021
Journal no.: 1

#	ACCOUNT	DEBITS	CREDITS	DESCRIPTION
1	Supplies Asset	500.00		
2	Miscellaneous		500.00	

11 Click **Save and close**.

The same process could be used to defer a cost that had been recorded as an expense but should be deferred as an asset at period end. Examples might include insurance to be deferred as either prepaid insurance or prepaid expenses or rent to be deferred as either prepaid rent or prepaid expenses.

Another example of this occurs when an expense is deferred in a prior period but is consumed in the current period. We will use the Supplies Asset created as an example assuming $100 of supplies were consumed in the month leaving $400 of supplies as an asset.

To record an adjusting journal entry to record the consumption of supplies, do the following:

1. Continue from where you left off. If you closed the Sample Company, follow the steps to reopen it found at the beginning of this chapter.

2. Click the **+ New** icon and then click **Journal Entry**.

3. Type the last day of the previous month into the Journal date text box (in this case, 10/31/2021).

4. Select **Supplies** from the drop-down list in line 1 of the Account column. (This is an expense account already in the Company's chart of accounts.)

5. Type **100** into the Debits column of line 1.

6. Select **Supplies Asset** from the drop-down list in line 2 of the Accounts column.

7. Accept **100** into the Credits column of line 2 to view the journal entry as shown in Figure 9.4.

Figure 9.4

Journal entry (recording the consumption of supplies)

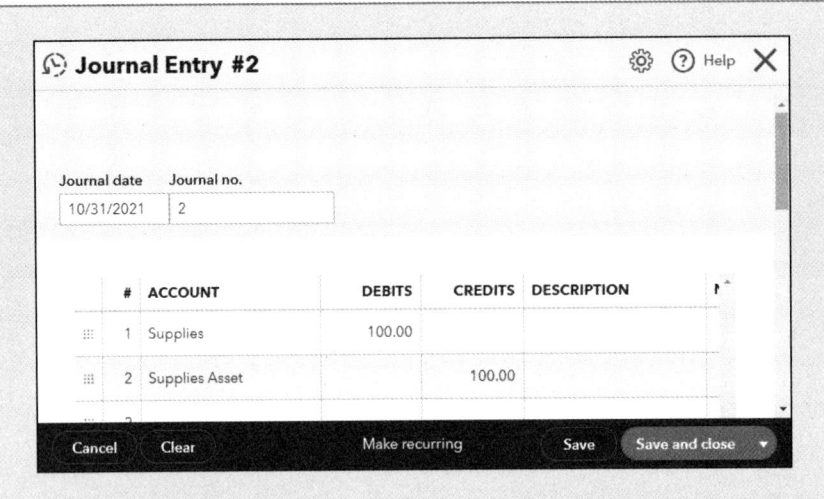

#	ACCOUNT	DEBITS	CREDITS	DESCRIPTION
1	Supplies	100.00		
2	Supplies Asset		100.00	

Journal date: 10/31/2021   Journal no.: 2

8 Click **Save and close**.

9 Closing the journal entry should reveal the trial balance created before. Make sure the custom dates reflect the prior month (in this case, 10/01/2021 to 10/31/2021). The trial balance has now been updated to reflect the supplies asset account as shown in Figure 9.5.

Figure 9.5

Trial Balance after supplies adjustments (partial view)

Craig's Design and Landscaping Services
Trial Balance
As of October 31, 2021

	DEBIT	CREDIT
Checking	2,101.00	
Savings	800.00	
Accounts Receivable (A/R)	5,281.52	
Inventory Asset	596.25	
Supplies Asset	400.00	
Undeposited Funds	2,062.52	
Truck:Original Cost	13,495.00	

10 Click the Supplies Asset **400** amount, (if necessary) adjust the report period like you've done previously, and then click **Run Report** to reveal a Transaction Report for the Supplies Asset account as shown in Figure 9.6.

11 Click **Back to report summary** to return to the Trial Balance report.

Figure 9.6

Transaction Report (for supplies asset)

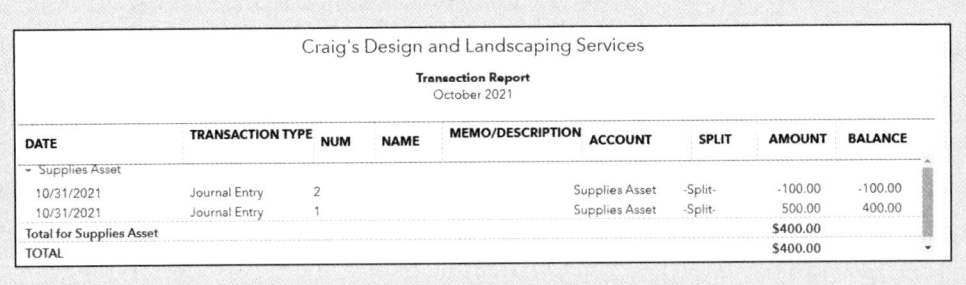

Craig's Design and Landscaping Services
Transaction Report
October 2021

DATE	TRANSACTION TYPE	NUM	NAME	MEMO/DESCRIPTION	ACCOUNT	SPLIT	AMOUNT	BALANCE
▼ Supplies Asset								
10/31/2021	Journal Entry	2			Supplies Asset	-Split-	-100.00	-100.00
10/31/2021	Journal Entry	1			Supplies Asset	-Split-	500.00	400.00
Total for Supplies Asset							$400.00	
TOTAL							$400.00	

The first entry deferred $500 from miscellaneous expense; the second entry recorded the consumption of supplies reducing the asset account.

Adjusting Journal Entries: Accrued Expenses

Further investigation of this trial balance and period end business activities indicates that a bill for $300 was received and recorded in the next month for advertising consumed in the current month. Thus, an adjusting journal entry needs to be made to accrue this expense. For our purposes, we will create a new accrued liabilities account to keep track of these accruals and keep them separate from accounts payable.

To record an adjusting journal entry to record the accrual of advertising expense, do the following:

1. Continue from where you left off. If you closed the Sample Company, follow the steps to reopen it found at the beginning of this chapter.
2. Click the **+ New** icon and then click **Journal Entry**.
3. Type the last day of the previous month into the Journal date text box (in this case, 10/31/2021).
4. Select **Advertising** from the drop-down list in line 1 of the Account column.
5. Type **300** into the Debits column of line 1.
6. Type **Accrued Liabilities** on line 2 of the Account column and then click **+ Add Accrued Liabilities**.
7. Select **Other Current Liabilities** from the drop-down list in the Account Type text box.
8. Select **Other Current Liabilities** from the drop-down list in the Detail Type text box.
9. Click **Save and close**.
10. Accept **300** into the Credits column of line 2 to view the journal entry as shown in Figure 9.7.

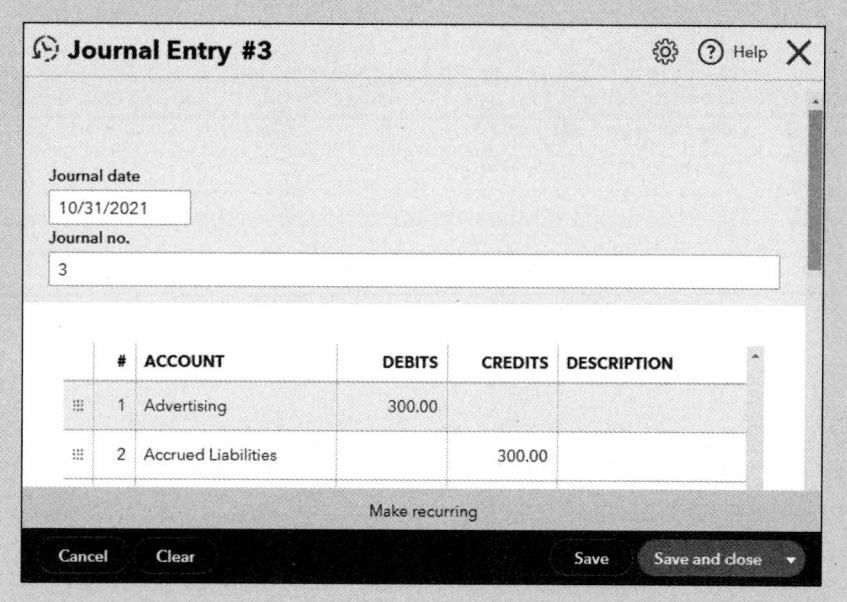

Figure 9.7

Journal entry (accruing advertising expense)

11. Click **Save and close**.
12. Closing the journal entry should reveal the trial balance created before but now updated to reflect the accrual of advertising expense to the accrued liabilities account.
13. Click the Accrued Liabilities **300** amount, (if necessary) adjust the report period like you've done previously, and then click **Run Report** to reveal a Transaction Report.
14. Click **Back to report summary** to return to the Trial Balance report.

Adjusting Journal Entries: Unearned Revenue

Further investigation of this trial balance and period end business activities indicates that design income recorded on sales receipt #1003 for $337.50 to Dylan Sollfrank were never performed even though cash had been received. Thus, the revenue had not been earned. Work is expected to occur next month; thus, this amount of revenue must be deferred and set up as an unearned revenue liability.

To record an adjusting journal entry to reflect earned revenue, do the following:

1. Continue from where you left off. If you closed the Sample Company, follow the steps to reopen it found at the beginning of this chapter.
2. Click the **+ New** icon and then click **Journal Entry**.
3. Type the last day of the previous month into the Journal date text box (in this case, 10/31/2021).
4. Select **Design income** from the drop-down list in line 1 of the Account column.
5. Type **337.50** into the Debits column of line 1.
6. Select **Dylan Sollfrank** from the drop-down list of customers in the Name column of line 1.
7. Type **Unearned Revenue** on line 2 of the Account column and then click **+ Add Unearned Revenue**.
8. Select **Other Current Liabilities** from the drop-down list in the Account Type text box.
9. Select **Other Current Liabilities** from the drop-down list in the Detail Type text box.
10. Click **Save and close**.

11 Accept **337.50** into the Credits column of line 2 and then select **Dylan Sollfrank** from the drop-down list of customers in the Name column of line 2 to view the journal entry as shown in Figure 9.8.

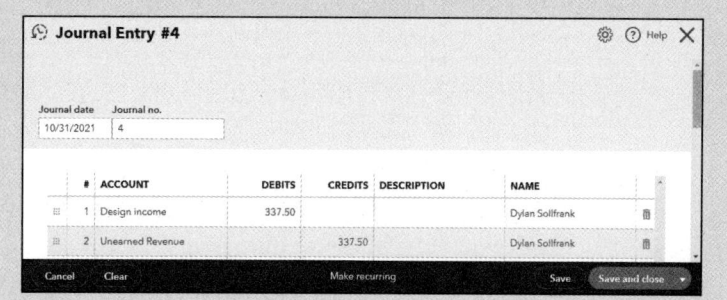

Figure 9.8

Journal entry (recording unearned revenue)

12 Click **Save and close**.

13 Closing the journal entry should reveal the trial balance created before but updated to reflect the deferral of revenue to the unearned revenue liability account.

14 Click the Unearned Revenue **337.50** amount, (if necessary) adjust the report period like you've done previously, and then click **Run Report** to reveal a Transaction Report.

15 Click **Back to report summary** to return to the Trial Balance report.

Adjusting Journal Entries: Accruing Revenue

Further investigation of this trial balance and period end business activities indicates that some landscaping services of $500 were performed on the last day of the month for Diego Rodriguez but not invoiced to the customer or recorded into the accounting records until a few days into the next month. Thus, you will need to record an adjusting journal entry to accrue revenue and an accrued receivable.

To record an adjusting journal entry to reflect earned revenue, do the following:

1 Continue from where you left off. If you closed the Sample Company, follow the steps to reopen it found at the beginning of this chapter.

2 Click the **+ New** icon and then click **Journal Entry**.

3 Type the last day of the previous month into the Journal date text box (in this case, 10/31/2021).

4 Type **Accrued Receivable** on line 1 of the Account column and then click **+ Add Accrued Receivable**.

5 Select **Other Current Assets** from the drop-down list in the Account Type text box.

6   Select **Other Current Assets** from the drop-down list in the Detail Type text box.

7   Click **Save and close**.

8   Type **500** into the Debits column of line 1.

9   Select **Diego Rodriguez** from the drop-down list of customers in the Name column of line 1.

10 Select **Landscaping Services** from the drop-down list in line 2 of the Account column.

11 Accept **500** in the Credits column of line 2.

12 Select **Diego Rodriguez** from the drop-down list of customers in the Name column of line 2 to view the journal entry as shown in Figure 9.9.

Figure 9.9

Journal entry (recording accrued revenue)

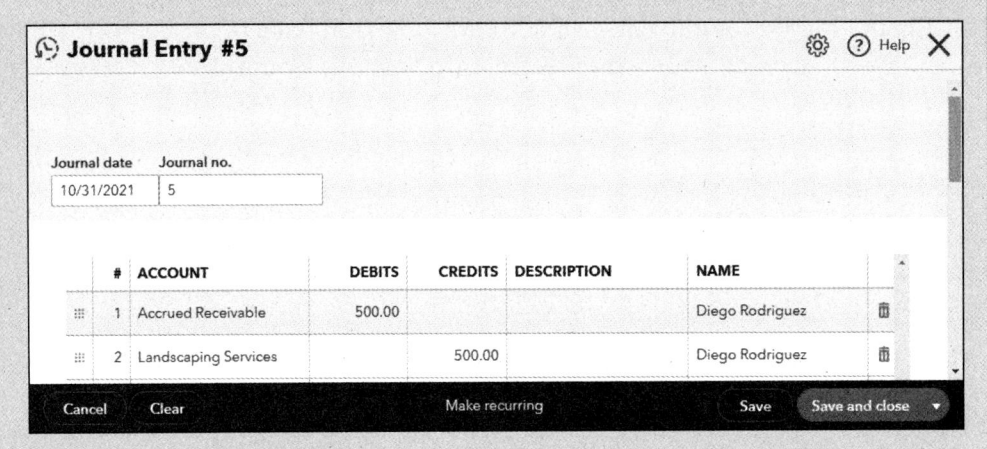

#	ACCOUNT	DEBITS	CREDITS	DESCRIPTION	NAME
1	Accrued Receivable	500.00			Diego Rodriguez
2	Landscaping Services		500.00		Diego Rodriguez

Journal Entry #5
Journal date: 10/31/2021
Journal no.: 5

13 Click **Save and close**.

14 Closing the journal entry should reveal the trial balance created before but updated to reflect the accrual of revenue to the accrued receivable account.

15 Click the Accrued Receivable **500** amount, (if necessary) adjust the report period like you've done previously, and then click **Run Report** to reveal a Transaction Report.

16 Click **Back to report summary** to return to the Trial Balance report.

Adjusting Journal Entries: Depreciation

Further investigation of this trial balance and period end business activities indicates the company's only fixed asset, a truck, needed to be depreciated for the month. Monthly depreciation is $1,000. Normally, the adjusting entry would debit depreciation expense and credit accumulated depreciation. However, the accounts set up in the Sample Company are both named depreciation. Thus, you decide to change the account names first and then record the depreciation adjusting journal entry.

Analysis and Recording of Adjusting Entries **Chapter 9** 215

To edit account names and then record an adjusting journal entry to record depreciation, do the following:

1. Continue from where you left off. If you closed the Sample Company, follow the steps to reopen it found at the beginning of this chapter.
2. Click the **Gear** icon, click **Chart of Accounts**, and then click **See your Chart of Accounts**.
3. Click **Edit** from the drop-down arrow next to the words View Register on the Depreciation line listed under the Truck account.
4. Type **Accumulated** *in front* of Depreciation in the Name text box and then click **Save and close**.
5. Scroll down to the bottom of the chart of accounts and select **Edit** from the drop-down arrow next to the words Run report on the Depreciation line listed above Miscellaneous.
6. Type **Expense** *after* Depreciation in the Name text box and then click **Save and close**.
7. Click the (+ New) icon and then click **Journal Entry**.
8. Type the last day of the previous month into the Journal date text box (in this case, 10/31/2021).
9. Select **Depreciation Expense** from the drop-down list in line 1 of the Account column.
10. Type **1000** into the Debits column of line 1.
11. Select **Truck:Accumulated Depreciation** from the drop-down list in line 2 of the Account column.
12. Accept **1000** as the Credits column amount. Your screen should look like Figure 9.10.

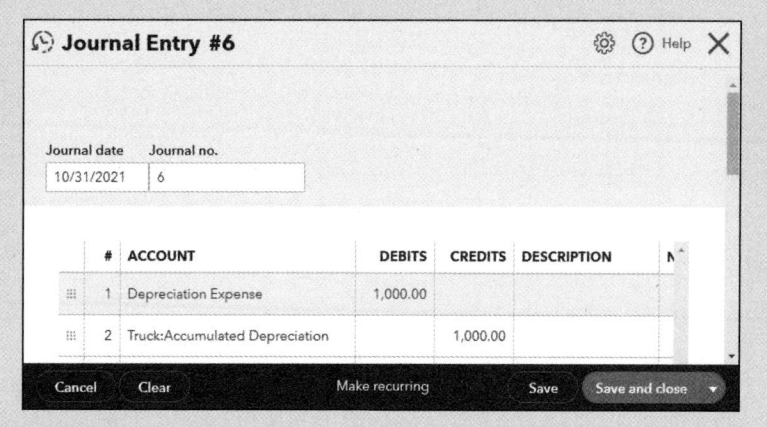

Figure 9.10

Journal entry (recording depreciation)

13. Click **Save and close**.
14. Click **Reports** from the navigation bar, type **Trial Balance** in the Find report by name text box, and then select **Trial Balance** from the drop-down list to view the trial balance.
15. Change the To: and From: dates like you did earlier in this chapter and then click **Run Report** to reveal a trial balance now updated to reflect the depreciation expense and accumulated depreciation just recorded.

216 Chapter 9 *Analysis and Recording of Adjusting Entries*

16. Click the Truck:Accumulated Depreciation **1000** amount, (if necessary) adjust the report period like you've done previously, and then click **Run Report** to reveal a Transaction Report.

17. Click **Back to report summary** to return to the Trial Balance report. Your completed Trial Balance report should look like Figure 9.11.

Figure 9.11

Revised Trial Balance report (partial view)

Craig's Design and Landscaping Services
Trial Balance
As of October 31, 2021

	DEBIT	CREDIT
Checking	2,101.00	
Savings	800.00	
Accounts Receivable (A/R)	5,281.52	
Accrued Receivable	500.00	
Inventory Asset	596.25	
Supplies Asset	400.00	
Undeposited Funds	2,062.52	
Truck:Accumulated Depreciation		1,000.00
Truck:Original Cost	13,495.00	
Accounts Payable (A/P)		1,602.67
Mastercard		1,003.73
Accrued Liabilities		300.00
Arizona Dept. of Revenue Payable		0.00
Board of Equalization Payable		370.94
Loan Payable		4,000.00
Unearned Revenue		337.50
Notes Payable		25,000.00

End Note

In this chapter, you recorded adjusting entries to create accrual accounting based records. In the next chapter, you will create financial statements and useful reports.

Chapter 9 Questions

1. What is an unadjusted trial balance?
2. What is an adjusted trial balance?
3. Why accrue an expense?
4. Why defer an expense?
5. Why accrue revenues?
6. Why defer revenues?
7. What QBO task is used to record accruals and deferrals?
8. Why depreciate a fixed asset?
9. Describe the new method you learned in this chapter to add a new account from within a journal entry.
10. Describe the method you learned in this chapter to add a customer to a transaction within a journal entry.

Chapter 9 Matching

a. Prepaid Expenses   _____ Debit this account when recording depreciation
b. Accrue   _____ Credit this account when accruing an expense
c. Unearned Revenue   _____ Debit this account when accruing revenue
d. Defer   _____ Supplies consumed
e. Depreciation Expense   _____ Credit this account when recording depreciation
f. Supplies Asset   _____ Expenses not yet consumed
g. Supplies Expense   _____ Revenue not yet earned
h. Accrued Receivables   _____ To increase
i. Accrued Liabilities   _____ Supplies not yet consumed
j. Accumulate Depreciation   _____ To postpone

Chapter 9 Cases

The following cases require you to open the company you updated in Chapter 8. Each of the following cases continues throughout the text in a sequential manner. For example, if you are assigned Case 01, you will use the file you modified in this chapter in all following chapters. Each of the following cases is similar in concepts assessed but differs in amounts and transactions.

To reopen your company, do the following:

1. Open your Internet browser.
2. Type **https://qbo.intuit.com** into your browser's address text box.
3. Type your user ID and password into the text boxes as you've done before.

Case 1

Now it is time to make some adjusting journal entries. Based on what you learned in the text using the Sample Company, you are to make the following changes to the Case 1 company you modified in Chapter 8:

1. Open and review your previously customized report named Trial Balance 1/31/24.

2. Record the appropriate adjusting journal entries on 1/31/24 based on the following:

    a. An inventory of supplies reveals that only $75 of supplies remain as of 1/31/24. You'll need to add a new Supplies account—Account Type: Expenses, Detail Type: Supplies & Materials, Name: Supplies.

    b. Prepaid expenses of $800 expired (representing prepaid rent) in the month of January.

    c. A bill for $150 was received and recorded in the next month for repairs and maintenance consumed in the current month. Create a new liability account as you did earlier in the chapter.

    d. Consulting services recorded on sales receipt #1004 for $2,500 to Surf Rider Foundation were never performed even though cash had been received. Thus, the revenue had not been earned. Create a new liability account as you did earlier in the chapter.

    e. Consulting services of $8,500 were performed on the last day of the month for a new customer Blazing Boards but not invoiced to the customer or recorded into the accounting records until a few days into the next month. Create a new asset account as you did earlier in the chapter.

    f. Depreciation Expense of $575 ($75 and $500 for Equipment and Furniture & Fixtures, respectively) needed to be recorded for the month. Before recording this journal entry, edit the "Depreciation" expense account so that the new name is "Depreciation Expense." Also, change the account title for Furniture & Fixtures accumulated depreciation from "Depreciation" to "Accumulated Depreciation" as you did earlier in the chapter. This also needs to be done for the Equipment accumulated depreciation account.

3. Open, print, and export to Excel your previously customized report named Trial Balance 1/31/24, which should now reflect your adjusting journal entries.

4. Open, print, and export to Excel your previously customized report named Transaction Detail by Account, which should now reflect your adjusting journal entries.

Case 2

Now it is time to make some adjusting journal entries. Based on what you learned in the text using the Sample Company, you are to make the following changes to the Case 2 company you modified in Chapter 8:

1. Open and review your previously customized report named Trial Balance 1/31/25.

2. Record the appropriate adjusting journal entries on 1/31/25 based on the following:
   a. An inventory of supplies reveals that only $200 of supplies remain as of 1/31/25. You'll need to add a new Supplies account—Account Type: Expenses, Detail Type: Supplies & Materials, Name: Supplies.
   b. Prepaid expenses of $1,800 expired (representing prepaid insurance) in the month of January.
   c. A bill for $750 was received and recorded in the next month for legal fees performed in the current month. Create a new liability account as you did earlier in the chapter.
   d. Custom painting services recorded on invoice #1003 for $4,500 to Hagen's toys were never performed even though invoiced. Thus, the revenue had not been earned. Create a new liability account as you did earlier in the chapter.
   e. Repair services of $6,298 were performed on the last day of the month for a new customer Kelly's Awesome Copters but not invoiced to the customer or recorded into the accounting records until a few days into the next month. Create a new asset account as you did earlier in the chapter.
   f. Depreciation Expense of $1,000 ($375 and $625 for Furniture and Machinery & Equipment, respectively) needed to be recorded for the month. Before recording this journal entry, edit the "Depreciation" expense account so the new name is "Depreciation Expense." Also, change the account title for Machinery & Equipment accumulated depreciation from "Depreciation" to "Accumulated Depreciation" like you did earlier in the chapter. This also needs to be done for the Furniture accumulated depreciation account.
3. Open, print, and export to Excel your previously customized report named Trial Balance 1/31/25, which should reflect your adjusting journal entries.
4. Open, print, and export to Excel your previously customized report named Transaction Detail by Account, which should reflect your adjusting journal entries.

Case 3

Now it is time to make some adjusting journal entries. Based on what you learned in the text using the Sample Company, you are to make the following changes to the Case 3 company you modified in Chapter 8:

1. Open and review your previously customized report named Trial Balance 1/31/26.
2. Record the appropriate adjusting journal entries on 1/31/26 based on the following:
   a. An inventory of supplies reveals that only $200 of supplies remain as of 1/31/26. (You'll need to add a new Supplies expense account—Account Type: Expenses, Detail Type: Supplies & Materials, Name: Supplies)
   b. Prepaid expenses of $1,500 expired (representing prepaid insurance) in the month of January.

c. A bill for $350 was received and recorded in the next month from FixIt, Inc. (new vendor) for repairs & maintenance performed in the current month. Create a new liability account like you did earlier in the chapter.

d. Phone Consulting services recorded on invoice #1003 for $210 to Diamond Girl, Inc. and recorded as Service income were never performed even though invoiced. Thus, the revenue had not been earned. Create a new liability account like you did earlier in the chapter.

e. Phone Consulting services of $1,800 were performed on the last day of the month for a new customer Graham Engineering, Inc. but not invoiced to the customer or recorded into the accounting records until a few days into the next month. Create a new asset account like you did earlier in the chapter.

f. Depreciation Expense of $1,200 ($850 and $350 for Computers and Machinery & Equipment respectively) needed to be recorded for the month. Before recording this journal entry, edit the "Depreciation" expense account so that the new name is "Depreciation Expense." Also change the account title for the Machinery & Equipment accumulated depreciation from "Depreciation" to "Accumulated Depreciation" like you did earlier in the chapter. This also needs to be done for the Computers accumulation depreciation account.

3 Open, print, and export to Excel your previously customized report named Trial Balance 1/31/26, which should now reflect your adjusting journal entries.

4 Open, print, and export to Excel your previously customized report named Transaction Detail by Account, which should now reflect your adjusting journal entries.

Case 4

Now it is time to make some adjusting journal entries. Based on what you learned in the text using the Sample Company, you are to make the following changes to the Case 4 company you modified in Chapter 8:

1 Open and review your previously customized report named Trial Balance 1/31/21.

2 Record the appropriate adjusting journal entries on 1/31/21 based on the following:

a. An inventory of supplies reveals that only $200 of supplies remain as of 1/31/21. You'll need to create a new Supplies Expense account (Account Type: Expenses, Detail Type: Supplies & Materials, Name: Supplies Expense).

b. Prepaid expenses of $1,500 expired (representing prepaid insurance) in the month of January.

c. A bill for $675 was received and recorded in the next month from FixIt, Inc. for advertising placed in the current month. Create a new liability account like you did earlier in the chapter.

d. Training services recorded on invoice #1003 for $3,750 to Flyer Corporation were only partially performed even though invoiced. Thus, the $2,000 of sales had not been earned. Create a new liability account like you did earlier in the chapter.

e. Training services of $750 were performed on the last day of the month for a new customer Jules, Inc. but not invoiced to the customer or recorded into the accounting records until a few days into the next month. Create a new asset account like you did earlier in the chapter and record additional sales.

f. Depreciation Expense of $1,500 ($500, $600, and $400 for Buildings, Furniture, and Machinery & Equipment, respectively) needed to be recorded for the month. Before recording this journal entry, edit the "Depreciation" expense account so that the new name is "Depreciation Expense." Also change the account title for the Buildings, Furniture, and Machinery & Equipment accumulated depreciation from "Depreciation" to "Accumulated Depreciation" like you did earlier in the chapter.

3 Print your Trial Balance 1/31/21 report that should now reflect your adjusting journal entries.

Case 5

Now it is time to make some adjusting journal entries. Based on what you learned in the text using the Sample Company, you are to make the following changes to the Case 5 company you modified in Chapter 8:

1 Open and review your previously customized report named Trial Balance 01/31/22.

2 Record the appropriate adjusting journal entries on 01/31/22 based on the following:

a. Prepaid expenses of $8,000 expired (representing prepaid insurance) in the month of January.

b. A bill for $2,800 was received and recorded in the next month from Indeed for recruiting services consumed in the current month. Create a new liability account like you did in the chapter.

c. Consulting services recorded on invoice #1003 for $32,000 to Boeing were only 50% complete as of 01/31/22 even though invoiced in the current month. Thus, $16,000 of consulting services had not been earned. Create an unearned revenue liability account like you did in the chapter.

d. Training services of $6,700 were performed on the last day of the month for a new customer Raonic but not invoiced to the customer or recorded into the accounting records until a few days into the next month. Create a new asset account like you did in the chapter.

e. Depreciation Expense of $11,000 ($6,000, 2,000, and $3,000 for Computers, Copiers, and Furniture, respectively) needed to be recorded for the month. Before recording this journal entry, edit the "Depreciation" expense account so that the new name is "Depreciation Expense." Also change the account title for the Computers, Copiers, and Furniture accumulated depreciation from "Depreciation" to "Accumulated Depreciation" like you did in the chapter.

3 Print your Trial Balance 01/31/22 report that should now reflect your adjusting journal entries.

Case 6

Now it is time to make some adjusting journal entries. Based on what you learned in the text using the Sample Company, you are to make the following changes to the Case 6 company you modified in Chapter 8:

1. Open and review your previously customized report named Trial Balance 1/31/23.

2. Record the appropriate adjusting journal entries on 1/31/23 based on the following:

   a. An inventory of supplies reveals that only $400 of supplies remain as of 1/31/23 and $1,000 of supplies were mistakenly recorded as Contractors (an expense). You'll need to create a new Supplies Asset account and journalize $1,000 of Contractors (expense) to the newly created Supplies Asset account. (Note: This a correction of an error journal entry.) Then you'll need to create a new Supplies Expense account (Account Type: Expenses, Detail Type: Supplies & Materials) and journalize $600 of Supplies Asset to the newly created Supplies Expense account. (Note: This requires an adjusting journal entry.)

   b. Prepaid expenses of $2,400 expired (representing prepaid insurance) in the month of January. (Note: This requires an adjusting journal entry.)

   c. A bill for $1,800 was received and recorded in the next month from Pacific Marketing for advertising placed in the current month. Create a new liability account like you did in the chapter. (Note: This requires an adjusting journal entry.)

   d. A Transmission Service of $350 and a Sewer System Repair of $600 were performed on the last day of the month for an existing customer (Deja Smith) but not invoiced to the customer or recorded into the accounting records until a few days into the next month. Create a new asset account like you did in the chapter and then record this as Sales. (Note: This requires an adjusting journal entry.)

   e. Depreciation Expense of $2,100 ($1,000, $300, and $800 for Buildings, Computers, and Machinery & Equipment, respectively) needed to be recorded for the month. Before recording this journal entry, edit the "Depreciation" expense account so that the new name is "Depreciation Expense." Also change the account title for the Buildings, Computers, and Machinery & Equipment accumulated depreciation from "Depreciation" to "Accumulated Depreciation" like you did in the chapter. (Note: This requires an adjusting journal entry.)

3. Print your Trial Balance 1/31/23 report that should now reflect your adjusting journal entries.

Preparing Financial Statements and Reports

chapter 10

Student Learning Outcomes

Upon completion of this chapter, the student will be able to do the following:

- Create an income statement
- Create a balance sheet
- Create a statement of cash flows
- Create an accounts receivable aging summary
- Create an accounts payable aging summary
- Create an inventory valuation summary
- Customize and save reports

Overview

Intuit has provided a Sample Company online to let new users test-drive its QBO product. In this chapter, you will open this Sample Company and practice creating reports in QBO. Prior to the creation of periodic financial statements, generally accepted accounting principles (GAAP) require that accounting records be adjusted to reflect accrual accounting. You completed that process in the previous chapter.

Four standard reports exist in financial accounting: the income statement, the statement of stockholders' equity, the balance sheet, and the statement of cash flows. QBO does not have a report for stockholders' equity. It does have the others along with a host of other reports so you can understand the underlying business events that have occurred during a particular accounting period. You will be exploring the A/R Aging Summary, A/P Aging Summary, and Inventory Valuation Summary reports. You will also be customizing them by adding columns and removing cents.

Remember, if you stop in the middle of this work, none of your work will be saved. So, when you return, the same Sample Company, without your work, will appear. In some parts of the chapter, you will be asked to sign out of the Sample Company and sign back in so the Sample Company is reset to its original state. In the end of chapter work, you will be asked to perform the same tasks completed on the Sample Company on your Student Company. That work, of course, will be saved.

Income Statement

In this section, you will create an income statement. Intuit decided years ago to call this report Profit and Loss rather than an Income Statement. Even though this may confuse the accounting professional and accounting student, it resonates with the small business user that uses QBO. This report is designed to communicate the revenues earned and expenses incurred for a business over a month, quarter, or year.

Intuit defines this report as follows: "Shows money you earned (income) and money you spent (expenses), so you can see how profitable you are." That is not exactly how an accounting professional or accounting student was taught but close enough. Accountants define the income statement as a report reflecting revenues less expenses to derive net income. Intuit is not about to change its wording to accommodate us, so we will accept it at face value. Thus, revenues are the same as income in the Profit and Loss report. For simplicity, we will refer to this as the Profit and Loss report.

To create a Profit and Loss report for the Sample Company, do the following:

1. Open your Internet browser.
2. Type **https://qbo.intuit.com/redir/testdrive** into your browser's address text box, and then press [**Enter**] to view the Sample Company Dashboard.
3. Click **Reports** from the navigation bar.
4. Type **Profit and Loss** in the Find report by name search box and then select the **Profit and Loss** text, which appears below the search text box.

You recall that when using the Sample Company, dates change based upon the system date of Intuit's servers on which these data reside. Scroll to the top of the report to reveal the report period information. The system date was 11/20/2021 when this report was created; therefore, the default dates for this report were from 01/01/2021 to 11/20/2021 as seen in the Report period text boxes at the top of Figure 10.1.

Figure 10.1

Profit and Loss Report (collapsed and partial views)

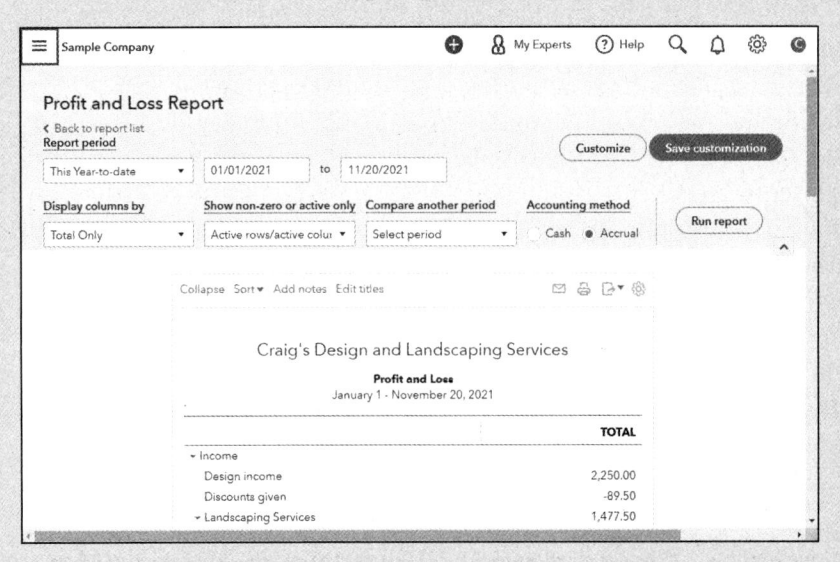

5 Change the Report period to **Last Month** and click **Run report**. Since the system date was 11/20/2021 when this report was created, the report shown in Figure 10.2 is for the period 10/01/2021 to 10/31/2021. Your report will have a different period than that shown next.

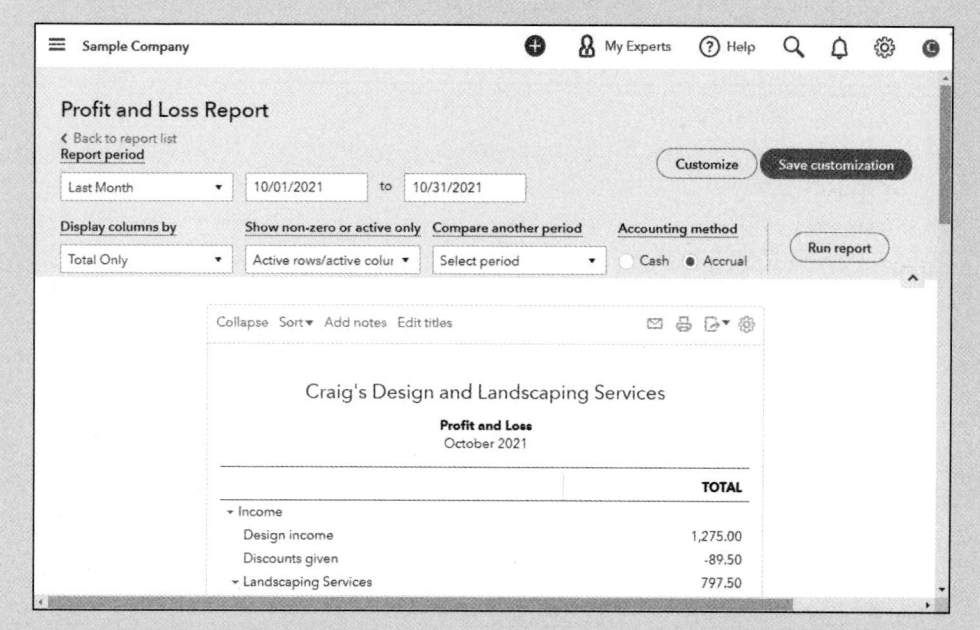

Figure 10.2

Profit and Loss Report (partial view)

Trouble? If you are doing this work in a different year, 2021, for example, you may have to type a different year and a different month to view the data.

By defining the accounting period as the month of October 2021, the only events reported are those recorded during that period. All reports in QBO allow you to drill down to specific transactions recorded in that period. You drill down by clicking an account on a report. That reveals a transactions report for that account for that period. Double-clicking a specific transaction in the transactions report reveals a specific source document, such as an invoice, sales receipt, cash receipt, and bill. Recall the **Trouble?** earlier. The amounts you are asked to investigate next will most likely be different than that stated in the steps. Remember you're just using the Sample Company to explore. You will not find these issues in the end-of-chapter case problems.

6 Click the **1,275.00** amount (or whatever amount is shown) next to the Design income account as shown in Figure 10.2 to view the Transaction report for the Design income account for the month of October shown in Figure 10.3, remembering that this figure illustrates the details behind the number you just clicked.

Figure 10.3

Transaction Report (for the design income account)

Craig's Design and Landscaping Services
Transaction Report
October 2021

DATE	TRANSACTION TYPE	NUM	NAME	MEMO/DESCRIPTION	ACCOUNT	SPLIT	AMOUNT	BALANCE
Design income								
10/20/2021	Sales Receipt	1003	Dylan Sollfrank	Custom Design	Design income	Checking	337.50	337.50
10/23/2021	Invoice	1010	Weiskopf Consulting	Custom Design	Design income	Accounts Receivable (A/R)	375.00	712.50
10/23/2021	Invoice	1015	Paulsen Medical Supplies	Custom Design	Design income	Accounts Receivable (A/R)	300.00	1,012.50
10/24/2021	Invoice	1033	Geeta Kalapatapu	Custom Design	Design income	Accounts Receivable (A/R)	262.50	1,275.00
Total for Design income							$1,275.00	
TOTAL							$1,275.00	

7   Click on the **Paulsen Medical Supplies** to view invoice #1015 shown in Figure 10.4.

Figure 10.4

Invoice #1015 (partial view)

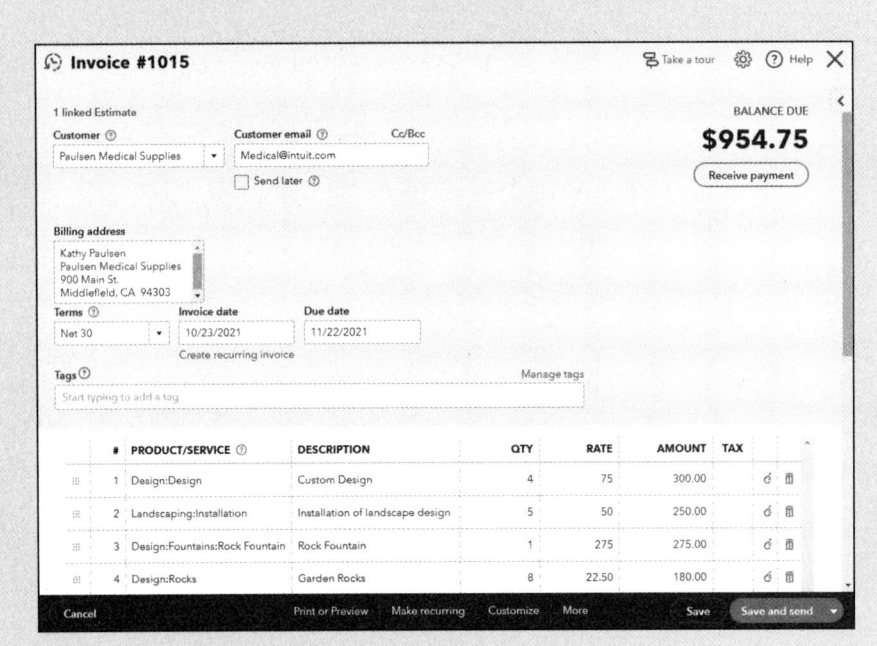

[Invoice #1015 screen showing Customer: Paulsen Medical Supplies, Balance Due: $954.75, Invoice date 10/23/2021, Due date 11/22/2021, with line items: Design:Design Custom Design qty 4 rate 75 amount 300.00; Landscaping:Installation Installation of landscape design qty 5 rate 50 amount 250.00; Design:Fountains:Rock Fountain Rock Fountain qty 1 rate 275 amount 275.00; Design:Rocks Garden Rocks qty 8 rate 22.50 amount 180.00]

8   Click **Cancel** to return to the transaction report, and click **Back to report summary** to return to the Profit and Loss report and then save this report as Profit and Loss Oct 2021 (your date will be different). Remember this report will be saved until you exit the Sample company. Once you exit, all Sample company changes are lost.

Balance Sheet

In this section, you will create a balance sheet that reports on your company's assets, liabilities, and stockholders' equity as of a specific date (not period). However, when creating this report, QBO provides you the ability to define the period in which underlying account balances will reflect in their transactions reports. QBO default is this Year-to-date. Recall the **Trouble?** earlier. The amounts you are asked to investigate next will most likely be different than that stated in the steps. Remember you're just using the Sample Company to explore. You will not find these issues in the end-of-chapter case problems.

To create a balance sheet, do the following:

1. Continue from where you left off. If you closed the Sample Company, follow the steps to reopen it found at the beginning of this chapter.

2. Click **Reports** from the navigation bar.

3. Type **Balance Sheet** in the Find report by name search box, and then select the **Balance Sheet** text, which appears below the search text box to view the partial balance sheet shown in Figure 10.5. Alternatively, the Balance Sheet can be accessed in the Sample Company by clicking **Balance Sheet** from the list of Favorites in the Reports section.

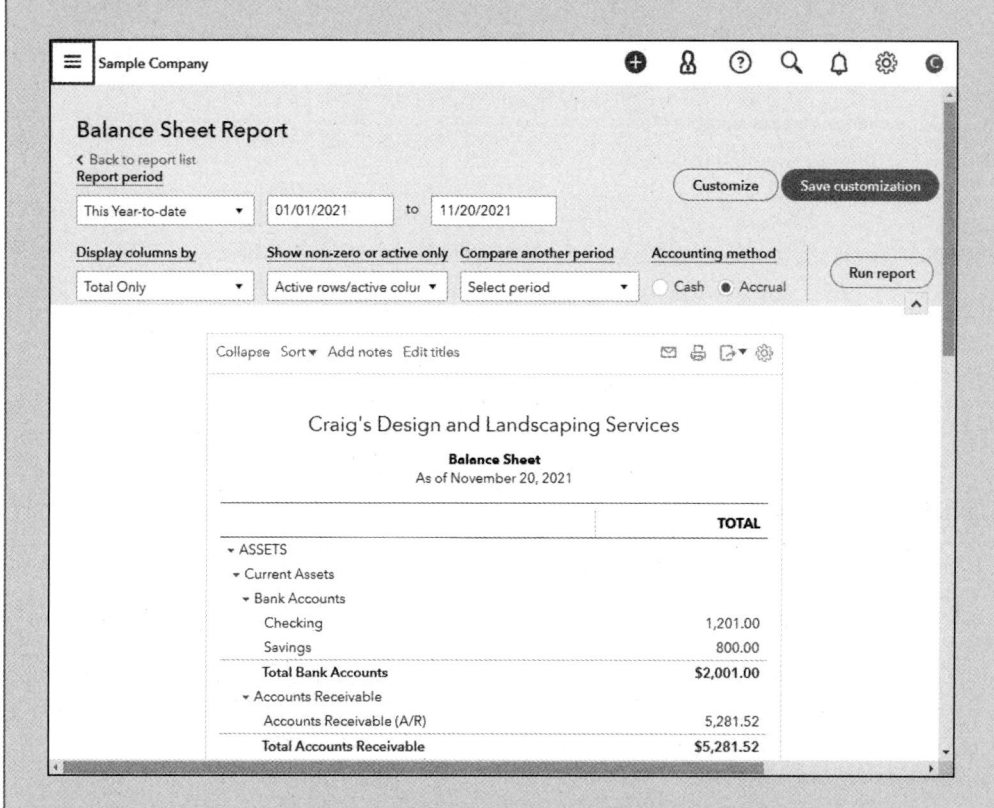

Figure 10.5

Balance Sheet (partial view)

4. The system date was 11/20/2021 when this report was created (yours will be your current system date); therefore, the default dates for this report were from 01/01/2021 to 11/20/2021 as seen in the Report period text boxes at the top of Figure 10.5. Change the Report period to **Last Month** like you did previously with the Profit and Loss statement, and click **Run report**. Since the system date was 11/20/2021 when this report was created, the report shown in Figure 10.6 is for the period 10/01/2021 to 10/31/2021. Your report will have a different period than that shown next.

Figure 10.6

Balance Sheet (partial view)

Craig's Design and Landscaping Services
Balance Sheet
As of October 31, 2021

	TOTAL
▼ ASSETS	
▼ Current Assets	
▼ Bank Accounts	
Checking	2,101.00
Savings	800.00
Total Bank Accounts	**$2,901.00**
▼ Accounts Receivable	
Accounts Receivable (A/R)	5,281.52
Total Accounts Receivable	**$5,281.52**

5 Click the Accounts Receivable (A/R) balance that, as shown in Figure 10.6, is **5,281.52** (or whatever balance is shown for Accounts Receivable) to view a transaction report for Accounts Receivable (A/R) for the month you specified. Figure 10.7 shows the top portion of this report.

Figure 10.7

Transaction Report for Accounts Receivable (A/R) (partial view)

Craig's Design and Landscaping Services
Transaction Report
October 2021

DATE	TRANSACTION TYPE	NUM	NAME	MEMO/DESCRIPTION	ACCOUNT	SPLIT	AMOUNT	BALANCE
▼ Accounts Receivable (A/R)								
Beginning Balance								1,739.00
10/02/2021	Payment		Amy's Bird Sanctuary		Accounts Receivable (A/R)	Checking	-105.00	1,634.00
10/03/2021	Invoice	1022	Jeff's Jalopies		Accounts Receivable (A/R)	-Split-	81.00	1,715.00
10/03/2021	Invoice	1021	Amy's Bird Sanctuary		Accounts Receivable (A/R)	-Split-	459.00	2,174.00
10/08/2021	Payment		Amy's Bird Sanctuary		Accounts Receivable (A/R)	-Split-	0.00	2,174.00
10/08/2021	Credit Memo	1026	Amy's Bird Sanctuary		Accounts Receivable (A/R)	Pest Control Services	-100.00	2,074.00
10/09/2021	Invoice	1017	Sushi by Katsuyuki		Accounts Receivable (A/R)	Landscaping Services	80.00	2,154.00
10/11/2021	Invoice	1012	Shara Barnett:Barnett Design		Accounts Receivable (A/R)	-Split-	274.50	2,428.50
10/13/2021	Invoice	1004	Cool Cars		Accounts Receivable (A/R)	-Split-	2,369.52	4,798.02

6 Note the ending balance of 5,281.52 (or whatever balance you have), which matches the Balance Sheet report shown in Figure 10.6.

7   Scroll down the report and then click **–1,675.52** (a payment from Cool Cars) to view the Receive Payment window shown in Figure 10.8.

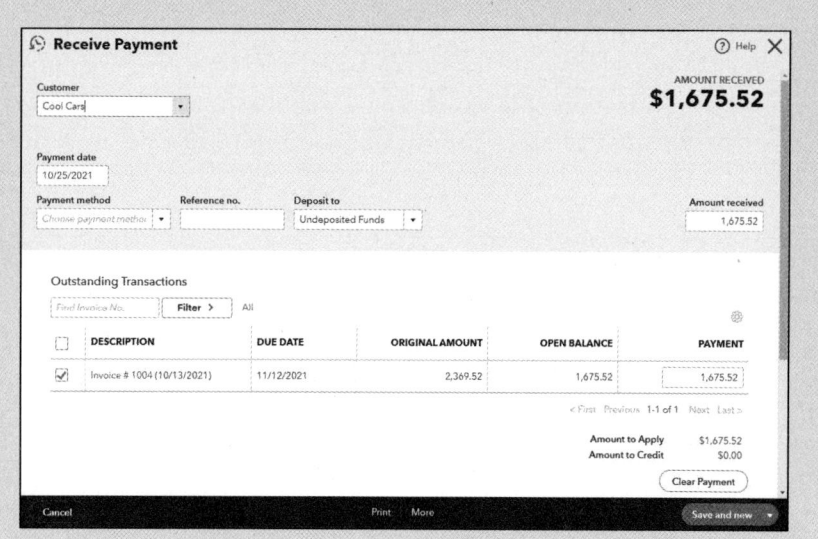

Figure 10.8

Payment received (from Cool Cars)

8   Click **Cancel** to return to the transaction report, and click **Back to report summary** to return to the Balance Sheet and then save this report as Balance Sheet Oct 2021 (your date will be different). Remember this report will be saved until you exit the Sample company. Once you exit all Sample company changes are lost.

Statement of Cash Flows

In this section, you will create a statement of cash flows, which reports on a company's operating, investing, and financing activities. Recall the **Trouble?** earlier. The amounts you are asked to investigate next will most likely be different than that stated in the steps. Remember you're just using the Sample Company to explore. You will not find these issues in the end-of-chapter case problems.

To create a statement of cash flows, do the following:

1   Continue from where you left off. If you closed the Sample Company, follow the steps to reopen it found at the beginning of this chapter.

2   Click **Reports** from the navigation bar.

3   Type **Statement of Cash Flows** in the Find a report by name search box, and then select the **Statement of Cash Flows** text.

4. The system date was 11/20/2021 when this report was created; therefore, the default dates for this report were from 01/01/2021 to 11/20/2021. Change the Report period to **Last Month** like you did previously with the balance sheet, and click **Run report**. Since the system date was 11/20/2021 when this report was created, the report shown in Figure 10.9 is for the period 10/01/2021 to 10/31/2021. Your report will have a different period than that shown next.

Figure 10.9

Statement of Cash Flows (partial view)

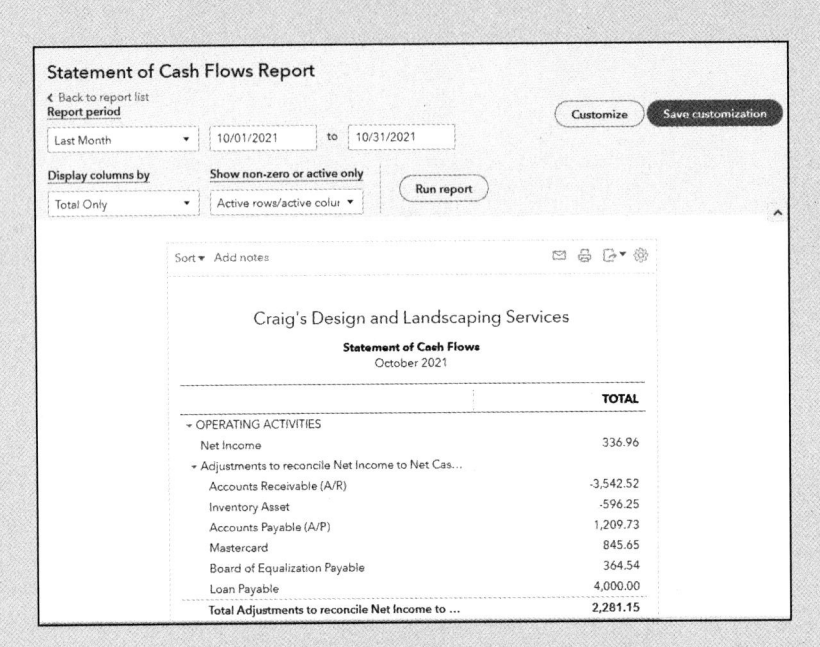

5. Scroll down the report and click the Notes Payable amount that is **25,000** to view a transaction report for Notes Payable for October as shown in Figure 10.10. (Your balance and dates will differ.)

Figure 10.10

Transaction Report (for Notes Payable)

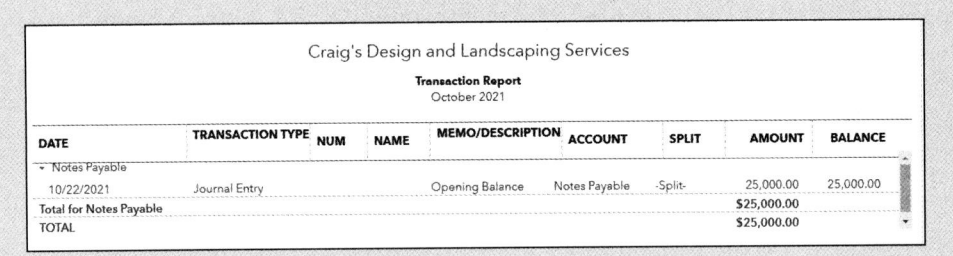

6   Click **25,000.00** to view the journal entry shown in Figure 10.11.

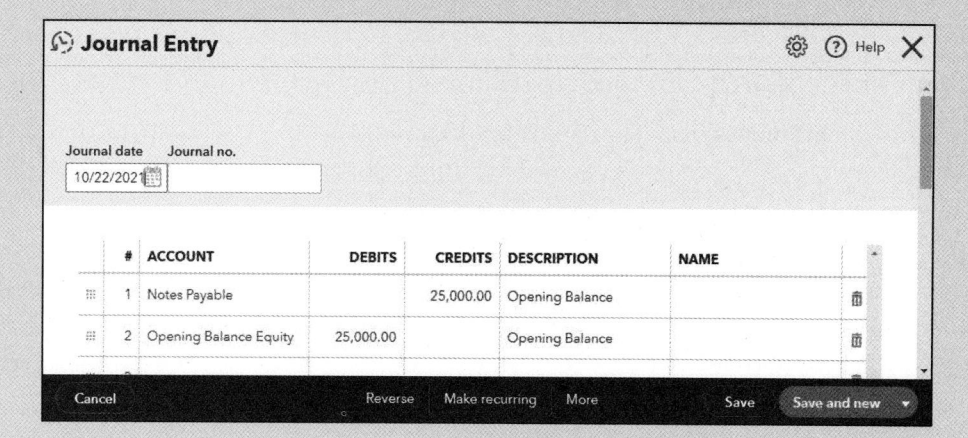

Figure 10.11

Journal Entry to record the Notes Payable Opening Balance

#	ACCOUNT	DEBITS	CREDITS	DESCRIPTION	NAME
1	Notes Payable		25,000.00	Opening Balance	
2	Opening Balance Equity	25,000.00		Opening Balance	

Journal date: 10/22/2021

7   Click **Cancel** to return to the transaction report, and click **Back to report summary** to return to the Statement of Cash Flows.

Accounts Receivable Aging Summary

In this section, you will create an accounts receivable aging summary, which reflects unpaid invoices for the current period and for the last 30, 60, and 90+ days as of a specific date. Aging summaries help find customers who may be delinquent in their payments and help a company estimate the need for an allowance for uncollectible accounts. Aging information must take into consideration the company's normal terms for a customer. For example, it would not be an issue if many customers are in the 60+ category, but the normal terms for those customers are net 60. However, it would be an issue if the normal terms are net 30 and the same situation existed. Recall the **Trouble?** earlier. The amounts you are asked to investigate next will most likely be different than that stated in the steps. Remember you're just using the Sample Company to explore. You will not find these issues in the end-of-chapter case problems.

To create an accounts receivable aging summary report, do the following:

1. Continue from where you left off. If you closed the Sample Company, follow the steps to reopen it found at the beginning of this chapter.

2. Click **Reports** from the navigation bar.

3. Type **Accounts receivable aging summary** in the Find a report by name search box, and then select the **Accounts receivable aging summary** text, which appears below the search text box to view the accounts receivable (A/R) aging report. Change the Report period to **Last Month**. In this case, the new "as of" date is 10/31/2021. Then click **Run report** to view the report shown in Figure 10.12.

Figure 10.12

Accounts Receivable (A/R) Aging Summary (partial view)

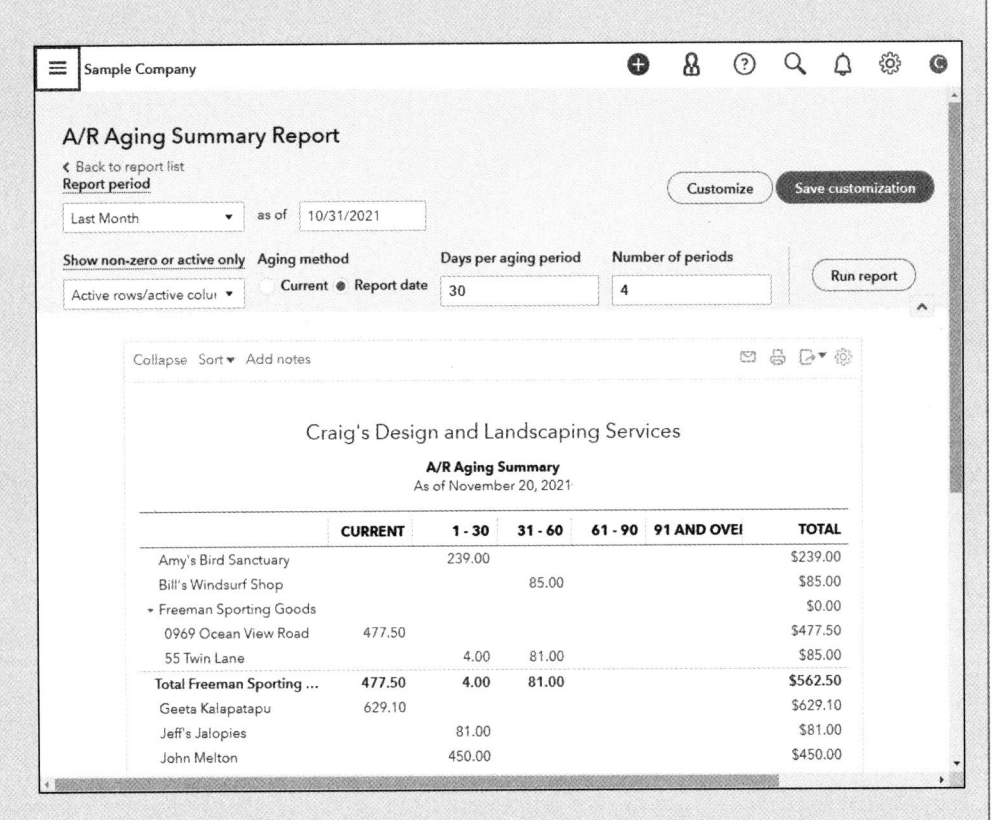

4. Click on the **85.00** owed by Bill's Windsurf Shop shown in Figure 10.12 to view A/R Aging Detail report shown in Figure 10.13.

Figure 10.13

Accounts Receivable (A/R) Aging Detail report (partial view)

5 Click **85.00** to view invoice #1027 shown in Figure 10.14.

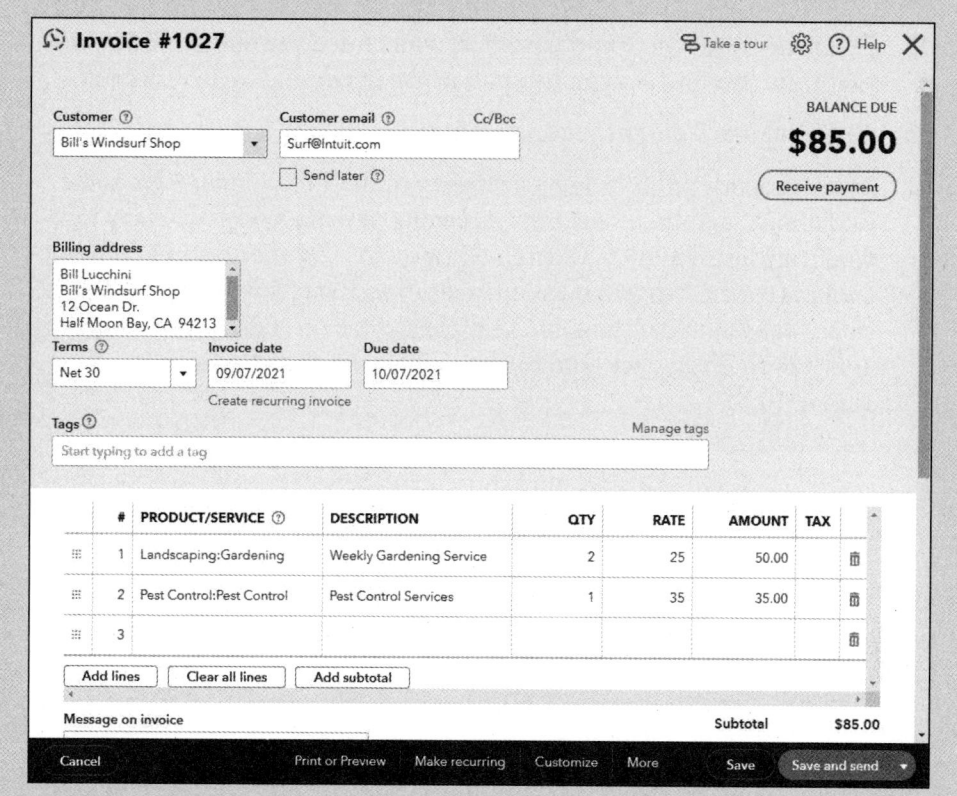

Figure 10.14

Invoice #1027 (to Bill's Windsurf Shop)

6 Call Bill to find out when he is planning to pay you. Actually, no, do not do that. Instead, click **Cancel** to return to the detail report, and click **Back to report summary** to return to the A/R Aging Summary report.

Accounts Payable Aging Summary

In this section, you will create an accounts payable aging summary, which reflects unpaid bills for the current period and for the last 30, 60, and 90+ days as of a specific date. Aging summaries help prioritize the payment of bills. Aging information must take into consideration the company's normal terms from a vendor. For example, it would not be an issue if a large amount of vendors bills are in the 60+ category, but the normal terms for those vendors are net 60. However, it would be an issue if the normal terms are net 30, and the same situation existed. Recall the **Trouble?** earlier. The amounts you are asked to investigate next will most likely be different than that stated in the steps. Remember you're just using the Sample Company to explore. You will not find these issues in the end-of-chapter case problems.

To create an accounts payable aging summary report, do the following:

1. Continue from where you left off. If you closed the Sample Company, follow the steps to reopen it found at the beginning of this chapter.
2. Click **Reports** from the navigation bar.
3. Type **Accounts payable aging summary** in the Find a report by name search box, and then select the **Accounts payable aging summary** text, which appears below the search text box to view the accounts payable aging report. Change the Report period to **Last Month**. In this case, since the system date was 11/20/2021, the "as of" date was changed to 10/31/2021. Then click **Run report** to view the report shown in Figure 10.15.

Figure 10.15

Accounts Payable (A/P) Aging Summary

Craig's Design and Landscaping Services
A/P Aging Summary
As of October 31, 2021

	CURRENT	1 - 30	31 - 60	61 - 90	91 AND OVER	TOTAL
Brosnahan Insurance Age…		241.23				$241.23
Diego's Road Warrior Bo…	755.00					$755.00
Norton Lumber and Build…		205.00				$205.00
PG&E		86.44				$86.44
Robertson & Associates		315.00				$315.00
TOTAL	$755.00	$847.67	$0.00	$0.00	$0.00	$1,602.67

4. Click on the **86.44** owed to PG&E shown in Figure 10.15 to view A/P Aging Detail report shown in Figure 10.16.

Figure 10.16

Accounts Payable (A/P) Aging Detail report

Craig's Design and Landscaping Services
A/P Aging Detail
As of October 31, 2021

DATE	TRANSACTION TYPE	NUM	VENDOR	DUE DATE	PAST DUE	AMOUNT	OPEN BALANCE
▼ 1 - 30 days past due							
09/10/2021	Bill		PG&E	10/10/2021	41	86.44	86.44
Total for 1 - 30 days past due						$86.44	$86.44
TOTAL						$86.44	$86.44

5. Click **86.44** to view the bill shown in Figure 10.17.

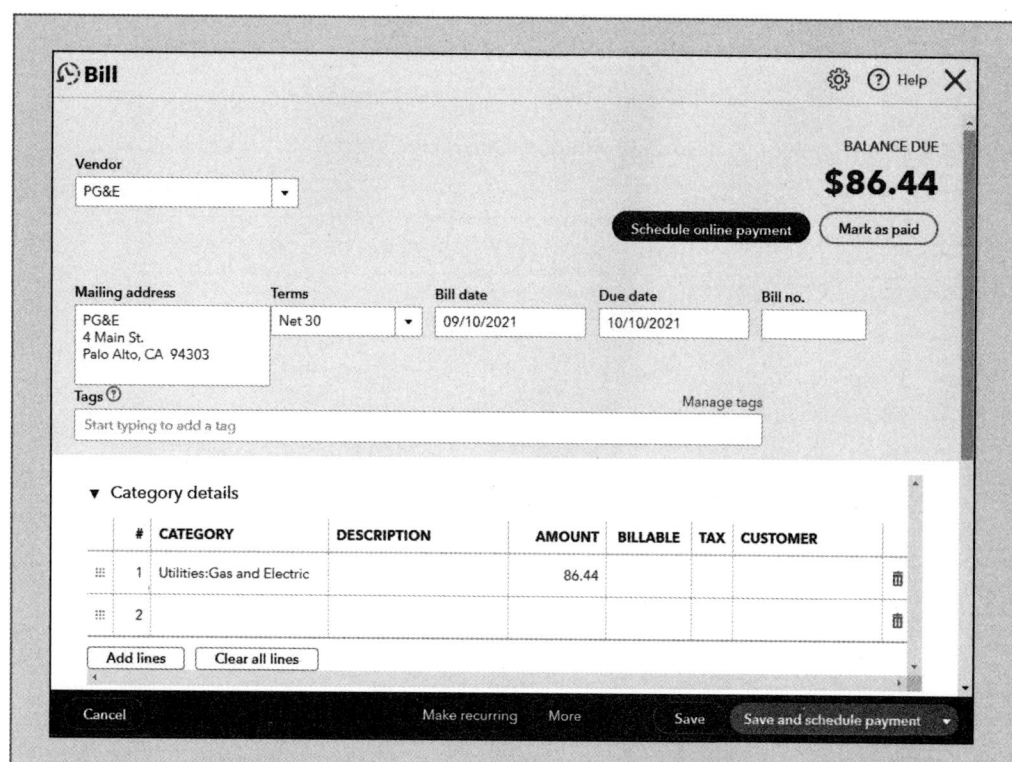

Preparing Financial Statements and Reports **Chapter 10** 235

Figure 10.17

Bill (from PG&E)

6. Write a check to PG&E before the power gets cut off. Actually, no, do not do that. Instead, click **Cancel** to return to the detail report, and click **Back to report summary** to return to the A/P Aging Summary report.

Inventory Valuation Summary

In this section, you will create an inventory valuation summary that reflects each inventory item's quantity on hand, its average cost, and the resulting valuation as of a specific date. Recall the **Trouble?** earlier. The amounts you are asked to investigate next will most likely be different than that stated in the steps. Remember you're just using the Sample Company to explore. You will not find these issues in the end-of-chapter case problems.

To create an inventory valuation summary report, do the following:

1. Continue from where you left off. If you closed the Sample Company, follow the steps to reopen it found at the beginning of this chapter.

2. Click **Reports** from the navigation bar.

3. Type **Inventory** in the Find a report by name search box, and then select the **Inventory Valuation Summary** text, which appears with other inventory reports below the search text box to view the inventory valuation summary report. Change the Report period to **Last Month**. In this case, since the system date was 11/20/2021, the "as of" date was changed to 10/31/2021. Then click **Run report** to view the report shown in Figure 10.18.

Figure 10.18

Inventory Valuation Summary

Craig's Design and Landscaping Services
Inventory Valuation Summary
As of October 31, 2021

	SKU	QTY	ASSET VALUE	CALC. AVG
▾ Design				
▾ Fountains				
Pump	P461-17	25.00	250.00	10.00
Rock Fountain	R154-88	2.00	250.00	125.00
Total Fountains			500.00	
Total Design			500.00	
▾ Landscaping				
▾ Sprinklers				
Sprinkler Heads	S867-56	25.00	18.75	0.75
Sprinkler Pipes	S867-62	31.00	77.50	2.50
Total Sprinklers			96.25	
Total Landscaping			96.25	
TOTAL			**$596.25**	

4. Click on the **25.00** representing the number of pumps on hand shown in Figure 10.18 to view an Inventory Valuation Detail report shown in Figure 10.19.

Figure 10.19

Inventory Valuation Detail

Craig's Design and Landscaping Services
Inventory Valuation Detail
October 2021

DATE	TRANSACTION TYPE	NUM	NAME	QTY	RATE	FIFO COST	QTY ON HAND	ASSET VALUE
▾ Design								
▾ Fountains								
▾ Pump								
10/25/2021	Inventory Qty Adjust	START		16.00	10.00	160.00	16.00	160.00
10/25/2021	Check	75	Hicks Hardware	3.00	10.00	30.00	19.00	190.00
10/25/2021	Bill		Norton Lumber and Buildin...	8.00	10.00	80.00	27.00	270.00
10/25/2021	Invoice	1036	Freeman Sporting Goods:0...	-1.00	10.00	-10.00	26.00	260.00
10/25/2021	Invoice	1037	Sonnenschein Family Store	-1.00	10.00	-10.00	25.00	250.00
Total for Pump				25.00		$250.00	25.00	$250.00
Total for Fountains				25.00		$250.00	25.00	$250.00
Total for Design				25.00		$250.00	25.00	$250.00

5. Click **Bill** reflecting the purchase of eight pumps shown in Figure 10.19 to view the bill shown in Figure 10.20.

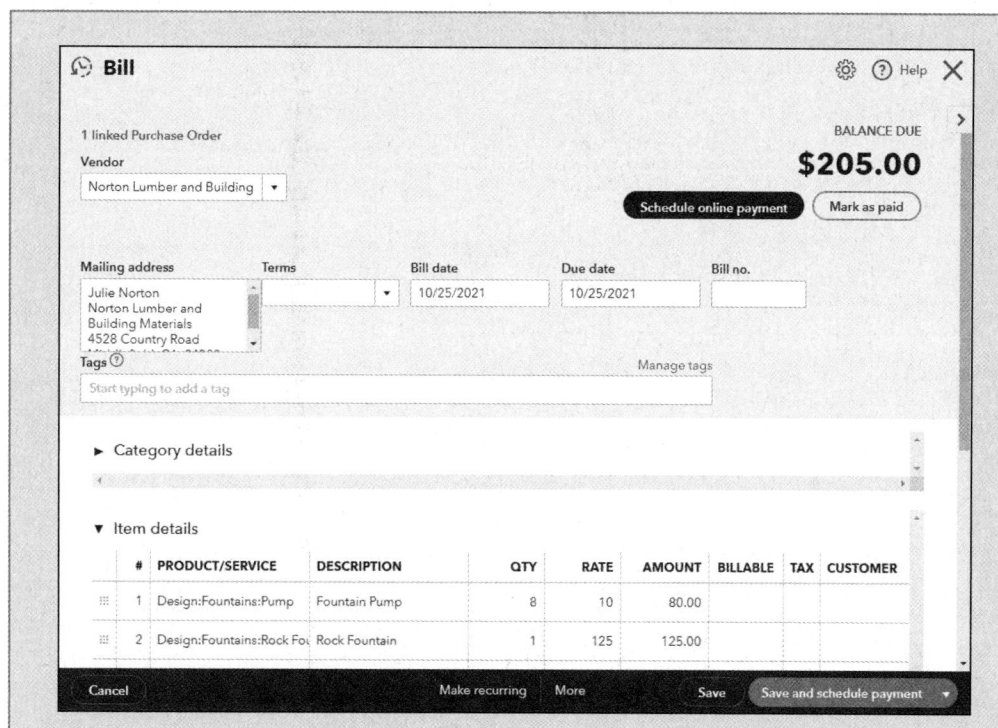

Preparing Financial Statements and Reports **Chapter 10** 237

Figure 10.20

Bill (from Norton Lumber for the purchase of eight pumps)

6 Click **Cancel** to return to the detail report, and click **Back to report summary** to return to the Inventory Valuation Summary report.

Customizing and Saving Reports

All of the reports available in QBO can be customized in some fashion and saved for later use. In this section, you will customize a Profit and Loss report as an example. Recall the **Trouble?** earlier. The amounts you are asked to investigate next will most likely be different than that stated in the steps. Remember you're just using the Sample Company to explore. You will not find these issues in the end-of-chapter case problems.

To customize and save a Profit and Loss report, do the following:

1 Continue from where you left off. If you closed the Sample Company, follow the steps to reopen it found at the beginning of this chapter.

2 Click **Reports** from the navigation bar.

3 Type **Profit** in the Find a report by name search box and then select the **Profit and Loss** text, which appears below the search text box.

4 Click **Collapse**.

5 Change the From: date to the first of the month, three months prior to your system date, and the To: date to the end of the previous month. In this case, since the system date was 11/20/2021, the From: date was changed to 08/01/2021 and the To: date was changed to 10/31/2021. Then click **Run report** to view the report shown in Figure 10.21.

Figure 10.21

Profit and Loss report

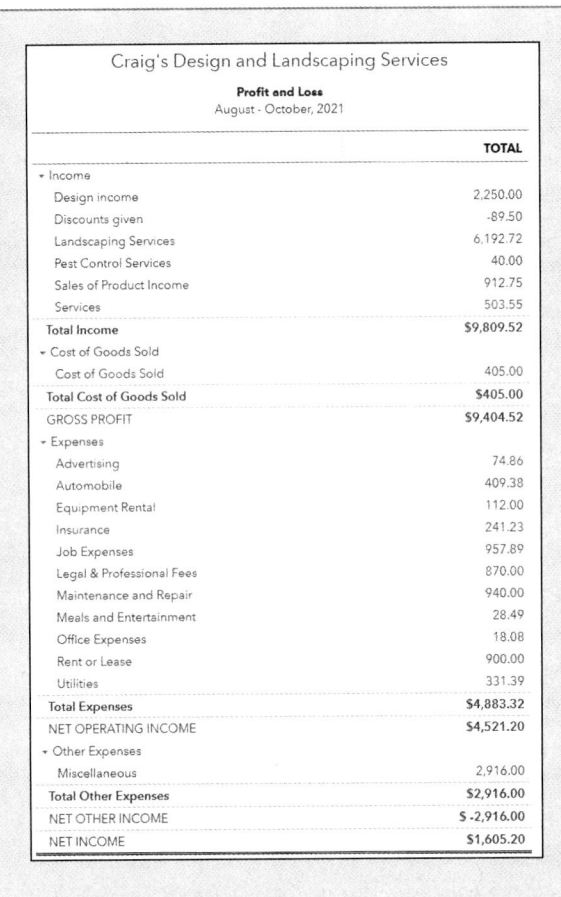

Craig's Design and Landscaping Services
Profit and Loss
August - October, 2021

	TOTAL
▼ Income	
Design income	2,250.00
Discounts given	-89.50
Landscaping Services	6,192.72
Pest Control Services	40.00
Sales of Product Income	912.75
Services	503.55
Total Income	**$9,809.52**
▼ Cost of Goods Sold	
Cost of Goods Sold	405.00
Total Cost of Goods Sold	**$405.00**
GROSS PROFIT	$9,404.52
▼ Expenses	
Advertising	74.86
Automobile	409.38
Equipment Rental	112.00
Insurance	241.23
Job Expenses	957.89
Legal & Professional Fees	870.00
Maintenance and Repair	940.00
Meals and Entertainment	28.49
Office Expenses	18.08
Rent or Lease	900.00
Utilities	331.39
Total Expenses	**$4,883.32**
NET OPERATING INCOME	$4,521.20
▼ Other Expenses	
Miscellaneous	2,916.00
Total Other Expenses	**$2,916.00**
NET OTHER INCOME	$ -2,916.00
NET INCOME	$1,605.20

6. Scroll to the top of the report and then click **Customize**, click **Rows/Columns**, and then select **Months** from the Columns drop-down list in the Rows/Columns section of the Customize Profit and Loss window shown in Figure 10.22.

Figure 10.22

Customize Profit and Loss report

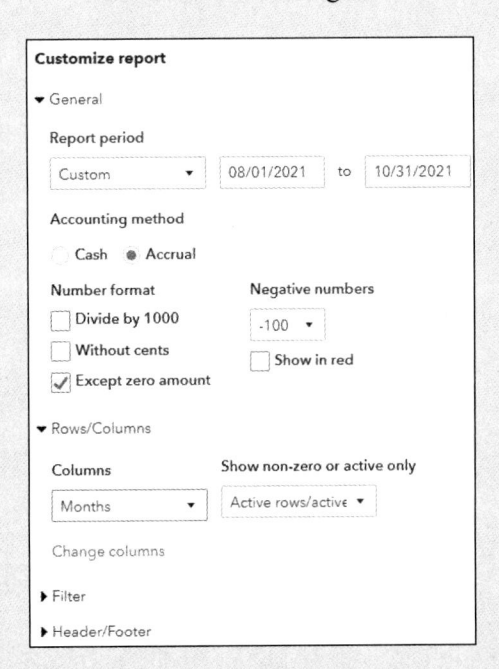

Customize report

▼ General

Report period

[Custom ▼] [08/01/2021] to [10/31/2021]

Accounting method

○ Cash   ● Accrual

Number format   Negative numbers

☐ Divide by 1000   [-100 ▼]
☐ Without cents   ☐ Show in red
☑ Except zero amount

▼ Rows/Columns

Columns   Show non-zero or active only

[Months ▼]   [Active rows/active ▼]

Change columns

▶ Filter
▶ Header/Footer

7. Click **Change columns** and then place a check in the **% of Income** check box.

8 Click **Run report** to view the customized Profit and Loss report shown in Figure 10.23.

Figure 10.23

Customized Profit and Loss report (partial view)

	AUG 2021		SEP 2021		OCT 2021		TOTAL	
	CURRENT	% OF INCOME	CURRENT	% OF INCOME	CURRENT	% OF INCOME	CURRENT	% OF INCOME
▼ Income								
Design income			975.00	50.86 %	1,275.00	17.30 %	$2,250.00	22.94 %
Discounts given					-89.50	-1.21 %	$ -89.50	-0.91 %
Landscaping Services	521.00	100.00 %	872.00	45.49 %	4,799.72	65.11 %	$6,192.72	63.13 %
Pest Control Services			70.00	3.65 %	-30.00	-0.41 %	$40.00	0.41 %
Sales of Product Income					912.75	12.38 %	$912.75	9.30 %
Services					503.55	6.83 %	$503.55	5.13 %
Total Income	$521.00	100.00 %	$1,917.00	100.00 %	$7,371.52	100.00 %	$9,809.52	100.00 %

Craig's Design and Landscaping Services
Profit and Loss
August - October, 2021

9 Click **Save Customization**.

10 Type **Profit and Loss Comparison** as the new name for this report and then click **Save**.

End Note

In this chapter, you did not add business events, but you did create the basic financial statement reports: profit and loss, balance sheet, and statement of cash flows. In addition, you drilled down beyond those reports to transaction detail reports and to source documents like payments, invoices, bills, and so on. You created some analytical reports to learn more about accounts receivable, accounts payable, and inventory. Lastly, you learned how to customize reports and save those reports for later use.

chapter practice 10

Chapter 10 Questions

View the Sample Company QBO file to answer these questions by creating reports:

1. Invoice 1015 was created for which customer?
2. What was the first item sold on invoice 1015?
3. What was the last item sold that was categorized as sales of product income?
4. Who sent a bill for $315 in accounting fees?
5. How many sprinkler heads are currently on hand?
6. What is the average cost per unit of sprinkler heads?
7. Who is the most delinquent customer?
8. What is the total amount of receivables that are current?
9. What amount of payables are 1–30 days past due?
10. What amount of cash was provided by financing activities?

Chapter 10 Matching

a. Income statement　　　　　　　_____ Click on an event in any transaction report
b. Balance sheet　　　　　　　　　_____ Click an account on any report
c. Statement of cash flows　　　　　_____ Click to add a new column in a report
d. AR aging report　　　　　　　　_____ Reflects unpaid bills for the current period
e. AP aging report　　　　　　　　_____ Reports revenues and expenses
f. Inventory valuation report　　　　_____ Includes operating, investing, and financing activities
g. Profit and Loss report　　　　　　_____ Reports inventory quantities on hand
h. To view a transaction report　　　_____ Reports assets, liabilities, and equities
i. To view a source document　　　　_____ Another name for the income statement
j. % of income check box　　　　　_____ Reflects unpaid invoices for the current period

Chapter 10 Cases

The following cases require you to open the company you updated in Chapter 9. Each of the following cases continues throughout the text in a sequential manner. Each of the following cases is similar in concepts assessed but differs in amounts and transactions.

> **To reopen your company, do the following:**
>
> **1** Open your Internet browser.
>
> **2** Type **https://qbo.intuit.com** into your browser's address text box.
>
> **3** Type your user ID and password into the text boxes as you have done earlier.

Case 1

Now it is time to create, customize, and print some new reports. Based on what you learned in the text using the Sample Company, you are to make the following changes to the Case 1 company you modified in Chapter 9:

1 Create, print, and export to Excel a Profit and Loss report for January 2024. Customize this report by adding a percent of income column and saving and by sharing your customization as Profit and Loss Jan 2024.

2 Using the Profit and Loss report created above, drill down to a Transactions Report for the Sales account. Print and export this report to Excel. Save and share this report as a Sales Transaction Report.

3 Create, print, and export to Excel a Balance Sheet report as of 1/31/24. Customize this report by adding a percent of column and saving and sharing your customization as Balance Sheet Jan 2024.

4 Using the Balance Sheet report created above, drill down to a Transactions Report for the Checking account. Print and export this report to Excel. Save and share this report as Checking Report.

5 Create, print, and export to Excel a Statement of Cash Flows report as of 1/31/24. Save and share your customization as Statement of Cash Flows Jan 2024.

6 Using the Statement of Cash Flows report created above, drill down to a Transactions Report for the Accounts Receivable account. Print and export this report to Excel. Save and share this report as an A/R SCF Report.

7 Create, print, and export to Excel an A/R Aging Summary report for the month of January 2024. Save and share your customization as A/R Aging Summary Jan 2024.

8 Create, print, and export to Excel an A/P Aging Summary report for the month of January 2024. Save and share your customization as A/P Aging Summary Jan 2024.

9 Create, print, and export to Excel an Inventory Valuation Summary report for the month of January 2024. Save and share your customization as an Inventory Valuation Summary Jan 2024.

Case 2

Now it is time to create, customize, and print some new reports. Based on what you learned in the text using the Sample Company, you are to make the following changes to the Case 2 company you modified in Chapter 9:

1. Create, print, and export to Excel a Profit and Loss report for January 2025. Customize this report by adding a percent of income column. Save and share your customization as Profit and Loss Jan 2025.

2. Using the Profit and Loss report created above, drill down to a Transactions Report for the Insurance account. Print and export this report to Excel. Save and share this report as an Insurance Transaction Report.

3. Create, print, and export to Excel a Balance Sheet report as of 1/31/25. Customize this report by adding a percent of column. Save and share your customization as Balance Sheet Jan 2025.

4. Using the Balance Sheet report created above, drill down to a Transactions Report for the Inventory Asset account. Print and export this report to Excel. Save and share this report as Inventory Report.

5. Create, print, and export to Excel a Statement of Cash Flows report as of 1/31/25. Save and share your customization as Statement of Cash Flows Jan 2025.

6. Using the Statement of Cash Flows report created above, drill down to a Transactions Report for the Prepaid Expenses account. Print and export this report to Excel. Save and share this report as PPE SCF Report.

7. Create, print, and export to Excel an A/R Aging Summary report for the month of January 2025. Save and share your customization as an A/R Aging Summary Jan 2025.

8. Create, print, and export to Excel an A/P Aging Summary report for the month of January 2025. Save and share your customization as an A/P Aging Summary Jan 2025.

9. Create, print, and export to Excel an Inventory Valuation Summary report for January 2025. Save and share your customization as Inventory Valuation Summary Jan 2025.

Case 3

Now it is time to create, customize, and print some new reports. Based on what you learned in the text using the Sample Company, you are to make the following changes to the Case 3 company you modified in Chapter 9:

1. Create, print, and export to Excel a Profit and Loss report for the month of January 2026. Customize this report by adding a percent of income column and saving and sharing your customization as Profit and Loss Jan 2026.

2. Using the Profit and Loss report created earlier, drill down to a Transactions Report for the Advertising & Marketing account. Print and export this report to Excel. Save this report as Advertising & Marketing Transaction Report.

3 Create, print, and export to Excel a Balance Sheet report as of 1/31/26. Customize this report by adding a percent of column and saving your customization as Balance Sheet Jan 2026.

4 Using the Balance Sheet report created earlier, drill down to a Transactions Report for the Accounts Receivable (A/R) account. Print and export this report to Excel. Save this report as AR Report.

5 Create, print, and export to Excel a Statement of Cash Flows report for the month of January 2026. Save your customization as Statement of Cash Flows Jan 2026.

6 Using the Statement of Cash Flows report created earlier, drill down to a Transactions Report for the Payroll Tax Payable account. Print and export this report to Excel. Save this report as Payroll Tax SCF Report.

7 Create, print, and export to Excel an A/R Aging Summary report for the month of January 2026. Save your customization as A/R Aging Summary Jan 2026.

8 Create, print, and export to Excel an A/P Aging Summary report for the month of January 2026. Save your customization as A/P Aging Summary Jan 2026.

9 Create, print, and export to Excel an Inventory Valuation Summary report for the month of January 2026. Save your customization as Inventory Valuation Summary Jan 2026.

Case 4

Now it is time to create, customize, and print some new reports. Based on what you learned in the text using the Sample Company, you are to make the following changes to the Case 4 company you modified in Chapter 9:

1 Create and print a Profit and Loss report for the month of January 2021. Customize this report by adding a percent of income column and saving your customization as Profit and Loss Jan 2021.

2 Using the Profit and Loss report you just created, drill down to a Transactions Report for the Advertising & Marketing account. Print and save this report as Advertising Transaction Report.

3 Create and print a Balance Sheet report as of 1/31/21. Customize this report by adding a percent of row column. Collapse, print, and save this report as Balance Sheet Jan 2021.

4 Using the Balance Sheet report you just created, drill down to a Transactions Report for the Accounts Receivable (A/R) account. Print and save this report as AR Report.

5 Create and print a Statement of Cash Flows report as of 1/31/21. Save your customization as Statement of Cash Flows Jan 2021.

6. Using the Statement of Cash Flows report you just created, drill down to a Transactions Report for the Payroll Tax Payable account. Print and save this report as Payroll Tax SCF Report.

7. Create and print an Accounts Receivable Aging Summary report for the month of January 2021. Save your customization as A/R Aging Summary Jan 2021.

8. Create and print an Accounts Payable Aging Summary report for the month of January 2021. Save your customization as A/P Aging Summary Jan 2021.

9. Create and print an Inventory Valuation Summary report for the month of January 2021. Save your customization as Inventory Valuation Summary Jan 2021.

Case 5

Now it is time to create, customize, and print some new reports. Based on what you learned in the text using the Sample Company, you are to make the following changes to the Case 5 company you modified in Chapter 9:

1. Create and print a Profit and Loss report for the month of January 2022. Customize this report by adding a percent of income column and saving your customization as Profit and Loss Jan 2022.

2. Using the Profit and Loss report you just created, drill down to a Transactions Report for the Advertising & Marketing account. Print and save this report as Advertising Transaction Report.

3. Create and print a Balance Sheet report for the month of January 2022. Customize this report by adding a percent of row column. Collapse, print, and save this report as Balance Sheet Jan 2022.

4. Using the Balance Sheet report you just created, drill down to a Transactions Report for the Accounts Receivable (A/R) account. Collapse, print, and save this report as AR Transaction Report.

5. Create and print a Statement of Cash Flows report as of 01/31/22. Save your customization as Statement of Cash Flows Jan 2022.

6. Using the Statement of Cash Flows report you just created, drill down to a Transactions Report for the Payroll Tax Payable account. Print and save this report as Payroll Tax SCF Report.

7. Create and print an Accounts Receivable Aging Summary report for the month of January 2022. Save your customization as AR Aging Summary Jan 2022.

8. Create and print an Accounts Payable Aging Summary report for the month of January 2022. Save your customization as AP Aging Summary Jan 2022.

9. Create and print an Inventory Valuation Summary report for the month of January 2022. Save your customization as Inventory Valuation Summary Jan 2022.

Case 6

Now it is time to create, customize, and print some new reports. Based on what you learned in the text using the Sample Company, you are to make the following changes to the Case 6 company you modified in Chapter 9:

1. Create and print a Profit and Loss report for the month of January 2023. Customize this report by adding a % of income column and saving your customization as Profit and Loss Jan 2023.

2. Using the Profit and Loss report you just created, drill down to a Transactions Report for the Payroll account. Print and save this report as Payroll Transaction Report.

3. Create and print a Balance Sheet report as of 1/31/23. Customize this report by adding a % of row column. (This is done in a similar manner to adding a % of income column done for the Profit and Loss report.) Collapse, print, and save this report as Balance Sheet Jan 2023.

4. Using the Balance Sheet report you just created drill down to a Transactions Report for the Prepaid Expenses account. Collapse, print, and save this report as Prepaid Expenses Transaction Report.

5. Create and print a Statement of Cash Flows report as of 1/31/23. Save your customization as Statement of Cash Flows Jan 2023.

6. Create and print an Accounts Receivable Aging Summary report for the month of January 2023. Save your customization as A/R Aging Summary Jan 2023.

7. Create and print an Accounts Payable Aging Summary report for the month of January 2023. Save your customization as A/P Aging Summary Jan 2023.

8. Create and print an Inventory Valuation Summary report for the month of January 2023. Save your customization as Inventory Valuation Summary Jan 2023.

appendix 1

Sales Tax

Some companies are required to collect sales tax from customers depending on the state(s) in which they do business. Collecting sales tax in QBO has gotten easier! Through the new Automated Sales Tax experience, you just need to answer a few simple questions and QBO will know what taxes apply to your business, set them up, and automatically track your sales taxes.

This means you no longer need to select a tax rate when you create an invoice or other transaction. As long as your Sales Tax Center and all applicable tax agencies are set up, the system will automatically do it for you!

Be advised that end-of-chapter Cases 1 and 2 do not require the collection of sales tax. Cases 3 to 6 do require the collection of sales tax using the new Automated Sales Tax system. Keep in mind that sales tax rates change year to year, state to state. The solutions provided by the author for each case were based on tax rates in effect for that particular year. If a rate changes your answers for sales, tax payable and related accounts may be different.

At the time of publication, Intuit had two different procedures for setting up sales tax. The first works for regular companies students and instructors. This is the process used in prior editions of QBO and this text. The second works for the Sample Company and is the new process used going forward. At some point this new process will be implemented and work for both types of companies.

The following are steps to set up the new Automated Sales Tax system. The following example assumes the company is in California. That is not true in all cases. Your case may be in a different state, and thus, your steps to create a company's sales tax will be different.

VIDEO LINK

Navigate your browser to the Video Tutorials provided by Intuit (See web site address specified in the Preface to this text) and then search on How to Set Up and use Automatic Sales Tax.

To set up a company's sales tax (QBO regular companies):

1. Click **Taxes** from the navigation bar.

2. Click the **Use Automatic Sales Tax** button (assuming you've already entered your company's address during the setup process), and then click Next to confirm your company's business address. Click No when asked if you need to collect sales tax out of the state and then click Next. Now view the window shown in Figure A.1.

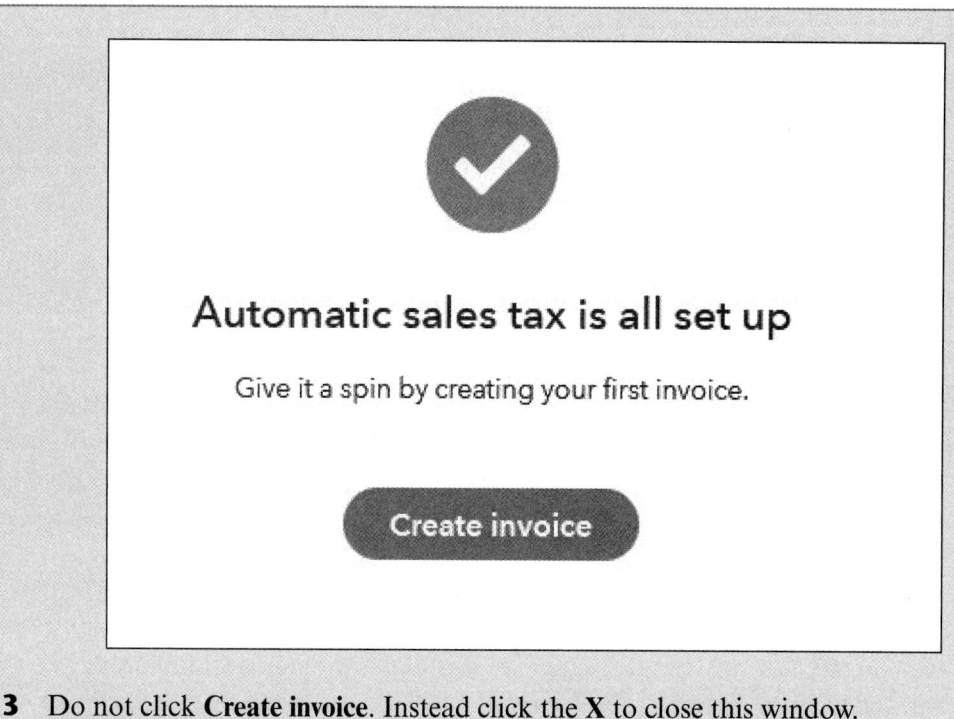

Figure A.1

Sales Tax Center

3. Do not click **Create invoice**. Instead click the **X** to close this window.
4. Select **Quarterly** from the Filing frequency drop-down text box, and then click **Save**.

To set up a company's sales tax: (QBO Sample Company only)

1. Click **Taxes** from the navigation bar.
2. Click the **Get Started** button (assuming you've already entered your company's address during the setup process) as shown in Figure A.2.

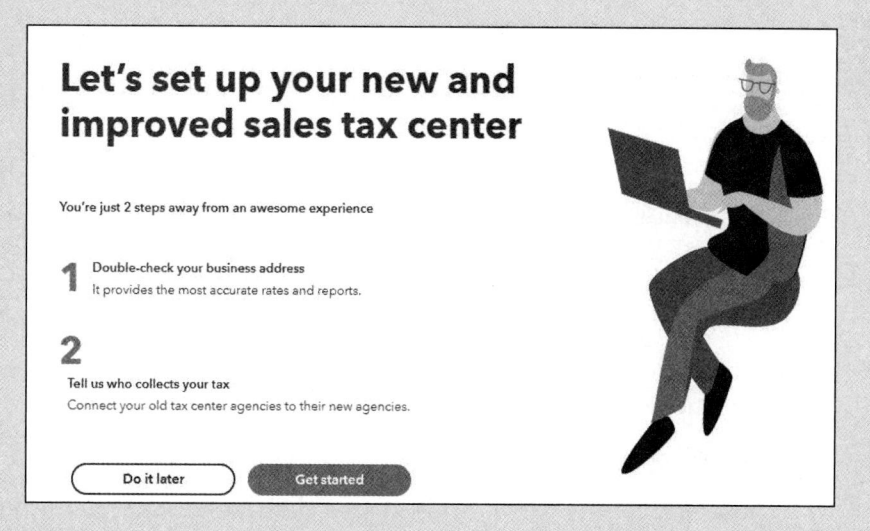

Navigate your browser to the Video Tutorials provided by Intuit (see website address specified in the Preface to this text) and then search on How to Set Up and use Automatic Sales Tax.

Figure A.2

Sales Tax Center

3. Click **Next** to accept the address you previously entered for your company. The address shown in Figure A.3 is the address of the Sample Company.

Figure A.3

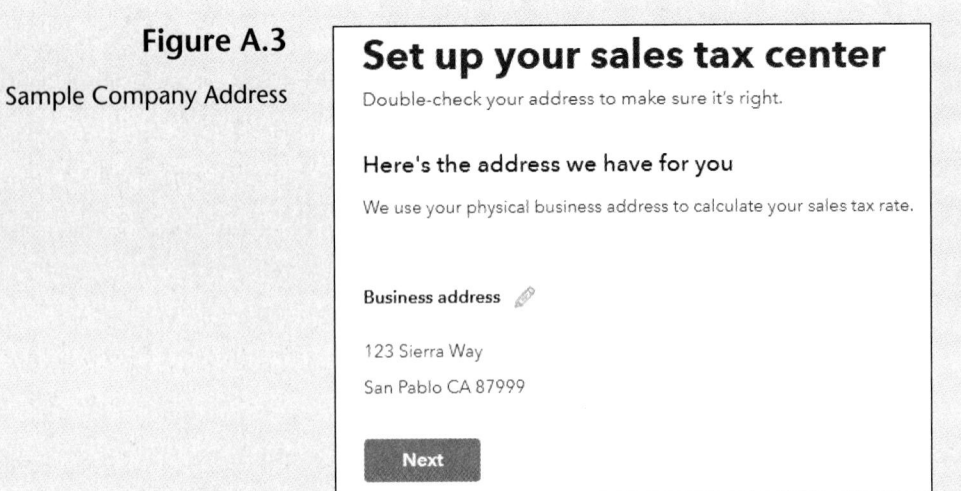

Sample Company Address

Set up your sales tax center
Double-check your address to make sure it's right.

Here's the address we have for you
We use your physical business address to calculate your sales tax rate.

Business address ✎

123 Sierra Way
San Pablo CA 87999

[Next]

4. Place a check in each **Tax Rate Name** check box and then select the appropriate Official Agency Name and then click **Next**. Note that in Figure A.4 the tax rate names are based on the Sample Company's zip code. Your company's address will be different depending on which case you are working on. Thus your screen will look different and reflect the tax rate unique to your company's address.

Figure A.4

Assigning a Tax Rate to your Company

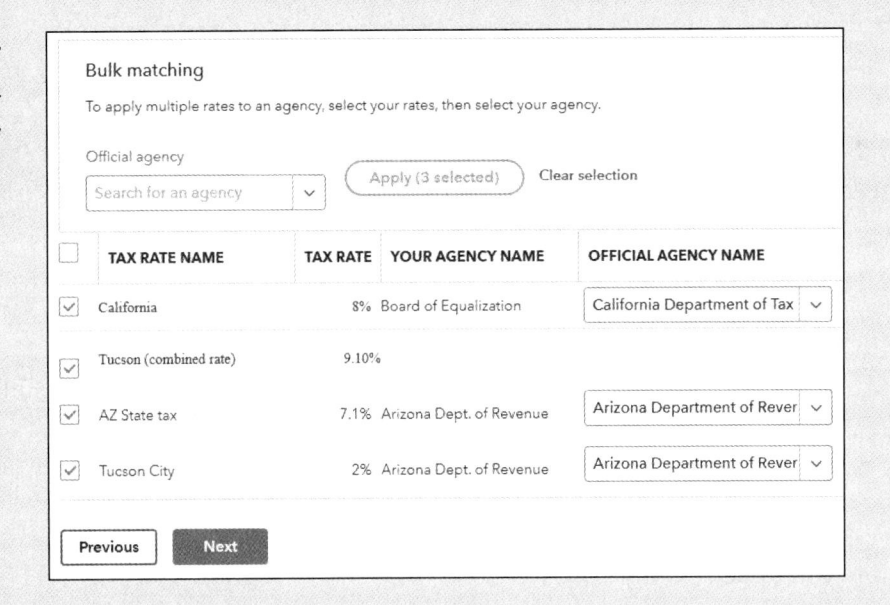

Bulk matching
To apply multiple rates to an agency, select your rates, then select your agency.

Official agency
[Search for an agency] [Apply (3 selected)] Clear selection

	TAX RATE NAME	TAX RATE	YOUR AGENCY NAME	OFFICIAL AGENCY NAME
✓	California	8%	Board of Equalization	California Department of Tax
✓	Tucson (combined rate)	9.10%		
✓	AZ State tax	7.1%	Arizona Dept. of Revenue	Arizona Department of Rever
✓	Tucson City	2%	Arizona Dept. of Revenue	Arizona Department of Rever

[Previous] [Next]

5. Click **Next** to save your work and then click **Continue** 2 times.
6. Click **View sales tax center** and then select **Quarterly** as the Filing frequency.
7. Click **Next agency** and once again select **Quarterly** as the Filing frequency.
8. Click **Save** to save your work and then click **Dashboard** to return to the main QuickBooks page.

Comprehensive Case Problems

appendix 2

Your instructor may assign you these comprehensive case problems after you complete all 10 chapters of the text. These are an *extension* of the cases assigned at the end of Chapters 3 to 10 of the *QuickBooks Online for Accounting*, fifth edition, text. Because QBO only allows you access to one company, Case 1 can be used by students only if they have *successfully completed* Case 1 through Chapter 10, Case 2 can be used by students only if they have *successfully completed* Case 2 through Chapter 10, Case 3 can be used by students only if they have *successfully completed* Case 3 through Chapter 10, and Case 4 can be used by students only if they have *successfully completed* Case 4 through Chapter 10. There is no Case 5 comprehensive problem. Case 6 can be used by students only if they have *successfully completed* Case 6 through Chapter 10.

Case 1 Comprehensive Problem

Case 1, which begins in Chapter 3, is a company that distributes surfboards and is in La Jolla, California. Business events in Case 1 occurred from 12/31/23 to 1/31/24 when presented in Chapters 3 to 10. The following is a description of business events that occurred in the month of February 2024.

Date	Description of Event	Chapter	Event
2/1/24	Add a new product	4	Add a new product with quantity tracked – Biscuit Bonzer, initial quantity on hand: 0, as of date: 2/1/24, price: $1,000, cost: $675, income account: Sales, expense account: Cost of Goods Sold. Vendor: Channel Islands.
2/1/24	Edit the chart of accounts	3	Change the name of the account Notes Payable to Notes Payable – Bank of CA.
2/1/24	Add a new service	4	Add a new service – Repairs, rate: $85, income account: Services.
2/1/24	Modify budget	8	Modify the following monthly budgeted amounts (Budget 1) for February 2024 through December 2024 as follows: sales: $35,000, services: $2,000, cost of goods sold: $21,500, interest expense: $800, payroll: $13,000, rent or lease: $2,500, travel: $500, utilities: $300.
2/1/24	Add a new employee	7	Add a new employee – Jane Price, 65 Ocean View Lane, La Jolla, CA 92037, Employee ID No.: 555-15-3537.
2/1/24	Add a new customer	4	Add a new customer – Awesome Surf, 501 Boardwalk Place, Santa Cruz, CA 95060.
2/5/24	Add a sales receipt	4	Add a new sales receipt #1005 for $2,810 – Customer: Awesome Surf, payment method: Check, reference no.: 984, deposit to: Undeposited Funds, product: The Water Hog, quantity: 1, and product: Rook 15, quantity: 3.
2/6/24	Add a new invoice	4	Add a new invoice #1006 for $820 – Customer: Surf Rider Foundation, terms: Net 30, service: Repairs, quantity: 2, and product: Rook 15, quantity: 1.
2/7/24	Add a cash receipt	4	Add a new cash receipt – Customer: Blondie's Boards, payment method: Check, reference no.: 1003, deposit to: Undeposited Funds, amount received: $8,000, applied to invoice #1003.
2/8/24	Make a bank deposit	4	Add a bank deposit to the checking account in the amount of $15,810, which represents payments from Blondie's Boards for $5,000 and $8,000 and Awesome Surf for $2,810.
2/9/24	Add a new vendor	5	Add a new vendor – BoardsWest, 36 Anacapa St., Santa Barbara, CA 93101, terms: Net 30.

Date	Task	Ch	Description
2/9/24	Add a new product	5	Add a new product with quantity tracked – Wiley One, initial quantity on hand: 0, as of date: 2/9/24, price: $4,000, cost: $2,400, income account: Sales, expense account: Cost of Goods Sold. Vendor: BoardsWest.
2/9/24	Add a new account	3	Add a new account – Account type: Other Current Assets, detail type: Other Current Assets, name: Employee Loans.
2/9/24	Add a new purchase order	5	Add a new purchase order #1003 for $9,600 to purchase 4 Wiley One boards from vendor BoardsWest.
2/10/24	Use credit card	5	Add a credit card charge – Vendor: Village Travel, using credit card: VISA, category Travel, amount: $775.
2/11/24	Record a check	5	Add check no. 1013 – Vendor: Office Depot, amount: $575, category: Supplies Asset.
2/11/24	Add a new purchase order	5	Add a new purchase order #1004 for $12,400 – Vendor: Channel Islands, ordered 10 Fred Rubbles, 6 Rook 15, and 8 The Water Hog boards.
2/12/24	Add a new bill	5	Add a new bill based on a purchase order #1002 for $4,700 – Vendor: Stewart Surfboards, terms: Net 30. All items ordered were received.
2/13/24	Add a new bill	5	Add a new bill without a purchase order – San Diego Gas & Electric, terms: Net 15, category: Utilities, amount: $150.
2/14/24	Add a new bill	5	Add a new bill without a purchase order – Prime Properties, terms: Net 15, category: Rent or Lease, amount: $2,500.
2/14/24	Pay a bill with a check	5	Pay bill $7,500 due to Prime Properties using check no. 1012.
2/15/24	Add new fixed asset accounts	6	Create four new fixed asset accounts – Account type: Fixed Assets, detail type: Buildings and Accumulated Depreciation (where appropriate), account names: Original Cost (a sub account of Building) and Accumulated Depreciation (a sub account of Building), and Land with Account type: Fixed Asset, detail type: Land.
2/15/24	Purchase land and building	6	Add the purchase of land and a warehouse building from Prime Properties, check no. 1014, amount: $2,000, as a down payment on land $5,000 and a building $15,000. The balance was paid by signing a long-term note for $18,000 (create a new account called Notes Payable – Chase, Account type: Long-Term Liabilities, detail type: Notes Payable).
2/19/24	Sell common stock	6	Add the sale of common stock to shareholders as a deposit of a $15,000 check.
2/19/24	Pay dividends	6	Add the payment of dividends to shareholders on 2/19/24, check no. 1015, in the amount of $500.
2/20/24	Make a loan payment	6	Add the payment of $339.68 to Chase Bank (a new vendor) as an installment on the land and building purchase made on 2/15/24, which included interest expense of $75 and principal amount of $264.68 using check no. 1016.
2/20/24	Make a loan payment	6	Record the payment of $1,132.27 to Bank of CA on 2/20/24 (as an installment on a loan received last month), which included interest expense of $250 and principal amount of $882.27 using check no. 1017.
2/20/24	Pay first payroll	7	Add payroll (as you did in the chapter) based on the information shown in Figure 1. (This payroll covers work through 2/15/24 but wasn't paid until 2/20/24.)
2/27/24	Add a new bill	6	Add a new bill based on purchase order #1003 on 2/9/24 – Vendor: BoardsWest, terms: Net 30. All items ordered were received.
2/27/24	Add a new invoice	4	Add invoice #1007 for $12,000 to Blazing Boards, terms: Net 30, for 3 Wiley One boards.
2/28/24	Pay second payroll	7	Add payroll (as you did in the chapter) based on the information shown in Figure 2 as follows.
2/28/24	Add a new bill	5	Add a new bill based on purchase order #1004 for $12,400 – Vendor: Channel Islands, terms: Net 15. All items ordered were received. (*Hint:* First clear all lines in the Item details section of the bill that are left over from a previous bill from Channel Islands.)
2/28/24	Add a new invoice	4	Add an invoice #1008 for $12,990 to Blondie's Boards, terms: Net 30, for 8 Fred Rubble, 3 Rook 15, and 4 The Water Hog boards.

Date	Action	Ref	Description
2/28/24	Add a sales receipt	4	Add a sales receipt #1009 for Sarah Hay at Hey Hays Surf for $12,210 to record their check no. 988, which was deposited to the checking account, for 1 California Nose Rider, 3 Fred Rubble, 1 Wiley One, 1 Water Hog, and 2 Rook 15 boards.
2/28/24	Reconcile bank account	4	Reconcile your company's checking account. No service charges or interest were incurred or earned. The ending bank statement balance on 2/28/24 was $39,896.91. All checks cleared the bank except checks no. 1021 to 1023. All deposits cleared the bank except a check from Sarah Hay for $12,210.
2/28/24	Adjust supplies	9	$250 of supplies were used in February. Use journal entry 10.
2/28/24	Adjust prepaid rent	9	$800 of prepaid expenses expired (representing prepaid rent) in the month of February. Use journal entry 11.
2/28/24	Accrue expenses	9	A bill for $450 was received and recorded in the next month for travel consumed in the current month. Use journal entry 12. In January, you accrued $150 in maintenance costs, which remains unpaid. No adjustment is necessary, but payment needs to be made next month.
2/28/24	Defer revenue	9	Consulting services recorded on invoice #1004 for $2,500 to Surf Rider Foundation were unearned as of 1/31/24 but were performed in February 2024. Thus, the revenue was earned. This requires the reversal of journal entry 7 recorded on 1/31/24. (*Hint:* Look at journal entry 7, and use journal entry 13 to reverse it on 2/28/24.)
2/28/24	Accrue revenue	9	Consulting services of $8,500 (340 hours) were performed as of 1/31/24 for Blazing Boards but not invoiced to the customer or recorded into the accounting records. Revenue was accrued using journal entry 8. Add invoice #1010 to bill Blazing Boards for this service. This also requires reversal of journal entry 8 recorded on 1/31/24. (*Hint:* Look at journal entry 8, and use journal entry 14 to reverse it on 2/28/24.)
2/28/24	Accrue depreciation	9	Depreciation Expense of $675 ($100, $75, and $500 for Building, Equipment, and Furniture & Fixtures, respectively) needs to be recorded for the month. Use journal entry 15 to record this depreciation.
2/28/24	Accrue revenue	9	Consulting services of $10,200 were performed on 2/28/24 for a new customer, Kyle Hain, but not invoiced or recorded into the accounting records. Use journal entry 16 to accrue this revenue.

Pay/Tax/Withholding	Ben	Betsy	Jane	Total
Hours if applicable	n/a	62	60	
Annual salary or hourly rate	95,000.00	21.50	20.00	
Gross pay	3,958.33	1,333.00	1,200.00	5,291.33
Federal withholding	542.29	182.62	164.40	724.91
Social security employee (6.2%)	245.42	82.65	74.40	328.07
Medicare employee (1.45%)	57.40	19.33	17.40	76.73
Employee withholding	845.11	284.60	256.20	1,129.71
Social security employer (6.2%)	245.42	82.65	74.40	328.07
Medicare employer (1.45%)	57.40	19.33	17.40	76.73
Employer payroll tax expense	302.82	101.98	91.80	404.80
Net Check amount	3,113.22	1,048.40	943.80	5,105.42
Check number	1018	1019	1020	

Figure 1

First semimonthly payroll

Figure 2

Second semimonthly payroll

Pay/Tax/Withholding	Ben	Betsy	Jane	Total
Hours if applicable	n/a	52	45	
Annual salary or hourly rate	95,000.00	21.50	20.00	
Gross pay	**3,958.33**	**1,118.00**	**900.00**	**5,076.33**
Federal withholding	542.29	153.17	123.30	695.46
Social security employee (6.2%)	245.42	69.32	55.80	314.74
Medicare employee (1.45%)	57.40	16.21	13.05	73.61
Employee withholding	**845.11**	**238.70**	**192.15**	**1,083.81**
Social security employer (6.2%)	245.42	69.32	55.80	314.74
Medicare employer (1.45%)	57.40	16.21	13.05	73.61
Employer payroll tax expense	**302.82**	**85.53**	**68.85**	**388.35**
Net Check amount	3,113.22	879.30	707.85	3,992.52
Check number	**1021**	**1022**	**1023**	

Requirements:

1. Create, save, and print a Profit and Loss report for February 2024.
2. Create, save, and print a Sales Transaction report for February 2024.
3. Create, save, and print a Balance Sheet report for February 28, 2024, with a % of column.
4. Create, save, and print a Checking report for February 2024.
5. Create, save, and print a Statement of Cash Flows report for February 2024.
6. Create, save, and print an A/R Aging Summary report for February 2024.
7. Create, save, and print an A/P Aging Summary report for February 2024.
8. Create, save, and print an Inventory Valuation Summary report for February 2024.
9. Create, save, and print a Transactions List by Date report for February 2024.
10. Create, save, and print a Budget vs. Actuals report for February 2024.

Case 2 Comprehensive Problem

Case 2, which begins in Chapter 3, is a company that distributes remote controlled toys and is in La Jolla, California. Business events in Case 2 occurred from 12/31/24 to 1/31/25 when presented in Chapters 3 to 10. The following is a description of business events that occurred in the month of February 2025.

Date	Description of Event	Chapter	Event
2/1/25	Add a new product	4	Add a new product – Speedy Whit, initial quantity on hand: 0, as of date: 2/1/25, price: $1,500, cost: $925, income account: Sales, expense account: Cost of Goods Sold.

Date	Action	#	Details
2/1/25	Add a new vendor	5	Add a new vendor – 3D Robotics, 36 Anacapa St., Santa Barbara, CA 93101, terms: Net 30.
2/1/25	Edit the chart of accounts	3	Change the name of the account Notes Payable to Notes Payable – Bank of San Diego.
2/1/25	Add a new service	4	Add a new service – Consulting, rate: $105, income account: Services.
2/1/25	Modify budget	8	Modify the following monthly budgeted amounts (Budget 1) for February 2025 through December 2025 as follows: sales: $22,000, services: $4,800, cost of goods sold: $11,000, interest expense: $400, payroll: $10,000, rent or lease: $2,500, travel: $500, utilities: $300. All other accounts remain the same.
2/1/25	Add a new employee	7	Add a new employee – Juan Perez, 65 Ocean View Lane, La Jolla, CA 92037, Employee ID No.: 555-15-3537.
2/1/25	Add a new customer	4	Add a new customer – Briggs Construction, 501 Boardwalk Place, Santa Cruz, CA 95060.
2/5/25	Add a sales receipt	4	Add a new sales receipt #1005 for $3,300 – Customer: Briggs Construction, payment method: Check, reference no.: 984, deposit to: Undeposited Funds, product: Broon F830 Ride, quantity: 1, and product: Sport Cub S, quantity: 3.
2/6/25	Add a new invoice	4	Add a new invoice #1006 for $2,250 – Customer: Hagen's Toys, terms: Net 30, service: Consulting, quantity: 10, and product: Sport Cub S, quantity: 2.
2/7/25	Add a cash receipt	4	Add a new cash receipt – Customer: Hagen's Toys, payment method: Check, reference no.: 5841, deposit to: Undeposited Funds, amount received: $1,425 (related to invoice #1002).
2/8/25	Make a bank deposit	4	Add a bank deposit to the checking account in the amount of $5,650 (Benson's RC $925, Brigg's Construction $3,300, and Hagen's Toys $1,425).
2/9/25	Add a new product	4	Add a new product – Pro View, initial quantity on hand: 0, as of date: 2/9/25, price: $2,500, cost: $1,200, income account: Sales, expense account: Cost of Goods Sold.
2/9/25	Add a new account	3	Add a new account – Account type: Other Current Assets, detail type: Other Current Assets, name: Security Deposits.
2/9/25	Add a new purchase order	5	Add a new purchase order #1003 for $11,550 to purchase 6 Speedy Whit and 5 Pro View drones from vendor 3D Robotics.
2/9/25	Use credit card	5	Add a credit card charge, new vendor: Village Travel, using credit card: AMEX, category: Travel, amount: $1,800.
2/11/25	Record a check	5	Add check no. 1011, vendor: Staples, Inc., amount: $750, account: Supplies Asset.
2/11/25	Add a new purchase order	5	Add a new purchase order #1004 for $3,695 – Vendor: E-flite for 5 Sport Cub S and 4 Mystique RES drones.
2/12/25	Add a new bill	5	Add a new bill based on a purchase order #1002 for $8,820 – Vendor: Kyosho, terms: Net 30. All items ordered were received.
2/13/25	Add a new bill	5	Add a new bill without a purchase order – San Diego Gas & Electric (a new vendor), terms: Net 15, category: Utilities, amount: $150.
2/13/25	Add a new bill	5	Add a new bill without a purchase order – Deluxe Properties (a new vendor), terms: Net 15, category: Rent & Lease, amount: $3,500.
2/13/25	Add new fixed asset accounts	6	Create four new fixed asset accounts – Account type: Fixed Assets, detail type: Buildings and Accumulated Depreciation (where appropriate), account names: Original Cost (a sub account of Building) and Accumulated Depreciation (a sub account of Building), and Land with Account type: Fixed Asset, detail type: Land.
2/13/25	Purchase land and building	6	Add the purchase of land and a warehouse building from Deluxe Properties, check no. 1012, amount: $10,000, as a down payment on land $15,000 and a building $35,000. The balance was paid by signing a long-term note for $40,000 to the Bank of San Diego (a new vendor).

Date	Action	#	Description
2/15/25	Pay first payroll	7	Add payroll (as you did in the chapter) based on the information shown in Figure 1.
2/19/25	Sell common stock	6	Add the sale of common stock to shareholders as a deposit of a $10,000, check no. 3009.
2/19/25	Pay dividends	6	Add the payment of dividends to shareholders on 2/19/25, check no. 1016, in the amount of $500.
2/20/25	Make a loan payment	6	Add the payment of $1,216.88 to the Bank of San Diego as an installment on the land and building purchase made on 2/15/25, which included interest expense of $200 and principal amount of $1,016.88, using check no. 1017.
2/22/25	Add a new bill	5	Add a new bill based on a purchase order #1003 – Vendor: 3D Robotics, terms: Net 30, amount: $11,550. All items ordered were received.
2/25/25	Add a new invoice	4	Add invoice #1007 for $10,500 to Kelly's Awesome Copters, terms: Net 30, for 4 Speedy Whit and 3 Broon F830 Ride drones.
2/25/25	Pay a bill with a check	5	Pay bill $3,500 due to Deluxe Properties using check no. 1018.
2/26/25	Receive payment	4	Receive payment on account from Hagen's Toys of $4,500 for invoice #1003 using check no. 938 and deposited to the Undeposited Funds account.
2/27/25	Add a new invoice	4	Add an invoice #1008 for $4,755 to A+ Engineering (a new customer), terms: Net 30, for 15 hours of consulting, 2 Speedy Whit drones, and 4 hours of custom painting.
2/27/25	Add a new bill	5	Add a new bill based on purchase order #1004 for $3,695 – Vendor: E-flite, terms: Net 15. All items ordered were received. (*Hint:* First clear all lines in the Item details section of the bill that are left over from a previous bill from E-flite.)
2/27/25	Add a sales receipt	4	Add a sales receipt #1009 for Fly by Night (a new customer) for $2,700 to record cash received, which was deposited to the checking account for 3 Sport Cub S and 2 Mystique RES drones.
2/27/25	Make a deposit	4	Deposited Hagen's Toys check for $4,500 into the checking account.
2/28/25	Add a new invoice	4	Add invoice #1010 to record repair services performed for Kelly's Awesome Copters. This transaction had been accrued on 1/31/25 via journal entry 8. (A variety of rates were used on this repair; thus, just enter $6,298 as the Rate for this invoice and 1 as the QTY.)
2/28/25	Add a bill	5	Add a bill for legal services rendered by Galas & Associates (new vendor) for $750. This had been accrued on 1/31/25 using journal entry 6.
2/28/25	Pay second payroll	7	Add payroll (as you did in the chapter) based on the information shown in Figure 2 as follows.
2/28/25	Reconcile bank account	8	Reconcile your company's checking account. No service charges or interest were incurred or earned. The ending bank statement balance on 2/28/25 was $29,835.47. All checks cleared the bank except checks no. 1019 to 1021. All deposits cleared the bank except a deposit from Hagen's Toys for $4,500.
2/28/25	Adjust supplies	9	$250 of supplies were used in February. Use journal entry 10.
2/28/25	Adjust prepaids	9	$1,800 of prepaid expenses expired (representing prepaid insurance) in the month of February. Use journal entry 11.
2/28/25	Accrue expenses	9	A bill for $850 was received and recorded in the next month for travel consumed in the current month. Use journal entry 12.
2/28/25	Reverse accrual	9	Legal fees accrued on 1/31/25 for $750 via journal entry 6 were properly recorded in February. Use journal entry 13 to reverse it.
2/28/25	Defer revenue	9	Consulting services recorded on invoice #1008 for $1,575 to A+ Engineering were not yet performed and thus were unearned as of 2/28/25. Use journal entry 14 to defer this revenue.
2/28/25	Accrue depreciation	9	Depreciation Expense of $1,125 ($125, $375, and $625 for Building, Furniture, and Machinery & Equipment, respectively) needs to be recorded for the month. Use journal entry 15 to record this depreciation.

2/28/25	Reverse accrual	9	$6,298 of revenue had been accrued on 1/31/25 via journal entry 8 for services rendered but not yet invoiced. These were then invoiced using invoice #1010 to Kelly's Awesome Copters. (*Hint:* Reverse journal entry 8 via a new journal entry 16.)
2/28/25	Accrue revenue	9	Consulting services of $15,000 were performed on 2/28/25 for a new customer, Wesley Ray, but not invoiced or recorded into the accounting records. Use journal entry 17 to accrue this revenue.

Figure 1

First semimonthly payroll

Pay/Tax/Withholding	Frank	Sara	Juan	Total
Hours if applicable	n/a	80	65	
Annual salary or hourly rate	72,000.00	18.75	17.00	
Gross pay	**3,000.00**	**1,500.00**	**1,105.00**	**4,500.00**
Federal withholding	411.00	205.50	151.39	616.50
Social security employee (6.2%)	186.00	93.00	68.51	279.00
Medicare employee (1.45%)	43.50	21.75	16.02	65.25
Employee withholding	**640.50**	**320.25**	**235.92**	**960.75**
Social security employer (6.2%)	186.00	93.00	68.51	279.00
Medicare employer (1.45%)	43.50	21.75	16.02	65.25
Employer payroll tax expense	**229.50**	**114.75**	**84.53**	**344.25**
Net Check amount	2,359.50	1,179.75	869.08	3,539.25
Check number	1013	1014	1015	

Figure 2

Second semimonthly payroll

Pay/Tax/Withholding	Frank	Sara	Juan	Total
Hours if applicable	n/a	75	70	
Annual salary or hourly rate	72,000.00	18.75	17.00	
Gross pay	**3,000.00**	**1,406.25**	**1,190.00**	**4,406.25**
Federal withholding	411.00	192.66	163.03	603.66
Social security employee (6.2%)	186.00	87.19	73.78	273.19
Medicare employee (1.45%)	43.50	20.39	17.26	63.89
Employee withholding	**640.50**	**300.24**	**254.07**	**940.74**
Social security employer (6.2%)	186.00	87.19	73.78	273.19
Medicare employer (1.45%)	43.50	20.39	17.26	63.89
Employer payroll tax expense	**229.50**	**107.58**	**91.04**	**337.08**
Net Check amount	2,359.50	1,106.01	935.93	3,465.51
Check number	1019	1020	1021	

Requirements:

1. Create, save, and print a Profit and Loss report for February 2025.
2. Create, save, and print a Total Income Transaction report for February 2025. (*Hint:* Click the **Total Income amount** in the Profit and Loss report for February 2025.)
3. Create, save, and print a Balance Sheet report for February 28, 2025.
4. Create, save, and print a Checking report for February 2025.
5. Create, save, and print a Statement of Cash Flows report for February 2025.
6. Create, save, and print an A/R Aging Summary report for February 2025.
7. Create, save, and print an A/P Aging Summary report for February 2025.
8. Create, save, and print an Inventory Valuation Summary report for February 2025.
9. Create, save, and print a Transactions List by Date report for February 2025.
10. Create, save, and print a Budget vs. Actuals report for February 2025.

Case 3 Comprehensive Problem

Case 3, which begins in Chapter 3, is a company that sells and services cell phones to consumers (retail business) and is in La Jolla, California. Business events in Case 3 occurred from 12/31/25 to 1/31/26 when presented in Chapters 3 to 10. The following is a description of business events that occurred in the month of February 2026.

Date	Description of Event	Chapter	Event
2/2/26	Add new products	4	Add two new taxable products – iPhone 8, initial quantity on hand: 0, as of date: 2/1/26, inventory asset account: Inventory Asset, price: $850, cost: $650, income account: Sales of Product Income, expense account: Cost of Goods Sold (taxable) and iPhone 8 Plus, initial quantity on hand: 0, as of date: 2/1/26, inventory asset account: Inventory Asset, price: $1,050, cost: $850, income account: Sales of Product Income, expense account: Cost of Goods Sold (taxable).
2/2/26	Change the name of a product	4	Change the name of the Apple iPhone 7 to iPhone 7.
2/2/26	Add a new vendor	5	Add a new vendor – LG Baker Distributing Company, 36 Sequoia St., Redlands, CA 92374, terms: Net 30.
2/2/26	Add a new product	4	Add a new taxable product – LG V30, initial quantity on hand: 0, as of date: 2/2/26, inventory asset account: Inventory Asset, price: $830, cost: $600, income account: Sales of Product Income, expense account: Cost of Goods Sold (taxable).
2/3/26	Add a new service	4	Add a new service – LG Repairs, rate: $95, income account: Services (not taxable).
2/3/26	Modify budget	8	Modify the following monthly budgeted amounts (Budget 1) for February 2026 through December 2026 as follows: sales of product income: $25,000, services: $9,000, cost of goods sold: $18,000, advertising and marketing: $2,000, insurance: $750, interest paid: $200, meals: $0, payroll: $11,000, utilities: $300.
2/3/26	Add a new employee	7	Add a new employee – Obi-Wan Kenobi, 65 Ocean View Lane, La Jolla, CA 92037, Employee ID No.: 555-22-9741.

Date	Action		Description
2/3/26	Add a bill	5	Add a bill from FixIt, Inc., terms: Net 15, for repairs made last month for $350. This bill was accrued as of 1/31/26. You will reverse this accrual at the end of this month.
2/4/26	Add a new customer	4	Add a new customer – United Air, 598 Terrace View, Santa Cruz, CA 95060.
2/5/26	Add a sales receipt	4	Add a new sales receipt #1004 for $1,293 – Customer: GHO Marketing, payment method: Check, reference no.: 1641, deposit to: Payments to deposit, product: iPhone 7, quantity: 1, and product: Samsung Galaxy 8, quantity: 1. (Click **See the math** to update amounts.)
2/6/26	Add a new purchase order	5	Add a new purchase order #1003 for $16,700 to purchase 10 iPhone 8 and 12 iPhone 8 Plus phones from vendor Apple Computer, Inc.
2/7/26	Add a new purchase order	5	Add a new purchase order #1004 for $9,000 to purchase 15 LG V30 phones from vendor LG Baker Distributing Company.
2/10/26	Add a new invoice	4	Add a new invoice #1005 for $9,751.38 – Customer: United Air, terms: Net 30, product: Pixel, quantity: 10, and product: Samsung Note, quantity: 3. (Click **See the math** to update amounts.)
2/10/26	Add a new invoice	4	Add a new invoice #1006 for $1,800 – Customer: Graham Engineering, Inc., terms: Net 30, service: Phone Consulting. Use 1 as the QTY and $1,800 as the Rate. (Not taxable.)
2/11/26	Add a cash receipt	4	Add a new cash receipt – Customer: Diamond Girl, Inc., payment method: Check, reference no.: 7419, deposit to: Payments to deposit, amount received: $6,728.88 (related to invoice #1003).
2/11/26	Pay bills	5	Pay $8,900 in bills from Hathaway Insurance, Google, Inc., and the News-Press, using checks no. 330 to 332.
2/11/26	Make a bank deposit	4	Add a bank deposit to the checking account in the amount of $8,021.88 to deposit previously received payments from GHO Marketing ($1,293) and Diamond Girl, Inc. ($6,728.88).
2/12/26	Record a credit card purchase	5	Purchase supplies from Staples, Inc. using the AMEX credit card $800. (Be sure to use the Supplies Asset account.)
2/12/26	Record a check	5	Add check no. 333 to E-Trade for $15,000 in additional investments.
2/12/26	Record a check	5	Add check no. 334 to Property, Inc. (a new vendor) for $12,000 to prepay one-year rent on a storage facility.
2/12/26	Add a new purchase order	5	Add a new purchase order #1005 for $16,500 – Vendor: Samsung, Inc. for 10 Samsung Galaxy 8 and 20 Samsung Note phones.
2/13/26	Add a new bill	5	Add a new bill based on a purchase order #1004 for $9,000 – Vendor: LG Baker Distributing Company, terms: Net 30. All items ordered were received.
2/14/26	Add a new bill	5	Add a new bill based on a purchase order #1003 for $16,700 – Vendor: Apple Computer, Inc., terms: Net 30. All items ordered were received.
2/14/26	Add a new bill	5	Add a new bill without a purchase order – San Diego Gas & Electric (a new vendor), terms: Net 15, category: Utilities, amount: $300.
2/15/26	Modify fixed asset accounts	6	Modify the Furniture & Fixtures account to track depreciation of this asset by adding two subaccounts: Original Cost and Accumulated Depreciation.
2/15/26	Record a credit card purchase and bank loan using a journal entry.	6	Add the purchase of $25,000 in furniture from Staples, Inc. On this purchase, $5,000 was charged to the AMEX credit card, and the $20,000 balance was paid by signing a note payable using journal entry 10. (Be sure to indicate Rabobank in the Name section of the notes payable entry and to record the purchase in the original cost sub account of Furniture & Fixtures.)
2/15/26	Pay first payroll	7	Add payroll (as you did in the chapter) based on the information shown in Figure 1. (Use checks no. 335 to 337.)

Date	Action	#	Description
2/17/26	Additional owner's investment	6	Received additional owner's investment and recorded it as a deposit of $10,000 (check no. 283) from owners.
2/17/26	Withdrawals	6	Record a withdrawal by owners using check no. 338, in the amount of $200.
2/18/26	Make a loan payment	6	Add the payment of $590.38 made to Rabobank as an installment on the furniture purchased on 2/15/26, which included interest paid of $66.67 and principal amount of $523.71, using check no. 339.
2/19/26	Make a loan payment	6	Add the payment of $944.77 to Chase Bank as an installment on the note payable on 1/16/26, which includes interest paid of $106.67 and principal amount of $838.10, using check no. 340.
2/20/26	Add a new bill	5	Add a new bill of $16,500 based on a purchase order #1005 – Vendor: Samsung, Inc., terms: Net 30. All items ordered were received. (*Hint:* First clear all lines in the Item details section of the bill that are left over from a previous bill from Samsung, Inc.)
2/25/26	Pay bills	5	Pay bills from Samsung, Inc. ($6,950) and Apple Computer, Inc. ($16,700) using checks no. 341 and 342.
2/25/26	Add a new invoice	4	Add invoice #1007 for $16,809 to Surfer Sales, terms: Net 30, for 10 iPhone 8 Plus and 6 iPhone 8 phones plus tax. (Click **See the math** to update amounts.)
2/25/26	Receive payment	4	Receive payment on account from Graham Engineering, Inc. of $1,800 from invoice #1006 using check no. 1641 into the Payments to deposit account.
2/27/26	Add a new invoice	4	Add an invoice #1008 for $13,738.13 to Diamond Girl, Inc., terms: Net 30, product: Samsung Note, quantity: 15. (Click **See the math** to update amounts.)
2/27/26	Add a new invoice		Add an invoice #1009 for $875 to Rooney Enterprises (a new customer), for 25 hours of Phone Consulting @ $35/hour, terms: Net 30.
2/27/26	Make a deposit	4	Deposited Graham Engineering, Inc.'s check for $1,800 into the checking account.
2/28/26	Pay second payroll	7	Add payroll (as you did in the chapter) based on the information shown in Figure 2 as follows. (Use checks no. 343 to 345.)
2/28/26	Reconcile bank account	8	Reconcile your company's checking account. No service charges or interest were incurred or earned. The ending bank statement balance on 2/28/26 was $6,043.24. All checks cleared the bank except checks no. 343 to 345. All deposits cleared the bank except a deposit from Graham Engineering, Inc. for $1,800.
2/28/26	Adjust supplies	9	Supplies worth $700 were used in February. Use journal entry 11.
2/28/26	Adjust prepaids	9	Prepaid expenses of $2,800 expired in the month of February ($1,800 related to insurance expense and $1,000 related to rent). Use journal entry 12.
2/28/26	Accrue expenses	9	A bill for $2,550 was received and recorded in the next month for legal fees consumed in the current month. Use journal entry 13.
2/28/26	Reverse accrual	9	Repair fees accrued on 1/31/26 for $350 via journal entry 6 were properly recorded in February. Use journal entry 14 to reverse this accrual.
2/28/26	Defer revenue	9	Phone Consulting services recorded on invoice #1009 for $875 for Rooney Enterprises were deemed unearned as of 2/28/26. Use journal entry 15 to defer this revenue.
2/28/26	Reverse deferral	9	Phone Consulting services deferred in the prior month of $210 were earned in February. Use journal entry 16 to reverse journal entry 7 recorded on 1/31/26.
2/28/26	Accrue depreciation	9	Depreciation Expense of $1,700 ($850, $500, and $350 for Computers, Furniture & Fixtures, and Machinery & Equipment, respectively). Use journal entry 17 to record this depreciation.
2/28/26	Accrue revenue	9	Phone Consulting services of $3,500 were performed on 2/28/26 for a new customer, Rigel Works, but not invoiced or recorded into the accounting records. Use journal entry 18 to accrue this revenue.

Figure 1

First semimonthly payroll

Pay/Tax/Withholding	Kira	Jedi	Obi-Wan	Total
Hours if applicable	n/a	72	80	
Annual salary or hourly rate	48,000.00	17.00	22.00	
Gross pay	**2,000.00**	**1,224.00**	**1,760.00**	**4,984.00**
Federal withholding	274.00	167.69	241.12	682.81
Social security employee (6.2%)	124.00	75.89	109.12	309.01
Medicare employee (1.45%)	29.00	17.75	25.52	72.27
Employee withholding	**427.00**	**261.33**	**375.76**	**1,064.09**
Social security employer (6.2%)	124.00	75.89	109.12	309.01
Medicare company employer (1.45%)	29.00	17.75	25.52	72.27
Employer payroll tax expense	**153.00**	**93.64**	**134.64**	**381.28**
Net Check amount	1,573.00	962.67	1,384.24	3,919.91

Figure 2

Second semimonthly payroll

Pay/Tax/Withholding	Kira	Jedi	Obi-Wan	Total
Hours if applicable	n/a	65	85	
Annual salary or hourly rate	48,000.00	17.00	22.00	
Gross pay	**2,000.00**	**1,105.00**	**1,870.00**	**4,975.00**
Federal withholding	274.00	151.39	256.19	681.58
Social security employee (6.2%)	124.00	68.51	115.94	308.45
Medicare employee (1.45%)	29.00	16.02	27.12	72.14
Employee withholding	**427.00**	**235.92**	**399.25**	**1,062.17**
Social security employer (6.2%)	124.00	68.51	115.94	308.45
Medicare company employer (1.45%)	29.00	16.02	27.12	72.14
Employer payroll tax expense	**153.00**	**84.53**	**143.06**	**380.59**
Net Check amount	1,573.00	869.08	1,470.75	3,912.83

Requirements:

1. Create, save, and print a Profit and Loss report for February 2026 that includes a % of income column.
2. Create, save, and print a Total Income Transaction report for February 2026. (*Hint:* Click the **Total Income amount** in the Profit and Loss report for February 2026.)
3. Create, save, and print a Balance Sheet report for February 28, 2026.
4. Create, save, and print a Checking report for February 2026.
5. Create, save, and print a Statement of Cash Flows report for February 2026.
6. Create, save, and print an A/R Aging Summary report for February 2026.
7. Create, save, and print an A/P Aging Summary report for February 2026.
8. Create, save, and print an Inventory Valuation Summary report for February 2026.
9. Create, save, and print a Transactions List by Date report for February 2026.
10. Create, save, and print a Budget vs. Actuals report for February 2026.

Case 4 Comprehensive Problem

Case 4, which begins in Chapter 3, is a sports gym that sells month-to-month memberships and related merchandise. Business events in Case 4 occurred from 12/31/20 to 1/31/21 when presented in Chapters 3 to 10. The following is a description of business events that occurred in the month of February 2021.

Date	Description of Event	Chapter	Event
2/2/21	Add new product	4	Add a new taxable product – Bowflex Xtreme Home Gym, initial quantity on hand: 0, as of date: 2/1/21, inventory asset account: Inventory Asset, price: $1,199, cost: $700, income account: Sales of Product Income, expense account: Cost of Goods Sold (taxable).
2/2/21	Change the name of a product	4	Change the name of the Yoga pants to Xtreme Yoga pants.
2/2/21	Add a new vendor	5	Add a new vendor – Sole Fitness LLC, 1844 Raven Rd., Diana, TX 75640, terms: Net 30.
2/2/21	Add a new product	4	Add a new taxable product – Sole E98 Elliptical, initial quantity on hand: 0, as of date: 2/2/21, inventory asset account: Inventory Asset, price: $2,300, cost: $1,500, income account: Sales of Product Income, expense account: Cost of Goods Sold (taxable).
2/3/21	Add a new service	4	Add a new service – Annual Fee – Individual, rate: $1,620, income account: Sales (not taxable).
2/3/21	Modify budget	8	Modify the following monthly budgeted amounts (Budget 1) for February 2021 through December 2021 as follows: sales of product income: $6,000, sales: $60,000, cost of goods sold: $3,000, advertising & marketing: $3,000, insurance: $2,100, interest expense: $325, payroll: $16,000, repairs & maintenance: $700.
2/3/21	Add a new employee	7	Add a new employee – Sammy Watkins, 300 Westwood Blvd., Westwood, CA 90037, Employee ID No.: 555-22-9741.
2/3/21	Add a bill	5	Add a bill from Supreme Marketing, terms: Net 15, for advertising performed last month for $675. This bill was accrued as of 1/31/21. You will reverse this accrual at the end of this month.
2/4/21	Add a new customer	4	Add a new customer – Fox Broadcasting Company, 10201 West Pico Blvd., Los Angeles, CA 90064, terms: Net 30.

Date	Action	Ch.	Description
2/5/21	Add a sales receipt	4	Add a new sales receipt #1005 for $6,480 – New customer: Harrison Ford, payment method: Check, reference no.: 1987, deposit to: Undeposited Funds, service: Annual Fee – Individual, quantity: 4.
2/5/21	Add a new purchase order	5	Add a new purchase order #1003 for $2,100 to purchase 3 Bowflex Xtreme Home Gyms from vendor Bowflex, Inc.
2/5/21	Add a new purchase order	5	Add a new purchase order #1004 for $7,500 to purchase 5 Sole E98 Elliptical machines from vendor Sole Fitness LLC.
2/8/21	Add a new invoice	4	Add a new invoice #1006 for $29,453.10 – Customer: Fox Broadcasting Company, terms: Net 30, service: Monthly Fee – Corporate Membership 50 Employees, quantity: 4, and product: Bowflex Dumbbells, quantity: 20. (Click **See the math** to update amounts.)
2/9/21	Add a new invoice	4	Add a new invoice #1007 for $12,000 – Customer: ABC Studios, terms: Net 30, service: Monthly Fee – Corporate Membership 50 Employees, quantity: 2.
2/11/21	Receive payment	4	Receive payment – Customer: ABC Studios, payment method: Check, reference no.: 98745, deposit to: Undeposited Funds, amount received: $7,368.75 (related to invoice #1002).
2/11/21	Pay bills	5	Pay $6,800 in bills from Bowflex, Inc. and Supreme Marketing, using checks no. 25511 and 25512.
2/11/21	Make a bank deposit	4	Add a bank deposit to the checking account in the amount of $13,848.75 to deposit previously received payments from ABC Studios ($7,368.75) and Harrison Ford ($6,480).
2/12/21	Record a credit card purchase	5	Purchase supplies from Wal-Mart (a new vendor) using the VISA credit card $1,800. (Be sure to use the Supplies asset account.)
2/12/21	Record a check	5	Add check no. 25513 to Barber Investments, Inc. for $10,000 in additional investments.
2/12/21	Record a check	5	Add check no. 25514 to Leaseco, Inc. (a new vendor) for $6,000 to prepay one-year rent on a storage facility (Prepaid Expenses).
2/12/21	Add a new purchase order	5	Add a new purchase order #1005 for $25,000 – Vendor: NordicTrack, Inc. for 5 new treadmills for use in the facility and not for resale (Equipment).
2/15/21	Add a new bill	5	Add a new bill based on a purchase order #1003 for $2,100 – Vendor: Bowflex Inc., terms: Net 15. All items ordered were received.
2/15/21	Add a new bill	5	Add a new bill without a purchase order – LADWP (a new vendor), terms: Net 15, category: Utilities, amount: $900.
2/15/21	Add new fixed asset accounts	6	Create new fixed asset accounts – Account type: Fixed Assets, detail type: Fixed Asset Computers, name: Computers. Track depreciation of this asset. Be sure to change the name of the Computer accumulated depreciation account from Depreciation to Accumulated Depreciation.
2/15/21	Record a credit card purchase and bank loan using a journal entry	6	Add the purchase of $45,000 in computers from Best Buy (a new vendor) for which $10,000 was charged to the VISA credit card and the $35,000 balance was paid by signing a note payable using journal entry 10. (Be sure to indicate Coast Bank in the Name section of the notes payable entry and to record the purchase in the original cost sub account of Computers.)
2/15/21	Pay first payroll	7	Using recurring transactions (as you did in the chapter), pay Graham, Beckett, and Allegra based on the information shown in Figure 1. Using the Check function, pay Sammy based on the information shown in Figure 1. Be sure to indicate that Sammy's check is a recurring transaction. (Use checks no. 25515 to 25518.)
2/17/21	Sell common stock	6	Add the sale of common stock as a deposit of $25,000, check no. 1974, from shareholders.
2/17/21	Pay dividends	6	Add the payment of dividends to shareholders, check no. 25519, in the amount of $1,000.
2/18/21	Make a loan payment	6	Add the payment of $2,000 made to Coast Bank as an installment on notes payable, which included interest expense of $300 and principal amount of $1,700, using check no. 25520.

Date	Action	Ch.	Description
2/19/21	Add a new bill	5	Add a new bill of $2,985 based on a purchase order #1002 – Vendor: Precor, terms: Net 30. All items ordered were received.
2/25/21	Pay bills	5	Pay bills from LADWP ($900) and Supreme Marketing ($675) using checks no. 25521 and 25522.
2/26/21	Add a bill	5	Add a new bill of $7,500 based on purchase order #1004 – Vendor: Sole Fitness LLC, terms: Net 30.
2/27/21	Add a new invoice	4	Add invoice #1008 for $7,555.50 to Jules, Inc., terms: Net 30, for 3 Sole E98 Elliptical machines plus tax. (Click **See the math** to update amounts.)
2/27/21	Receive payment	4	Receive payment on account from ABC Studios of $12,000 from invoice #1007 using check no. 19981 into the Undeposited Funds account.
2/27/21	Add a new bill	5	Add a new bill of $25,000 based on purchase order #1005 – Vendor: NordicTrack Inc., terms: Net 30.
2/27/21	Add a sales receipt	4	Add a new sales receipt #1009 for $3,280.62 to Taylor Swift (a new customer), product: Bowflex Xtreme Home Gym, quantity: 2, and product: Power Block Elite Dumbbells, quantity: 2, deposit to: Undeposited Funds. (Click **See the math** to update amounts.)
2/27/21	Make a deposit	4	Deposited ABC Studios check for $12,000 into the checking account.
2/28/21	Pay second payroll	7	Add payroll (as you did in the chapter) based on the information shown in Figure 2 as follows. (Use checks no. 25523 to 25526.)
2/28/21	Reconcile bank account	8	Reconcile your company's checking account. No service charges or interest were incurred or earned. The ending bank statement balance on 2/28/21 was $19,173.16. All checks cleared the bank except checks no. 25524 and 25526 for $1,671.31 and $1,275.70, respectively. All deposits cleared the bank except a deposit from ABC Studios for $12,000.
2/28/21	Adjust supplies	9	Supplies worth $1,700 were used in February. Use journal entry 11.
2/28/21	Adjust prepaids	9	Prepaid expenses of $3,000 expired in the month of February ($2,000 related to insurance and $1,000 related to rent & lease). Use journal entry 12.
2/28/21	Reverse accrual	9	Reverse journal entry 6 made on 1/31/21 to accrue advertising & marketing expenses of $675 to Supreme Marketing using journal entry 13.
2/28/21	Accrue expenses	9	A bill for $1,300 was received and recorded in the next month for legal & professional services consumed in the current month. Use journal entry 14.
2/28/21	Reverse accrual	9	Sales accrued on 1/31/21 for $750 via journal entry 8 were properly recorded in February. Use journal entry 15 to reverse this accrual.
2/28/21	Defer revenue	9	Sales of product income recorded on sales receipt #1009 for $3,280.62 to Taylor Swift were deemed unearned as of 2/28/21. Use journal entry 16 to defer this revenue and reduce sales tax payable. You'll need to review this sales receipt to determine amounts by account.
2/28/21	Reverse deferral	9	Training services recorded on invoice #1003 for $3,750 to Flyer Corporation were only partially performed even though invoiced. Sales of $2000 had not been earned and thus were deferred in the prior month. Use journal entry 17 to reverse journal entry 7 recorded on 1/31/21.
2/28/21	Accrue depreciation	9	Record Depreciation Expense of $1,600 ($500, $600, $400, and $100 for Building, Furniture & Fixtures, Machinery & Equipment, and Computer, respectively). Use journal entry 18 to record this depreciation.
2/28/21	Accrue revenue	9	Training (Sales) of $2,500 was performed on 2/28/21 but not invoiced or recorded into the accounting records. Use journal entry 19 to accrue this revenue.

Figure 1

First semi-monthly payroll

Pay/Tax/Withholding	Graham	Allegra	Beckett	Sammy	Total
Hours if applicable	n/a	70	80	90	
Annual salary or hourly rate	75,000.00	25.00	22.00	20.00	
Gross pay	**3,125.00**	**1,750.00**	**1,760.00**	**1,800.00**	**8.435.00**
Federal withholding	428.13	239.75	241.12	246.60	1,155.60
Social security employee (6.2%)	193.75	108.50	109.12	111.60	522.97
Medicare employee (1.45%)	45.31	25.38	25.52	26.10	122.31
Employee withholding	**667.19**	**373.63**	**375.76**	**384.30**	**1,800.87**
Social security employer (6.2%)	193.75	108.50	109.12	111.60	522.97
Medicare company employer (1.45%)	45.34	25.38	25.52	26.10	122.34
Employer payroll tax expense	**239.09**	**133.88**	**134.64**	**137.70**	**645.31**
Net Check amount	2,457.81	1,376.37	1,384.24	1,415.70	5,218.42

Figure 2

Second semimonthly payroll

Pay/Tax/Withholding	Graham	Allegra	Beckett	Sammy	Total
Hours if applicable	n/a	85	72	83	
Annual salary or hourly rate	75,000.00	25.00	22.00	20.00	
Gross pay	**3,125.00**	**2,125.00**	**1,584.00**	**1,660.00**	**8,494.00**
Federal withholding	428.13	291.13	217.01	246.60	1,182.86
Social security employee (6.2%)	193.75	131.75	98.21	111.60	535.31
Medicare employee (1.45%)	45.31	30.81	22.97	26.10	125.19
Employee withholding	**667.19**	**453.69**	**338.18**	**384.30**	**1,843.36**
Social security employer (6.2%)	193.75	131.75	98.12	111.60	535.31
Medicare company employer (1.45%)	45.34	30.81	22.97	26.10	125.22
Employer payroll tax expense	**239.09**	**162.56**	**121.18**	**137.70**	**660.53**
Net Check amount	2,457.81	1,671.31	1,245.81	1,275.70	5,374.93

Requirements:

1. Create, save, and print a Trial Balance report for February 2021.
2. Create, save, and print a Profit and Loss report for February 2021.
3. Create, save, and print a Total Income Transaction report for February 2021. (*Hint:* Click the **Total Income amount** in the Profit and Loss report for February 2021.)
4. Create, save, and print a Balance Sheet report for February 28, 2021.
5. Create, save, and print a Checking report for February 2021.
6. Create, save, and print a Statement of Cash Flows report for February 2021.
7. Create, save, and print an A/R Aging Summary report for February 2021.
8. Create, save, and print an A/P Aging Summary report for February 2021.
9. Create, save, and print an Inventory Valuation Summary report for February 2021.
10. Create, save, and print a Transactions List by Date report for February 2021.
11. Create, save, and print a Budget vs. Actuals report for February 2021.

Case 5 Comprehensive Problem

Note: Be aware that there is no Case 5 comprehensive problem provided in this text.

Case 6 Comprehensive Problem

Case 6, which begins in Chapter 3, is a Recreational Vehicle (RV) dealership in the state of Washington. They sell new RVs and related accessories to individuals and businesses. In addition, they repair and service RVs. Business events in Case 6 occurred from 12/31/22 to 1/31/23 when presented in Chapters 3 to 10. The following is a description of business events that occurred in the month of February 2023.

Date	Description of Event	Chapter	Event
2/1/23	Add a new vendor	5	Add a new vendor – R-Pod, 888 SE Sheridan Road, Sheridan, OR 97378, terms: Net 30.
2/2/23	Add new product	4	Add a new product – Name/Description/Purchasing information: RP-171, initial quantity on hand: 0, as of date: 2/2/23, inventory asset account: Inventory, Sales price: $26,900, cost: $21,520, income account: Sales of Product Income, expense account: Cost of Goods Sold, Sales tax category: Taxable – standard rate, Preferred vendor: R-Pod.
2/2/23	Change the name of a product	4	Change the name/description of the service Basic 6,000-mile service to Basic 8,000-mile service.
2/2/23	Add a new product	4	Add a new product – Name/Description/Purchasing information: RP-179, initial quantity on hand: 0, as of date: 2/2/23, inventory asset account: Inventory, Sales price: $22,800, cost: $18,240, income account: Sales of Product Income, expense account: Cost of Goods Sold, Sales tax category: Taxable – standard rate, Preferred vendor: R-Pod.
2/3/23	Add a new service	4	Add a new service – Detailing, rate: $50, income account: Sales, Sales tax category: Nontaxable.
2/3/23	Modify budget	8	Modify the following monthly budgeted amounts (Budget 1) for February 2023 as follows: sales of product income: $400,000, sales: $15,000, cost of goods sold: $320,000, advertising & marketing: $18,000, contractors: $3,000, insurance: $4,000, interest expense: $600, payroll: $22,000, repairs: $700, utilities: $5,000, and depreciation: $1,200. Leave budgets for March through December as is.
2/3/23	Add a new employee	7	Add a new employee – Anastasia Quinn, 507 N 169th St., Shoreline, WA 98133, Social Security No.: 555-54-1111.
2/3/23	Add a bill	5	Add a bill from Pacific Marketing, terms: Net 15, for advertising performed last month, for $1,800. This bill was accrued as of 1/31/23. You will reverse this accrual at the end of this month.
2/4/23	Add a new customer	4	Add a new customer – Apple Travel, terms: Net 30.
2/6/23	Add a sales receipt	4	Add a new sales receipt #1003 – New customer: Rose Ski, 241 St., Andrews Way, Santa Maria, CA 93454, payment method: Check, reference no.: 355, deposit to: Undeposited Funds, product: 2022 Winnebago Revel 44E, price: $150,000 quantity: 1, amount received: $163,950.
2/7/23	Add a new purchase order	5	Add a new purchase order #1003 to purchase two RP-171 and three RP-179 trailers from vendor R-Pod for a total cost of $97,760.
2/8/23	Add a new purchase order	5	Add a new purchase order #1004 to purchase two 2023 Thor Motor Coach Palazzo 33.2 motorhomes from vendor Thor Motor Coach for a total cost of $288,000.
2/8/23	Add a new invoice	4	Add a new invoice #1004 for $108,207 – Customer: Apple Travel, terms: Net 30, product: one 2023 Airstream Flying Cloud 27FB TWIN. (Click **See the math** to update amounts.)
2/10/23	Add a new invoice	4	Add a new invoice #1005 for $700 – Customer: Rose Ski, terms: Net 30, service: one Basic 8,000-mile service and five hours of Detailing.
2/13/23	Receive payment	4	Receive payment – Customer: Deja Smith, payment method: Check, deposit to: Undeposited Funds, amount received: $153,020 (related to invoice: #1002).
2/14/23	Pay bills	5	Pay $322,000 in bills from Winnebago, Inc., and Pacific Marketing, using checks no. 601 and 602.

Date	Action		Description
2/15/23	Make a bank deposit	4	Add a bank deposit to the checking account in the amount of $316,970 to deposit previously received payments from Deja Smith and Rose Ski.
2/15/23	Record a credit card purchase	5	Purchase supplies from Best Buy using the AMEX credit card $3,000. (Be sure to use the Supplies Asset account.)
2/15/23	Record a check	5	Add check no. 603 to McConnel Investments, Inc. for $20,000 in additional investments.
2/15/23	Record a check	5	Add check no. 604 to Global Leasing (a new vendor) for $24,000 to prepay one-year rent on a warehouse (Prepaid Expenses).
2/15/23	Add a new bill	6	Add a new bill without a purchase order – Seattle City Light (a new vendor), terms: Net 15, category: Utilities, amount: $3,000.
2/15/23	Add new fixed asset accounts	6	Create new fixed asset accounts – Account type: Fixed Assets, detail type: Vehicles, name: Vehicles. Track depreciation of this asset. Be sure to change the name of the Vehicles accumulated depreciation account from Depreciation to Accumulated Depreciation.
2/15/23	Record a vehicle purchase and bank loan using a journal entry	6	Add the purchase of a truck for $95,000 from Seattle Ford (a new vendor) and the signing a note payable to Seattle Bank for the full purchase price using journal entry 10.
2/15/23	Pay first payroll	7	Using recurring transactions (as you did in the chapter), pay Rhett, Oliver, and Emelia based on the information shown in Figure 1. Using the check function, pay Anastasia. Be sure to indicate that Anastasia's check is a recurring unscheduled transaction. (Use checks no. 605 to 608.)
2/17/23	Sell common stock	6	Add the sale of common stock as a deposit of $20,000 from shareholders (Common stock $200, Paid-In Capital $19,800).
2/20/23	Pay dividends	6	Add the payment of dividends to shareholders, check no. 609, in the amount of $500.
2/21/23	Make a loan payment	6	Add the payment of $3,542.88 made to Seattle Bank as an installment on notes payable, which included interest expense of $390 and principal amount of $3,152.88, using check no. 610.
2/22/23	Add a new bill	5	Add a new bill of $97,760 based on a purchase order #1003 – Vendor: R-Pod, terms: Net 30. All items ordered were received.
2/25/23	Pay bills	5	Pay bills from State Farm Insurance ($18,000), National Covers ($4,000), and Airstream, Inc. ($180,000) using checks no. 611 to 613.
2/27/23	Add a new invoice	4	Add invoice #1006 for $29,401.70 to Donald Biden, terms: Net 30, for one RP-171 plus tax. (Click **See the math** to update amounts.)
2/27/23	Receive payment	4	Receive payment on account from Apple Travel of $108,207 from invoice #1004 recorded into the Undeposited Funds account.
2/27/23	Add a sales receipt	4	Add a new sales receipt #1007 for $153,020 to Ebony Williams for one 2022 Winnebago View 24G deposited to Undeposited Funds. (Click **See the math** to update amounts.)
2/27/23	Add a new invoice	4	Add invoice #1008 for $950 to Deja Smith, terms: Net 30, for a transmission service ($350) and sewer system inspection and repair ($600).
2/28/23	Make a deposit	4	Deposited Apple Travel and Ebony William's checks for a total of $261,227 into the checking account.
2/28/23	Add a new bill	5	Add a new bill without a purchase order, vendor: Pacific Marketing, terms: Net 15, category: Advertising & Marketing, amount: $1,800.
2/28/23	Pay second payroll	7	Add payroll using recurring transactions for Rhett, Oliver, Emelia, and Anastasia based on the information shown in Figure 2. (Use checks no. 614 to 617.)
2/28/23	Reconcile bank account	8	Reconcile your company's checking account. No service charges or interest were incurred or earned. The ending bank statement balance on 2/28/23 was $182.49. All checks cleared the bank except checks no. 613 through 617. All deposits cleared the bank except a deposit made on 2/28/23 for $261,227.
2/28/23	Adjust supplies	9	Supplies worth $1,200 were used in February. Use journal entry 11.
2/28/23	Adjust prepaids	9	Prepaid expenses of $4,400 expired in the month of February ($2,400 related to insurance and $2,000 related to rent & lease). Use journal entry 12.

Date	Action	Ref	Description
2/28/23	Reverse accrual	9	Reverse journal entry 7 made on 1/31/23 to accrue advertising & marketing expenses of $1,800 to Pacific Marketing using journal entry 13.
2/28/23	Accrue expenses	9	A bill for $2,500 was received from Elite Events and recorded in March 2023 for contractors expense consumed in the current month. Use journal entry 14 to accrue this liability.
2/28/23	Reverse accrual	9	Sales accrued on 1/31/23 for $950 via journal entry 8 were properly recorded in February. Use journal entry 15 to reverse this accrual.
2/28/23	Defer revenue	9	The sale of a motorhome to Donald Biden on 2/27/23 for $29,401.70 was deemed unearned as of 2/28/23 since it wasn't delivered until March. Use journal entry 16 to defer this revenue to a new Unearned Revenue account and reduce sales tax payable. You'll need to review invoice #1006 to determine amounts by account.
2/28/23	Accrue depreciation	9	Record Depreciation Expense of $3,000 ($1,000, $300, $800, and $900 for Buildings, Computers, Machinery & Equipment, and Vehicles, respectively). Use journal entry 17 to record this depreciation.
2/28/23	Accrue revenue	9	Services of $16,000 were performed for Sam Ski on 2/28/23 but not invoiced or recorded into the accounting records until the next month. Use journal entry 18 to accrue Sales and Accrued Receivables.

Figure 1 First semimonthly payroll

Pay/Tax/Withholding	Oliver	Rhett	Emelia	Anastasia	Total
Hours if applicable	n/a	n/a	83	65	
Annual salary or hourly rate	85,000.00	60,000.00	35.00	40.00	
Gross pay	3,541.67	2,500.00	2,905.00	2,600.00	8,946.67
Federal withholding	485.22	342.50	397.99	356.20	1,225.70
Social security employee (6.2%)	219.58	155.00	180.11	161.20	554.69
Medicare employee (1.45%)	51.35	36.25	42.12	37.70	129.73
Employee withholding	756.15	533.75	620.22	555.10	1,910.11
Social security employer (6.2%)	219.59	155.00	180.11	161.20	554.70
Medicare company employer (1.45%)	51.38	36.28	42.12	37.70	129.79
Employer payroll tax expense	270.97	191.28	222.23	198.90	684.48
Net Check amount	2,785.52	1,966.25	2,284.78	2,044.90	7,036.55

Figure 2 Second semimonthly payroll

Pay/Tax/Withholding	Oliver	Rhett	Emelia	Anastasia	Total
Hours if applicable	n/a	n/a	73	72	
Annual salary or hourly rate	85,000.00	60,000.00	35.00	40.00	
Gross pay	3,541.67	2,500.00	2,555.00	2,880.00	8,596.67
Federal withholding	485.22	342.50	350.04	394.56	1,177.75
Social security employee (6.2%)	219.58	155.00	158.41	178.56	532.99
Medicare employee (1.45%)	51.35	36.25	37.05	41.76	124.65
Employee withholding	756.15	533.75	545.49	614.88	1,835.39
Social security employer (6.2%)	219.59	155.00	158.41	178.56	533.00
Medicare company employer (1.45%)	51.38	36.28	37.05	41.76	124.71
Employer payroll tax expense	270.97	191.28	195.46	220.32	657.71
Net Check amount	2,785.52	1,966.25	2,009.51	2,265.12	6,761.27

Requirements:

1. Create, save, and print a Bank Reconciliation report as of 2/28/23 (click **Hide additional information** when generating this report).
2. Create, save, and print a Trial Balance report as of 2/28/23.
3. Create, save, and print a Profit and Loss report for the month of February 2023 with a % of income column.
4. Create, save, and print a Balance Sheet report as of 2/28/23 with a % of row column.
5. Create, save, and print a Statement of Cash Flows report for February 2023.
6. Create, save, and print an A/R Aging Summary report as of 2/28/23.
7. Create, save, and print an A/P Aging Summary report as of 2/28/23.
8. Create, save, and print an Inventory Valuation Summary report as of 2/28/23.
9. Create, save, and print a Transactions Detail by Account report for all dates.
10. Create, save, and print a Budget vs. Actuals report for the two months ended 2/28/23.

Overview—Do I Need to Become QuickBooks Online Certified?

appendix 3

There are two schools of thought here. The first is that becoming certified provides employers/clients independent confirmation of an individual's skill and proficiency in using QBO. Thus, certification is a good résumé builder. The second is that any employer/client that relies solely on certification to assure competency in using QBO will eventually find themselves looking for a new QBO professional.

Does it hurt? No. Does it help? Maybe. Is it necessary? No. What is important is the knowledge, skill, and proficiency in using QuickBooks as a tool to help businesses better understand the financial implications of their decisions.

In the author's opinion, certification takes a back seat to accounting education and experience. Thus, it is in the student's best interest to gain accounting knowledge (the more, the better) through courses at accredited institutions in the topics of bookkeeping, financial accounting, managerial accounting, cost accounting, and tax accounting, as well as the application of QuickBooks to different business situations. The next step is to gain experience through internships or part-time jobs working under a QuickBooks/Accounting professional. Add that to certification and you're ready for gainful employment.

The following is a summary overview of the topics covered by the QuickBooks certified user online exam.

What Topics Are Covered in the QBCU Certification Exam?

1   QuickBooks setup and maintenance
    a. List management
    b. Sales and money-in
    c. Purchases and money-out
    d. Basic accounting
    e. Reports
    f. Customization and saving time
    g. The Intuit QBCU Desktop exam covers the following topics:
2   QuickBooks set-up
    a. QuickBooks utilities and general product knowledge
    b. List management
    c. Items
    d. Sales
    e. Purchases

f. Payroll
   g. Reports
   h. Basic accounting
   i. Customization and shortcuts

Links to QuickBooks Certification Information

https://certiport.pearsonvue.com/Certifications/QuickBooks/Certified-User/Overview

https://quickbooks.intuit.com/accountants/training-certification/certifications/

Index

A

account(s). *See also* charts of accounts
   Accounts Payable
      establishing beginning balance, 43–45
      journalizing, 49
      Transaction Report, 117
   Accounts Receivable
      establishing beginning balance, 43–45
      journalizing, 49
      reports, 18
      Transaction Report, 228
   charts of, 13–14
   creating, 2, 24
   Inventory Asset, 117
   Opening Balance Equity, 51–53
   Payroll (expense), 157
   Payroll Tax Payable (liability), 157
Account Quickreport, 14
Accounts Payable (A/P) account
   establishing beginning balance, 49–50
   journalizing, 49–50
   Transaction Report, 117
Accounts Payable (A/P) Aging Detail Report, 232
Accounts Payable (A/P) Aging Summary report, 232
Accounts Payable (A/P) Register page, 14
Accounts Receivable (A/R) account, 49–50
   establishing beginning balance, 49–50
   journalizing, 49–50
   reports, 18
   Transaction Report, 228
Accounts Receivable (A/R) Aging Detail Report, 234
Accounts Receivable (A/R) Aging Summary reports, 231–233
accrued expenses, 211–212
accruing revenue, 213–214
adjusting entries, 206–216
   accrued expenses, 211–212
   accruing revenue, 213–214
   creating trial balance, 206
   depreciation, 214–216
   overview, 206
   prepaid expenses
      deferring supplies as asset, 208–209
      recording consumption of supplies, 209–210
   types of, 206
   unearned revenue, 212–213
Advanced settings, 20
aging summaries
   Accounts Payable Aging Summary report, 233–235
   Accounts Receivable Aging Summary reports, 231–233
A/P account. *See* Accounts Payable (A/P) account
A/P (Accounts Payable) Aging Detail Report, 234
A/P (Accounts Payable) Aging Summary report, 233–235
A/P (Accounts Payable) Register page, 14
A/R account. *See* Accounts Receivable (A/R) account
A/R (Accounts Receivable) Aging Detail Report, 234
A/R (Accounts Receivable) Aging Summary reports, 231–233
Automated Sales Tax system, 246

B

balance sheet, creating, 51–53, 226–229
Balance Sheet page, 53
Balance Sheet reports, 17
Bank and Credit Cards page, 8
bank deposit, inputting, 86
bank deposits, 9
Bank Register (partial view), 8
banking transactions, viewing, 7–9
bank reconciliations, 189–192
   creating, 189–192
   overview, 189
   Summary Reconciliation Report, 192
bill(s). *See also* invoices
   adding purchase order information, 109
   after adding purchase order information, 110
   credit card, 114–115
   entering, 109

paying, 112–115
    for prepaid expenses, 112
    for services, 111
    from vendors for receipt of products or services, 108–112
budget(s)
    Budget Overview reports, 187–188
    Budget *vs.* Actual reports, 188–189
    creating, 182–185
    overview, 182
    reports, 185–189
Budgeting window, 183
Budget Overview reports, 187–188
Budget *vs.* Actual reports, 188–189
Business Overview reports, 16

C

case studies, 248–268
    adjusting entries, 217–212
    budgets and bank reconciliations, 193–205
    financial statements and reports, 240–245
    investing and financing activities, 143–154
    operating activities, purchases and cash payments, 119–133
    operating activities, sales and cash receipts, 88–103
    payroll, 165–181
    setting up company, 55–75
Cash Flows report, statement of, 17, 18
cash receipts, 83–86
charts of accounts, 13–14. *See also* account(s)
    modifying, 43–50
        adding additional accounts, 48–49
        adding checking accounts, 43–44
        adding products and services, 46–48
    viewing, 13–14
check payments, 114–115
common stock
    definition of, 138
    recording deposit of funds from sale of, 138–139
companies
    closing Opening Balance Equity account, 51–53
    establishing beginning balances, 43–50
    modifying chart of accounts, 43–50
    setting for, 42–43
Company settings, 18–20

Create (+) menu, 2
Create window, 80, 82, 84, 86, 106, 109, 113
Credit card charge, 115
credit card payment, 114–115
customer
    accessing information about, 34–35
    adding, 79–80
Customer Information window, 79
Customers window, 3
customizing
    Budget Overview report, 187–188
    Budget *vs.* Actuals report, 188–189
    Profit and Loss report, 237–239
    reports, 237–239

D

dashboard, 2
deferring
    definition of, 206
    supplies as asset, 208–209
Deposit window, 86
depreciation, 134–135, 214–216
dividends
    definition of, 138
    payment of, 139
due on receipt, 114

E

employees
    accessing information about, 6–7, 38
    adding, 156
    paying, 158–164
        recording payment, 158–164
        Recurring Transactions, 161
        semi-monthly payroll information, 158, 162
        Transaction Report, 160, 163–164
        Trial Balance, 160, 163
Employees window, 6–7
equipment, purchase of, 135–136
equity accounts, 9
equity transactions, 138–139
Expenses settings, 20
expense transactions, viewing, 9–11
Expense window, 11

F

financial reports, 223–239
financial statements
   balance sheet, 226–229
   income statements
      creating, 224–226
      definition of, 224
      Invoice, 226
      Profit and Loss Report, 224–225
      Transaction Report, 226
   overview, 223
   Statement of Cash Flow, 229–231
financing activities. *See* investing and financing activities
fixed assets
   acquisition of in exchange for long-term debt, 141–142
   definition of, 134
   depreciation, 134–135
   recording purchase of, 135–136, 141

G

Gear icon, 11, 13
Gear window, 35
generally accepted accounting principles (GAAP), 206, 223

H

Help feature
   QuickBooks Online, 31–32

I

income statements
   creating, 224–226
   definition of, 224
   Invoice, 226
   Profit and Loss Report, 224–215
   Transaction Report, 226
Intuit, 1, 34
Inventory Asset Account, 117
Inventory Valuation Detail, 236
Inventory Valuation Summary report, 235–237
investing and financing activities
   acquisition of fixed assets in exchange for long-term debt, 141–142
   common stock and dividends, 138–139

   fixed assets, 134–136
   long-term debt, 140–141
   long-term investments, 136–137
investments
   long-term, 136–137
   owner, 138–139
invoices
   Accounts Payable Aging Summary, 234, 235
   Accounts Receivable Aging Summary, 234, 235
   adding, 82–83
   income statements, 226
   sales, 80–83

J

journalizing
   Accounts Payable (A/P) account, 49–50
   Accounts Receivable (A/R) account, 49–50

L

lists
   of products and services, 77
   in QBO, 14–15
   viewing
      list of lists, 15
      list of terms, 15
long-term debt, 140–141
   acquisition of fixed assets in exchange for, 141–142
   recording receipt of funds from borrowing, 140–141
   repayment with interest, 141
long-term investments
   definition of, 136
   recording purchase of, 137

M

Medicare taxes, 157

N

+ New menu, 33

O

Opening Balance Equity account, 51–53
operating activities
   paying bills, 112–115

purchases and cash payments, 104–118
  adding vendors, 104–105
  purchase orders, 105–108
  recording bills, 108–112
  recording check payments, 114–115
  recording credit card payments, 114–115
  trial balance, 115–133
sales and cash receipts, 76–87
  adding services, products, and customers, 76–80
  recording cash receipts, 83–86
  sales invoices, 80–83
  sales receipts, 80–83
  Transaction Detail by Account reports, 86–87
owner investments, 138–139
owner withdrawals, 138–139

P

payments
  check, 114–115
  credit card, 114–115
  receipts of, 83–86
  recording, 158–164
payroll
  adding employees, 156
  adding payroll-related accounts, 157–158
  paying employees, 158–164
    recording payments, 158–164
    Recurring Transactions, 161
    semi-monthly payroll information, 158, 162
    Transaction Report, 160, 163–164
    Trial Balance, 160, 163
Payroll (expense) account, 17
Payroll Tax Payable (liability) account, 157
prepaid expenses
  bills for, 112
  deferring supplies as asset, 208–209
  recording consumption of supplies, 209–210
products
  adding, 77–78, 105–108
  lists of, 77
  purchase order, 105–108
  recording bills from vendors for receipt of, 108–112
Product/Service information window, 47

Profit and Loss budget, 183–185
Profit and Loss report, 17. *See also* income statements
  creating, 224–225
  customizing, 237–239
  saving, 237–239
purchase of equipment, 135–136
purchase orders, 105–108
purchases and cash payments, 104–118
  adding vendors, 104–105
  paying bills, 112–115
  purchase orders, 105–108
  recording bills, 108–112
  recording check payments, 114
  recording credit card payments, 114–115
  trial balance, 114–133

Q

QuickBooks Accountant (QBDT), 23–24
QuickBooks/Accounting professional, 268–269
QuickBooks certified user online exam objectives, 268–269
QuickBooks Online (QBO)
  assigning instructor as company's "accountant", 36–37
  creating accounts, 23–24
  definition of, 22
  vs. desktop version of QuickBooks Accountant, 23–24
  navigating, 31–36
  overview, 22
  video tutorials for, 37–39

R

receipts of payment (cash receipts), 83–86. *See also* sales and cash receipts
Receive Payment window, 84
Reconcile–Checking form, 191
Reconcile window, 190
reconciliation process, 192
Recurring Transactions, 161
report(s)
  accessing customers information, 3–4
  accessing employee information, 6–7
  accessing vendor information, 4–6

report(s) (*Continued*)
   Accounts Payable Aging Detail, 234
   Accounts Payable Aging Summary, 233–235
   accounts receivable, 18
   Accounts Receivable Aging Detail Report, 234
   Accounts Receivable Aging Summary, 231–233
   account and settings window, 12
   Balance Sheet, 17
   banking transactions, viewing, 7–9
   budget, 185–189
   Business Overview, 16
   chart of accounts, viewing, 13–14
   customizing and saving, 237–239
   expense transactions, viewing, 9–11
   financial, 223–239
   Inventory Valuation Summary, 234–237
   Profit and Loss, 17, 224–225
   sales transactions, viewing, 9–11
   Statement of Cash Flows, 18
   Transaction
      for Accounts Receivable (A/R), 228
      income statements, 226
      for notes payable, 230
      for supplies asset, 210
   Transaction Detail by Account
      creating, 53–54
      exporting, 53–54
      printing, 53–54
   Transaction Detail by Account reports, 86–87
      creating, 86–87
      exporting, 86–87
      printing, 86–87
revenue
   accruing, 213–214
   unearned, 212–213

S

sales and cash receipts, 76–87
   adding services, products, and customers, 76–80
   recording cash receipts, 83–86
   sales invoices, 80–83
   sales receipts
      adding, 80–83
      definition of, 80
   Transaction Detail by Account reports, 86–87
Sales Receipt after Sales Tax, 81
Sales Receipt before Sales Tax, 81
sales receipts
   adding, 80–83
   definition of, 80
Sales settings, 19
sales tax, 246
Sales Tax Center, 246
sales transactions, viewing, 9–11
Sample Company
   accessing customer information, 34–35
   accessing employee information, 38
   accessing vendor information, 33–35
   adding customers, 79–80
   adding new employees, 156
   adding new services, 76–80
   adding products, 77–78
   adding sales invoices, 80–83
   banking transactions, viewing, 7–9
   cash receipts, 83–86
   chart of accounts, viewing, 13–14
   expense transactions, viewing, 9–11
   list of lists, viewing, 14–15
   list of terms, viewing, 15
   payroll for, 158–164
   receipts of payment, 83–86
   recording purchase of long-term investment, 137
   recording purchase of new equipment, 135–136
   sales transactions, viewing, 9–11
   settings management
      Advanced settings, 20
      Company settings, 18–20
      Expenses settings, 20
      Sales settings, 19
Sample Company Home page, 7, 8
Save Report Customizations, 53
saving
   Profit and Loss report, 237–239
   reports, 237–239
semi-monthly payroll information, 158, 162
services
   adding, 76–80
   lists of, 77
   paying bills for, 111
   recording bills from vendors for receipt of, 108–112
   settings management
      Advanced settings, 20
      Company settings, 18–20

Expenses settings, 20
Sales settings, 19
Sign In window, 56
social security, 157
Statement of Cash Flows, 18, 229–231
Summary Reconciliation Report, 192

T
taxes
  Medicare, 157
  sales, 246
Transaction
  for Accounts Payable account, 117
  for checking account, 117
  for Inventory Asset Account, 117
Transaction Detail by Account, 86–87
  creating, 53–54, 86–87
  exporting, 53–54, 86–87
  printing, 53–54, 86–87
Transaction reports
  for Accounts Payable account, 117
  for Accounts Receivable (A/R), 228
  for checking account, 117
  income statements, 226
  for Inventory Asset account, 117
  for notes payable, 230
  for supplies asset, 210
trial balance, 115–133
  creating, 115–133, 206
  investigating, 115–133
Trial Balance report, 160, 163, 206

U
unearned revenue, 212–213
Users window, 31
U.S. Treasury, 157

V
Vendor Information window, 104–105
vendors, 3–7
  accessing information about, 4–5, 33–35
  adding, 104–105
  recording bills from vendors for receipt of products or services, 108–112
Vendors window, 5, 34–35
video tutorials
  online navigating QuickBooks, 33–34
  for QuickBooks Online, 33–34

Notes

Notes

Notes

Notes